THE VOYAGES OF ADRIAAN VAN BERKEL TO GUIANA

Sidestone Press

THE VOYAGES OF ADRIAAN VAN BERKEL TO GUIANA

-DUTCH RELATIONSHIPS

N 17TH-CENTURY GUYANA

EDITED BY

MARTIJN VAN DEN BEL

LODEWIJK HULSMAN

LODEWIJK WAGENAAR

Published by Sidestone Press, Leiden
www.sidestone.com

ISBN 978-90-8890-263-5

English edition of the original Dutch text by M. van den Bel and L. Hulsman

Proof reading by P. Richardus

Lay-out & cover design: Sidestone Press
Photograph cover: Timhesterphotography | Dreamstime.com
Drawing ship cover: after replica of the Halve Maen door, by K. Wentink, Sidestone Press

Contents

Foreword

The present-day Lokono of Guyana reside between *c.* 60 and 90 miles inland from the Atlantic seacoast. Their villages are strategically situated on high sandy ridges, on the edge of the forest and are connected by bridges and roads that criss cross the forests and savannahs. The Lokono remain, therefore, in contact with their relatives in other villages, which in most cases are located no more than a day's journey apart.

Inspired by Adriaan van Berkel's journey from the Demerara to the Berbice, I set off from Georgetown for the Berbice River in 1986. My goal was not only to relocate the Lokono villages Van Berkel had encountered while travelling across the savannahs but also to acquire pottery samples from the now abandoned village sites in the Abary River area. Having traversed the various land and river routes with my elders, I decided to follow a well-known trail that had served my ancestors. It connected the Lokono villages on the Demerara River to those on the Berbice River continuing from the Berbice to the Canje River and then towards the Courentyne River and into Surinam.

After travelling from Georgetown to Linden by bus I got off at the junction of the Linden Highway and the road leading to St. Cuthbert's Mission.[1] From here I walked to the Mahaica River and having stayed the night at St Cuthbert's Mission, continued on the trail to Kibilery Creek, accompanied by a resident of the village, departing before daybreak. After an almost 7-hour long hike, we paused only very briefly in order to refresh ourselves at a stream, enjoyed a snack and arrived at the abandoned village of Kibilery in mid-afternoon. From here we paddled downstream towards the Mahaicony River in a dugout and then set off up Captain Creek, a tributary of the Mahaicony River, towards Saint Francis Mission (now named Marikobai). The night was passed at Marikobai. We proceeded towards the Andabo Creek, a tributary of the Abary River, the next morning.

At Marikobai, having asked the direction towards the Berbice River, we were informed the upper Abary River area had been flooded due to a dam constructed across the Abary River in 1970. The entire savannah separating the Abary and the Berbice Rivers is now inundated. Villagers fished the Andabo Creek area but did not venture far out towards the Berbice River for fear of the dangerously rough "sea". However, determined to reach this river, we boarded a dugout, navigated the grassy sheet of water until nightfall and then took a break in order to cook a meal in our canoe and have a rest. Unable to sleep, we continued our journey, carefully finding our way, under a very clear moon, through the savannah. We stopped again at around 4 o'clock in the morning, as we were heading into a forest island.

Woken up by a loud banging sound in the distance, we excitedly decided to follow the signal telling us we were not alone. Sure enough in the distance we could see a couple comfortably seated in their canoe cleaning fish. Having approached

1 Linden is located 90 km south of Georgetown. The route via the Soestdyke-Linden Highway is about 100 km. This highway follows more or less the bends of the Demerara River. The village of Hitia is *c.* 70 km east of Linden as the crow flies. Direct road connections do not exist.

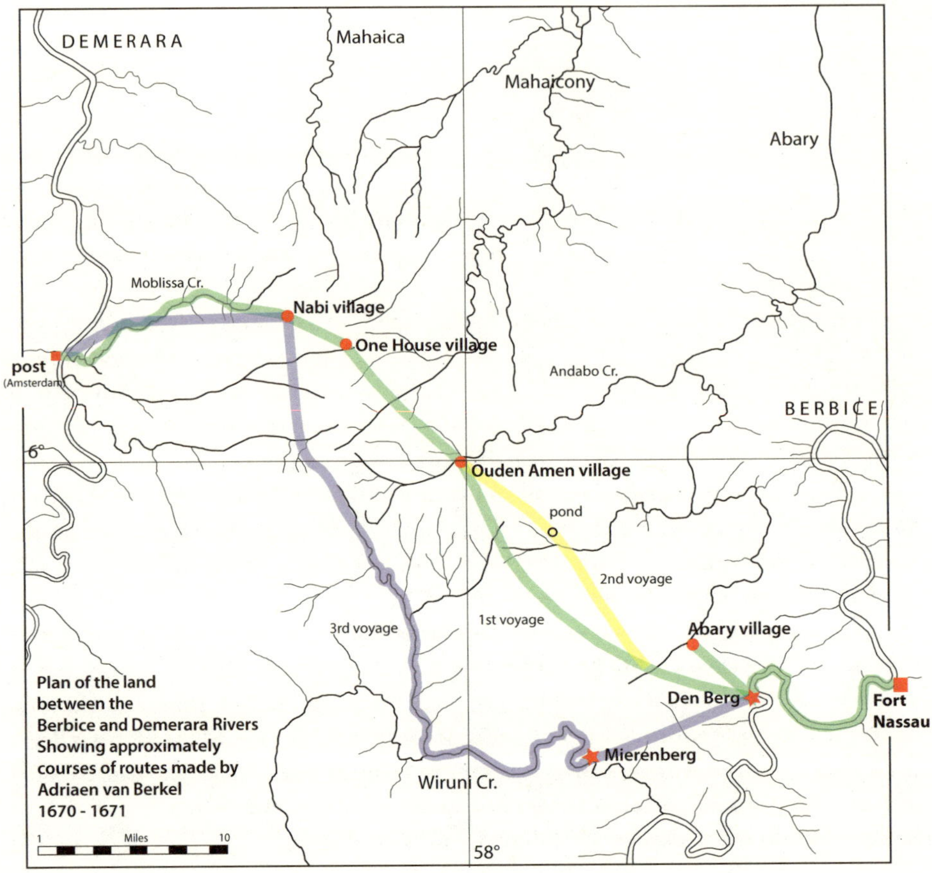

Figure 1: Map of the Guiana plateau with the voyages of Adriaan van Berkel.

them and introducing ourselves, they showed us the way to Coffee Landing on the Abary River adding that the 10-mile road from this landing would take us to the Berbice River. Indeed, after a 3-hour walk through the forest, a house appeared in the distance. We had arrived at the village of Hitia, near the former Dutch plantation *Den Berg*, visited by Adriaan van Berkel. It turned out this village is one of the earliest Lokono villages in the Berbice![2]

George Simon, Lokono Archaeologist
Georgetown, 1 August 2014

2 Whitehead, N.L., M.J. Heckenberger, G. Simon, Materializing the Past among the Lokono (Arawak) of the Berbice River, Guyana, *Antropológica* 114, 2010.

Preface

The former Dutch colonies in the Co-operative Republic of Guyana are probably the least known part of the Dutch colonial heritage in the Caribbean. The early history of the colonies along the Berbice, Demerara and Essequibo Rivers is still full of mysteries.[3]

Adriaan van Berkel's *American Voyages* to Berbice and Surinam represents one of the first printed reports on the Dutch Colonies of Berbice and Essequibo during the second half of the 17th century.[4] This book, published in 1695, has never been reprinted in Dutch. The first part consists of Van Berkel's voyage (1670-1674) to the Colony of Berbice; the second part describes a fictitious journey to Surinam, allegedly made between April 1680 and August 1689.

Van Berkel was appointed a 'Merchant and Secretary' by the owners ('patrons') of the Berbice Colony, the Zeeland-based entrepreneurs Abraham van Pere Jr. and his brother-in-law Pieter van Rhee. During a sojourn of more than 3 years, Van Berkel made three journeys on foot through the interior of the eastern parts of Guyana and one voyage over sea, from Berbice to Essequibo. His description hereof contains the only existing information on Berbice dating from this period.

American Voyages deals with the daily life of the local Arawak population in great detail. Moreover, it reports profusely on two Amerindian ceremonies: (a) becoming a Captain and (b) the capture and sentence of a enemy which resulted in his execution and his body being consumed. Van Berkel informs us not only of his work but also of the observations made during his voyages, for instance to

3 Prior to the British takeover, the Dutch named the colony Essequebo. The Zeelanders often applied the name Isekepe, for example: 'Directie der Nieuwe Colonie op Isekepe', in 1657. Now and again the English named the colony Desseceeb. From 1814 on, the name Essequibo was adopted while the other Zeelander colony was called Demerary or Demerarie. This edition adopts the British names, unless cited otherwise in the sources.
Marinus Netscher's study published in 1888 is as yet the best book on the general history of this subject. However, in recent years, Dutch historians have taken up researching this forgotten chapter of Dutch colonial history e.g., G.J. Oostindie, 'British Capital, Industry and Perseverance' versus Dutch 'Old School'? The Dutch Atlantic and the Takeover of Berbice, Demerara and Essequibo, 1750-1815, *Low Countries Historical Review BMGN* 127(4), 2012; J.C. van Langen, *De Britse overname van de Nederlandse koloniën Demerary, Essequebo en Berbice (Guyana); van economische overvleugeling naar politieke overheersing (1740-1814),* Master Thesis University of Amsterdam, 2004; M. Kars, Policing and Transgressing Borders: Soldiers, Slave Rebels, and the Early Modern Atlantic, *New West Indian Guide* 83, 2009; 'Wij beleven hier droevige tyden': Europeanen, indianen en Afrikanen in de Berbice slavenopstand, 1763-1764, *Geweld in de West: een militaire geschiedenis van de Nederlandse Atlantische wereld, 1600-1800*, V. Enthoven, H. den Heijer, H. Jordaan (eds). In: Caribbean Series 33, Leiden: E.J. Brill, 2013, pp. 183-216; E.W. van der Oest, The Forgotten Colonies of Essequibo and Demerara, 1700-1814, *Riches from Atlantic Commerce: Dutch Transatlantic Trade and Shipping, 1585-1817*, J. Postma & V. Enthoven (eds), Leiden: E.J. Brill, 2003, pp. 343-346; L. Bosman, *Nieuw Amsterdam in Berbice (Guyana): de planning en bouw van een koloniale stad, 1764-1800*, Hilversum: Verloren, 1994. In the Republic of Guyana the 250th anniversary of the Berbice slave revolt was commemorated recently. *The Berbice Uprising 1763*, Georgetown: Caribbean Press, 2007, by A. Benjamin, under her maiden name A.J. McR. Cameron, was reprinted in 2013. The National Museum in Georgetown commemorated the slave revolt with an exhibition organized by Lodewijk Wagenaar.

4 Certain Dutch surnames have a specific spelling. The 'v' in *Adriaan van Berkel* is noted in lower case only if the surname prefix is preceded by a given name; otherwise the surname prefix includes the upper case 'V'.

fort Kyckoveral, located on the Essequibo River. As was rather common in those days, he composes a general survey of the rivers, flora, fauna, merchandise, and the inhabitants of Guiana. Various sections of this description have been derived from existing French and German literature concerning this part of the New World.

After this traditional description, Van Berkel continues with a factual report on the troublesome provision of rations resulting in the mutiny of October 1673. The Commander of Berbice was taken prisoner by mutineers who even forced the appointment of a new commander. After these events Van Berkel was sent to the lower Berbice River where he had to divert a possible Carib attack. These and earlier episodes are good examples of true events he reported on as an eyewitness. When his successor arrived in early 1674 Van Berkel left in March for the roadstead of Flushing on board the *Eendracht*, commanded by Captain Adriaen de Vyver. With his arrival here, at the end of May or the beginning of June 1674, this travellogue ends.

The second part of *American Voyages* pretends to report on a sojourn in Surinam between 1680 and 1689. This fictitious travelogue starts with the offer made to Adriaan van Berkel to represent an owner of a plantation in Surinam who had come to the Netherlands in order to liquidate an inheritance. Van Berkel then boards the *Juffrou Sophia* to arrive in Surinam on 23 June 1680, a date punctionally referred to in Chapter I of this second journey. Chapter II starts with a description of the Surinam River, its fish and the falls upstream. However, Chapter II all the way to Chapter XI were taken from the Dutch translation (1669) of a booklet by George Warren entitled, *An Impartial description of Surinam upon the Continent of Guiana in America* […], published in 1667. W.E. Roth was the first to discover the source of these chapters. Though not at all original, they describe the flora, fauna and products of the colony in brief. Moreover, they present us with interesting information on the indigenous Indians and the enslaved at the plantations.[5]

The final chapter of *American Voyages*, for which this publication is best known, was supposed to be an eyewitness report of two important events that occurred in the Colony of Surinam: (a) the tragic death of Governor Cornelis van Aerssen, Lord of Sommelsdijck, on 19 July 1688 and (b) the attack carried out by the French pirate Ducasse on the fort of Paramaribo in May 1689. However, in the below segment on 'Dutch newspapers reporting on the Guianas, 1650-1700', Lodewijk Wagenaar proves that the stories concerning this specific intersection on actual news from Surinam (Chapter XII) had already been made public by Dutch newspapers and Yearbooks covering the events of 1688 and 1689.

This publication presents a new and annotated translation of the *American Voyages* as published in 1695. In order to better understand not only the historical background of the *American Voyages* but also its history and reception an in-depth

5 W.E. Roth, *Adriaan van Berkel's Travels in South America between the Berbice and Essequibo Rivers and in Surinam 1670-1689*, Translated and Edited by Walter Edmund Roth [1925], The Guiana Edition 2 (3rd Impression) of reprints and original works dealing with all phases of life in British Guiana, Edited by Vincent Roth, Georgetown: The Daily Chronicle, 1948, p. ix. See also J. van Donselaar, De boeken van Warren (1667, 1669), Van Berkel (1695) en Herlein (1718) en hun onderlinge betrekkingen, *OSO Tijdschrift voor Surinamistiek en het Caraïbisch gebied* 12(1), 1993.

Introduction precedes the texts. The first chapter of this Introduction focusses on the news concerning the Guianas as published by the Dutch newspapers of that time. The second chapter continues with a historiographic discussion of *American Voyages* and its various editions.

Subsequently, the character of *American Voyages* is discussed. Which parts of the text have been derived from existing literature, and which can be seen as original reports written by an eyewitness? What was the publisher's precise role? Next full attention is paid to revealing the true identity of Adriaan van Berkel, who as yet was a mere shadow. In the third chapter of the Introduction, the historical context of *American Voyages* is examined. The Introduction ends with a short note on the edition of the Dutch text and its present English translation.

Part I

Introduction

Chapter 1

Dutch newspapers reporting on the Guianas, 1650-1700

Printed information on the Dutch Colonies

As was tradition in those days, Adriaan van Berkel asked his readers to forgive him for his impertinence, for it was only because he could not resist the 'unceasing encouragements by his good friends' that he succumbed and decided to publish his recollections of the journeys to Rio de Berbice and Surinam. His book, as the author emphasizes in his 'To the reader', was not a novel, but a truthful description of facts. That could be useful, he says, as so little had been written about those two colonies inhabited by so many fellow countrymen. As if to guarantee the reader he had no hidden motives, in the very beginning of the first chapter, Van Berkel obediently follows the standard recipe assuring the reader it was only 'the noble desire to visit foreign climes and countries' that caused him to travel abroad. Trust me! Of course, such phrases were the traditional tools publishers applied in order to convince the reader he had not wasted his money, but on the contrary, had bought a true and useful book.

Contemporary readers, living more than three centuries after the 1695 Dutch publication of the *American Voyages to the River Berbice and Surinam*, must indeed question if this publication can be trusted and considered a useful source on the countries and peoples the author claims to have visited. In order to discuss the quality of the contents passed down to us, we have to find out which information those interested were able to gather concerning the two countries in the period between Van Berkel's departure in 1670 and the publication of his travelogue in 1695. Generally speaking, during the second half of the 17th century, the printed information on the Dutch ventures overseas was quite abundant and widely varying in scope. Dozens of titles were available with information on the countries where the Dutch East India Company had settlements. Often richly illustrated, a number of these publications will have been acquired only by the wealthy elite. However, information on the Dutch Indies was not restricted to the higher social classes. The information market did indeed also serve people with a smaller purse by means of cheap editions, the majority being travelogues recanting fascinating stories of disasters at sea, remarkable rescues and divine intervention. Contrary to the situation of information on the East Indies, literature concerning the West Indies in that period was scarce. Books on Berbice and Surinam were even limited to one or two titles.

Of much interest is the publication by David Pietersz de Vries (*c.*1592-post 1655) on his travels between 1618 and 1644. His descriptions of destinations located in the continents of Europe, Africa, Asia and America were published in 1655.[6] A second voyage 'to the coast of America or the Wild Coast of the West Indies' in 1634 had brought him to the Wild Coast, where he had to disembark thirty colonists. With his ship *Coninck David* he left Texel on 10 July 1634 and arrived at the Oyapock River (the border of Brasil and French Guyana) on 4 September to procede to Cayenne where the colonists disembarked. Next De Vries sailed to Surinam. Here 150 Indians (fearing the Caribs would kill them) requested to be transferred to Demerara, which De Vries fulfilled.[7]

Explaining the variations in focus on these two dissimilar parts of the world is not very difficult. The East India enterprises had good fortune from the very start when, in 1595, the first Dutch sails left the ports of Holland and Zeeland. The foundation of Batavia on the island of Java (1619) can be seen as proof that within 25 years the first phase of a Dutch East India trade empire had been successfully completed. Albeit the Dutch had modest success in America when founding New Amsterdam, activities in the Caribbean and South America had to wait till 1621 when the truce between Spain and its rebellious Dutch provinces was discontinued. Only then did the newborn Dutch West India Company (WIC) commence its operations, although private companies were already trading at the Wild Coast before this date. The WIC functioned initially mainly as part of the military machinery against Spain and its Iberian affiliation Portugal. Van Pere's first venture in the Guianas, then called the 'Wild Coast', started in 1627. However, the enterprise at the *Rio de Berbice* was very limited in size, and for decades it had very little impact on the economy of the Dutch Republic. During the Second Dutch-Anglo War (1665-1667) the Dutch took over Surinam, as formalized in the Treaty of Breda (31 July 1667). During its early stages, Surinam was as yet a modest undertaking. In 1695, when Van Berkel's *American Voyages* was published, the colony had showed some progress. The plantation economy was nonetheless not booming as it would be during the century that followed.

Nevertheless, the early profits of both Berbice and Surinam were arguments for *courantiers*, Dutch newspaper publishers, to collect information on these regions as well as on the connected trade. The networks of correspondents had expanded impressively since the printing of the first newspapers in 1618. At the

6 D. Pietersz de Vries, *Korte Historiael ende Journaels Aenteykeninge van verscheyden Voyagiens in de Vier Deelen des Werelds-ronde, als Europa, Africa, Asia, ende Amerika gedaen door David Pietersz de Vries.* Alkmaar: Symon Cornelisx Brekegeest, 1655. Modern edition by H.J. Colenbrander. In: Werken van de Linschoten Vereniging 3, 1911, Den Haag: Martinus Nijhoff.

7 D. Peterson de Vries, *Voyages from Holland to America, A.D. 1633 1644.* Translated from the Dutch by Henry C. Murphy. New York: Billin & Brothers, 1853, p. 97: 'Here [in Timmerarie] we disembarked the Indian men and women, who immediately prepared their habitation with pieces of wood, as they were near their friends. While we were lying here, Jan vander Goes came with a canoe from the River of Isekebie, where he was commander for the West India Company.' Jan Adriaensz van der Goes had officiated as commander of Essequibo since 1626. The Indians were members of the Sapaya tribe who 'were apprehensive that the Caribs would kill them', ibid., p. 96. This publication only contains De Vries' travels to America. The translation is not perfect but it is the only English edition of De Vries' sixth journey to the Wild Coast and the West Indies.

same time recently dug waterways facilitated the fast transfer of mail by canal boats connecting major towns. Supplementary services linked maritime centres (e.g., Den Helder in the north of Holland, Flushing and Middelburg in Zeeland) with the metropolis Amsterdam and Haarlem, its neighbouring competitor in the rapidly expanding information industry. Correspondents were located in The Hague, the residence of the States-General, the States of Holland and the Stadtholder. Between 1650 and 1672, however, the maritime provinces of Holland and Zeeland had no acting Stadtholder. For the newspaper correspondents, The Hague was an important source of information: all the ambassadors, envoys and other representatives of foreign countries and of towns were stationed there. The network of the *courantiers* covered the capitals and commercial centres all over Europe. Therefore within weeks, sometimes within days, any relevant business news or incoming information from abroad on wars and the like was presented to the reader. Eager to obtain the latest news were: politicians, administrators, merchants, shipbuilders, entrepreneurs and members of the financial elite. For each of them the consumption of information was essential in order to avoid risk or to understand fresh opportunities. In 1665, newspapers in several towns served the reader with weekly, bi-weekly and even three-weekly editions. The booming economy of the Dutch Republic was paralleled by the information industry which offered the relevant information the members of commercial and governmental circles required.[8]

In addition to newspapers, the entrepreneurs had another important source of commercial news: the weekly price lists of the commodities dealt in at the Amsterdam Exchange. Copies of the *Cours van Coopmanschappen tot Amsterdam* was published every Monday and sent to merchants across Europe. The commodities were classified in categories, e.g., 'pepper and spices', 'olive oil', 'seeds, seed oil and soap'. Sugar was listed as No. 3 and consisted of the imported raw sugar as well as several kinds of sugar refined in Amsterdam. Lists indicate that wars caused prices to rise. Weekly papers listed not only commodities: category No. 29 consisted of costs of marine assurances, grouped according to destination. No. 30 concerns the rate of the so-called exchange letters, listed per location of exchange.[9]

News on Berbice and Surinam selected from the *Oprechte Haerlemse Courant*, *La Gazette d'Amsterdam*, and the *Amsterdamsche Courant*, 1665-1688

Amsterdam and Haarlem were not the only towns where *courantiers,* or publishers of newspapers, had set up shop. Amsterdam witnessed the first newspapers in 1618. Initially the size of the paper was rather small. On occasion only one side of a sheet was printed. Jan van Hilten and Broer Jansz respectively were the first

8 See M. Schneider and J. Hemels, De Nederlandse Krant 1618-1978. Van 'nieuwstydinghe' tot dagblad. Baarn: Het Wereldvenster, 1979.

9 The issue of 5 September 1693 served as an example. See the collection of copied price papers procured at the International Institute for Social History/Netherlands Archive for Economic History (IISG/NEHA), Amsterdam, Special Collections 674: AMS.1.01 fol. C 'Cours van Koopmanschappen tot Amsterdam', 1674 and 1683-1783.

entrepreneurs regarding news in Amsterdam. From the late 1660s on their papers received the mutual title *Amsterdamsche Courant*, printed on Tuesdays, Thursdays and Saturdays. Although they applied one and the same title, the newspapers were edited and printed by four *courantiers* who published by means of rotation. *La Gazette d'Amsterdam* from 1663 on. Haarlem can be seen as the second centre of the information industry, thanks to Abraham Casteleyn's remarkable drive. His *Weeckelijcke Courante van Europa* ('Weekly European Newspaper') was first printed on 8 January 1656. It was such a success that, from June 1658 on, he was able to publish this paper on Saturdays and Tuesdays. In 1664 he renamed his *Haerlemse Saturdaeghse Courant* and *Haerlemse Dinsdaeghse Courant* to *Oprechte* (= true) *Haerlemse Courant*, by far the best informed newspaper in the Dutch Republic.

Adriaan van Berkel left for Rio de Berbice in 1670. It cannot be confirmed if he had read George Warren's *Impartial Description* (1667) which dealt with the people and the country of neighbouring Surinam. Nor do we know if Van Berkel owned a copy of the translation of this work which was published in 1669, only a year before his departure to the Wild Coast. Moreover, we only can speculate on the possibilities that he had read the relevant newspapers of his time. Therefore we only can discuss the nature of the news published by contemporary newspapers keeping in mind that the very existence of such papers served immensely to diffuse information otherwise kept behind the doors of meeting rooms of institutions governed by the commercial and political elite of that time. Although the East and West India Companies were state sponsored bodies, most information was kept secret by their respective governing boards of directors. Only news directly related to auctions or other facts the public must know in the sheer interest of the Companies themselves was made public. Of course, any individual could go to the port of Amsterdam, stretched out along the IJ, or visit nearby inns where sailors and the like would stay and spend their money, and try to interview recently arrived personnel. We know that certain individuals did so in order to acquire for themselves or for their patrons rarities from faraway shores. Correspondents of the various newspapers may possibly have strolled from the one place to the other collecting news. Captains and steersmen may even have established permanent contacts with such newspapermen, presumable receiving gratuities or even small payments for their information. Albeit speculation, we of course can guess within reason, based upon clues retrieved from the very news articles.

Early information on Surinam, 1665-1670

At present it is taken for granted that fort Willoughby was taken by Abraham Crijnssen (?-1669), commander of the Admiralty of Zeeland, shortly after his arrival at the Surinam River on 25 February 1667. Crijnssen was sent during the final stage of the Second Anglo-Dutch War (1665-1667) to attack the British strongholds in the West. His squadron consisting of three frigates and four small vessels counted 500 sailormen and 200 soldiers. On 6 March, Crijnssen gained full control over the colony, but after 6 months Surinam was retaken by the English, who of course renamed fort Zeelandia again to fort Willoughby. On

20 April, Crijnssen returned to Surinam with three ships and after a week he regained control over the colony. The first newspaper procured at the Koninklijke Bibliotheek (Royal Library, The Hague) containing news on the war dates from 22 December 1667. *La Gazette d'Amsterdam* reports that a ship had arrived in Texel delivering mail from the French isle of Guadeloupe. From these letters the newspaper had learned that, on 26 September of the same year, English troops had taken Cayenne and that they were en route to Surinam 'sur la coste Sauvage'.[10] It is apparently reported that the fleet would eventually retake Surinam in October. On 26 April 1668 the same newspaper writes that letters from Surinam 'sur la coste Sauvage' informed that troops from Zeeland had retaken the colony, but that the English still held the fort on the Surinam River, as they had not yet received orders from London to hand it over. The newspaper also mentions that ships from London had confirmed this news.[11] Three weeks later ships having arrived in Flushing bring the news that the English still refused to surrender, even though they had received orders to do so. In order to enforce their departure the Admiralty of Zeeland had sent men-of-war transferring troops. 'One believes they will surrender once they see the fleet approaching', *La Gazette d'Amsterdam* wrote on 17 May 1668.[12] It informs on 8 June that, on request of the Dutch ambassadors in London, King Charles II had agreed to accept the legal consequences of the treaty, and to surrender the fort.[13] A month later a report from London states that the king had sent orders to William Willoughby, Governor of Barbados and Vice-Roy of the British possessions in the West Indies to hand over Surinam.[14] On 24 January 1669 the above mentioned *Gazette* wrote that Major James Bannister, the former Governor of Surinam, had returned from Zeeland were he had been detained after having been taken prisoner of war by Crijnssen in 1668. The report adds: 'One is busy to bring the affairs of this Colony in order, so that no more

10 Koninklijke Bibliotheek (KB), Den Haag, *La Gazette d'Amsterdam* (GA), 22-12-1667. The collection of newspapers kept in the depostitory of the Royal Library (KB), The Hague, has been scanned and made accessible through www.Delpher.nl. The large collection, however, is incomplete. Therefore in certain cases other collections should be consulted e.g., the Amsterdam City Archives (SAA), the library of the University of Amsterdam (UvA) and its Special Collections and the archives of the province of North-Holland in Haarlem (NHAH). After a spot check it was decided to mainly utilise the collection of the Royal Library.

11 KB_GA, 26-04-1668: '*D'Amsterdam le 26 Avril.* Les lettres de Surinam sur la coste Sauvage donnent avis que les Zelandois ont repris tout le païs sur les Anglois, mais que ceux-ci tienent encore le Fort; parce qu'ils n'ont pas encore reçu l'ordre que sa M. B. leur a envoyé de le rendre. On écrit de Vlessingue qu'il y est arrivé divers bastiments de Londres qui confirment la même chose.'

12 KB_GA, 17-5-1668: '*D'Amsterdam le 17 May*: '(..) on croit qu'ils l'auront rendu dés qu'ils les aurons veu paroitre'.

13 KB_GA, 14-6-1668: '*De Londres le 8 Juin*: 'Sur le memoire presenté à sa M. pas Messieurs les Ambassadeurs des Provinces Unies, le Roy a resolu de leur faire droit, & de faire rendre au plutôt aux Zelandois le chateau de Surinam sur la coste Sauvage que nos Gens tennent encore'. The Treaty of Breda (31 July 1667) stipulated that hostilities in the West must cease no later than 24 April 1668.

14 KB_GA, 19-7-1668: '*De Londres le 13 Juillet*: Le Roy a dépeché de nouveaux ordres au Millord Willougly Gouverneur & Viceroy des Barbados & autres terres que sa M. possede dans les Indes Occidentales, pour rendre Surinam aux Zelandois selon qu'il a esté stipulé par les articles du Traité de pax de Breda'.

differences will arise between the two nations'.[15] However, the full execution of the treaty dragged on for quite some time. On 13 June 1669 *La Gazette* informs that, on request of the British ambassador in The Hague, the States-General, the supreme authority of the Dutch colonies, had sent an instruction to the Governor of Surinam, ordering him to permit the Englishmen residing there to leave and to favour them as much as possible.[16] Then, at last, on 10 August 1669, the *Oprechte Haerlemse Courant* brings the first 'normal' news from Surinam: a small galleot had arrived, but the ship was only half loaded, because continuous rains had caused a lack of sugar.[17] Apparently the situation regarding the English residents of Surinam remained unsolved. Therefore, on 5 November, Sir William Temple, ambassador in The Hague, presented the States-General with a memoir asking permission for the English residents to leave the colony with their properties.[18] The Haarlem newspaper dated 24 December 1669, informs us of the decision the States-General had taken with regard to this issue. The English residents would be allowed to take with them all their goods and slaves they were not willing to sell, but with only one exception: slaves they had acquired after the Dutch had conquered the colony had to be left behind. The Dutch Governor would compensate them fairly, i.e., 25 to 30 guilders above the sum they had originally paid.[19] On 26 December 1669 *La Gazette* published the same news. The States-General's decision, it wrote, must be understood to have been taken 'out of their consideration for his Majesty the King of England, and to give evidence one greatly complies with his friendschip'.[20]

News on Berbice and Surinam compared

Berbice, 1665-1688

No news at all is known concerning Rio de Berbice between 1665 and 1670 i.e., during the years preceding the departure of Adriaan van Berkel who was presumably fully dependent of information transferred by those who had offered him his

15 KB_GA, 24-1-1669: '*De Londres le 11 Janvier*: (..) on travaille à mettre ordre aux affaires de céte Colonie en sorte qu'il n'y arrive plus de différents entre les 2 Nations'.

16 KB_GA, 13-6-1669: '*De la Haye le 11 Juin*: A la requeste de M. l'Ambass. d'Angleterre, on dit que Mess. les Estats ont envoyé ordre au Gouverneur de Surinam d'en laisser partir les Anglois qui y sont, & de les favoriser en tout ce qu'il pourra'.

17 Koninklijke Bibliotheek (KB), Den Haag, *Oprechte Haerlemse Courant* (OHC), 10-8-1669: '*Vlissingen den 6 Augusti*: Op Eergisteren arriveerden hier een kleyn Galjootje van Suriname, zynde maer half vol, om dat aldaer soo weynigh ghemaeckte Suycker was; want het alle Dagen niet deed als regenen, dat een quaet Gewas veroorsaeckte'.

18 KB_GA, 7-11-1669: '*De la Haye le 5 Novembre*: (..) Mons. Tempel Ambassadeur d'Angleterre a communiqué un memoire à Mess. les Estats touchant Surinam & les Anglois qui y sont'.

19 KB_OHC, 24-12-1669: '*'s Gravenhage den 22 december*: (..) men verstaet mede, dat, op 't aenhouden van den Heere Ambassadeur van Engelandt, by haer Hoog. Mog: is geresolveert in de saecken van Suriname, om te betoonen dat so veel wel willen defereren aen de vrientschap van sijn Majest. van Groot Brittagne, namentlijk dat aen de Engelse ingesetenen in Suriname toestaen haer Transport van daer, met hare Slaven en Meub'len die sy in de Colonie niet en willen verkoopen, uytgenomen alleen de Slaven, welcke na 't veroveren van Suriname hebben gekocht, welcke van haer by den Gouverneur sullen overgenomen werden, voor 25 a 30 gulden meer, als die eerst hebben gekocht, &c'.

20 KB_GA, 26-12-1669: '*De la Haye le 24 Decembre*: (..) ce qu'ils ont fait à la consideration seule de sa M. Brittannique, & pour lui temoigner qu'on defère beaucoup à son amitié'.

position as a Secretary of the governing body of Berbice, located at fort Nassau. Only a small number of ships will have plied between the Zeeland colonies along the Wild Coast each year. Seamen arriving at Flushing may have spoken of their adventures. However, such information would not be made public for decades to come. We first read in the newspapers dated August 1684 about Rio de Berbice, when the *Oprechte Haerlemse Courant* printed news provided by the correspondent in Flushing, reporting that several ships destined for Lisbon and Cadiz were ready to sail, and that this also applied to the *Abraham and Isaac* destined for the 'Berbisjes'.[21] The colony played a modest role in the newspaper collection procured by the Royal Library in The Hague. Until 1695, when Van Berkel's travel stories were published, Berbice was mentioned only on nine occasions, while Surinam is referred to on around one hundred occasions between 1665 and 1695.

By and large Berbice was not mentioned at all. We do learn of ships ready to depart, or ships that had arrived in Flushing, the home town of the Van Pere family. The Berbice Colony was a private enterprise founded and exploited by the *patron* Abraham Van Pere Sr. The WIC had granted this colony as a kind of feudal fief, of which Van Pere would be the 'lord of the land'. In 1678 this fief officially acquired a hereditary status. In 1683 therefore his son Cornelis was automatically appointed the incoming *patron* after his father Abraham Van Pere Jr. had passed away (see 'Berbice and Van Pere in Chapter 3, 'Historical context of *American Voyages*' for more information on the Van Pere family). This new ownership did presumably not bring many changes. Nevertheless, Berbice will certainly have profited from the growing demand for sugar as did Surinam. Be that as it may, annually only a few ships set off for and arrived from Berbice, such as on 13 June 1685 when, again, the *Abraham and Isaac* arrived.[22] The journey from Berbice under Captain Pieter Van Goethem had taken 12 weeks, almost the same time Captain Pieter Van Hatte had needed to bring his ship *De Klock* safely from Surinam, arriving in Flushing only 2 days later.[23] On 24 February 1686 the *Abraham and Isaac* set off again to Berbice. Its owner seemingly maintained a more or less regular service. Apparently this ship was not involved in the triangular route: Europe-Africa-America, transporting goods to the coasts of West Africa, then transferring enslaved Africans to America before returning to Europe with sugar and other cargo. On 15 July 1687 the *Abraham and Isaac* had returned to Flushing, after a journey of 8 weeks from Berbice.[24] Considering this short space of time one wonders which the other ports of call had been during this voyage, for no shipowner would like to see his ship rest idle at faraway roadsteads.

On 30 March 1688, readers of the *Oprechte Haerlemse Courant* for the very first time learn of serious unrest in the Berbice Colony. A ship from Surinam reported 'that the *Naturellen* of Berbice had destroyed the colony, burnt down all the sugar mills except two, killed people and cattle alike, and had built a fort opposite the

21 KB_OHC, 31-8-1684. Rio de Berbice then was referred to as 'Berbisjes', 'Berbicies', 'Berbisies' and 'Barbisjes'. As geographical names were not standarized at that time, research is complicated.

22 KB_OHC, 19-6-1685.

23 KB_OHC, 5-3-1686.

24 KB_OHC, 15-7-1687.

fort [Nassau] that only was occupied by a small number of Christians'.[25] The Dutch term 'Naturellen' here refers to the Indians, the indigenous inhabitants of Berbice. 'Christians' as the colonist then also called themselves in reports, meant 'Europeans' or 'whites'.

We find no follow up at all to this shocking news. The following mention of this colony dates from 1694. In it the simultaneous arrival of three ships from Berbice is reported. This seems to be a rare occasion, even more exceptional as we read in the same newspaper that a fourth vessel had arrived at Berbice. It was a 'Surinaemsvaerder' named the *Son* and had been in Berbice prior hereto. Perhaps the colony could not provide enough return cargos. A fifth Zeeland ship had returned from Essequibo, a destination mentioned only once during this period. Ships possibly made combined journeys to neighbouring colonies along the Wild Coast. However, the information provided by newspapers at hand does not confirm this.

Surinam, 1665-1688

The very first time Surinam was mentioned in *La Gazette d'Amsterdam* was on 14 April 1667, the very same month negotiations in the Dutch town of Breda had started. This eventually resulted in the treaty of Breda which was signed on 31 July 1667.[26] The news acquired in London on 25 March concerned a party dispatched by the English Governor of Surinam to the mines of 'Thuian' (an apparent misspelling of Guiana). We read that the enslaved labourers and the free specialists at work at the foundry were taken. However, as further details are lacking, it is not clear if these mines were located in Cayenne, French Guiana, or in the Corantyne region.[27] The news is interesting because the Dutch refused the offer the British negotiators forwarded in Breda to hand back New Amsterdam, insisting in keeping Surinam. What was the background of this Dutch policy? Did they esteem the potential profits from the sugar plantations? Did they have a hidden agenda, related to old rumours originating from the early visit Sir Walter Ralegh had paid to this region in 1595? Tradition has it that, at the mouth of the Corantyne River, Ralegh had heard stories from local Indians that the gilded city of El Dorado was to be found in upstream Guiana. The news concerning the mines in Guiana was perhaps an extra argument for the Dutch to keep Surinam. Further news from the period preceding Adriaan van Berkel's first journey has already been dealt with in the

25 KB_OHC, 30-3-1688: '*Middelburg den 27 Maert.* (..) een Schip van Suriname [is] gearriveert, 't geen in Engelant niet heeft willen inlopen, maer 7 weecken oosten wint gehad en 3 Weken voor 't Canaal gelaveert: de Schipper rapporteert, dat de Naturellen op de Berbisies deselve Colonie geruineert, al de Suycker-Molens, except 2, verbrant, menschen en vee omgebracht en een fort tegens 't Fort, dat noch met eenige Christenenen beset was, opgeworpen hebben'.

26 KB_GA, 14-04-1667: '*De Londres le 25 Mars.* Les lettres de Surinam donnent avis du retour d'un Party que le Gouverneur avoit envoyé à 7 milles hors de Thuian; là où il a fait détruite une mine d'argent & emporter les armes & instruments, & emmener les esclaves & les Maitres de Fonte qui y travailloient'.

27 This news might be related to Baron Gerbier's frustated expedition (1659-1660). See for example M. van den Bel & L. Hulsman, Une colonie néerlandaise sur l'Approuague au début de la deuxième moitié du XVIIe siècle, *Bulletin de la société d'histoire de la Guadeloupe* 164, 2013.

Figure 2: Pen drawing of a Dutch 'driemast-galjoot' at sea by Cornelisz van der Salm (1660-1720) c.1675.

above section titled 'Early information on Surinam, 1665-1670'. Here the news published in Dutch papers will be taken up from 1670 on, the time that Surinam was firmly in Dutch hands. Again, the newspapers during this period dealt with captains leaving and arriving with their cargo. However the news is not entirely restricted to the purely commercial issues. Soon the Dutch Republic was at war again. In 1672 England and France together with two minute German states had declared war.[28] The Third Anglo-Dutch War ended with the signing of the Treaty of Westminster on 19 February 1674. The Franco-Dutch War continued until the signing of the Treaty of Nimwegen, on 11 August 1678. Peace was, nevertheless, short-lived. After the Dutch Stadtholder William III had crossed the North Sea in 1688 to be crowned King of Britain and Scotland, the Dutch Republic was involved in a major battle between France and the 'Great Alliance' resulting in the Nine Years' War (1688-1697).[29] The contemporary Dutch newspapers amply

28 These states were led by the Archbishop of Cologne in his capacity of Prince Elector of Cologne (consisting exclusive the town of Cologne) and the Bishop of Munster in his capacity of Head of State of the temporal possessions of the Diocese of Munster.

29 The Dutch often speak of England when referring to the U.K. As to the 17th century, the situation is indeed confusing. Newspapers such as the *Amsterdamsche Courant* speak of Brittagne. Likewise the adjective Brittannique is used by *La Gazette d'Amsterdam*. In 1603, England, Wales and Scotland were united into a personal union: James I of England was at the same time James II of Scotland. Formally, till the Act of Union of 1707, the island counted two kingdoms: Britain (consisting of England and Wales) and Scotland. The United Kingdom of Great Britain and Ireland dates from 1801. Wales was not known as a seafaring nation. It is thus quite understandable that Dutch newspapers also use the terms 'English' and 'Englishman', especially when identifying ships and their captains hailing from English ports.

report on the respective war years, and as ships plying over the Atlantic routes were threatened by men-of-war and privateers alike, a large part of the economic news on Surinam concerned hostile attacks overseas and commercial ships threatened or taken by the enemy.[30] Little wonder that business people as well as administrators (often merchants or affiliated with commercial circles) read this kind of news. It is striking that these contemporary newspapers report on the relation with the Indians in Surinam too. For present-day readers this is of interest as it corresponds with the information on the relation between the Zeeland colonists along the Berbice River and the indigenous Indians in *Amerikaansche Voyagien*. In that respect Van Berkel and the newspapers provide us with much more actual inside information when compared with George Warren's publication.[31] The latter merely mentions the fact that Indians 'made several attempts upon the English at their first settling [in Surinam, 1651], which were always frustrated, and they soundly smarted for their folly: now the Colony is grown potent they dare not but be humble.'[32]

The first reference to the recent war with England and its impact on the maritime connection with Surinam we find in the *Oprechte Haerlemse Courant* dated 18 July 1673. It presents us with a good insight into the misery inflicted upon common sailormen, who were very often defenseless victims of war. A positive exception hereto consists of the case of the ship *Maria* that along with another vessel from Curaçao had lost contact with its convoy to be subsequently taken by a Scottish privateer. However, a Zeeland vessel on its way to Surinam attacked this privateer, rescued the *Maria* as well as a boat from Sweden, laden with grains. Both were safely taken to Durgerdam near Amsterdam.[33] In 1676, the Franco-Dutch war ongoing, the Haarlem newspaper reported in February on the rumour that six French ships were spotted near Surinam. This was followed a month later by a statement that the convoy from London had safely arrived, including a ship from Surinam.[34]

---

30 The National Archives (Kew, Surrey) procures the so-called Prize Papers, which the High Court of Admiralty applied in order to judge if taken ships were legitimate bounty. Files from this era provide insight into the risky business of the merchant navy.

31 G. Warren, *An Impartial Description of Surinam upon the Continent of Guiana in America.* London, 1667 was published in a Dutch edition titled *Een onpartydige beschrijvinge van Surinam, Gelegen op het vaste Landt van Guiana in Africa*, Amsterdam: Pieter Arentsz, 1669.

32 G. Warren, op. cit., 1667, p. 26. Apart from several minor differences, one finds the same text in the Dutch translation of *An Impartial Description*, as is the case with Van Berkel's 'stolen' version. See A. van Berkel, op. cit., 1695, p. 133.

33 KB_OHC, 18-7-1673: '*Amsterdam den 17 Julij*. Het Scheepje de Maria, met de Hoecker de Elisabeth van Curassouw komende, van sijn Compagnie afgeraekt als gemelt, is door een Schotse Caper genomen geweest; maer een Zeeuws Schip, de wil hebbende nae Suriname, heeft gemelde Schotse Caper gerencontreert, hem meer gemelde Scheepje de Maria afgenomen, nevens noch een Sweets Schip met Graen, dat de Schotten hebben moeten verlaeten, soo dat sy niet een Mensch daer op gevonden hebben, en is gemelde Zeeuw, met de geseyde Prysen op komende, al voor Durckendam [Durgerdam] gekomen'.

34 KB_OHC, 4-2-1676: '*Amsterdam den 3 Februari* (..) Daer heeft hier een Gerucht van Suriname gelopen, al of de Fransse met 6 Schepen daer geweest waren, maer sonder seeckerheyt, en heeft geen vervolgh; 10-3-1676: *Amsterdamden 6 Maert* In Tessel is gearriveert het Convoy van Londen, ende met het selve verscheyde Koopvaerdy-schepen, daer onder het Gekroonde Radt, komende van Suriname'.

Several weeks after the Treaty of Nimwegen was signed in 1678, a ship commanded by Captain Willem de Vlaming had arrived in Plymouth, in the surprising space of time of merely 4 weeks and 3 days.[35] The war was over. 'All is well that ends well', it seemed. However, that was not the case: on 4 April 1679 the Haarlem newspaper describes the situation in Surinam at the time of the arrival of the incoming Governor Johannes Heinsius (*c.*1625-1680) who found 'the colony in a dismal condition due to the insurrection of the Indians'. They had killed one hundred slaves and forty whites, burnt five sugar mills to the ground and ruined several plantations. Soon after his arrival this Governor harvested his first modest success: a number of Indians had defected from their tribe members even assisting the Dutch in their struggle against them. The result hereof was that the revolting Indians could not escape and were forced to send envoys to negotiate peace. 'That is why', the paper writes, 'that one hopes that [the colony] will be set to rest again'.[36] The unrest had already started in *c.*1678, at a time the number of white inhabitants of Surinam had dropped from *c.*1500 to *c.* 500. In Governor Johannes Heinsius's view, as communicated to the commander of Essequibo, the raids of the Indians had to do with the peace treaty concluded between the two most important local groups: the Caribs of the Corantyne River and the Arawak, predominantly residing along the Berbice River. Heinsius therefore asked the commander of Essequibo to assist in ending their alliance. Only then could the Dutch successfully evade the Indians. He also suggested that the Arawak could be brought to the Dutch side if they obtained those Caribs the Dutch previously had captured as booty.[37] Regretably Adriaan van Berkel had not sent letters from his outpost in Berbice to the Netherlands containing further information on the relations with the Indians during his sojourn. In his 1695 narrative, he refers to the Caribs as 'the archenemies of the Arawaks' and as 'the Indians from the Corantyne River, enemies of ours'.[38] His remarks would have been a welcome addition to the scarce information printed in newspapers. Here the content of official missives sent from Surinam is not reflected. However, the policy of Governor Johannes Heinsius (who died in April 1680) that aimed at starting separate peaceful relations with the Indian groups in the Maroni District as well as with the Caribs in the Corantyne District proved to have had no long-term effect. Indeed the Dutch and

35 KB_OHC, 13-9-1678: '*Londen den 6 September* In Pleymuyen is een Nederlants Schip gearriveert, Schipper Willem de Vlaming, komt in 4 weecken en 3 dagen van Suriname'.

36 KB_OHC, 4-4-1679: '*Middelburg den 31 maart* Met de Schepen van Suriname gekomen, heeft men particulariteyt, dat den heer Heynsius als Gouverneur den 21 December aldaer was aengekomen, vindende die Colonie in een bedroefden staet, alsoo d'Indianen in een oproer wel 100 Slaven en 40 Blanken hadden doodt geslagen, 5 Moolens verbrandt en verscheyde Plantagien geruineert: doch met sijn komste, en dat eenige Indianen waren afgevallen, en by d'onse komende, de Oproermakers hadden helpen resisteren, waren sy genootsaekt geweest een Besending te doen, om van Vrede te tracteren, so dat men hoope heeft het weder tot ruste sal gebracht zijn. Sedert mijn laetste is hier noch gearriveert 't Schip de Maria, Schipper Joris Prijs, mede van Suriname komende, doch heeft een seer lange reys en vol rampe gehad, want is wel 7 maenden dat men van daer vertrock'. See R. Buve, 'Gouverneur Johannes Heinsius. De rol van Van Aerssen's voorganger in de Surinaamse Indianenoorlog, 1678-1680'. *Nieuwe West-Indische Gids* 45 (1966), pp. 14-26.

37 Zeeuws Archief (ZA), Middelburg, [Gids 102] Staten van Zeeland en Suriname, nr. 314, Johannes Heinsius to the commander of Essequibo, letter dated 31 December 1678.

38 A. van Berkel, op. cit., 1695, pp. 41, 97.

certain Indian groups clashed again. On 7 April 1681 letters arrived from Surinam, reporting the news that the incoming military commander of Surinam had had 'a lucky encounter with the Indians, resulting in the killing of 80 of them, and that afterwards they had not seen any more of them, so that they felt quite relieved.'[39] In June and September of the same year, reports on Indians in Surinam indicated the ongoing unrest. Captain Adriaen Tant, having arrived in Flushing on Saturday 12 June, wrote 'a new tumult had risen with the indigenous people.'[40] Both sources do not name the tribes involved. It was alarming news that certain French individuals had been caught while pretending to have come in peace to negotiate. On closer inspection, however, it appeared 'that they had with them a shipment of fire arms to be sold to the Indians.'[41] It was difficult to really comprehend all that occured during those years. On 20 March 1683 the above Haarlem newspaper reported that no skirmishes had recently occurred between colonists in Surinam and Indians. However, two months later, it was mentioned 'that the troubles with the Indians were still continuing.'[42] A captain who had arrived from Surinam on 15 June confirmed this news from Flushing.[43]

On several occasions, from 22 June 1683 on, the *Oprechte Haerlemse Courant* as well as the *Amsterdamsche Courant* reported on the departure of the Governor of Surinam, Cornelis van Aerssen, Lord of Sommelsdijck (1637-1688). He was supposed to leave on 6 July of that year, 'having contracted a great many people, even whole families are traveling with him'.[44] The Haarlem newspaper of the same date includes an advertisement, inviting those interested to enlist as a soldier and join Van Sommelsdijck's expedition, to come to the inn named *Plaets Royal* in

39 KB_OHC, 8-4-1681: '*Amsterdam den 7 April*: Uyt Tessel heeft men, dat aldaer een Scheepje, van St Valery komende, was gearriveert: Als mede een Hoecker, genaemt de Gedion, komende van Suriname; met het selve heeft men Brieven van daer van de 25 February, waer in vermelt werdt, dat die van die Colonie een nieuwe Commandant hadden bekomen, en onder deselve een geluckige rescontre met de Indianen hadden gehad, invoegen dat sy wel 80 van de selve hadden doodt geslagen, en 't sedert geen andere meer hadden vernomen, soo dat men daer wat beter gemoedt was'.

40 KB_OHC, 21-6-1681: '*Vlissingen den 18 Junij*: Voorleden Saturdag arriveerde hier Capiteyn Adriaen Tant, komende van Suriname; hy segt, dat aldaer weder een nieuw Tumult met de Naturellen was ontstaen'.

41 KB_OHC, 16-9-1681: '*Middelburg den 13 September*: Met het Schip Suriname, komende van die Colonie, heeft men, dat met een Chaloup aldaer 9 Franssen waren gekomen, om te negotiëren, maer men bevond, âls men haer aenhaelde, dat sy een party Vuur-Roers in hadden, om aen de Indianen te verkopen, onder voorgeven, dat sy een ordre van den Koningh by haer hadden; doch na examinatie bevond men de selve vals te zijn'.

42 KB_OHC, 20-3-1683: '*Amsterdam den 19 Maert*: Op gisteren arriveerde hier Schipper Paulus Jansz, manquerende 11 weecken van Suriname: met de Indianen was sedert laest geen Schermutseling voorgevallen; zijnde ons Volck thuys: de geweecken Indianen verkeerden met de Hollanders vreetsaem, en begonden haer met de Plantagie te bemoeyen'; idem KB_OHC 17-6-1683: '*Londen den 11 Junij*. Een Hollandts Schip, nu laetst tot Cowes [on the island of Whight] van Suriname gearriveert, rapporteert, dat de Troublen met de Indianen in die Colonie noch blyven continueren'.

43 KB_OHC, 19-6-1683: '*Vlissingen den 15 Juny*: Op heden is hier gearriveert Pieter Roey, komende van Suriname in drie Maenden geseylt; het stont daer noch als voor desen'.

44 KB_AC, 22-6-1683: ''*s Gravenhage den 20 Juny*. (..) In de aenstaende maent, staet de Heere van Somelsdijck na de Colonie van Suriname te vertrecken, hebbende seer veel volck aengenomen, selve gaen veel heele Familien mede'.

Amsterdam.[45] Apart from the daily rations, the advertisement states that a salary of 5 *stuyvers* would be paid.[46] In order to make this proposal more attractive contracts could be terminated without notice.[47] We may thus conclude that it was difficult to find sufficient people to enter service in Surinam. Van Sommeldijk's departure was postponed on more than one occasion not only due to his dealing with personal affairs but also the passing of his vessels across Pampus, the treacherous sandbank in the Zuyder Zee.[48] On 15 April 1684 the *Oprechte Haerlemse Courant* reported on the arrival of the Governor in Surinam.[49] Here he learned of the safe arrival of 200 horses which were very much in need in the colony.[50]

In subsequent years news on Surinam is limited to short messages dealing with the arrival and departures of ships. Interestingly the transport of slaves is mentioned now and again. Although the system as such was not the subject of a public discussion, news concerning the trade in enslaved Africans, their transport to America and employment in the colonial plantations must have been widely known, albeit that few will have been familiar with details. Chapters 'On the plantations' and 'On the Negroes or Slaves' in the translated edition of George Warren's description of Surinam were perhaps the first reliable accounts of this subject, accessible to an interested readership. We do not know how many copies of the Dutch translation of Warren's *An Impartial Description* were printed. Nonetheless his sharp remarks echoed in the *American Voyages* in which Chapter VIII titled 'Of the Negroes or Slaves' was literally copied via the translation of 1669. Its readers must have come across the remark on the sale of enslaved Africans in Surinam 'where they are sold like dogs.'[51] Warren's conclusions regarding the treatment of the slaves (copied again in the second part of Van Berkel's voyages, Chapter IX) were not less critical.

---

45 The inn named *Plaets Royal* was located outside the town walls, possibly near the present Amstelveenseweg.

46 An artisan could earn *c.* 20 *stuyvers* a day i.e., *c.*1 guilder.

47 KB_OHC, 22-6-1683: 'Also het vertrek van den Heere van Somelsdijck na Suriname blijft vastgestelt tegen den 6. July, staet sijn Hoog-Ed. sekerlijck op die tijd te vertrecken, met een considerabel getal Familien; en wert een yder geadverteert, die genegen zijn mede te gaen, hier noch aen te geven, op dat bequame commoditeteyt tot haer overbrengen genieten; en wie als Soldaet sig sal willen engageren, kan sig adresseren tot Amsterdam, in de Plaets Royal, sal boven sijn dagelijckse rantions, 5 Stuyvers 's daegs tot Soldy ontvangen, en daer afscheyt bekomen, als sy het sullen versoeken'.

48 KB_OHC, 5-8-1683: '*Amsterdam den 4 Augusti.* Sijn Excell: den Heere van Sommelsdijck onthout sig noch alhier; wachtende maer alleen, dat sijn Schip over 't Pampus sal zijn, om sig dan van hier te begeven, en sijn Reyse na Suriname voort te setten'. For earlier short references to his departure, see: KB_OHC 10-7-1683; KB_OHC 15-7-1683; KB_AC, 27-7-1683.

49 KB_OHC, 15-4-1684: '*Amsterdam den 14 April.* Volgens schryven van Zeelandt was de Heer van Sommelsdijck tot Suriname gearriveert'.

50 KB_OHC, 29-2-1684: '*Amsterdam den 14 April.* Tot Suriname waren wel 200 Paerden aengekomen'. The ship with the news concerning the supply of 200 horses must have left Surinam at least a few days before 24 November 1683. The newspaper continues with the remark that the incoming Governor had not yet arrived ('Den Heer van Sommelsdijck was daer noch niet gearriveert'). These horses mentioned may well have been imported from Ireland. A later news item mentions Cork as a port from which horses were shipped to Surinam KB-OHC, 6-5-1688).

51 G. Warren, *An Impartial Description*, 1667, p. 19; A. van Berkel, *American Voyages*, 1695, pp. 126-127.

Needless to say, only a limited number read this remark. In general, any business information exchanged between the administrators in the colonies and relevant governing bodies in the Netherlands remained secret. Therefore only those with inside information knew of the constant flow of slaves to the West Indies. Now and again, however, the public newspapers mention these transports. On 5 March 1686, for instance, the above Haarlem newspaper reports the arrival of the ship *Johanna*. The steersman Cornelis Antheunisz states it had transported slaves to Surinam and another would follow shortly.[52] We read that, in December, the Sociëteit van Suriname (i.e., the governing body of the colony since 1683) had been informed that the *Coning Salomon* had arrived in the Meuse River with sugar from Surinam, 'where another slave ship had arrived.' A more comprehensive version of this report was published in a special edition of the above Haarlem newspaper. Here it is added that the slaver had brought slaves from Angola. Interestingly it continues with the remark that another ship had arrived directly from the Gulf of Guinea, carrying 120 *Marck*[53] weight of gold.[54] This indicates that certainly not all ships destined for West Africa were involved in the triangular trade route Europe-Africa-America. The ship laden with gold named '*t Wapen van Englant* may have acquired its precious cargo from the 'Gold Coast' at a time this trade was still important, as was the trade in ivory from the 'Ivory Coast'.

We read on the slave trade again in March 1687. The correspondent in Flushing forwarded the news of the arrival of shipper Jan Boom, who in turn had reported that 'in Surinam shipper Mouris of the Calbary had arrived with Negroes.'[55] Once more the subject of the relation with the Indians is touched upon. Letters brought from Surinam by the *Apolonia*, dated 4 March 1687, advised that the *Sara* had arrived in Flushing after a 6-week voyage, adding: 'that one had a very good relation with the Indians; that everything in that country went well, and that all was at rest and in peace.'[56]

---

52 KB_OHC, 5-3-1686: '*Vlissingen den 25 Februarij.* Op den 24 desen is alhier gearriveert Schipper Cornelis Antheunisz., voerende 't Schip de Johanna, komende in 9 weken van Suriname, van waer 't Schip van de West-Indische Compagnie, voor de kamer van Enckhuysen, dat aldaer Slaven hadde gebracht, daegs daer aen stont te volgen (..)'.

53 Marck: one mark weighing *c.*230.4 grams can be divided into 8 ounces weighing *c.*28.8 grams. Several standards of measuring the weight of gold were utilised during this period.

54 KB_OHC, 12-12-1686: '*Vlissingen den 25Februarij.* De Societeyt heeft Brieven, dat 't Schip de Coning Salomo, komende met Suyker van Suriname, alwaer noch een slave schip gearriveert was, in de Maes gekomen is'; KB_OHC, special edition, 12-12-1686: 'Amsterdam den 11 December. (..) 't Schip de Coning Salomon, den 4 October van Suriname vertrocken, alwaer het Slaven van Angola had gebracht, is te Goeree binnen gelopen; en noch een ander schip, 't Wapen van Engelant, te Rotterdam, dat van den 29 Augusti van Guinee manqueerde, 't welck 120 Marck Gout heeft mede gebracht; maar geen ander nieuws, als dat de saken van de Commercie alle wel stonden'.

55 KB_OHC, 22-32-1687: '*Vlissingen den 18 Maert.* (..) En heden [is gearriveert] Schipper Jan Boom, in 9 weeken van Suriname, na Middelburg gedestineert; welcke rapporteert, dat te Suriname Schipper Mouris van de Calbary met Negers aengekomen is'.

56 KB_OHC, 22-32-1687: '*Amsterdam den 28 Meij* Met het Schip de Apolonia, 't welk in Zeelant van Suriname aengekomen is, zijn Brieven van den 4 Maert van die Plaets, dewelke adviseren, dat 't Schip de Sara daer in 6 weecken van hier gearriveert is; dat men seer goede Correspondentie met de Indianen had; dat het in 't Lant seer wel stont, en dat alles in rust en Vrede was'.

The above-mentioned Amsterdam and Haarlem newspapers contain interesting information on the arrival and sojourn of two 'Little Kings' or Indian chieftains. Initially it was written that they hailed from Surinam. A second report, however, stated these men were from the region neighbouring Surinam and that they were allies of the Dutch. Apparently Governor Van Sommelsdijck had urged them to visit his homeland in order to learn more about the Dutch. Their visit included 'a tour à la mode in the Voor-Hout', the square where the *beau monde* met.[57] In addition to The Hague, the 'Little Kings' visited Rotterdam as well as *'t Loo*, the hunting lodge of the Prince of Orange-Nassau located just outside the town of Apeldoorn, in order to meet the Stadtholder and his wife Mary Stuart. Both chiefs then travelled to Amsterdam and returned to their homeland from here.[58]

The *Amsterdamsche Courant* dated 9 October 1688 refers shortly to the news provided by Adriaan Dankers, the Captain of the *Sommelsdijck* (sic!), 'confiming the rebellion and the death of the Heeren Van Sommelsdijck and Verboom' adding that another ship named *St. Andries* would follow and depart from Surinam not later than August.[59]

The murder of Van Sommelsdijck (19 July 1688) and the French raid (6-11 May 1689)

No earlier editions mentioned the events in Surinam. We may therefore presume the above Amsterdam newspaper referred to the information published by the *Oprechte Haerlemse Courant* on 5 October. As is obvious from the newspapers quoted prior hereto, the *courantier* Abraham Casteleyn devoted a large amount of copy on the West Indies, much more than his Amsterdam colleagues and competitors did. An as yet unexplained personal interest might have inspired him to expand his network to towns in Zeeland (e.g., Flushing, Middelburg). Whereas the *Amsterdamsche Courant* spent only twenty-seven words on news from Surinam, Casteleyn in his *Oprechte Haerlemse Courant* utilized as many as 179 words, providing readers with a good impression of the events in Surinam. A real mutiny had taken place in the course of which soldiers had complained about

57 KB_OHC, 6-4-1688: '*'s Gravenhage den 4 April.* (..) Twee van de voornaemste Edelen van Suriname, welke gesegt werden, twee Heydense Koningen van die Quartieren te wesen, zijn alhier gearriveert ende van den Gouverneur, den heere van Sommelsdijck herwaerts gesonden, om dese Landen te besigtigen: Sy reden van de namiddag in 't Voor-Hout den Tour à la mode en waren alvorens in 't Bosch alles besien'. Ibidem KB_OHC, 6-4-1688: '*'s Gravenhage den 5 April.* De twee kleyne Koningen (waervan wy op gisteren in onse voorgaende gewag gemaeckt hebben) zijn van de Naburige Landen van Suriname ende met onse Natie aldaer in Alliantie'.

58 KB_OHC, 8-4-1688: '*'s Gravenhage den 8 April* (..) De twee kleyne Koningen van Suriname, laest gearriveert, en na Rotterdam, om die Stad te besichtigen, vertrocken. Sy wierden gisteren nevens andere Heeren door de Vrouwe van Sommelsdijck getracteert ende staen in 't kort na hare Hoogheden tot Loo te gaen'; KB_OHC, 17-4-1688: '*'s Gravenhage den 15 April.* (..) Ondertusschen zijn de twee kleyne Koningen van de gewesten van Suriname, na alles, wat besiens waerdig is, alhier besichtigt te hebben, na Amsterdam vertrocken'.

59 Koninklijke Bibliotheek, Den Haag, *Amsterdamsche Courant* (AC), 9-10-1688: '*Amsterdams den 8 October.* (..) Tot Middelburg was van Suriname gearriveert het Schip Sommelsdijck, Schipper Adriaan Dankers, met de confirmatie van de rebellie en doot van de Heeren van Sommelsdijck en Verboom. 't Schip de St. Andries stont in 't laest van Augusti hem te volgen'.

their meager rations and had threatened Governor, Cornelis Van Aerssen, Lord of Sommelsdijck. After several days of a insurgence Van Sommelsdijck met with a delegation from the rebels. Next instead of talking in a pacifying manner, he stepped forwards, his sword pointed at the rebels. Their reaction was unheard of: they aimed their muskets at the Governor and fired. Van Sommelsdijck fell to the ground, struck by three bullets. The report states he did not die instantly. Standing up with his sword in his hand he ran at the soldiers who then fired several rounds and 'as a result of that he fell dead to the ground with 30 wounds'. His commander Jan Verboom, who wanted to assist him, was shot dead as well. Later, '11 of the main ringleaders were caught, 8 hanged and 3 broken on the wheel; 20 others have been caught as well and sent back to the Netherlands'.[60]

In order to understand more about the role the Casteleyn news agency possibly played in the realization of Adriaan van Berkels's *Amerikaansche Voyagien*, we must closely examine Casteleyn's other asset i.e., the renowned yearbook entitled the *Hollandse Mercurius*.[61] Tome 39, 'telling the most important affairs of the state and other incidents occurred in and about the United Netherlands and elsewhere in Europe in the year 1688' reports on the events resulting in Governor Van Sommelsdijck's demise.[62] The first lines differ slightly from the report previously presented in the *Oprechte Haerlemse Courant*. The first part of the story told by Adriaan van Berkel is much more exhaustive, providing more detailed information on the background of the rebellion as well as on the facts linked to that disastrous 19 July. The second part of the story deals with the 140 and 150 rebels who first appointed officers of their own choice, before extorting 3,500 guilders from civilians in the expectation they could escape from the colony with two ships taken by force. However, this did not unfold as hoped. Indeed, the mutineers as described above were sentenced and punished. Van Berkel applies exactly the same

---

60 KB_OHC, 5-10-1688: '*Amsterdam den 4 Oktober.* In Tessel is gearriveert 't Schip Salamander van Suriname, en met 't selve Brieven van den 7 Augusti, meldende, dat eenige Soldaten van 't Guarnisoen den 19 July tegen den Gouverneur, den Heer van Sommelsdijck, hadden beginnen te rebelleren, uyt oorsaeck, dat men haer Rantsoen trachtte te verminderen; dat dit ettelijcke dagen continueerde en eyndelick soo ver quam, dat de heer van Sommelsdijck selfe personelijk met de Sabel in de Hant nevens sommige assistenten de Rebellen mosten resisteren; dat hy in die ontmoeting door drie musquet-schoten, op hem gelost, ter aerde neder-viel; doch echter niet doot; dat hy, opstaende, de Rebellen met de Sabel in de Vuyst weder te keer ging; maer dat sy een geheele Charge op hem losten en hy daer door met in de 30 Wonden doot ter Aerde storte: desselfs Commandeur, Jan Verboom, die hem wilde assisteren, is oock doot geschoten. Na dat dit volbracht was, heeft men 11 van de principaelste Belhamels gevangen gekregen, 8 gehangen en 3 geradbraeckt: 20 andere zijn insgelijcks by de kop gevat en herwaerts overgesonden'. There is also a detailed descriptino of this mutiny, the trial and execution to be found in: T. Pistorius, *Korte en zakelijke beschrijvinge van de Colonie van Zuriname*, Amsterdam: Theodorus Crajenschot, 1763, pp. 100-157.

61 Abraham Casteleyn (*c.*1628-1681) was succeeded by his son Gerard (1665-1702). See G. Verhoeven en S. van der Veen, De Hollandse Mercurius. Een Haarlems Jaarboek uit de zeventiende eeuw. Haarlem: Bubb Kuyper Veilingen, 2011.

62 University of Amsterdam, Special Collections, *Hollandse Mercurius,* Tome 39 (1688), Haarlem 1689, p. 151.

words as the 113 printed in the *Hollandse Mercurius*.[63] The present reader may easily compare this source with the Dutch text published in the *Amerikaansche Voyagien*.[64]

Let us not jump to premature conclusions, but first look into the manner in which the *Amsterdamsche Courant*, the *Oprechte Haerlemse Courant*, the *Hollandse Mercurius* and the *Amerikaansche Voyagien* deal with the following event: the French raid on Surinam on 6-11 May 1689. The Haarlem newspaper dated 6 August 1689 presents us with an in-depth report, based on letters dated 27 May 1689, which *De Kroon*, *De Juffrou Gordina* and *De Postellion* delivered from Surinam.[65] Exactly the same story on an attack the privateer Jean-Baptiste du Casse (1646-1715) carried out by means of a small fleet commanded from his ship *Le Hasardeux*, can be found in *Amerikaansche Voyagien*. Only a small number of words had been changed in order to adapt the text to personal taste. The only dissimilarity with the newspaper version is that Van Berkel relates the story of an accident that befell François, the Lord of Châtillon (1669-1740) and second son to the late Governor Van Sommelsdijck.[66] Being in command of a battery and, without the required artillerists, François had attempted to discharge a cannon entirely on his own. However, while doing so he was seriously hurt as it fired prematurely.[67] Close examination of the text on the French raid published by Casteleyn[68] teaches us that this text is exactly the same as the one printed in the *Amerikaansche Voyagien*.

Based on this, one may speculate in an attempt to comprehend what had actually occurred. It is certain that the texts published in the *Oprechte Haerlemse Courant* (1688, 1689) and in the *Hollandse Mercurius* appeared between 5 and 7 years prior to the *Amerikaansche Voyagien*. It is quite probable, as shown in this Introduction (see below), that Van Berkel had really existed and had traveled to the Berbice River and had written about his adventures. However, as will be proven later, he never visited Surinam. The publisher Johan ten Hoorn simply copied

---

63 'De soldaten bemachtigden het fort/ versterckten haer tot 140 a 150 man/ wierpen keur-overstens in plaets van de officiers van het fort op/ overweldighden twee schepen op de rivier/ voorsagen se met behoeften uyt het magasijn/ persten de burgers/ na haer ontwapent te hebben/ 3500 guldens af en vervaerdigden alles tot haer vertreck: de Politijcke Raetsheeren van het Lant deden haer weten/ dat de geene/ die wilden blijven/ quijtgescholden souden werden: 40 à 50 lieten haer geseggen: de overige raeckten t scheep; maer gaven haer, op het t'samenrotten der gantsche Colonie en beloften/ dat alleen de schuldige gestraft souden werden/ over: 8 van de belhamels wierden opgehangen/ 3 gerabrackt en de rest ontslagen.' Hollandse Mercurius, Tome 39 (1688), Haarlem 1689, p. 151.

64 A. van Berkel, op. cit., 1695, pp. 136-137.

65 KB_OHC, 5-10-1688: '*Amsterdam den 5 Augusti.* Amsterdam den 5 Augusti (..) De 3 Schepen de Kroon, Sipke Pietersz Blaeu; de Juffr. Gordina, Andries Martensz. en de Postellion, Jan Langman, in omtrent de 10 weken van Suriname gearriveert, brengen de volgende tyding (..)' [followed the report, dated Suriname, 27 May 1689, on the French raid].

66 François, the second son of Cornelis van Aerssen, Lord of Sommelsdijck, had joined his father to travel to Surinam in August 1683, arriving here at the beginning of 1684. In 1687 the former returns to the Netherlands in the company of three free and four enslaved Indians. Having received the news of his father's demise, he left for Surinam in order to settle the affairs here as is reported in the *Oprechte Haerlemse Courant* dated 12 October 1688 ('The Hague, 10 October: Rumour has it that the son of the late Lord of Sommelsdijck, governor of Surinam, will depart for Surinam shortly').

67 A. van Berkel, op. cit., 1695, p. 138.

68 University of Amsterdam, Special Collections, *Hollandse Mercurius,* Tome 40 (1689), Haarlem 1690, pp. 159-161.

Figure 3: View of the Oudezijds Heerenlogement in Amsterdam, opposite Johan ten Hoorn's office. Anonymous print, c.1664.

Warren's booklet on Surinam which had been published in a Dutch translation in 1669, utilising Adriaan van Berkel as a *nom de plume*. Ten Hoorn removed the final paragraph 'Hast, and an unfaithful Memory, made me omit an Observation..' replacing it with a few new lines, beginning with 'After the reader has thus been given a description of the most important things which can be noted for the Colony of Surinam, I shall return to other business which happened therein my time (..).'[69] In order to add flavour, Ten Hoorn gratefully adopted texts from the *Hollandse Mercurius*, bridging the story of Van Sommelsdijck's murder in 1688 with the French raid in 1689 by means of a small number of words he had to invent himself. Having inserted 'Nine or ten months after that, when we were again involved in an open war with the King of France' he simply continued with the report published in the *Hollandse Mercurius*, 'several French men-of-war in the West Indies seized the island of St. Christopher from the English and fancied to do the same with Surinam shortly after the arrival of Mr. Van Scherphuysen, the incoming Governor.'[70] Having heard the news concerning the arrival of French sails, the Governor ordered all military officers to concentrate their troops inside the fort, and so they did. 'Even the Jews' entered the fort, the *Hollandse Mercurius* wrote, 'notwithstanding the Sabbath.' This interesting observation Johan ten Hoorn omitted, albeit he dutifully followed the remaining part of the report. He ends the paragraph on the French raid with a fine ruse, again inserting several

69 G. Warren, op. cit., 1667, pp. 27-28; A. van Berkel, op. cit., 1695, p. 135.

70 University of Amsterdam, Special Collections, *Hollandse Mercurius*, Tome 40 (1689), Haarlem 1690, pp. 159-160.

simple lines: 'Three to four weeks after this incident, my stay in Surinam came to an end.'[71] Yes of course, for Ten Hoorn himself had introduced the incoming secretary as a *deus ex machina*, who solved the problem of how to get rid of this Adriaan van Berkel by means of his unexpected arrival. The former secretary could now board the first vessel leaving for Zeeland. Moreover, Johan ten Hoorn could close the episode concerning this fictitious journey. Remarkably he was too lazy to steal more (fragments) of text, for instance news the *Amsterdamsche Courant* published on 29 August 1689, too, on letters from Saint-Christophe stating: 'that the French ships which earlier had attacked Surinam had arrived in Martinique beyond repair and have thrown overboard many dead bodies.[72]

Conclusion

The information on Surinam forwarded by Johan ten Hoorn in 1695 had already been made public during the late 1660s and 1680s. Although we may be confident of the fact that the story about the Berbice River consists of authentic first-hand material recorded during the 1670s, no further contents had been added to the descriptions of both colonies. This would have been quite possible: now and again the *Amsterdamsche Courant* and the *Oprechte Haerlemse Courant* reported on the two colonies. Several examples hereof will indicate which material Johan ten Hoorn could have applied in order to fabricate an appealing, updated story covering the years between 1689 and 1695. Adriaan van Berkel's sojourn in Surinam being an invention and his name a mere pseudonym, his publisher Ten Hoorn had no excuse whatsoever not to postpone his departure and to invent a later arrival date in Middelburg.[73] In that case Van Berkel could have witnessed the arrival of the incoming Governor, Johan Van Scharphuizen (?-1699) on 12 March, on whom the *Oprechte Haerlemse Courant* reported several times, from his departure on 14 January 1689 till his arrival in February of the same year.[74]

The issues of the *Oprechte Haerlemse Courant* dated 10 February and 28 August 1689 both reported on the improvements of the fort. In addition they reassure that 'all was in good order'. Nevertheless, on 28 August, it adds 'there was a great desire for more cannons and troops'.[75] The Dutch Republic and its ally, the British Isles, fought the French all over the world during the Nine Years' War (1688-1697). Now transport over the high seas was not without risks. For this reason newspapers mention the safe arrival of ships time and again. As to the plantation colonies

71 A. van Berkel, op. cit., 1695, p. 138.

72 KB_AC, 29-8-1689: '*Amsterdam den 29 Augusti.* Brieven van St. Christoffel, melden dat de Fransse schepen die de attaque op Suriname gedaan hebben, seer reddeloos aen Martinique gekomen waren, hebbende veel dooden over boort geset'.

73 A. van Berkel, op. cit., 1695, p. 139: 'I stepped ashore on the 6th of August of the year 1689 at Middelburg'.

74 KB_OHC, 18-1-1689 (departure) and 7-6-1689 (arrival).

75 KB_OHC, 10-2-1689: 'Alles was in goede Staet en men was doende, met het Fort te verstercken'; KB_OHC, 28-8-1689: 'De Vogel Phoenix, Gerrit Warnicker, van Suriname, in Tessel binnen, brengt Brieven van den 15 Juny, van inhout, dat alles wel stont, de Fortificatien verbetert werden, er na meer Geschut en Volk groot Verlangen was; en de Rotterdamse Koopman met een ander Schip na 't vaderlant vertrocken'.

the transfer of enslaved Africans via the Middle Passage was crucial for their economies. Therefore Captain Tang's statement, upon arrival from Surinam, 'that the ship *Europe* had arrived with negroes from Angola', must have greatly assured readers who had invested their money in the West Indies. Such news could have been inserted into George Warren's description. Yet again, Johan ten Hoorn was not interested in investing time and money in order to upgrade his publication. Considering the general lack of information on the Berbice River and Surinam during that period, this unofficial reprint-*cum*-stolen newspaper reports was in his view sufficiently appealing to the Dutch readership.

Chapter 2

History and reception of *American Voyages*

Introduction

It is only during the second half of the 18th century that Van Berkel's work is referred to by other Dutch historians such as Jan Jacob Hartsinck. It had however been copied by J.D. Herlein in his *Beschryvinge van de volk-plantinge Zuriname*, published in 1718.[76] For some reason, later historians, e.g., D. Nassy (1788) and A. Kappler (1854), do not refer to *American Voyages*. C. van Sijpestijn (1854), J. Wolbers (1861), and P.M. Netscher (1888) do so only incidentally. Apparently Van Berkel's publication was bound for oblivion.[77] In 1913, the Dutch historian J. Knuttel presents us with excerpts from *American Voyages* in an anthology of travelogues and poetry dating from the 17th century.[78]

---

76 J.J. Hartsinck *Beschrijving van Guiana of de Wilde Kust, in Zuid-America* [...], Amsterdam: Gerrit Tieleburg, 1770, p. 280; J.D. Herlein, *Beschryvinge van de Volk-Plantinge Zuriname* [...], Leeuwarden: Meindert Injema, 1718; J. van Donselaar, *Werken van Warren*, 1993, p. 87.

77 D. Nassy, *Geschiedenis der Kolonie van Suriname*, 1788 (facsimile ed. by S. Emmering, Amsterdam 1974); A. Kappler, *Zes Jaren in Suriname. Schetsen en tafereelen uit het maatschappelijke en militaire leven in deze kolonie*, 2 Vols., Utrecht: W.F. Dannenfelser, 1854; C. A. van Sijpesteijn, *Beschrijving van Suriname, Historisch-, Geographisch- en Statistisch Overzigt, uit officiele bronnen bijeengebragt*, Den Haag: De Gebroeders van Cleef, 1854, p. 267; J. Wolbers, Geschiedenis van Suriname, Amsterdam: De Hoogh, 1861, p. 178 (facsimile edited by S. Emmering, Amsterdam, 1970); P.M. Netcher, *Geschiedenis van de Koloniën Essequebo, Demerary en Berbice, van de vestiging tot op onze tijd*, Den Haag: Martinus Nijhoff, 1888, pp. 80-82. Interestingly, none of these works refer to Andreas Seyler's German translation: *Adrian van Berkel's Beschreibung seiner Reisen nach Rio de Berbice und Surinam: Aus dem Holländischen übersetzt, Sammlung seltener und merkwürdiger Reisegeschichten*, Memmingen: Andreas Seyler, 1789.

78 J.A.N. Knuttel, Adriaan van Berkel, Amerikaanse Voyagien behelzende een reis na Rio de Berbice [...], *Proza uit de 17e eeuw*, Verzameld en toegelicht door J. Knuttel, Redacteur van het 'Woordenboek der Nederlandse taal', met reproducties van Titelbladen en Titelprenten, Amsterdam: S.L. van Looy, 1913, pp. 228-242.

In Guyana, historians, e.g., H. Bolingbroke (1807), W. Brett (1851), J. Rodway J. Watt (1888), D. Brinton (1871) and H. Dalton (1855) do not refer to Van Berkel, despite the fact the latter historian was a good friend of P.M. Netscher.[79] At the end of the 19th and the beginning of the 20th century, neither E.F. Im Thurn (1883), C. Harris & J. Villiers (1911) nor Walter E. Roth himself mentions Van Berkel's *American Voyages*.[80] In 1924 it is finally included in the bibliography of Roth's renowned publication entitled *An Introductory Study of the Arts, Crafts, and Customs of the Guiana Indians*.[81]

Walter E. Roth and the first English translation of Van Berkel's *American Voyages*

Before arriving in British Guiana in 1907, Roth had worked as an ethnologist among the aborigines of Australia. Appointed by the Imperial government in British Guiana as stipendiary magistrate, he also served as a medical magistrate and district commissioner. Having continued his anthropological work, he carried out three extended field expeditions which provided a basis for various articles and three monographs. Having taken up an interest in the history of Guyana, Roth started translating works by German and Dutch explorers and historians, e.g., the *Travels of Richard Schomburgk* (1922).[82] As the translation of Richard Schomburgk's travels does not mention *American Voyages*, one might conclude that Roth 'discovered' its author after 1922, but certainly prior to 1924, when Roth's book on the Guiana Indians was published. Roth seems to have been enthusiastic about his discovery. In this 1924 publication he often quotes from Van Berkel and

79 H. Bolingbroke, *A Voyage to the Demerary, containing a statistical account of the Settlements there, and of those of the Essequibo, the Berbice, and other contiguous Rivers of Guyana*, Norwich: Richard Philips, 1807; W.H. Brett, *Indian Missions in Guiana*, London: George Bell, 1851; J. Rodway & J.T. Watt, *Chronological History of the Discovery and Settlement of Guiana, 1493-1668*, Georgetown: Royal Gazette Office, 1888; D. G. Brinton, *The Arawack Language of Guiana in its Linguistic and Ethnological Relations*, Philadelphia: McCalla & Stavely Printers, 1871; H.G. Dalton, *The History of British Guiana comprising a General Description of the Colony*, 2 Vols., London: Longman, Brown, Green & Longmans, 1855); P. M. Netscher, *Geschiedenis van de Koloniën*, 1888, p. ix.

80 E.F. Im Thurn, *Among the Indians of Guiana, Being sketches chiefly anthropologic from the interior of British Guiana*, London: Kegan Paul, Trench & Co, 1883; C. A. Harris & J. A. J. de Villiers, *Storm van 's Gravesande, The Rise of British Guiana*, Vol. 1. Works issued by The Hakluyt Society, Second Series 26, London, 1911; W.E. Roth, *An Inquiry into the Animism and Folk-lore of the Guiana Indians*, Extract from the Thirtieth Annual Report of the Bureau of American Ethnology, Washington DC: Government Printing Office, 1915, pp. 113-116.

81 W.E. Roth, *An introductory study of the Arts, Crafts, and Customs of the Guiana Indians.* In: Thirty-Eighth annual report of the Bureau of American Ethnology to the Secretary of the Smithsonian Institution 1916-1917, Washington DC: United States Government Printing Office, 1924, p. 63.

82 *Richard Schomburgk's Travels in British Guiana, 1840-1844*, translated and edited, with Geographical and General Indices, and Route Maps by Walter E. Roth, Daily Chronicle, Georgetown, 1922. A few years before his death in 1933, Roth publishes *The History of the Colonies Essequibo, Demerary and Berbice form the Dutch Establishment to the present day*, The Daily Chronicle, 1929, the *magnum opus* of the Dutch historian P. M. Netscher.

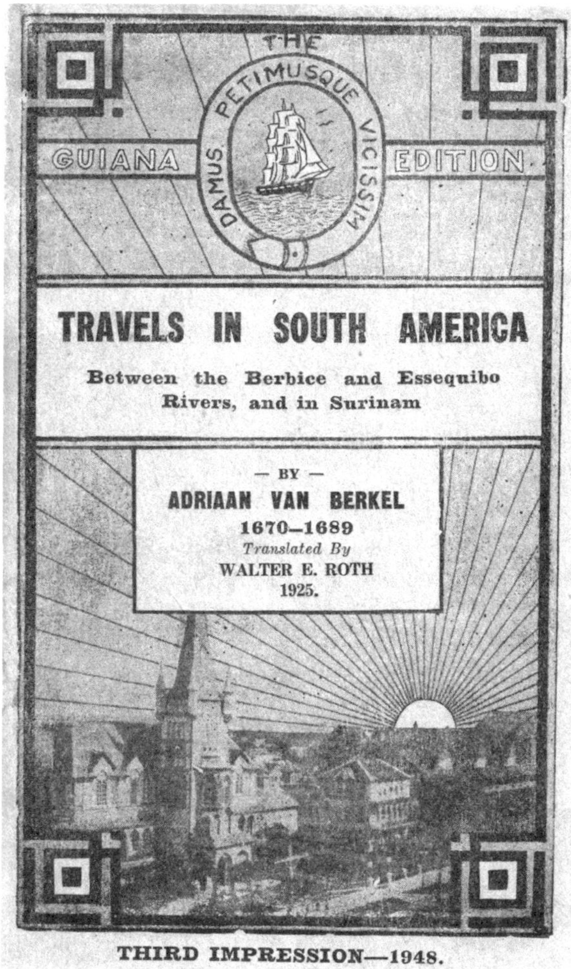
THE
PETIMUSQUE DAMUS VICISSIM
GUIANA EDITION

TRAVELS IN SOUTH AMERICA

Between the Berbice and Essequibo
Rivers, and in Surinam

— BY —
ADRIAAN VAN BERKEL
1670–1689
Translated By
WALTER E. ROTH
1925.

THIRD IMPRESSION—1948.

Figure 4: Title page of Walter E. Roth, Adriaan van Berkel's Travels in South America between the Berbice and Essequibo rivers and in Surinam, 1670-1689 (1948).

it appears that Roth had planned to start another translation project much earlier. The first results of his new project appeared in 1926, as a series in *The Daily Chronicle*.[83]

However, the 'Translator's Preface' of the posthumous publication of the complete translations, published in 1948, reveal that Roth had completed the translation of the entire book on 22 January 1922.[84] How can this early date be explained? The answer lies in in the acknowledgments of this posthumous publication. Here Roth thanks G. Wolff-Sybolts of Paramaribo for assisting him with the translation of Van Berkel's book. She was married to J.W. Wolff, bacteriologist and Chief Health Inspector of the Netherlands Indies who in 1921 was sent temporarily to

---

83 W.E. Roth, *Adriaan van Berkel's Travels,* 1948, p. v. The title page however gives 1925 as publication date.

84 W.E. Roth, *Adriaan van Berkel's Travels in South America between the Berbice and Essequibo Rivers and in Surinam 1670-1689*. Georgetown: *The Daily Chronicle*, 1948. This edition is currently very rare. The 3rd edition (*Adriaan van Berkel's Travels*, 1948) was consulted for this publication. In it the reference including the date of translation is given on p. xi.

Surinam.[85] Having arrived that same year, J.W. Wolff travelled to British Guiana in order to attend a medical conference in Georgetown, held on 27 June 1921. This conference predates Roth's signature of January 1922 in the Van Berkel translation and may fit the idea that this translation project had already began in 1921. J.W. Wolff may possibly have met Roth in Georgetown and introduced him to his wife who worked in the Colonial Library of Paramaribo and may have known Adriaan van Berkel's book (now held at the library of the Anton de Kom University). Once Dr. Wolff resigned in 1923[86] the couple probably returned to Sumatra later that year.[87] If Roth had already purchased a copy of Van Berkel's book prior to the 1921 conference, thus only demanding corrections of his translation, remains unknown. Whatever the case may be, Roth appreciated the information he retrieved from Van Berkel stressing in his own work the importance of Van Berkel's descriptions, notably of the inauguration of an Amerindian Captain and of the treatment of Indian slaves.[88]

The English anthropologist Neil L. Whitehead was another researcher to pick up the ethnographic information Van Berkel provided, notably the story on Carib warfare and the way one traded with the Dutch.[89] In a note referring to the print by Casper Luijken, that served to illustrate the front cover of his study, Whitehead writes it depicts 'a whipping scene Van Berkel seemed to have witnessed', expressing his doubts if Van Berkel had indeed really been present at such an event.[90]

As will be discussed in this Introduction (see below), we should be careful and critical when accepting any information provided in *American Voyages* at first glance. The interest shown by certain historians regarding Van Berkel because of his detailed narrative concerning the Van Sommelsdijck murder (as discussed above) has proven to be ill-founded.[91]

Original text or compilation?

The possibility that *American Voyages* contained plagiarism and even included fictitious segments was made clear by Walter E. Roth when pointing out that its second part was an almost literal translation of G. Warren's *An Impartial Description*

85 Handelingen der Staten-Generaal (HSG) 1922-1923.

86 HSG 1923-1924.

87 *Sumatra Post*, 36ste Jaargang, No. 62, Donderdag 15 Maart 1934.

88 W.E. Roth, op. cit., 1924, pp. 570-571, 593.

89 The Dutch archaeologist Arie Boomert quotes from Van Berkel in his historical research on the Arawak of Trinidad, See A. Boomert, The Arawak Indians of Trinidad and Coastal Guiana, ca 1500-1650, *Journal of Caribbean History* 19, 1984, p. 137. See also D. Roos, *Zeeuwen en de Westindische Compagnie (1621-1674)*, Hulst: van Geyt Productions, 1992, pp. 38-40.

90 N.L. Whitehead, *Lords of the Tiger Spirit: A History of the Caribs in Colonial Venezuela and Guyana 1498-1820*, PhD Dissertation University of Oxford (1984). In: KITLV Caribbean Series 1, Dordrecht: Foris Publishers, 1988.

91 E.g., P. van der Meiden, *Betwist bestuur. Een eeuw strijd om de macht in Suriname 1651-1753*, Amsterdam: De Bataafsche Leeuw, 2008 [1987].

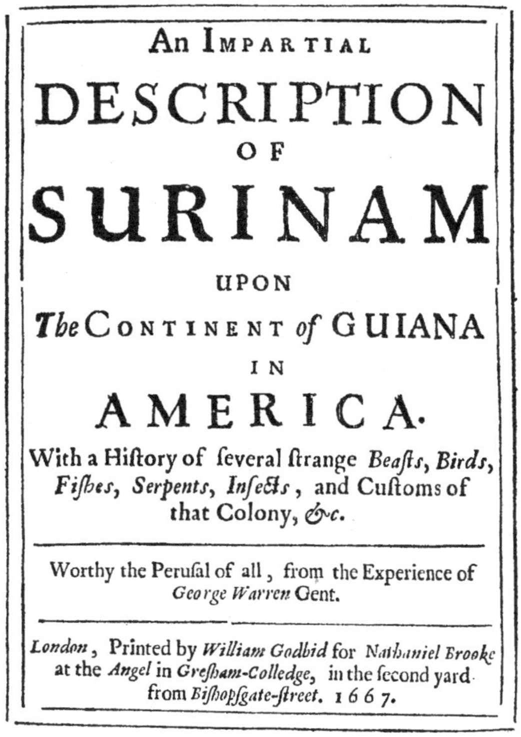

An IMPARTIAL
DESCRIPTION
OF
SURINAM
UPON
The CONTINENT *of* GUIANA
IN
AMERICA.
With a History of several strange *Beasts*, *Birds*, *Fishes*, *Serpents*, *Insects*, and Customs of that Colony, *&c.*

Worthy the Perusal of all, from the Experience of *George Warren* Gent.

London, Printed by *William Godbid* for *Nathaniel Brooke* at the *Angel* in *Gresham-Colledge*, in the second yard from *Bishopsgate-street*. 1667.

Figure 5: Title page of George Warren, An Impartial Description of Guiana (1667).

of Suriname.[92] The Dutch historian J. van Donselaar further contextualized this "borrowing" when mentioning that various 18th-century Dutch historians in turn had copied Van Berkel without indicating their source.[93]

It is evident that Van Berkel did not translate Warren's book. His publisher Johan ten Hoorn simply utilised the Dutch translation published by Pieter Arentsz (*c.*1633-1688) in Amsterdam in 1669, only two years after its original English release. Ten Hoorn even confused the Guianas in South America with the region along the Gulf of Guinea, and came up with the title *Een onpartydige beschrijvinge van Surinam, gelegen op het vaste landt van Guiana in Afrika* i.e., 'an impartial description of Surinam, located on the mainland of Guiana in Africa.'[94]

92 W.E. Roth, op. cit., 1948, p. ix. See also note 82.

93 J. van Donselaar, *De boeken van Warren*, 1993, p. 91.

94 G. Warren, *Een onpartydige beschrijvinge van Surinam, gelegen op het vaste landt van Guiana in Afrika. Mitsgaders een verhael van alle vreemde beesten, vogels, visschen, slangen ende wormen: gelijck mede van de gewoonheden ende manieren van deze colonie. Ende overgeset uyt het Engels*, Amsterdam: Pieter Arentsz, Amsterdam, 1669 (UBU T4°230^{13}). Warren's publication on Suriname or Willoughby-Land, as well as the manuscript of three times elected Governor of Suriname William Byam (see V. Harlow, *Colonising expeditions to the West-Indies and Guiana, 1623-1667*. Works of The Hakluyt Society, Second Series 56, London, 1925) reveal a rather flourishing colony based on African slave labour for the production of sugar (see F. Oudeschans Dentz, Suriname vóór de verovering door Abraham Crynssen, *Bijdragen en Mededelingen van het Historisch Genootschap* 39, 1918, pp. 173-213; J.A. Williamson, *English colonies in Guiana and on the Amazon, 1604-1668*, Oxford: Clarendon Press, 1923, pp. 160-161) as the Blathwayt map in the John Carter Brown Library illustrates: see H.C. van Renselaar, Oude Kaarten van Suriname, *Nieuwe West-Indische Gids* 45 (1966), Fig. 2.

The printing workshop and office of the publisher Johan ten Hoorn, named after its signboard '*In de Historieschrijver*', was situated opposite the *Oudezijds Herenlogement* at the Oudezijds Voorburgwal, one of the earliest Amsterdam canals. As discussed in the previous chapter 'Dutch newspapers reporting on the Guianas, 1650-1700', Ten Hoorn did not really modernize the existing Dutch translation, but omitted certain sections restricting himself to a small number of straightforward adaptations and minor changes to the existing text (e.g., applying the term *French* pox instead of *Spanish* pox when referring to syphilis). Hereto the publisher added but a few sections in order to update the text, e.g. on the Christian sect of the Labadists.[95] Moreover, he wrote a new introduction serving to evoke a plausible connection between the first travel to Berbice and the new journey to Surinam. Ten Hoorn also added a final chapter that pretended to be an eye-witness report on the murder of Governor Cornelis van Aerssen, Lord of Sommelsdijck in 1688 as well of the French attack on Paramaribo in 1689. Chapter I (see above) informs us that publisher Johan ten Hoorn had by and large copied the information of this final chapter from news already printed in Dutch newspapers and yearbooks. By doing so, he may have tried to render the publication more appealing to his readership.

Nevertheless, the first part of the *American Voyages* contains trustworthy and firsthand eyewitness reports containing useful ethnographic information on the Amerindians residing in the vicinity of these Dutch colonies, on their way of life and their contacts with the colonies. It is quite understandable, however, that numerous scholars have neglected this interesting information due to its supposedly doubtful content. Indeed, certain segments were taken from other sources and 'can be understood as principally synthetic and second-hand.'[96] Be that as it may, many parts of Van Berkel's narrative are of great value to present-day scholars. In fact, important descriptions are given, and illustrated by two prints depicting the inauguration ceremony of an incoming Captain and the treatment of captives. It further appears that the Amerindian population of this region was locked in eternal warfare with regard to revenging the deaths or enslavement of friends and kin by their enemies.[97]

In order to be a Captain one must endure the most horrible pain. In the future Captains could be confronted with similar pains once captured by their enemies. Therefore, each bashing, whipping, being poked with fire or smoked in a hammock, etc. represented a test. However, all this was probably considered merely child's play when compared with hardships inflicted by enemies. Van Berkel describes all this in detail. As an eyewitness he had trembled when learning how local Arawak treated a captured Carib. Yes, he was given something to eat which was the positive part of the treatment. On the other hand, prisoners would be mocked, despised, displayed in public, and dragged through the village with ropes

95 See also L. Knappert, De Labadisten in Suriname, *West-Indische Gids* 8 (1926).

96 N.L. Whitehead & M. Harbsmeier, *Hans Staden's True History: An Account of Cannibal Captivity in Brazil*, Durham: Duke University Press, 2008, p. xvii.

97 See F. Santos-Granero, *Vital Enemies: Slavery, Predation, and the American Political Economy of Life*, Austin: University of Texas Press, 2009.

tied around their legs. Burning torches would be pushed into their bodies, notably into the vital parts. They were told they would never see the sun again and indeed before sunrise be killed by a single blow to the head with a wooden club. Next the bodies would be torn apart, roasted, and consumed. Such cruelties, according to Van Berkel, were a result of revenge, affecting the various tribes as an eternal and unavoidable fate.

The first Europeans to reside among the Amerindian populations of the Guiana Coast had often witnessed a similar treatment. An early version of such a story can be found in the journal recorded by John Wilson of Wansteed. After visiting the Oyapock River, he wote:

> *They are armed in their warres with naked skins, and Indian Armes, their Artillery are Bowes and Arrowes, their Weapons wooden Swords and Bucklers. They choose their Captaines at their drunken Feasts; he is placed in the middest a patient of the whole company, holding his hands on his head. After they have made an Oration unto him to be valiant, and not to be treacherous unto them, with such like speeches: they whip him with a Whip which maketh the bloud spring out of his bodie at every stroke, and he never once mooveth thereat. By these meanes they try his patience and courage.*[98]

Flogging is a rather common phenomenon in Amazonia.[99] Father Antoine Biet provides us with an outstanding description of this tradition among the Carib of Cayenne. Before going to war, a warlord is chosen after testing candidates by means of scourging. Having selected a leader, much precaution was taken during the journey while approaching the enemy village as not to be spotted and in order to kill and take as many prisoners as possible by surprise. Once the village was surrounded, a terrible slaughter followed. Men, women and children were killed, tortured by means of torches, their vital parts cut off. Corpses were either smoked on fires or removed in canoes. If one desired a certain individual to be his prisoner, one only had to touch his hair in order to let his fellow tribesmen know he was his captive. He would then be led to his village and supplied with food.

> *Estant de retour chez eux, ceux qui ont des prisonniers, si ce sont des femmes ou des enfans, ils les laissent aller & les traitent comme s'ils estoient leurs propres enfans. Pour les hommes, ils les lient & attachent bien soigneusement, les nourrissent tres bien, leur faisant experimenter tous les plaisirs possibles jusqu'au jour de leur mort, qui estant arrivé selon le nombre de nœuds, qu'ils ont envoyez par les habitations, tous se trouvent à cette cruelle ceremonie bien ajustez de tous leurs plus beaux ornemens. Quand ils arrivent à la Case, ils font de grands cris & heurlemens*

98 J. Wilson of Wansteed, *The Relation of Master John of Wansteed in Essex, one of the last ten that returned into England from Wiapoco in Guiana 1606, Purchas His Pilgrimes: In Five Bookes: The First, Contayning the Voyages ... Made by Ancient Kings, ..., Others, to and thorow the Remoter Parts of the Knowne World, etc.*, Part 4, Chapter 14, London: W. Stansby for H. Fetherstone, 1625, p. 1262.

99 See S. Fritz, *Journal of the Travels and Labours of Father Samuel Fritz in the River of the Amazons between 1686 and 1723*, translated from the Evora Ms and edited by the Rev. Dr. George Edmundson, Works issued by The Hakluyt Society, Second Series 51, London, 1922, p. 61; A. Biet, *Voyage de la France Equinoxiale en l'Isle de Cayenne, entrepis par les françois en l'année MDCLII*, Paris: François Clouzier, 1664, pp. 380-384.

allant comme en cadence au son de leurs instruments. Il faut sçavoir que pour faire ce massacre le Chef de l'habitation, où demeure celuy qui a pris le prisonnier, a preparé un grand vin, car pour exercer cette cruauté il faut boire jusqu'à l'excez & s'enyurer.

Estans tous assemblez, on fait venir le pauvre miserable que l'on doit faire mourir, après l'avoir orné de tout ce qu'ils ont de plus beau, comme de rassade, de grains de [p. 383] cristaux, & d'un chapeau de belles plumes. Ils le tiennent droict au milieu d'eux, lié d'une corde aux deux poings, luy faisant étendre les bras en croix; puis celuy qui l'a fait prisonnier sort du Carbet, & le voyant il prend sa course, pendant que ceux qui le tiennent le font baisser, afin que celuy qui a pris sa course saute sur son dos; comme les enfans qui joüent au cheval fondu. Après quoy, on presente au patient un petit siege neuf & on le fait asseoir dessus bien lié & garoté. Les femmes commenent autour de luy une estrange danse, elle sortent toutes du Carbet comme des Furies, tenant chacune un baston à la main, elles dansent autour de luy avec un chant lugubre, elles pleurent, elles heurlent & font des cris épouventables, en sautant & faisant trois tours à l'entour de luy, en luy baillant l'une du baston, l'autres des soufflets, une autre des nazardes, & luy disant: 'Tien, voila pourquoy tu as tué mon frere', l'autre dit, 'mon compere, mon amy', & choses semblables. Il ne leur dit rien autre chose, sinon qu'elles font bien de luy faire souffrir ce mal, que s'il estoit en liberté, & qu'il tint un des leurs, sa femme luy en seroit tout autant, & encore pis.

Cette danse estant achevée & ce premier Acte de la Tragedie estant finy, on remeine le patient dans le Carbet, où chacun luy fait caresse, le mettant sur son lict, l'appelant son frere, son compere, l'autre son amy. On le fait boire & manger tant qu'il veut & tant qu'il peut, en quoy il ne s'épargne pas, pour faire voir qu'il le méprise tous ; ils n'oublient pas aussi tous de bien boire. Environ sur les trois heures apres midy, on commence une grande danse qui environne le grand Carbet, où ils font des postures estranges; l'on fait danser ce pauvre miserable, & pendant qu'il danse, les jeunes Sauvages préparent des flambeaux d'un certain bois gommeux qui brusle comme un flambeau de cire, & quand il passe par un certain endroit, ils luy appliquent ce flambeau ardent sur diverses parties de son corps, par tout où ils peuvent, ce qui devient tout en grosses ampoules. Je laisse à pense quelle douleur souffre ce pauvre mal-heureux, sans se plaindre aucunement, taschant seulement de se conserver le visage. On ne laisse pas [p. 384] de le faire danser en cet équipage, ce qu'il fait avec un grand courage ou plutost de rage. Les Sauvages sont brusler de la cassave & appliquent toute bruslante contre ces ampoules, qui se crevent & humectent cette cassave, qu'ils mangent avec grand appetit, & boivent en la mangeant, recommençans la danse, pendant laquelle l'un luy coupe l'oreille droite, l'autre la gauche, un autre luy coupe le nez, un autre le membre viril, & font griller ces choses qu'ils mangent en sa presence. Ce miserable au lieu de se plaindre les anime encore davantage, leur disant: 'Tu ne me fais rien, que je n'en aye fait autant à un tel ou tel de tes amis, ou à ton père; si j'estois en liberté, & que tu fusses entre mes mains, je t'en ferois bien d'autres'.

La danse cesse pour un peu de temps, afin de se donner le loisir de boire & manger, pendant lequel temps on jette de l'eau fraische sur ses playes, pour en appaiser un peu la douleur, afin de le faire vivre davantage, & luy faire souffrir de plus grands maux. On luy en fait endurer d'étranges toutes la nuict. Comme il est à demy mort, & presque devenu insensible, celuy qui l'a pris prisonnier de guerre, vient par derriere en luy donnant un coup de boutou sur la teste, duquel il tombe mort sur la place.

Quand il est mort, les Sauvages preparent des feüilles, sur lesquelles ils portent le corps, l'éventrent, & en tirent les entrailles qu'ils jettent au nez de leurs femmes. Chacun prend un morceau de la fressure, l'un du cœur, l'autre du foye, &c. Ils l'embrochent dans des brochettes de bois, & le font rostir, c'est le commencement de leur festin. Ils coupent en pieces, ostant les jambes, les cuisses, les bras, & le reste ils boucannent, & le mangent ; cela dure deux jours, s'enyurant & saoulant comme des pourceaux. Celuy qui l'a tué, en boucanne une partie de sorte qu'il le conserve pour le moins six mois, afin de le faire voir à ses amis.[100]

Here we clearly recognize similarities with Van Berkel descriptions with regard to the treatment of prisoners. Whether he was inspired by Father Antoine Biet to refresh his mind when he finally sat down to record his memories, perhaps even 20 years later, remains unknown. However, the similarity between both texts is striking and requires further exploration. There are certainly a number of differences. In Father Biet's story the captured Amerindian said, before the torture started, that he himself had tortured many enemies, which made him feel at ease. In *American Voyages,* the captured Amerindian states that one day his kin will revenge him. Van Berkel inserted the Amerindian term 'maquary' in order to indicate the torches thereby suggesting he had witnessed such events. Of course, it is difficult to establish if he had derived this knowledge from personal observation or from existing literature. However, according to Roth, the word *maquari* refers to a whip, not to a torch, which various Amerindian populations of the Guianas utilize during specific ceremonies and dances.[101] This specific whip was probably associated with the Arawak *morakuyuha* or 'a white crane or stork, of which the Tupi term is *magoary* [...]'.[102] In addition, Roth remarks that 'Van Berkel applies the term maquary to the torch used in putting the prisoners to death' but does not give any further explanation as to the contradictory meaning of the word.[103]

Although stressing 'the authority of Van Berkel, an eyewitness on the Berbice in the middle half of the seventeenth century' concerning descriptions of the capturing and treatment of the two Caribs, Roth never evokes any similarities between the Dutch and French books, despite the fact he had listed Biet's work as one of his sources.[104] It is noteworthy that, when citing non-English sources, Roth actually applies English translations when available. This is predominantly the case

100 A. Biet, *Voyage de la France Equinoxiale en l'Isle de Cayenne,* Chapitre IX, 1664, pp. 382-384.

101 Whip or *makoüali,* see also P. Boyer Sieur du Petit-Puy, *Véritable relation de tout ce qui s'est passé au voyage que monsieur de Bretigny fit à l'Amérique occidentale* [...]. Paris: Chez Pierre Rocolet, 1654, p. 409.

102 W.E. Roth, op. cit., 1924, p. 646.

103 See C. de Goeje, *The Arawak Language,* Cambridge: Cambridge University Press, 2009, p. 161: 'van Berkel *maquary,* whip used in the flogging ceremony (also: torch), Sm. *makoali,* a whip, S. *a-makoalitedi-,* to flog (Karib languages: Cumanagota *macuare,* Kalina *macoali*).'

104 W.E. Roth, op. cit., 1924, p. 593.

with French publications i.e., Rochefort and De la Borde, from which we may conclude that Roth had not mastered French very well.[105]

The term 'maquary' was perhaps erroneously inserted by the translator and modifier of Biet's description on behalf of the publisher Johan ten Hoorn. Another possibility may be that the burning torches in Van Berkel's book were either borrowed from Rocheforts publication *Histoire naturelle et morale des îles Antilles de l'Amerique* or from a publication by Samuel Champlain, who had observed torches during Amerindian ceremonies held in early 17th-century Québec, thus revealing plagiarism originating from North America![106]

In fact, we can confirm that Van Berkel copied from other works. For example, when on deck during Atlantic crossings, he observes 'marvellous events' as he describes them, notably the rare Saint Elmo's fire or the spectacular catching of sea hogs.[107] However, these sections appear to be translations from books published during the second half of the 16th century i.e., by Hans Staden and Jean de Léry respectively. The report on the capture of sea hogs states:

> *(...) L'un d'entre eux, des plus stylez et façonnez à telle pesche, se tenant au guet près du mats du beaupré, au devant de la navire, ayant en la main un arpon de fer, emmanché en une perche, de la grosseur et longueur d'une demie pique, et lié à quatre ou cinq brasses de cordeaux, quand il en void approcher quelques troupes, choississant entre iceux celuy qu'il peut, il luy jette et darde cest engin de telle roideur, que s'il l'attaint à propos, il ne faut point de l'enferrer. L'ayant ainsi frapé, il file et lasche la corde, de laquelle neantmoins retenant le bout ferme, après que le Marsouïn, qui en se debattant et s'enferrant de plus en [30] plus perd son sang dans l'eau, s'est un peu affoibli, les autres mariniers pour aider à leur compagnon*

105 C. de Rochefort, *Histoire naturelle et morale des îles Antilles de l'Amérique* [...], Rotterdam: Arnould Leers, 1658; *Voyages curieux et nouveaux de Messieurs Hennepin & De La Borde* [...], Amsterdam: Aux depens de la Compagnie, 1674. Concerning P. Fermin, he had probably read the Dutch version *Nieuwe algemeene beschryving van de colonie van Suriname. Behelzende al het merkwaardige van dezelve, met betrekkinge tot de historie, aardryks- en natuurkunde*, Harlingen: V. van der Plaats jr, 1770 and not the earlier French *Description générale, historique géographique et physique de la colonie de Surinam*, 2 Vols., Amsterdam: E. van Harrevelt, 1769.

106 C. de Rochefort, *Histoire naturelle et morale des îles Antilles de l'Amérique* [...], Rotterdam: Arnould Leers, 1658, p.482 ; F. Jameson, *Voyages of Samuel de Champlain 1604-1618*. In: Original Narratives of Early American History 4, New York: Charles Scribner's Sons, 1907, pp. 166-167, 184-185. Historic links between the mouth of the Amazon and/or northeastern Brazil (Tupi), the Guianas, and the Antilles have been demonstrated by comparative linguistic research (see B.J. Hoff, Language contact, war, and Amerindian historical tradition: The special case of the Island Carib, *Wolves from the Sea: Readings in the Anthropology of the Native Caribbean*, Neil L. Whitehead (ed.). In: Caribbean Series 14, Leiden: KITLV Press, 1995, p. 53, note 14). However, it may also be 'the product of the French ethnography', N.L. Whitehead, Ethnic plurality and cultural continuity in the native Caribbean: Remarks and uncertainties as to data and theory, *Wolves from the Sea: Readings in the Anthropology of the Native Caribbean*, Neil. L. Whitehead (ed.). In: Caribbean Series 14, Leiden: KITLV Press, 1995, p. 93, note 4.

107 Seamen consider this natural phenomenon known as *Corpo Santo*, or St. Elmo's fire, a sign of protection provided by St. Elmo (St. Erasmus), an early Christian martyr and patron saint of sailors, N.L. Whitehead & M. Harbsmeier, *Hans Staden's True History*, 2008, p. 25, note 19. The phenomenon can be explained as a kind of ball lightning.

vienent avec un crochet de fer qu'ils appelent gaffe (aussi emmanché en une longue perche de bois) et à force de bras le tirent ainsi dans le bord: en allant nous en prismes environ vingt cinq de ceste façon.[108]

Hans Staden describes the Saint Elmo's fire as follows:

(...) Da begab es sich eyn nacht, das wir eynen grossen sturm hatten, ware in grosser mühe, da erschienen uns vil blawer liechter in dem schiff, dero ich nit mehr gesehen hatte. Da die bulgen vor ins schiff schlugen, da giengen der liechter auch. Die Portugaleser sagten, Das die liechter eyn zeychen gutes zukünfftigen wetters weren, sonderlich von Gott gesant in nöten zu trösten. Theten Gott eyne dancksagung darfür mit eynem gemeynen gebett, Darnach verschwinden sie wider. Und diese liechter heysse Santelmo, oder Corpus Santon.[109]

It is obvious that Van Berkel, or more probably his editor, Johan ten Hoorn, consulted numerous books on the Americas in order to enlarge or enhance the former's fieldnotes recorded at Berbice. Issues concerning the exact number of additions and their sources demands further research. Nevertheless, Van Berkel obtained an intriguing amount of specific information, for instance the Arawakkan expression *Bockja wattili*, the names of various types of manioc beer (e.g., *payewar, beltieri, pernou, bassia, commany, cassyry*), the names of local fish, etc. This information indicates that part of the story of the Berbice travels in *American Voyages* were probably based on notes, even on a journal, which is now lost or hidden somewhere.

In sum, it is evident that numerous 17th-century and 18th-century authors (and publishers) borrowed from other books. To which degree the *American Voyages* is a compilation of earlier books, and its original segments are difficult to ascertain. It probably contains a true history based an original journal which has been hugely embellished in order to improve sales.

Who was Adriaan van Berkel?

The discussion on the originality of *American Voyages* and the editor raises serious doubts regarding the author's existence. Was it a pseudonym or did Adriaan van Berkel really exist?

One of the first obstacles is the lack of uniformity in the spelling of Dutch names during the 17th century. Adriaan could be Adriaen, Adrijaen, Adrijaan, etc., whereas Van Berkel could also be Van Berckel. The name itself derives from a village near Rotterdam. Members of the Van Berckel family occupied important posts in Rotterdam. Adriaen Van Berckel is perhaps a possible 'candidate' for the author Adriaan van Berkel.[110] However, in 1640, he was engaged as a high official

108 J. de Léry, *Histoire d'un voyage faict en la terre de Brésil, autrement dite Amerique* [...], La Rochelle: Antoine Chuppin, 1578, pp. 29-30.

109 H. Staden, *Warhaftige Historia und beschreibung eyner Landtschafft der Wilden Nacketen, Grimmigen Menschfresser-Leuthen in der Newenwelt America gelegen*, Marburg: Kolb, 1557, caput 2, a3.

110 E.A. Engelbrecht, *De vroedschap van Rotterdam 1572-1795*, Rotterdam: Gemeentelijke Archiefdienst, 1973, p. 138.

in the Admiralty and therefore could not have embarked as a junior to Berbice 30 years later. In Delft, another branch of the family Van Berckel formed part of the local elite. The Van Berckel family of Leiden included the renowned Abraham Van Berckel, a medical doctor appointed at the University of Leiden.

The above-mentioned Van Berkels counted several men named Adriaan, but none can be linked to *American Voyages*. However, in a notarial deed dating from 1670, a certain Adriaan van Berkel empowered Abraham van Berckel 'Medical Doctor', or a *Doctor in de Medicina*, to take care of his share in the heritance bequeathed to him, Adriaan, by his father Dirck Abrahamsz van Berckel.[111] This deed matches the profile of the author we are looking for, because it was common practise for people who were about to travel to empower a third person to see to their matters..

Father Dirck Abrahamsz was born in Rotterdam. Information dating from 1644 found in the Leiden archives indicated he purchased a house.[112] He was married to Susanna Pieters van Maldegem with whom he had eight children.[113] Adriaen van Berckel was their fifth child and was baptized on 17 November 1647 in the Hooglandse Kerk in Leiden.[114]

Dirck Abrahamsz van Berckel made his last will in 1661, perhaps motivated by the plague that swept through the town. Residing at the Coepoortsgracht, he testified to be a merchant in brandy (Dutch *brandewijn*). Adriaan (14) and his two sisters Maria (12) and Anna (10) witnessed the demise of both their parents in 1662, perhaps victims of the plague.[115] In 1665 the tutors of Adriaen, Maria and Anna presented a claim.[116] The next year, Adriaen officiated as a witness when his niece Geertruid Pauw, daughter of Gerard Pauw and Hester van Berckel, was baptized on 7 March 1666.[117] Adriaan is mentioned in 1669 with an attestation

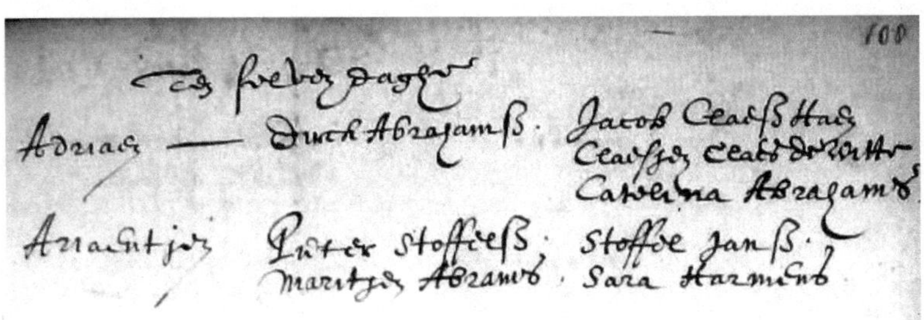

Figure 6: Entry of the baptism of Adriaen [van Berkel], 17 October 1647. Register of Baptisms, Hooglandse Kerk, Leiden.

111 NL-LdnRAL_AR_506_1136_f. 113.
112 NL-LdnRAL_0501A_6611_f. 134.
113 NL-LdnRAL_1004_235; 222.
114 NL-LdnRAL_1004_235_f. 108.
115 NL-LdnRAL_0501A_ 1323_f. 155.
116 NL-LdnRAL_0501A_ 6618_f. 81v.
117 NL-LdnRAL_1004_223.

Veniam Aetatis, implying he legally held the status of an adult.[118] Apparently he left shortly after empowering his uncle Abraham van Berckel on 19 October 1670. This is proven by means of another document, dated 29 October 1670, which states he is abroad.[119] Interestingly, Van Berckel reappears in Leiden in September 1675 as a witness. These facts correspond to the chronology of *American Voyages*.[120] The profile of this historical Adriaen van Berckel also fits well in with the Adriaan van Berkel who travelled to Berbice in 1670. This young man from a well-to-do family was, because of the demise of his parents, not without means and connected to the intellectual circles of Leiden through his uncle, Dr. Abraham van Berckel.

However, the historical figure of this Adriaan van Berckel remains inadequately documented. A recently found reference concerns an event in May 1685, when Adriaan appeared before notary Van Tielt in relation with the settlement of the inheritance left by his parents. This fact casts genuine doubt on the historical validity of the second part of *American Voyages*, confirming the conclusions reached on other grounds.[121] In sum, the first part of the book can be connected with an historical person who was born in Leiden and who did live there, perhaps even close to the *Theatrum Anatomium*. This institution is referred to as the writer-*cum*-traveller Adriaan van Berkel describes the anteater he saw there.

118 NL-LdnRAL_0501A_ 6618_f. 81v.
119 NL-LdnRAL_0501A_ 6618_f. 81v.
120 NL-LdnRAL_1004_239.
121 NL-LdnRAL_0501A_ 6618_f. 81v

Chapter 3

Historical context of *American Voyages*

The period described in *American Voyages* entailed major changes for most colonies along the Wild Coast, as the Dutch named the coast of the Guianas located between the Amazon and Orinoco Rivers. At the time Van Berkel's book begins, the region was recovering from the Second Anglo-Dutch War (1665-1667). The early history of the Dutch colony in Berbice is inadequately documented. However, existing sources suggest it was intimately linked to the Dutch colony of Essequibo and the later Dutch colony of Surinam. The present editors have enhanced the historical context of *American Voyages* by means of information retrieved from literature and archival documents mainly originating from the WIC archives.[122] The early administration of Berbice, which was a private company, has been lost.[123] An important source consists of the Surinam Papers procured at the Archive of the Staten van Zeeland and covers the period between 1667 and 1683.[124] We have focused on the first part of these papers that concern Van Berkel's stay in Berbice. The part of *American Voyages* dealing with Surinam has largely been copied from other sources. Moreover, the few descriptions of historical events add little to the already ample documentation on this period found in the Archive of the Sociëteit van Suriname, kept at the National Archives (Nationaal Archief, NA), The Hague.

Berbice and Van Pere

The Berbice Colony was named after the river it was located on, as was the case with most colonies on the Wild Coast.[125] It lies within the present-day Co-operative Republic of Guyana, henceforth referred to as Guyana. The Berbice River runs through eastern Guyana, ascending from the highlands of the Rupununi region. It flows northwards for 595 km traversing dense forest to reach the coastal plain. To the east runs the Corantyne River which currently forms the boundary between

---

122 As to literature we mainly consulted J.J. Hartsinck, *Beschrijving van Guiana*, 1770; P.M. Netscher, *Geschiedenis van de Koloniën*, 1888; C. Goslinga, The *Dutch in the Caribbean and on the Wild-Coast (1580-1680)*, Groningen: Van Gorcum, 1971. The archives of the 'old' WIC (1621-1674) are digitalized and can be consulted at the website of the Nationaal Archief: www.gahetna.nl.

123 This colony was later managed by the *Sociëteit van Berbice*.

124 Many documents included in the Suriname collection can be consulted online: www.zeeuwsarchief.nl. Zeeland was one of the seven provincies of the Dutch Republic. They were considered independent units within the framework of the United Provinces. The 'Staten van Zeeland', with representatives from the towns and a small number of noblemen, governed the province.

125 Examples hereof are the Pomeroon, Essequibo, Surinam, Sinnamary, Approuague, and Oiapoque.

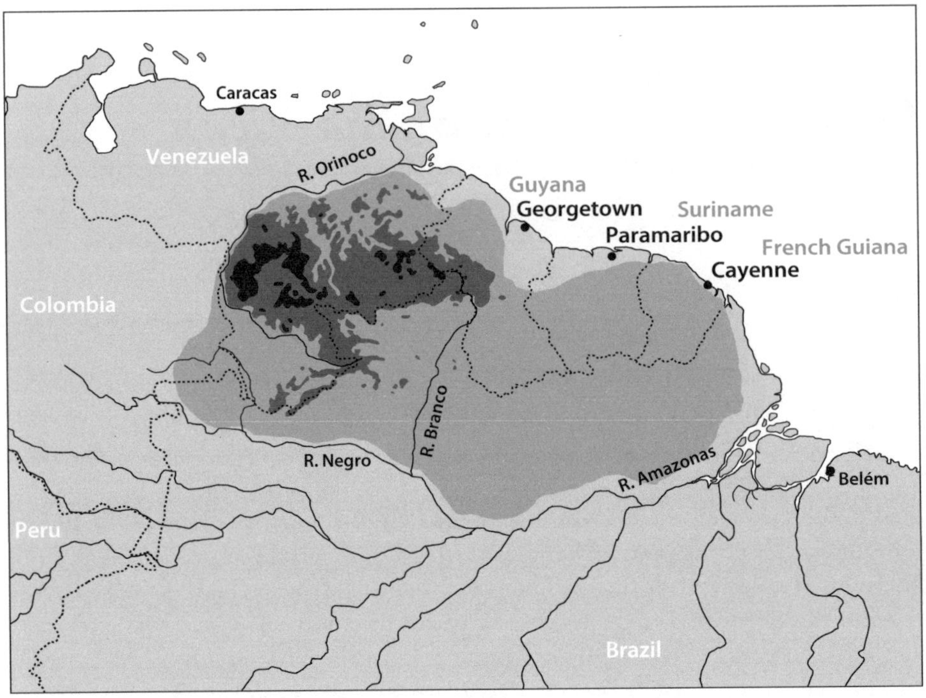

Figure 7: Map of the Guiana Plateau.

Guyana and Surinam. To the west lies the Demerara River, where the present capital Georgetown is situated, beyond which the Essequibo River flows. This is the largest river between the Amazon and the Orinoco Detas. It rises in the Acarai Mountains on the Brazilian border and flows northward for *c.*1010 km.[126]

Berbice's early history is intimately associated with the Van Pere family from Zeeland (the Netherlands). Abraham van Pere Sr. had moved from Sandwich in England to Vlissingen. Here he was involved with shipping to the Wild Coast in 1602 when the newly founded Dutch Provinces were still fighting Spanish troops for independence.[127] Van Pere Sr. married Agnieta Cornelis daughter van Couwenburchs van Duveland in 1603.[128] Their son Cornelis was baptized in November 1606. Abraham van Pere Jr. was baptized in August 1609, the year the Republic and Spain reached a 12-year truce.[129]

Abraham van Pere Sr. was one of the Directors of the Zeeland Chamber of the WIC who attempted to stimulate colonisation by granting patronages to private entrepreneurs. The Dutch WIC was founded in 1621 after the truce with Spain had ended. It counted five 'Chambers', of which the Zeeland chamber

126 The present Democratic Republic of Guyana became independent in 1966. Prior hereto it was known as British Guiana being officially a British colony from 1814 on, when the colonies of Essequibo, Demerara and Berbice were ceded by the Dutch in the Treaty of Vienna.

127 I. Beeckman, *Journal tenu par Isaac Beeckman de 1604 à 1634, publication avec une introduction et des notes par C. de Waard*, IVième Supplément, La Haye: Martinus Nijhoff, 2007, p. 286 [1953].

128 NL-VsGA_357_531_f. 62v.

129 NL-VsGA_387_5673.

was specifically involved with the Wild Coast.[130] The Directors of the WIC, the Gentlemen XIX, granted him a patronate for the Berbice River in 1627.[131] The WIC drew up a contract with Van Pere, stipulating detailed conditions. He was to send forty colonists who could settle in Berbice, but should not infringe the Essequibo territory (of which the dimensions were not defined in the contract). The WIC was to control all trade. The colonists obtained exemption from certain taxes during the first 10 years and were bound to stay there for 7 years. Several articles on relations with the indigenous population ordered them to spread the Christian faith and prohibit the harassment of local women and girls.[132]

The States-General and the WIC then published several regulations which largely amounted to the condition that the patron would own the colony as a hereditary fief, for which he had to pay his dues. The colonists remained subjects of the States-General and must be represented in the colony by a council that advised the commander. This implied that Abraham van Pere gained the rights of possession of the colony he was to establish in Berbice, but also that he should abide to several regulations the WIC and the States-General had laid down. Thus Van Pere had to purchase permits from the Zeeland Chamber for each and every ship he wanted to send to his colony. The charter of the patronate was renewed in July 1632.[133]

Abraham Jr. succeeded his father after his demise in 1639.[134] On 18 June 1640, he and his friend-*cum*-associate Pieter van Rhee signed a renewed charter as the incoming patrons of Berbice.[135] According to Zeeland law, he had to pay 20 guilders for the *heergewaad*, the recognition of his feudal authority.[136] It may be added here that Maria, a younger sister of Abraham Jr. was married to Pieter van Rhee, a clear proof of the close ties between the Van Pere and Van Rhee families who shared the Berbice patronate.[137]

Abraham Jr. married Caterine Beeckmans from Rotterdam on 13 April 1642.[138] The couple had several children: Angenita (born 18 January 1643), and Abraham whom we shall henceforth refer to as the third (b. 18 November 1646), Isaac (b.

130 C. Goslinga, *The Dutch in the Caribbean and in the Guianas 1680-1791*, 1985, pp. 89-94, 102-105. The Wild Coast fell within the area patented by the Dutch West India Company founded in 1621. It consisted of five separate chambers: Amsterdam, Zeeland, Maze, Noorderkwartier, and Stad en Ommelanden.

131 C. Goslinga, *The Dutch in the Caribbean,* 1985, p. 102. The Zeeland chamber had proposed a regulation for the colonization of the Wild Coast which the Gentlemen XIX had adapted. The patronate implied that the colony must be populated and ordered for a council of colonists to advise the Commander governing for the patron. Van Pere's patent granted him hereditary right to the colony, G.J. Grol, *De grondpolitiek in het West-Indische domein der Generaliteit*, 's-Gravenhage: Algemene Landsdrukkerij, 1942, p. 25.

132 NL-HaNA_1.05.01.01_41_ff. 32-38.

133 NL-HaNA_1.05.01.01_41_ff. 61-62.

134 NL-HaNA_1.05.01.01_41_f. 75.

135 P.M. Netscher, *Geschiedenis van de Koloniën*, 1888, p. 60.

136 NL-HaNA_1.05.01.01_23_16400802.

137 I. Beeckman, *Journal tenu par Isaac Beeckman,* 2007, p. 286.

138 Ibidem.

23 February 1649), Johannes (b. 11 October 1654), Susanna Maria (b. 3 October 1658) and Cornelis (b. 14 July 1667).[139]

Van Pere and Van Rhee signed a new charter confirming their patronship in 1660, when the WIC was virtually bankrupt after losing northeastern Brazil.[140] In October 1657 the Zeeland Chamber had transferred the Essequibo Colony to the *Nova Zeelandia* conglomerate.[141] The Van Peres succeeded in retaining their patronship when the WIC finally succumbed in 1674 to be re-founded in a downsized version. Their position as patrons was confirmed on 14 September 1678.[142] The Van Pere family moved in the higher circles of the Zeeland society and, in the 18th century, became well-known as the Lords of the Estate of West-Souburg. The juridical construction of Van Pere's concession led to continuous conflicts until 1720 when the Van Pere family abandoned its rights on Berbice to the *Sociëteit van Berbice*.[143]

Berbice 1627-1665

The first 1627 expedition counted the ships *Swarten Arent* owned by Master Jacob Bart and the *Hazewindt* owned by Master Cornelis Cornelisz and did not include women, only some twenty men and ten boys.[144] Recruiting boys from Dutch orphanages was common practice at that time.[145] Gelein van Stapels visited the colony in 1629. He described its main post located near the confluence of the Berbice and Wiruni Rivers where the commander Cornelis van Pere, Abraham Sr.'s eldest son, resided. This wooden house with two floors and a tile roof probably formed the centre of the later plantation called *Peereboom*, which Van Berkel named *De Mierenberg*. At that time the Dutch had already settled along the Canje River, where a plantation owned by a certain Buven Marijnisz has been founded.[146]

Gelein van Stapels described how colonists lived in small bands in the Amerindian villages in order to grow tobacco. The majority seemed to be in a poor condition according to Gelein, who adds that the terrain was not very suitable for growing tobacco. The colonists had agreed with Governor Cornelis van Pere to be exempt of the obligation to work for the patron and pay 33% of their harvest as a tribute. The annatto trade however, would remain the monopoly of the patron:

> *They did not want any part of the dye [annatto], only that the general would provide them merchandise to trade for their provisions. Once the general had deliberated about everything and recognised the condition of the men because of*

---

139 NL-VsGA_387_5673. The dates are those entered in the baptism registers.

140 NL-HaNA_1.05.01.01_41_ff. 76-78

141 P.M. Netscher, op. cit., 1888, p. 71.

142 Ibid., pp. 152-153.

143 Ibid., pp. 159-160.

144 Ibid., p. 59. Possibly, the *Swarten Arent* ('Black Eagle') already visited the Wild Coast in 1625 under the command of Admiral Lucifer, R. de Forest, *A Walloon Family in America. Lockwood de Forest and his Forbears 1500-1848. Together with A Voyage to Guiana being the Journal of Jesse de Forest And his Colonists 1623-1625*, 2 Vols., Boston/New York: Houghton Mifflin Company, Vol. 2, 1914, p. 268.

145 Ibid., pp. 345-354.

146 M. van Wallenburg, Het reisverhaal van Gelein van Stapels, *Zeeuws Tijdschrift* 1995(1), 1995b, p. 12.

Figure 8: Map of the Berbice River by Jean Mousnier de la Montagne, c.1625.

> *the aforementioned reasons, he saw only the annatto dye as profit that he could gather easily enough with three to four men without running any risk and granted this to them.*[147]

Gelein deemed the annatto trade to be far more profitable if the Amerindians brought the annatto as a semi-finished product to the Dutch, who would then only need a small number of men to collect it and store it in barrels. The annatto could be sold in the Netherlands with large profits:

> *The ultimate means –in my opinion– to derive any future profit from this colony would be to cut all unnecessary costs that are made here in abundance, and to send back the greater part of the people, because they don't accomplish much with all the boys that are of little help. It would be better to send them home and leave 6 to 7 good young lads with a capable person in charge, who having learned the language, could replace the general. [...] The yearly return would amount to over 9,000 pounds of annatto dye. [...] This is in my opinion the best way to derive some gain from this river, because it cannot support many people.*[148]

Berbice was not the first Dutch settlement in this region. When the WIC was founded it was agreed that its Chambers should incorporate existing colonial settlements within its patented territory. Especially the Zeeland Chamber was interested in the Wild Coast and had taken over the majority of the trading posts established here prior to 1621, among them fort Kyckoveral.

147 NL-MbgZA_MS_182_f. 4r. This quotation is an excerpt from the forthcoming transcription and translation of the journal of Gelein van Stapels by M. van den Bel, M. van Wallenburg, A. Bright & L. Hulsman.

148 NL-MbgZA_MS_182_ff. 4r-4v.

There is considerable historical controversy with regard to the settlement of the Dutch in this region. Many historians opine they settled in 1616 in fort Kyckoveral which is strategically situated on a small island where the Mazaruni and Cuyuni Rivers enter the Essequibo.[149] The Dutch often call this colony *Ysekepe*. In 1629 Van Stapels visited the Essequibo Colony in his sloop. Although not arriving at fort Kyckoveral, he contacted several traders in an Arawak village led by Chief Balliskus and located downstream opposite three islands.[150]

Apparently Abraham van Pere Sr. heeded Van Stapels' advice. He performed better in Berbice than the WIC in Essequibo as the references regarding Van Pere equipping ships for his colony with consent of the WIC between 1630 and 1650 indicate. Now and again, Van Pere's vessels provided the Essequibo Colony with necessities and imported their annatto (the main produce of Essequibo as it was of Berbice) for the WIC to Zeeland.[151] The small colonies of Berbice and Essequibo were the only stable settlements on the Wild Coast between 1621 and *c.*1650. Other Dutch, English and French endeavours during this period invariably met with disaster (with the exception of the Normand colony located at the Counamama and Sinnamary Rivers), often because of conflicts with the local indigenous population.[152]

The Dutch in Berbice seemingly succeeded in establishing local alliances in Berbice. Van Stapels discusses several indigenous nations in the Berbice River of which the Arawak was the most important. Today, the Arawak of the Guianas are generally identified as the Lokono. Moreover, they appear to have been the principal allies of the Dutch, allowing them to establish small colonies at Berbice and Essequibo, whereas other colonial settlements along the coast were destroyed by the indigenous population.[153]

The conquest of the WIC in northeastern Brazil (now and again referred to as New Holland) had succumbed in 1654 to a rebellion of the Portuguese population. Now a renewed interest for colonization of the Wild Coast awoke in

---

149 See G. Edmundson, The Dutch in Western Guiana, *The English Historical Review* 16(64), 1901, pp. 640-675; H. den Heijer, *De geschiedenis van de WIC*, Zutphen: Walburg Pers, 1994; D. Roos, *Zeeuwen en de Westindische Compagnie (1621-1674)*, Hulst: van Geyt Productions, 1992; J.J. Hartsinck, *Beschrijving van Guiana*, 1770; P.M. Netscher, *Geschiedenis van de Koloniën*, 1888; L. Bosman, *Nieuw Amsterdam in Berbice* (Guyana), 1994. However, no reliable historical sources document this event. The discussion on the foundation of fort Kyckoveral is left to more qualified scholars. The first solid evidence with regard to the Dutch settlement on the Essequibo River is linked to Jean Mousnier de la Montagne.who visited the Essequibo River in 1625. The Resolutions of the Zeeland Chamber of the WIC preserved from the year 1626 on contain further proof hereof, see R. de Forest, *A Walloon Family*, Vol. 2, 1914, p. 264. In 1626, too, commander Jan Canijn returned to the Netherlands to be replaced by Jan van der Goes, see P.M. Netscher, op. cit., 1888, p. 61.

150 NL_MbgZA_MS_182_f. 6r.

151 L.A.H.C. Hulsman, *Nederlands Amazonia. Handel met indianen tussen 1580 en 1680*, PhD Dissertation University of Amsterdam, 2009, p. 133; P.M. Netscher, op. cit., p. 60, note 2.

152 J.A. Williamson, *English colonies in Guiana and on the Amazon*, 1923.

153 L.A.H.C. Hulsman, op. cit., 2009. Gelein van Stapels described the Dutch in Essequibo as staying in the village of Arawak Captain Balliskus in 1629. Other coastal groups (e.g., the Sapaye or Shebayo) have now disappeared, but are considered to belong to the Arawak language family. See P. Grenand, Que sont devenus les Amérindiens de l'Approuague? Réflexions autour d'une histoire peu documentée, *L'histoire de la Guyane, depuis les civilisations amérindiennes*, Serge Mam Lam Fouck & Jacqueline Zonzon (eds), pp. 105-126, Matoury: Editions Ibis Rouge, 2006, p. 111.

the Netherlands. In 1659 the Zeeland chamber of the WIC granted a patent for the colonisation of the Essequibo region to a conglomerate founded by merchants in the Zeeland towns of Middelburg, Veere and Vlissingen. The main goal of this Company aimed at producing sugar on the Pomeroon River. Here a settlement was to be built with the name: Nieuw Middelburg. This colony was called *Nova Zeelandia*.[154] The contract with the *Nova Zeelandia* conglomerate also specified that the annatto trade remained the monopoly of the WIC.[155]

The *Nova Zeelandia* colony on the Pomeroon seems to have had a certain degree of success in producing sugar. Nevertheless, the references in the resolutions of the Zeeland Chamber of the WIC indicate it was not the commercial success certain historians claim.[156] The situation of fort Kyckoveral in the Essequibo River remained unchanged under Aert Adriaensz Groenewegel who had been in command since 1644.[157] Although efforts were made to start sugar plantations here, the commercial mainstay continued to be the annatto trade.

The most successful sugar producing colony on the Wild Coast at that time was actually Surinam. Englishmen from Barbados had managed to forge an alliance with the local Carib population establishing a colony orientated towards sugar production in 1650. Five years later this rapid-growing colony counted a population of 1500 Europeans and 3500 enslaved Africans.[158]

Berbice 1665-1670

The development of Surinam had a considerable impact on the development of Berbice during the Second Anglo-Dutch War. Especially English sources document the role Berbice played in the course of these events. The war in the Caribbean had begun with hostilities carried out by English troops. In 1665 an attack on Berbice was countered by means of the assistance of the local Arawak population.[159] Van Berkel refers to this when recounting the episode of Captain 'Kakkebaretje', or Shit Hat, ridiculing the courage of the latter Arawak. The English troops led by Major John Scott met with more success in the *Nova Zeelandia* colony and

154 C. Goslinga, *The Dutch in the Caribbean*, 1971, pp. 422-423.

155 L.A.H.C. Hulsman, op. cit., 2009.

156 C. Goslinga, op. cit., 1971, pp. 424-425. A contingent of Jews from Livorno was accidently left on the island of Tobago. Several ships with enslaved Africans did not arrive. A constant stream of references of people knocking on the door of the Zeeland WIC chamber in order to claim payment for services to the Nova Zeelandia conglomerate.

157 P.M. Netscher, op. cit., 1888, pp. 72-75. There is some controversy concerning the name Groenewegel vs. Groenewegen. G. Edmundson, *The Dutch in Western Guiana*, 1901 suggests the Cromweagle Scott mentioned in his manuscript was in fact Groenewegen, the son of a Delft notable. Goslinga, den Heijer, and Roos follow Edmundson while Netscher opines that the name mentioned in the sources was clearly Groenewegel (P.M. Netscher, op. cit., 1888, pp. 68-69). Harris agrees with Netscher that Groenewegel who died in 1664, is not the founder of the colony (C.A. Harris & J.A.J. de Villiers, *Storm van 's Gravesande*, 1911, pp. 146–153). In fact, the Zeeland Archives documents proves there was indeed a family called Groenewegel (an unusual, remarkable name) then living in Scherpenisse: NL-MbgZA_995-SRP-01B Scherpenisse 1B NG Trouwregister 1610-1684.

158 C. Goslinga, op. cit., 1985, p. 425.

159 Anonymous, *Een vertoogh van de considerable colonie, by de Staten van Hollandt uitgeset op de vaste kust van America* [...], Den Haag: Jacob Scheltus, 1676, p. 67.

Essequibo. The former commander Aert Adriaensz Groenewegel had passed away on 19 August 1664. His son Adriaen, succeeding in command, rendered the fort to Scott.[160] William Byam wrote:

> *In few Months his great Fortune and Gallantry, prudent and industrious Conduct made him Master of all the great Provinces New Zealand and Desseceeb, settled a Peace with the Arrowayes, left both Colonies in a flourishing Condition and well garrisoned for the King of England, now Zealand under the Conduct of one Capitaine Boxlion and Desseceeb under the Command of one Capt. Renn, both old soldiers and sober Gentleman.*[161]

This excerpt from the William Byam's report spells Essequibo as Desseceeb. Arawak are called Arrowayes. The English colony in Surinam had been hit by an epidemic earlier in 1665 and, despite these successes, it felt threatened by the continuing Dutch presence in Berbice, which made it unwise to send troops from Surinam in order to destroy the French settlements on the Wild Coast:

> *At this Time the Assembly presented to me and the Council the great Danger of sending so many of our best Men to windward while we lay exposed to the threatened Invasion of Borganasy, governor of Barboto, and the Arwacas from Leeward (...).*[162]

The name 'Borganasy' must be read as Matthijs Bergenaer, the then Governor of Berbice. The English had got it right, because Bergenaer had gathered strong troops in order to attack the English who had occupied fort Kyckoveral. English reinforcements were sent from Surinam in order to hold the fort:

> *(...) nor was Capt. Rondar unsuccessful at Leeward having stormed two Warehouses of the Arwacas and had other Rickornings* [encounters] *with them wherein he slew about 30 Men and took 70 Captives. But for the Release of our men at Dissekebo he came to late, who about 3 weeks before thorough Want of Ammunition and irresistible Hunger were forced to surrender themselves and 12 hundred Slaves which they had taken to Burgunas a Dutch General who besieged them. But on good articles which those Complain he afterwards broke (...).*[163]

The reference to 1200 slaves in Essequibo raises questions and seems rather exaggerated. Fort Kyckoveral was situated on a small island with certainly not sufficient room for such a large number of people. Bergenaer's conquest of Kyckoveral in 1666 led to disagreements concerning the presence of slaves (see below). French troops attacked the English garrison that occupied *Nova Zeelandia* on the Pomeroon and Moruka Rivers and was forced to surrender due to a lack of provisions towards the end of 1666. In both cases, the local Indian population discontinued its trading relationships with the English shortly after Scott had left with the larger part of his troops.[164]

---

160 P.M. Netscher, op. cit., 1888, p. 75.

161 William Byam Journal of Guiana, Mss No. 3662, ff. 27-37, referring to July 1666.

162 Ibid., also referring to July 1666.

163 V. Harlow, *Colonising expeditions*, 1925, p. 203.

164 C. Goslinga, op. cit., 1971, p. 425.

The States of Zeeland reacted to the British actions by sending a naval expedition under command of Abraham Crijnssen. The objectives included, for instance, retaking the Dutch possessions on the Wild Coast and attacking the English colony in Surinam. Arriving here in February 1667 Crijnssen succeeded in capturing Surinam. To his delight he learned he did not need to bother with the conquest of fort Kyckoveral as Matthijs Bergenaer had already taken it. The latter, commander of the patroonship of Berbice, did not cause any trouble with regard to ceding fort Kyckoveral. In April 1667, he even signed a paper while visiting Crijnssen's fleet, which was ready to sail to Tobago.[165]

The situation Crijnssen faced in Essequibo, after his return to Surinam in February 1668, was quite complicated. Acting as a naval commander for the States of Zeeland, which had granted the Essequibo colony to the *Nova Zeelandia* consortium, he cooperated with the WIC Zeeland, which wished to recuperate their former colony. In June 1668, Crijnssen resolved to compose a contract with Bergenaer concerning the manner of governing fort Kyckoveral. Bergenaer was to take care of the annatto trade on behalf of the States of Zeeland.[166] This provided Bergenaer, and through him the patrons Van Pere and Van Rhee, with the effective control over the trade in the entire region located between the Corantyne and the Moruka Rivers.

The Directors of the WIC Zeeland intended to regain control of Essequibo. Therefore Hendrick Rol was sent as the WIC commander to fort Kyckoveral in the summer of 1667.[167] The situation of the WIC Zeeland was complicated due to the bankruptcy of the *Nova Zeelandia* consortium. In addition, the States of Zeeland formally controlled the entire region through their military and naval officers. In the meantime the effective control lay in the hands of Berbice and its private patrons because of the contract between Crijnssen and Bergenaer. The Berbice manner of governing Kyckoveral soon led to disputes. Captain Hendrik Rol, incoming commander of the WIC colony of Essequibo, complained that after his arrival in the spring of 1668 people from Berbice had stolen his merchandise.[168] Bergenaer quarrelled in August 1668 with Jolijt, the military commander of Kyckoveral, over the use of slaves.[169] In August 1668, the WIC Chamber of Zeeland decided officially to notify the patrons of Berbice because of their illegal occupation of fort Kyckoveral. Negotiations with the States, the Admiralty, and the *Nova Zeelandia* consortium began.[170]

165 Ibid., pp. 400-401; Anonymous, *Waerachtich Verhael van de heerlijke overwinning van Pirmeriba*, Johannes Rammazeyn, boekdrukker, wonende op de Stadssingel over de nieuwe Haven, 1667, A3-A4.

166 NL-MbgZA_2035_36 1668 06 20 concerns the agreement between Bergenaer and Crijnssen.

167 NL-HaNA_1.05.01.01_29_16670710.

168 NL-HaNA_1.05.01.01_29_16680524;16680820.

169 NL-MbgZA_2035_90_166808 concerns the declaration by Lanslot Kraeckou, Laurens Woutersen and Lambert van Oserne on behalf of Mathijs Bergenaer regarding the comportment of Commandeur Jolijt in fort Kyckoveral on the Essequibo.

170 NL-HaNA_1.05.01.01_29: 16680524; 16680820.

The liquidation of the Essequibo account proved very difficult. An issue the WIC wished to settle concerned the Company's slaves located in fort Kyckoveral. On 12 November 1668, Groenewegel Jr. had been interrogated regarding this matter by the WIC Zeeland Directors. Groenewegel then stated that thirty-five African slaves had been sent to Jacob Cools, his father's brother-in-law, who lived on the island of Martinique. Cools had not employed those slaves and said they belonged to Master Jan Doense.[171]

In October 1668 Crijnssen wrote from Paramaribo that Bergenaer had requested the patrons and the States of Zeeland to allow him to return home in order to plead his case, having appointed competent businessmen to take care of the annatto trade.[172] Apparently given permission, he wrote to the States of Zeeland on 6 March 1669 he had appointed an incoming commander in Kyckoveral.[173] Governor Lichtenberg, the successor of Crijnssen who had unexpectedly passed away, wrote in April 1669 he had called back Jolijt as well the soldiers, except for twelve men placed under the command of Lansloet Krakau [Lanslot Kraeckau], who had been appointed on Bergenaer's advice.[174]

The tension between the patrons of Berbice and the other Directors of the Zeeland Chamber abated due to the involvement of politicians, including the State Pensionary Johan de With. In March 1669, negotiations concerning the restitution of Essequibo to the WIC resulted in a draft agreement. The WIC could take possession of Essequibo without costs, but Bergenaer or his patrons must be compensated for the work carried out in order to consolidate the defence works in Essequibo.[175] The contract for the restitution of Essequibo was finally signed in May 1670.[176]

The restitution was based on an ingenious juridical argumentation: it was by way of force that the States of Zeeland had conquered the territory of Essequibo, which prior hereto had been granted to the *Nova Zeelandia* conglomerate. However, as this territory had been devastated by the invasions of English and French troops, it had become *terra nullius*. Thus the States of Zeeland had this occupied territory to their full disposal. Moreover, the States were legally free to hand over Essequibo as a grant to the WIC. The contract contained an article regulating the encampment in fort Kyckoveral consisting of a garrison of ten soldiers, formally financed by the States of Zeeland, but in practice funded by the duties the colony of Surinam owed to the States of Zeeland.[177]

---

171 NL-HaNA_1.05.01.01_29: 16681112. On 20 January 1667 Doense claimed payment from the WIC Zeeland Chamber because he was acting guardian of the children of the deceased Commander Groenewegel (NL-HaNA_1.05.01.01_29: 16670120).

172 NL-MbgZA_2035_76a and 77.

173 NL-MbgZA_2035_117.

174 NL-MbgZA_2035_128_16690401_Lichtenberg.

175 NL-HaNA_1.05.01.01_29: 16690312.

176 NL-HaNA_1.05.01.01_30: 16700524.

177 *Nederlandsch gedenkboek of Europische Mercurius*, Vol. LXII, eerste deel van 't jaar 1751, 's Gravenhage: Frederic Hendric Scheurleer, p. 29.

Contracted by the WIC Zeeland in order to take up the command in Essequibo, Hendrick Rol set off in the summer of 1670. The ship *Kinderdans* under Master Matheus van den Bossche took him to Essequibo, together with troops, artisans as well as free planters, and a cargo consisting of merchandise, victuals and building bricks.[178] Rol must have reached his destination several months before Van Berkel. The incoming commander wrote a letter dated 26 February 1671 to the WIC's Zeeland Directors, informing them that only an order from the Gentlemen XIX could force the commander of Berbice to evacuate all illegally occupied locations.

Van Berkel writes that he arrived on 20 January 1671. Not mentioning Bergenaer, he informs us that the Master of his ship had replaced the commander. Netscher assumed that this was Matthijs Bergenaer. However, Bergenaer's successor is probably referred to because the latter must have passed away between 1670 and 1672 to never return to the Netherlands. In the resolutions of the WIC's Zeeland Chamber not a single word is found with regard to Bergenaer's return. Had he indeed returned, he would have claimed his share of the financial compensation for the costs related to fort Kyckoveral. A resolution of a board meeting dated May 1672 includes a reference to Bergenaer's widow who had managed a plantation in Essequibo and was involved in a dispute over slaves confiscated by Hendrick Rol.[179]

Berbice 1670-1674

Van Pere required a licence for every ship he wished to dispatch to Berbice as was the case in the spring of 1669, when the WIC's Zeeland Chamber granted a licence to the *Nassau* owned by Master Cornelis Marinus.[180] That very same vessel took Van Berkel to Berbice in the autumn of 1670. He described Berbice in 1671 as a rather small colony. Its progress since being founded in 1627 had seemed fairly modest:

> *During my stay, there were five plantations, including the head-plantation of the fort, which produced yearly a fair quantity of sugar; the most important (next to the Oriane, of which is shipped about one hundred barrels), merchandise that is traded here. They are all located at the riverside, yet not equally attractive, nor equally easy of access.*[181]

Fort Nassau and its population

The centre of the colony was fort Nassau, situated at a bend of the Berbice River. Between 1629 and 1670, the colony's main post had been moved from the confluence with the Wiruni down the Berbice River. At a distance of 14 leagues, *c.* 80 km from the sea, ships could utilise the incoming tides to reach this fort. Unfortunately, Van Berkel did not describe it. We therefore know little

178 NL-HaNA_1.05.01.01_30: 16700724;16700804.
179 P.M. Netscher, op. cit.,1888, pp. 359-360.
180 NL-HaNA_1.05.01.01_29_16690401.
181 A. van Berkel, op. cit, 1695, p. 90.

about its dimensions etc. It probably included earthen walls with palisades and other defence works made of wood. The images of fort Nassau published by Hartsinck in 1770 are probably not representative of its earlier stages: the Van Pere family renewed the fort after 1678, after Van Berkel had left Berbice.[182] When the inhabitants of the plantation feared an enemy attack in 1673, they found shelter inside the fort. According to Van Berkel it then housed eighty people, for whom the accommodation was insufficient. The fort certainly would have counted a storage room and lodgings for the garrison. There may well have been a larger building, possibly multifunctional, with a meeting and staff rooms. The Chief's room was upstairs implying that this building had at least two floors. Van Berkel also describes that he handed something through the window of his room, which was apparently located on the ground floor. Near the fort was a plantation, but we are not informed on buildings or structures outside the fort. In his 1770 publication Hartsinck presents a church and several other buildings, but it is not known whether this situation existed during the 1670s.[183] Van Berkel does not include any information on the plan of the main plantation near the fort or on the locations of the slave quarters. The layout may well have been identical to the plantations in Surinam, of which the earliest pictorial evidence dates from the first decade of the 18th century.[184]

The staff of the fort consisted of the Chief and his secretary. The cook, artisans (e.g., coopers, carpenters, blacksmiths) and perhaps several other employees were omitted by Van Berkel.[185] The contingent of soldiers in the fort comes apparent when they rebel and lock up the Chief. Van Berkel is quite reticent on this matter and does not inform us how many troops were involved or who commanded them. He only mentioned the constable Dirk Roosekrans from Flushing, overseer of the artillerists and spokesman of the mutineers.

The colony included a parson who, according to Van Berkel, was associated with the l'Église wallonne, the Walloon Reformed Church, in Flushing. This clergyman cannot have been an old hand because the Rev. Westhuijsen, who visited Berbice in April 1667, mentions that his departure was delayed due to the fact that nobody was available to baptize eleven children.[186] Van Berkel did not mention any houses in the vicinity of the fort, but did report the parson's house where a barrel of ale was delivered. This parson probably left with Cornelis Marinus (see below) in 1671.

---

182 NL-HaNA_1.10.69_614_Rademacher 18e eeuw.

183 For a discussion on fort Nassau, see M. van Wallenburg, Sites of Fortifications and Administrative Headquarters of Early Dutch Colonists on the Berbice River, *Archaeology and Anthropology* 10, pp. 1-18, 1995a; A. Benjamin, Fort Nasau and the van Wallenburg Thesis: A Re-evaluation of the Evidence, *Archaeology and Anthropology* 12, pp. 8-21, 1998; L. Bosman, *Nieuw Amsterdam in Berbice (Guyana),* 1994; D. Roos, *Nederlandse forten in Guyana*, Vlissingen: Stichting Menno van Coehoorn, 1996.

184 See Dirk van Valkenburg's (1675-1721) drawings of the plantations Palmeneribo and Surimonbo in Surinam, Collection Rijksmuseum, Amsterdam.

185 For a description of the population of the fort during the 18th century, see L. Bosman, *Nieuw Amsterdam in Berbice (Guyana),* 1994, pp. 16-21.

186 Anonymous, *Waerachtich Verhael,* 1667, A3-A4.

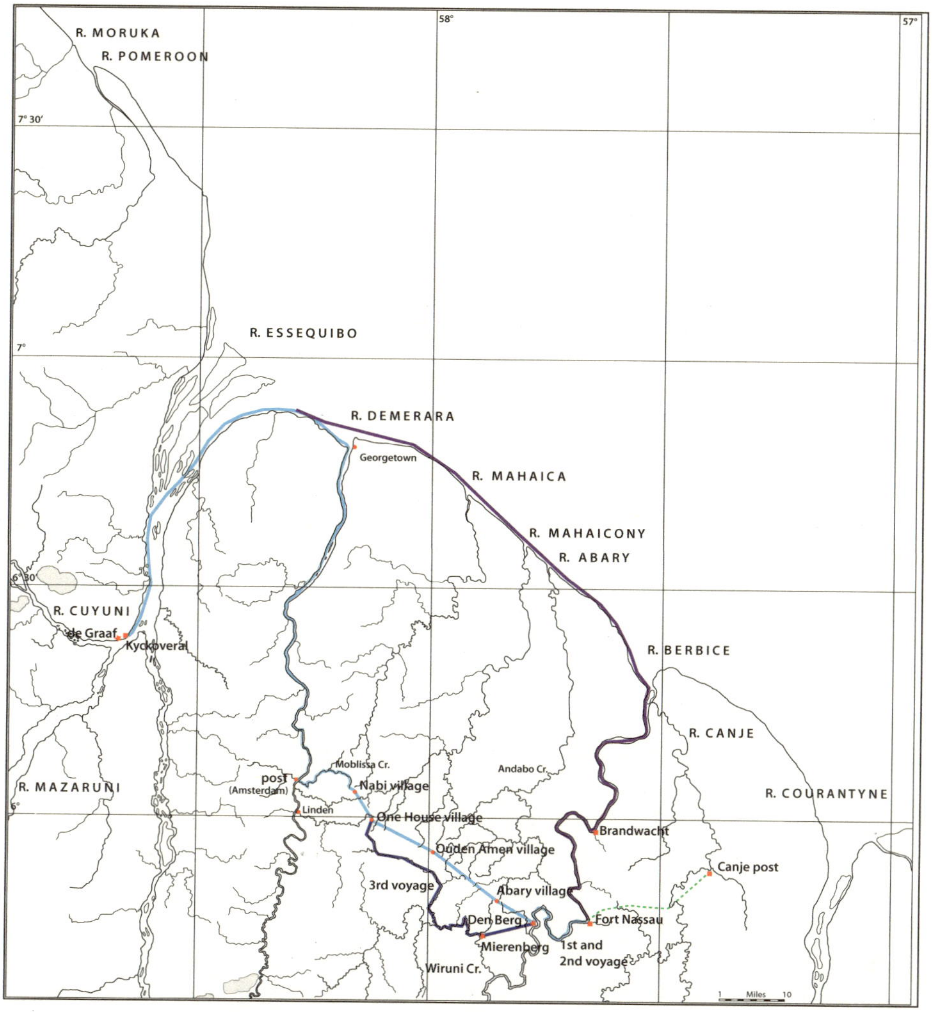

Figure 9: Map of the area between the Corantyne and Essequibo Rivers.

The Chief was assisted by a council of planters in accordance with the regulations of the States-General and the WIC. Van Berkel is vague about the number of planters in this council. According to later regulations the council counted five or six members, in addition to the chairman, the Commander of Berbice.

The colony's Commander, or Chief, was often a shipmaster closely associated with the patrons.[187] Again, Van Berkel is extremely vague regarding the names of individuals. He only informs us that his shipmaster was called Cornelis Marinus and that the latter had assumed the position of Chief on Sunday 25 January 1671, a few days after his arrival. He adds that the Chief had left the colony after signing the final treaty with Essequibo. This must have occurred in July 1671 when a ship

187 Such as the commission of WIC Captains and Commanders.

arrived with an incoming Commander, the very same ship took Marinus home. Only after 18 months did the next vessel arrive, as we learn from Van Berkel:

> *In the month of June of the year 1673, we received tidings about Essequibo, by means of a vessel that arrived there from Holland, telling how the d'Eendracht, sent to us according to the old custom, had captured an English ship coming from the East Indies and had sailed with the same to Bergen in Norway, and from there to Elbe. We had received no tidings for 17 months.*[188]

The final arrival from the Netherlands Van Berkel reported of, relates to shipmaster Marinus. According to his chronology, it was 17 months prior to June 1673 that he reached his destination in December 1671. Newspaper reports inform us that an Atlantic crossing took between 8 and 12 weeks. How many days were spent on unloading, maintenance and reloading remains unknown, but may have taken a month or more. Therefore Marinus must have left Berbice between 15 April and 15 May in order to arrive at Berbice again in December. In this case, he only can have served as Commander for *c.* 3 months. This calculation does not include trips to Essequibo or other colonies along the Wild Coast, on the way to or from Zeeland. It may be added here that such journeys were no exception.

The Third Anglo-Dutch War (1672-1674) and the Franco-Dutch War (1672-1678) put transports across the Atlantic at risk. As a result no supplies reached Berbice. In fact, the Republic nearly succumbed to the combined attack of English and French, leaving the overseas colony Berbice temporarily unattended. The 1674 peace treaty with England allowed maritime communication to be resumed, much to the relief of the inhabitants of Berbice, who had to wait 2 years to receive any relief. Van Berkel wrote 'While the things were in this state, we received in the month of January 1674 the tidings from the fort concerning the arrival of two ships.'[189]

The resolutions of the Zeeland Chamber of the WIC state that Van Pere requested in September 1673, a commission for the *Eendracht* under command of Master Jan Laurens to visit Berbice. He also asked for two commission letters in 1674 to send two privateering ships i.e., the *America* and the *Eendracht* under Master Cornelis Marinus. In fact, further proof exists that these two ships arrived on the Berbice coast in 1674: on 13 August Van Pere informed the Directors of Zeeland's WIC Chamber that one of these corsairs carried a letter of marque and and thus did not need to pay any recognition because it did not carry any goods.[190] This probably concerned the frigate *America* transporting booty slaves to Curaçao in 1674.[191] Van Berkel wrote that he returned home on board of the *Eendracht*

188 A. van Berkel, op. cit., 1695, p. 94.

189 Ibid., p. 100.

190 NL-HaNA_1.05.01.01_32, 24 July 1670. In this period the *patrons* had to pay recognition for the goods they transported.

191 NL-MbgZA 2035_242, 7 June 1673; 430, 2 May 1680.

under command of Adriaen van de Vyver, whose commission for the *Regenboge* was paid later by Abraham van Pere, as is registered by the States of Zeeland.[192]

Plantations, sugar and slavery

The vicinity of fort Nassau counted four other plantations, all situated on the Berbice River, which Van Berkel described as follows:

> *The plantations, called den Berg and Mierenberg, are situated fairly high up; with a wealthy pasture around them and a lovely view of the forest at the rear. The two others, on the contrary, are on places where a large and long stretch of forest has been felled, but at a lower level, and on clay ground; therefore, when it has rained heavily, [and] the rain reaches over there, it [the ground] is useless. In the savannahs, or pastures, on the other hand, one has sandy ground; subsequently the roads [are] always useable, along which one can travel from the two first-mentioned plantations towards various villages in the land.*[193]

When comparing Van Berkel's description with the report Van Stapels compiled in 1629, we can note that the Dutch still lived in more or less the same areas (i.e., in the vicinity of Amerindian villages) as they did 40 years earlier, in upriver plantations. Van Berkel merely mentions plantations at the Canje River in 1671, not describing them further.

Planters are seldom mentioned by name. We do however come across Master De Feer, owner of the plantation *Den Berg* and father of Matthijs de Feer, who in 1687 was appointed Commander of the colony.[194] From his letter to his colleague in Essequibo we learn that Indians and slaves had attacked the Dutch settlements.[195] Life in Berbice was nevertheless comfortable according to Van Berkel:

> *Moreover, one lives there in an excellent way; because one takes care in having all things on the plantation, such as chickens, turkeys, tame ducks, all sorts of greens, and everything else one needs [91] for necessities and pleasure. The cows supply fresh milk daily, of which butter is also made; the Indians, who serve the Lords Planters for a small consideration, hunt many kinds of tasty game for them. The others, who dwell in the surrounding villages, provide them with everything they may get a hold of, etc.* [196]

192 NL-MbgZA_2.1 Staten van Zeeland en Gecommitteerde Raden_1670, 12 September 1674, f.160v. Registers van commissiën en instructiën 1578-1809: 'Adriaen van de Vijver, schipper op het schip genaamd de Regenboge, groot 140 lasten, varende van Vlissingen naar Suriname. Permissie verleend aan Abraham van Pere, betalende het lastgeld' (Register of Commissions and Instructions, 1578-1809: 'Adriaen van de Vijver, Master of the ship the Rainbow, 140 lasts, sailing from Flushing to Surinam. Permission granted to Abraham van Pere, paying the duties for it').

193 A. van Berkel, op. cit., 1695, p. 90.

194 P.M. Netscher, op. cit., 1888, p. 329.

195 Ibid., p. 154. On the war with Indians, see also Chapter 1 of this Introduction, pp. 25-26.

196 A. van Berkel, op. cit., 1695, pp. 90-91.

Sugar was an important product:

> *And since we are describing the plantations here, we must not forget to speak about the preparation of the sugar, and what it further concerns; a matter appropriate to arouse the curiosity of the attentive readers. See here, how, from the beginning till the end, the whole thing happens.*[197]

In 1671, the sugar production at Berbice Van Berkel spoke of was as yet in an incipient stage, compared to the scale it reached during the 18th century.[198] Van Berkel's task as a secretary provided him with inside information on the colony's population and production. He mentioned compiling an inventory soon after his arrival, but no inventories from this period have been kept in the archives, only a small number dating from the 18th century. However, certain 17th-century inventories from Essequibo have survived. Van Berkel writes that in 1670 the Essequibo Colony counted only three plantations, of which Master de Graaf's plantation with about thirty slaves was the largest.[199] The other two had only twelve slaves each. This corresponds more or less with the 1686 inventory of Essequibo. It lists a similar number of African and Amerindian slaves in three locations: the fort, the plantation *West-Souburg* and the plantation *Nieuw Vlissingen*.[200]

Van Berkel's book indicates the small scale production of sugar. With five Company plantations against three, Berbice was probably larger than Essequibo. Van Berkel did describe private plantations, e.g., at the Canje or Demerara Rivers. The population would have been limited, perhaps only fifty Europeans and between 150 and 300 slaves.

We have hardly any information on the Africans living in Berbice in 1670. It is therefore a great pity Van Berkel does not deal with enslaved Africans. Linguistic research into Berbice creole languages has shown the presence of Eastern Ijo from the Bight of Biafra.[201] Van Berkel only mentions an accident in a sugar mill killing two male slaves, commenting that the people at the plantation did not care about their sad fate. The Dutch Atlantic slave trade was now expanding rapidly. It is interesting to note that the patrons of Berbice were involved in the conquest and occupation of the island of Arguin situated off the coast of Mauretania. This major slave port was in Dutch hands between 1633 and 1678.

---

197 Ibid., p. 91.

198 On Berbice during the 18th and 19th centuries, see A. J. McR. Cameron, *The Berbice Uprising*, 2007; A.O. Thompson, *Unprofitable servants: crown slaves in Berbice, Guyana, 1803-1831*, Barbados: University of the West Indies Press, 2002.

199 A. van Berkel, op. cit., 1695, p. 43.

200 NL-HaNA_1.05.01.02_1025.

201 S. Kouwenberg, The invisible hand in Creole Genesis, Reanalysis in the formation of Berbice Dutch, *Complex processes in New Languages*, Enoch O. Aboh & Norvan Smith (eds). In: Creole Language Library 35, Amsterdam: John Benjamins Publishing Company, 2009, pp. 120-121.

Amerindians, food and annatto

Van Berkel documents an intimate relationship between Europeans and the indigenous population of Berbice. He reveals no trace of tension between the Dutch and the Amerindians, pointing to a rebellion Commander Matthijs de Feer reported in 1687.[202] The relation of Van Berkel ressembles the one Gelein van Stapels described 40 years earlier. The 1629 situation when most Dutch inhabited indigenous villages is seemingly continued. Although residing at their plantations near the fort during the 1670s, the Dutch maintained a lively trade with the surrounding indigenous villages, i.e., the 'Maikony' outpost. Amerindians of neighbouring villages supplied the plantations with cassava, fruits and game. It is noteworthy that Van Stapels reported the presence of several ethnic groups on the Berbice in 1629, while Van Berkel mainly mentions the Arawak and Warau in the vicinity of the Berbice Colony.

Van Berkel applies the derogatory term *Bokjes* when referring to the Amerindian population. It may be added here that *bokje* is the Dutch word for a small billygoat and was probably derived from the English *buck* which even today characterizes youngsters. Theophilus S. Schumann,[203] who led a Moravian mission named Pilgerhut on the Wiruni River, wrote in 1748 that the term *Bockjes* was applied to all members of the indigenous population, such as the Carib, Warau and Arawak, who called themselves 'Lukunu'.[204] Schumann also discusses Jephta, a converted payé, or shaman, describing the contemporary relations between the Lokono of Berbice and eighteen other indigenous peoples inhabiting the Guianas and Amazonia.[205] Van Berkel also describes the Lokono who accompanied him to Essequibo, indicating how familiar they were with the situation in this Dutch colony.

An interpreter, or *tolk* (Dutch) perhaps of Amerindian descent, considering his ability to fish *loulouw* in between 'thousand-legs trees' and to translate the lyrics of the mourning song 'Little Daddy, little Daddy', often accompanied Van Berkel.[206] Again when the Indians asked permission to attend the ceremonies in the village of Abary, this interpreter gave detailed answers to all his questions concerning this event. In addition to asking his interpreter, Van Berkel makes his own observations on the daily Arawak way of life: their way of counting, conversing and raising

202 See also the report in the *Oprechte Haerlemse Courant*, 30 March 1688, discussed in Chapter 1 of this Introduction.

203 After his arrival in the Arawak region, Theophilus Solomon Schumann (1719-1760) founded the mission post named Pilgerhut. In letters written to his fellow brothers in Hernnhut (Saxony, Germany) he described his work and life in Berbice. In 1758 he returned to Europe and traveled Surinam in 1760 to only spend some time there among the Surinamese congregation; having returned to Berbice that same year he passed away in the village of Pilgerhut which he had founded. Due to his early demise, he was not able to finish his Arawakkan-German dictionary containing religions songs and hymns in the Arawak language which his son Carl Wilhelm completed eventually.

204 F. Staehelin, *Die Mission der Brüdergemeine in Suriname und Berbice im achtzehnten Jahrhundert: eine Missionsgeschichte hauptsächlich in Auszügen aus Briefen und Originalberichten*, Herrnhut, Vol. 2, 1918, p. 8.

205 Ibid., pp. 173-176; G. Bos, *Some recoveries in Guiana Indian ethnohistory*, PhD Dissertation Free University, Amsterdam: VU University Press, 1998.

206 A. van Berkel, op. cit., 1695, p. 18.

children. He also deals with theft, religion, the appearance of men and women, warfare, burials, body painting, daily food and its preparation, feasting, and sexuality.[207] Although Van Berkel views the Arawak *rites de passage* to be valiant, he mocks the Amerindian fear of European weaponry, which he relates in the story locals tell about Captain *Kakkebaretje* during the English attack on Fort Nassau in 1665.[208]

The short visit to the village of Abary was made departing from the plantation *Den Berg*. Van Berkel returned in the night to his host De Feer without the Amerindian porters because they wanted to attend the nightly ceremonies. He could not persuade them to come with him, Van Berkel wrote. We read: 'These folk cannot be driven by force. They are engaged by Christians to undertake journeys, to carry goods, and to convey them by day and night; for which they are paid on their return; but they do not stand under the bond as slaves, and wish not to be forced.'[209] This is an interesting remark: in the Amerindian societies of the Guianas, however, slavery was quite common. Moreover, the Dutch in Essequibo applied this indigenous system at their benefit. Later inventories of the colony of Berbice indicate that Indian slaves served in the same way as in Essequibo too. These Amerindian slaves may have been sold to the Dutch by their Arawak allies, after raiding a Carib village, or perhaps they have been brought from the interior and sold by trading partners such as the Akawaio. On several occasions Van Berkel himself mentions the phenomenon of indigenous slavery, for instance when he speaks of an enslaved Amerindian midwife.[210] Whatever indigenous slavery in this specific timeframe actually represents does require further study. These relations were clearly quite complex.[211]

The annatto trade deserves attention too. The colony exported *c.*100 barrels of annatto annually. Amerindian tradesmen sold it to the Dutch. Van Berkel writes:

> *While I was busy preparing the said merchandise, some Indians came to the fort with their wares which my interpreter sent off; in accordance with his notes I wrote down the shares. They are ignorant people where counting is concerned as I have*

---

207 Ibid., pp. 25-26. A similar ceremony has been described by Antonio Vásquez de Espinosa in *Compendio y Descripcion de las Indias Ocidentales* (*c.*1630). See: C. de Goeje, 'Een oud bericht over Arowakken en Karaiben', *West-Indische Gids* 12 (1930-31), p. 485-491, especially p. 489. There Vásquez mentions the Arawak words for wife (*soco*), son (*dadite*), father (*dajuna*) and friend (*dabuquei* or *tapane*). This Spanish manuscript has been found in the library of the Vatican (Biblioteca Apostolica Vaticana) and published in 1942 (English translation) and 1948 (publication of the original Spanish text). See: Antonio Vásquez de Espinosa, *Compendium and description of the West Indies.* Translated by Charles Upson Clark. Smithsonian Miscellaneous Collection, Vol. 102. Washington: [Smithsonian Institution,] 1942, pp. 72-73. Chapter XVI, 'Of the Rites, Ceremonies, and Customs of This Aruaca Tribe' describes the customs related to death, funeral and remarriage of the widow (paragraps 183-185), and dwells on other family affairs (paragraph 186). For the Spanish edition see: [Antonio Vásquez de Espinosa,] *Compendio y Descripcion de las Indias Occidentales por Antonio Vazquez de Espinosa.* Transcrito del manuscrito original por Charles Upson Clark. In: Smithsonian Miscellaneous Collections 108, Washington: Smithsonian Institution, 1948, pp. 66-67.

208 Ibid., pp. 26-27.

209 Ibid., p. 27.

210 Ibid., p. 55.

211 See F. Santos-Granero, *Vital Enemies: Slavery, Predation, and the American Political Economy of Life*, Austin: University of Texas Press, 2009.

Figure 10: The public execution of a prisoner. Print in André Thevet, Cosmographie universelle.

> *noted on so many different occasions. Because, when they come to sell a set of thirty balls of paint, called oriane, they do not know how to count them in succession. They put five balls together, according to the number of fingers of the hand, and then again five others.*[212]

In addition to the fort of Berbice, several outposts (e.g., in Demerara) were engaged in trading annatto. Van Berkel reported on Demerara that fifteen or sixteen men were stationed here to market a pigment called 'oriane' [annatto] with the Indians.[213] Another post was located along the 'Maikony', most certainly the Mahaicony River.

Neighbouring Amerindians often visited the colony in order to sell their products. For instance, the Warau sold fish to the Dutch or showed up whenever a ship arrived. The Dutch also maintained trading connections with the Akowaios

---

212 A. van Berkel, op. cit., pp. 17-18. Cf. the European way of counting by scores of five.
213 Ibid., p. 30.

or Akawaio. They resided in the highlands and visited the Dutch at a trading post called *Markaay* higher up the Berbice River.[214]

In 1670, the Caribs of the Corantyne River are pictured as the archenemy of both the Arawak and the Dutch, as van Gelein van Stapels wrote in 1629. The Dutch maintained economic and military contacts with the Arawak, whom they considered their allies. This is proven by the fact that the Arawak had a so-called 'strong-house' in Naby,[215] not far from fort Nassau. The collaboration was strengthened when the Dutch and the Arawak combined forces in 1677 in order to drive the English out of the Essequibo Colony and to fight against the Caribs and the English in Surinam.[216]

Surinam at the time of the fictitious voyage of Adriaan van Berkel, 1680-1689

The Dutch-Arawak alliance in Berbice was a factor of great importance as was proven when the Dutch in Surinam were surprised in 1678 by an uprising of the indigenous population. Lucas Caudri, the then Commander of Berbice, sent troops to assist his colleague in Surinam. However, Governor Johannes Heinsius did not much appreciate this contribution, alleging that the Arawak had made a pact with the Carib of the Coppename River.[217]

The historical documentation of the 1680s concerning Surinam is very scarce. Not one document referring to Van Berkel or the *Juffr. Sophia* on which he claimed to have travelled has been found. Even if more documents had survived, Van Berkel and his ship would not have been mentioned in any of them, for, as we already have seen, this voyage to Surinam was a fictitious one.

As Surinam during this period already has been dealt with in Chapter 1 of this introduction, here only one topic needs attention. The Colony of Surinam was at that time plagued by attacks of Amerindians, who had also liberated a number of the African slaves. The runaways or Maroons were able to create autonomous communities in the hinterland of the plantations with the help of Amerindians. This striking phenomenon is completely omitted by Johan ten Hoorn, who made up this part of *American Voyages*. As we have seen earlier, the publisher was not interested to supply updated information on the actual situation of Surinam.

214 For a historiography of the Akawaio, see C. Carrico, Akawaio-European relations during the Dutch colonial Era in Guyana, *From Historical paths to the cultural processes between Brazil and Guyana*, R. Gomes & I. Melissa (Orgs.). Boa Vista: EdUFRR, 2011. See also A.J. Butt-Colson, *Land. Its occupation, management, use and conceptualization: the case of the Akawaio and Arekuna of the Upper Mazaruni District, Guyana*. Panborough: Last Refuge, 2009.

215 Perhaps Naby resembles the Dutch preposition *nabij* meaning 'near'. Another suggestion is 'potato', as *nabi* in Cariban refers to an old garden.

216 P.M. Netscher, op. cit., 1888, p. 77.

217 R. Buve, *De positie van de indianen in de Surinaamse plantagekolonie gedurende de 17e en de 18e eeuw*, typoscript, 1962.

Chapter 4

Notes to the edition of *American Voyages*

The translation presented here is based on a literal transcription of the original publication of *Amerikaansche Voyagien*, Amsterdam 1695, kept in the Special Collections of the Library of the University of Amsterdam (OTM: O 60-5542).[218] A second copy is bound in with two other publications (OTM: O 629698).[219] The Amsterdam-based publisher Johan ten Hoorn dealt through 'In de Historischrijver', a bookstore located opposite the 'Oudezijds Heerenlogement'. His publications were also sold in ''t Zinnebeeld' which was owned by his brother Timotheus ten Hoorn and established in de Nes (Amsterdam).[220]

As to this translation, the text has been harmonized, implying that the application of uppercase and undercase has been normalized. However, the capital letters have been maintained not only for titles (e.g., Master, Chief, Council, Director, Lord, Captain, Gouvernor, Commander, Lieutenant, etc.), but also for names, days of the week as well as for Rivers, Indians, Negroes, Christians, Whites, and Europeans. Dutch names and certain specific terms are placed within single quotation marks and quotations in double inverted commas. Words from other languages are set in italics (Arawakkan, Cariban, Latin, etc.).

As to the translation as well as in the reissue of the Dutch text, the original paginating of the 1695 publication is provided between square brackets, indicating the page breaks. The numbers referring to the sections are omitted being of relevance only to the bookbinder. A Dutch glossary is added to the transcription indexed according to the original paginating.

---

218 A. van Berkel, *Amerikaansche voyagien, behelzende een reis na Rio de Berbice, gelegen op het vaste land van Guiana, mitsgaders een andere na de colonie van Suriname, gelegen in het Noorder deel van het gemelde landschap Guiana : Ondermengd met alle de byzonderheden noopende de zeden, gewoonten, en levenswijs der inboorlingen, boom- en aard-gewassen, waaren en koopmanschappen, en andere aanmerkelijke zaaken. / Beschreven door Adriaan van Berkel.* Tot Amsterdam: by Johan ten Hoorn 'tegenover het Oudezijds Heren Logement, in de Historischryver', 1695.

219 This volume consists of three books: P. van der Burg, *Curieuse beschrijving van de gelegentheid, zeden, godsdienst, en ommegang van verscheyden Oost-Indische gewesten en machtige landschappen, en inzonderheit van Golkonda en Pegu: alles uyt de eygen ondervinding by een vergadert door P.V.D.B.* Rotterdam: I. Naeranus, 1677; A. van Berkel, *Amerikaansche Voyagien*, and Th. Aletheus, *Discursus politicus de polygamia*. Friburgi: apud Henricum Cunrath, 1676.

220 For the study on Ten Hoorn's publishing house, see H. Korten, '*Boeckeniers zijn gaeuw in het schieten': Jan ten Hoorns uitgave 'Americaensche zee-roovers'*, Master Thesis University of Amsterdam, 2011.

Part II

Texts & glossary

Figure 11: Title print in A. van Berkel, Amerikaansche Voyagien.

[i]

AMERICAN VOYAGES
to
RIVER BERBICE and SURINAM
See Fol. 64

[ii] blanco

[iii]

AMERICAN VOYAGES
containing a journey to
BERBICE RIVER
situated in the continent of Guiana
on the wild coast of America
Together with another to the Colony of
SURINAM
situated in the northern part of the said
Country GUIANA
intermingled with all the details
concerning the customs, manners and ways of living of the natives, fruits and vegetables, commodities and merchandise, and other remarkable things.
Written by
ADRIAAN VAN BERKEL
EMBELLISHED WITH COPPER PLATES

AT AMSTERDAM
by Johan ten Hoorn. Bookseller opposite
the Oude Heeren lodging-house 'At the Historian' 1695

[iv] blanco

[v]

TO THE READER

I would never have thought of publishing these American voyages of mine, and undoubtedly they would have shared my grave, had not the continuous persuasions of good friends, with whom I had spoken about my early expeditions many times, and who finally made me decide to share with the world that which for a long time had been buried in my brain. It is commonly said of authors that they have been forced to publish their works in order to show, as it were, a certain kind of reservation. But I can truthfully say that has indeed been the case with me. I have known for a long time what little honour is to be gained by such an effort and for that reason was not very eager to be included in the [vi] category of book writers. But they [my friends] talked these scruples out of my head, and tried to show me I would do a great benefit to publish a description of countries of which no one had talked about yet. As a matter of fact, it is of grand negligence to describe the whole world, so to speak, and not to mention two colonies where so many of our countrymen reside; from which we should be able to obtain sufficient information to at least sketch them without being obliged to travel to those places ourselves. Meanwhile, this has been neglected, and as it seems, the task has been left to me to put a hand to this canvas. I have exercised my diligence so that it may appear somewhat agreeable to the eyes, yet that is why, however, the truth has never in the least been detracted. This has been my principal aim, [vii] and if I had had no scruples in overstepping it as loosely as many travellers have done, I would have been able to tell the reader the most remarkable things in the world, especially about the Berbice River, as being less travelled than Surinam. But the truth, quite naked, has always charmed me more than falsehood stacked with all the jewellery with which one tries to make her attractive. Here I ought and may assure my readers that, as far as I know, I have said nothing in the entire work which I could not, at any time, confirm by the testimony of others. If elegant stories and strange events are wanting, remember it is no novel, but a true description of facts, of which people will be convinced when they shall have heard others speak of the same things. I thus set myself at ease against all slander, and wish the impartial reader the best.

[viii]

ON THE VOYAGES OF ADRIAAN VAN BERKEL

Here the reader sees, by van Berkel, in print:
The condition and ways of the wild Americans.
The fertility and potential of the land, its customs and manner.
On religion, marriage and death; its rivers, forests, roads.
Thus is shown by him, like on a canvas,
which wonders occur in that other part of the globe.
J. Schriek.

[1]

VOYAGE
To
RIVER BERBICE
situated on the mainland of
GUIANA
on the Wild Coast of
AMERICA

CHAPTER I.

The author is engaged to go to the Berbice River. Driven back by bad weather, on several occasions he puts to sea. Peculiarity of the trade winds. Method of catching sea hogs, or porpoises. Remarks concerning the same. Description of the sharks, bonito; and flying fish. Description of a waterspout. Danger of waterspouts. Waterspouts of another kind called 'pypen'. Arrival at the River Berbice.

Incited by a noble desire to visit foreign climates and countries, I found an opportunity for partially satisfying my wishes when the Lords Van Ree and Van Peere, the Principals[221] of the River and Colony of Berbice were fitting out a ship which was soon bound for those parts. The intercession of good [2] friends paved the way that smoothly engaged me on the same as trader and secretary. Having previously despatched my baggage to 'Vlissingen' [Flushing], I went there in person on 24 October of the year 1670, where, having waited 4 weeks long for a favourable wind, and the same beginning at last to blow, I was conveyed on board. Here I found everything ready for the expedition and on 24 November we put to sea with an easterly wind; the ship which carried sixteen pieces of cannon being a frigate named *Nassau* and the Captain Cornelis Marinus.[222] But the next day, just as we came in sight of 'Grevelingen', the wind turned, and we returned with the same to Zealand.[223] Yet, before we could reach port, the unusualness of the sea, although we were taken along with but a slight breeze, made such a change in my body, and turned everything so upside-down, that, in spite of whatever effort I employed to retain it, all the food and drink was given in return through the same way as they were consumed. And this difficulty being accompanied with a heavy headache and strange dizziness, I found myself quite indisposed. Shortly after, however, by sticking my nose in the wind, and keeping the sea in view, I recovered immediately.

221 As to the spelling of Dutch surname prefixes, see note 5. The term Principals serves as a translation of the Dutch 'Patronen'. The Dutch WIC granted the right to found a colony within its patented area to individuals who then were called *patroon* (Eng. 'patron').

222 Van Berkel spells Marinus which also can render the patronym Marinuszoon (son of Marinus), often abbreviated as Marinusz or Marinussen.

223 'Grevelingen' a small port located between Calais and Dunkirk, the present day Gravelines.

After the course of 8 days, we once more got a favourable wind, upon which they began to weigh anchor,[224] but just as we were clear, an East Indiaman came in front of our bow which damaged our galleon,[225] so to repair the damage, we were forced to stay there until next day. The following day it was that we set sail, and we again put to sea in the afternoon. In the evening, some people down below in the ship called out that we were sinking; upon hearing the call, I, quite ignorant of these tricks, and consequently in a mortal fright, came rushing forward. But 'Jan Hagel',[226] seeing how fear had taken me, laughed at my ignorance saying it was because the hawse pipes were not closed. Then I went back to my bunk, a bit [3] more at ease than when I got out, and slept that night without any further interruption. The next day, just as we had gotten into the channel at 'Bevesier' [Beachy Head] the wind turned again, it blew harder and harder, and during the night turned into such a gale it wanted to smash the ship to pieces. But a disastrous faith struck the East Indiaman of which I have just spoken. It hit a sandbank, called the 'Gom' or 'Gonje' [The Goodwins], burst open, and shortly after the bow went under; nevertheless, except for the steersman, the entire crew and the greater part of the goods were saved. Another ship, coming from Bilbao and laden with Spanish wool and 40000 pieces of eight, also sunk on this particular place. We saw it lying near us before we went to supper, and when we had finished, the night watch told us it had sunk, but that the people had all been saved by a ship that lay to leeward of them. Considering ourselves after this storm, which had carried us between Dover and Calais, we had to return despite a contrary wind, and on the fifth day [we] reached Flushing once more, where my landlord, with whom I had now lodged on two occasions, welcomed me with great joy, as he deemed we had perished, because a ship had sunk near Zealand.

Two days later, the wind blew from the East again, whereupon we set sail in the afternoon for the third time. We made such good time that, at day watch, we saw the fires of England's Foreland, and when I awoke, we found ourselves in sight of Pevensey where the tempest had previously overtaken us. The cold, which hitherto had given us some trouble, now began to lessen daily; the favourable wind continued, speeded our voyage and carried us to the latitude of the Canaries, but here it subsided, and we drifted a while in the calm.

Meanwhile a change occurred shortly afterwards. For, coming into sight of the Island of Madeira, I was [4] told we had met the trade winds, to great joy of all the sailorfolk. These winds always blow from the same quarter, between North and East, and during that period one need not worry much about the rigging and sails. On the other hand, since they are moderate, they temper the heat of the sun which would be unbearable without them. They are usually found around the latitude of the said island and when met with, one makes an average run of between 40 and 50 miles a day, without almost even feeling the motion of the ship or the pounding of the sea.

---

224 Outgoing ships waited for favourable winds. If possible they stayed together in order to prevent solitary ships from being attacked by pirates from Dunkirk.

225 The curve of the prow (Dutch: *galjoen*).

226 'Jan Hagel' is a Dutch expression referring to 'common people.'

In the meantime, throughout the day, we amused ourselves catching fish. Almost daily, we saw a very large quantity of all sorts of them; especially sea hogs, or porpoises, which swam around the ship in large schools. They are caught as follows. At various places on the ship, but especially on the bow, several sailors took position, each with in his hand a harpoon, to the end of which was fastened a rope about as thick as one's little finger. Now, when the sea hogs swam past them, they threw the harpoon with such force they pierced them on several occasions. They let it stay in the wound, holding it all the time by the rope which they release that long until the fish, weakened by the loss of blood, lets itself be hauled in without any resistance and be brought on deck. Several were caught in this manner. This fish is rightly called a sea hog, because it looks like a hog or pig, not only because of the flesh and fat, but also because of its shape both on the inside and the outside. The flesh, however, has absolutely no delicacy and tastes somewhat of whale oil.

It is a common idea among many people who have never seen porpoises, that the blood of these animals is not warm; but I experienced the contrary and can speak with absolute certainty because I had the stomach of one of them cut open and had the curiosity to stick my hand into the guts and found [5] its blood to be almost as warm as that of a pig. Likewise, I could not doubt they breathed when I saw their lungs as suitable for breathing as those of animals which live out of water. They have no gills like other fish but only two holes on both sides of the head to breathe through; it is certain, on this account, that from time to time they heave their heads, and occasionally the whole body, out of the water, and always swim close to windward. Hence when sailors, during calms, see porpoises setting off for a certain direction, they say that the wind must come from that quarter. Besides the porpoises, or sea hogs, we also caught many sharks. These fish are a sort of sea dogs, with a very broad and flat head and a very deep throat because the lower jaw is much shorter than the upper; thus when they want to bite they have to lie on the side, and sometimes on their back. A little below the head, their skin consists of a kind of shagreen, which is rather coarse, with six openings on either side, which close by means of a kind of very thin skins that serve as gills or guts. They are the greediest animals of all that men can mention, because, although they may have been pricked with the hook three or four times one after the other, their mouths smothered in blood, they always come after it again as keen as before until they are either caught or end up with the bait. Moreover, when they get hold of someone, he is done for, as they never let go. The reason for this extraordinary gluttony is the size of their liver. They have three rows of teeth, of which one is curved, and the others straight and of various shapes; the teeth in third row are triangular, select at the front and tapering upwards like a saw. They are always accompanied by certain small fish which form their retinue and are that inseparably clasped to them they prefer to be caught rather than forsake them. They are named their steers [6] men or pilots, because it is said they serve as guides to lead them to places where food is to be found.[227] They eat the remnants of the catch and keep themselves attached

227 Steermen or pilots: *Remora* sp.

to the shark's skin by means of a crease-like piece of oval-shaped skin which they have on their head and is fit with grooves.

Nearby we also found a number of bonitos, the implacable enemies of the flying fish which they are always chasing. This fish has the size of the stoutest homeland carp, but much thicker; it is furthermore without scales [but] with a silvery skin and its back is marked with long dark and golden stripes. The bonitos are easily caught because, due to their inordinate preference for flying fish, one makes use of the same shape made of feathers [lure] which is tied securely to the end of a line. One bobs this feather work back and forth on the water where, deceived by the resemblance, they jump at it that greedily that often that with only two or three lines, thirty or forty are caught within the hour. The taste is good.

Concerning the flying fish, we saw various schools raise themselves in flight to the height of *c.* 8 or 10 feet, and cover 50 or 60 paces before they fell back in the water again to moisten their wings, and acquire renewed strength against the bonitos who sometimes catch them as they descend, or jump out of the water to catch them as they fly. Besides bonitos, the flying fish have yet another enemy: a certain kind of bird which shoots down on them as they fly out of the water to save themselves from the bonitos. Our constable brought me the first flying fish which, followed by one of the said birds nearby, had happened to fall onto our ship. It had the shape, colour, and size of a herring, the back slightly thicker, and the front part of the head roundish, like a sea beam, with wings abo- [7] ve the cheeks, very much like that of a bat.

We thus sailed along up to 17 January 1671, a Sunday,[228] when at about noon a large black cloud appeared from which, shortly afterwards, a part detached itself; when this separated part was driven away by a powerful gale, it changed its shape entirely to form a long column descending from the sky to the surface of the sea. We, as passengers,[229] who had never been to sea before, observed this apparition in amazement, which was sufficiently far away not to cause anxiety; we learned from the steersman, who discussed this with us, that these phenomena, or water spouts, are very dangerous (not only when one is forced to sail into them) and that they slice through the ship's yards and masts due to the water which then comes to fall onto the ship, but also due to the sudden violence and excessive pressure of the whirlwind, with which it is carried off and which is capable of wrenching the masts from the largest ships as well as running them into danger of being wrecked. And as their encounter is that perilous, everything possible is done to avoid them. Meanwhile, they are often knocked down without anything happening: to wit, when one tries to break the wind's movement by thinning the nearby atmosphere by firing cannons and muskets, on which occasion the water, now no longer supported, falls down in great abundance, and the entire spout immediately disappears. Albeit from afar, these water spouts look small and appear to be columns measuring between 6 and 7 feet in diameter, they are in reality of

228 Van Berkel is mistaken here: 17 January 1671 was a Saturday.

229 'Kajuitsgasten' (lit. guests of the cabin) means passengers.

much greater size; our steersman assured us that, at a distance of a pistol shot, he had seen them measuring more than 100 feet in circumference.

One sees, however, at sea other kinds of water spouts, called 'pypen' by some, on account of their length: [8] but these are not dangerous and only manifest themselves in the lowest regions of the atmosphere, appearing at sunrise and sunset at just about the same place the sun then happens to be. They are long, thick clouds surrounded by other lighter and transparent clouds. They do not fall down but after a time become entangled, one with the other, and gradually disappear. Whereas the water spouts are driven by force, these last a long while and are always accompanied with rains and whirlwinds causing the sea to boil and become covered with foam.

On that same day, to wit, 17 January, one saw the sea violently ablaze as if it was covered with fire; therefore we, inexperienced sailors, amazed or astonished at the least sight of unusual things, asked the Captain and steersman the reason for this; they told us that we might well see land within 2 or 3 days. The lead [for sounding] was also being prepared and a depth of 43 fathoms of water was found; on the second occasion, more, and at the third time, 40 [fathoms]. The Captain now shouted that the steersman should tack two points. The next day, at about noon, we sighted land which appeared dark and, coming closer, we found it to be the Devil Islands [Îles du Salut]. On that day, namely Monday, as well as Tuesday, we sailed 'over land,' a way of expression, customary among seafaring people, who thereby wish to imply one is to high [of latitude] and makes for land before the wind. In the afternoon (having passed the River Surinam, as well as the Coppenam and Suramkeka[230]) the anchor was cast in the ground, and the River Corantyne, belonging to Surinam, was in view. Not accustomed to the sea, I already yearned with all my heart to place my feet on firm land; yet I had to be patient until we arrived at the River Berbice, situated 7 hours from here. The next day the anchor was weighed, as to run conveniently at higher water into the river; having been occupied with the journey for 5 weeks and having set sail for the third time on a Wednesday afternoon into the sea, [9] this occurred on a Wednesday evening, [and] after casting the anchor 1 mile within the river.

CHAPTER II.

The author travels up the Berbice River. He steps on land. Is mistakesn by eating atty. Returns on board. Is dispatched to the fort. Drink made from the mastication of women. Charm of the Berbice River. Arrival at the fort.

That evening, just as we entered the river, as related in the preceding chapter, we could not see much but the pleasant forests, from which now and again, sometimes even continuously a very confused sound, made by monkeys and other animals, was heard. In the morning, at sunrise, I went up the topstays to see what the land looked like; from here it struck me that the weariness caused by the sea was

230 The Saramacca River.

immediately driven off by the delightful view of the green trees and fresh air. At about 9 o'clock the anchor was weighed and we were pushed on slowly by the tide. There was little wind and having not covered more than between 3 and 4 miles [an hour] we had to drop the anchor again. We then observed some Indians, commonly called 'bokjes' [bucks]. A few sailors, who had been here before, asked permission to take the boat ashore to cut palmyt,[231] which was allowed. I was curious to see this kind of people and went along with them; when landed I came across men, women, and children who were stark naked, except for with which they cover their private parts, of which we will speak later. In the meantime, while I stood looking on in astonish [10] ment at these people, my eye fell upon a black pot containing red pepper, a soup they always consume.[232] Just as strangers who are often very curious and usually too much than necessary, I craved to taste it straightaway, [and] took a piece of their bread and dipped it in it. But this nibbling did not turn out well, for scarcely was the bread down my throat or my mouth started to burn as much as if it had stood on fire. I accordingly asked those who had been there often what kind of food this was; the answer: it was called *atty* and served as the common food of the Indians who in general took it as a meal, as we will relate more extensively further on.

Meanwhile we approached the forest to continue here [on foot] a bit along unbeaten paths, where our people were cutting palmyt; of which we will likewise speak later. We then returned to the river, stepped into the boat, and were conveyed to the ship. Here we were visited by some Indians with women and children. Several of our ship's crew, who had been there several times and knew something of the language, began to talk with them and do business by means of a few knick knacks. Meanwhile, while the Indians were still on board, someone shouted: "A sail". The large boat of the fort set off to fish at sea. Our Captain signalled them aboard, and we thus obtained information as to the situation there. A certain friend, who had already been there once, received orders, besides me, to sail with the same boat to the fort; when we would have arrived there, we sent letters to the plantations in order to make our arrival known. We then changed boats, lifted the anchor, and gave one another a gun salute. Being carried along for *c.*2 hours, my thirst was awful due to the heat and I accordingly asked the skipper if he had anything to drink. "Drink enough" he answered and next a Negro, who did duty as a cook, was given orders [11] to look after my wants; he then washed his black hands, went off to draw clean water, and took a handful of a certain substance which was scarcely unlike porridge from a quake [basket]. He rubbed it with his hands until the water turned white, poured it into a calabash, applied in that country as cups, and handed it to me. Without asking anything, I put the calabash to my mouth and got a good pintfull out of it. While drinking, the Master said I must keep my teeth slightly apart whereby the drink could slip down more easily. I found this indeed to be the case, because this beverage, resembling a kind of

231 Palmyt is the edible heart found in numerous species of palm trees. In this case it was probably that of the 'podon' (Sr.) or 'manicole' (G.) palm (*Euterpe oleracea*). The pith inside the trunk is scraped out, washed, and dried in order to produce flour.

232 To this day pepperpot is a national dish in Guyana.

pap, lets the liquid through, whereas the crumbles remain stuck in front of the teeth. Meanwhile, the Master could not restrain himself from smirking along; upon which I wanted to know the reason; when he asked me if I really knew what I had drunk, I said: "No"; but as I had suffered from a terrible thirst, the drink, it might be what it is, had tasted reasonably good. "It is the mastication of women," the Master said, of which one must make use of here in this country for want of better. Meantime, we drifted on nicely, of which opportunity I had the pleasure of observing the river at ease. It is usually very lushfull; its high green trees provides a very pleasant view, accompanied by a continuous screeching of apes, meerkats, baboons, parrots, etc. The latter flew above our heads in complete droves from time to time, and made such a noise, one could scarcely have heard a cannon shot. Having arrived at a *c.* 2-hour distance from the fort, the oars were put out, because otherwise we should have waited again for the next tide. In the meantime, as the evening was beginning to fall, and I could therefore no longer enjoy the pleasure of seeing things, I lay myself down to rest, but had not slept for long, or I was awakened, as we found ourselves in front of the fort. Two hours earlier we had fired our cannon, in order to notify the arrival of our ship, which can be easily [12] heard from there, because the river runs in a large bend, and the arrival at the same would have been delayed a bit. We then stepped over into the little boat, were carried to shore and, in the night between a Friday and Saturday, reached the fort, called Nassau, where one showed a great happiness upon our arrival. And here we were received by the Chief with all imaginable friendliness; after we had held some jolly good speeches with eachother, we were each assigned a hammock as to spend the remainder of the night in.

CHAPTER III.

Letters despatched by the author to the plantations. Lovely avenue of orange and lemon trees. Arrival of the ship in front of the fort. Installation of a new Commander, or Chief. Departure of the ship for the plantations. The author goes there to take stock. Does the same at the fort. Distribution of linen to the slaves. The ship, with its freight, again at the fort. Arrival of an English ship in the river. Quarrel arises between women over a jug of ale. The author proceeds to the mouth of the river. Strange kind of shelters. Departure of the ship. Attempt at trading in the Poomeroon River.

Although rather sleepy, I could not however get much sleep that night, since I had never lain in a hammock.[233] I also did not know, although I had not asked about it, how to lie in it, because in such hammocks which are 8, 10, and *c.* 12 feet [13] wide, one lies crossways. As soon as it was day, I got up, and prepared my letters which were immediately sent to the plantations. Now, I was anxious to see where I was. I was charmed with everything. Not far from the fort there is an avenue of orange trees, each of them as large as a linden tree in the homeland; upon which

233 Roth translated: 'Although I had a *tolerable compartment*, I could not however, get much sleep, *and also*, I had never lain in a hammock' (emphasis added). However, Van Berkel writes he is rather sleepy ('redelijke vaek') because he had never slept in a hammock, W.E. Roth, op. cit., 1948, p. 13.

there is always an abundance of blossoms, green and ripe fruits to be seen. This avenue is hedged with lemon trees which, as to beauty, need not make way for the orange trees and together with the same produce a very pleasant sight and delightful scent. Having went out walking here for between 1 and 1½ hours after which, after returning to the fort, I was shown to my room which I found large and spacious enough for what I should have to do. At about noon our ship arrived in front of the fort; immediately a few cannon shots were now fired from both sides; next all the passengers went ashore, followed by the Captain, who was the last to do so, and who had come to relieve the Chief whose place he was to occupy from now on.

In the meantime, the Lords Planters, who are Councillors of the Colony, having received the letters we mentioned before, arrived on Saturday night and Sunday morning at the fort, and a fine sermon was presented by the Parson; next they all sat at table according to their rank. The table was set elegantly, but we had been seated only half a quarter of an hour when I had to get up as I felt very sick. When going outside, I vomited a little which made me suffer from a huge pain in the head. Getting into my hammock I was pulled out by the Lieutenant, or Second-person [in charge,] who told me I must not lie down but stay on my legs, or I should get land disease. I got back on my feet, took my place at the table, ate something more washing it down with a large beaker, and found myself completely recovered after some 2 hours. In the afternoon the [14] bell rang; subsequently in the presence of all the Councillors, the new Commander or Chief, whose Commission I read out, was installed, after which the remainder of the day, even a good portion of the night was devoted to merrymaking.[234]

The following morning a start was made with the unloading of our ship; some cases and casks were brought ashore which I had to take charge of together with some other goods for the servants at the fort. Then, the ship went up stream to the plantations. The Chief and I followed in a canoe filled with of naked Indians, as we had to carry out inventories and to muster the slaves, to learn how many of them had died, and how many had been born. At the first plantation, I worked between 3 and 4 hours after which we were invited to excellent food and drink. Everywhere we came the wine was entirely broached, so we would not feel much of the biting mosquitoes during the night. In short, it was a Gentlemen's life and I really wished it might have lasted somewhat longer.

Having spent a few days on this [work], we returned to the fort again, where the same thing was done, first concerning the merchandise and then the slaves, who furthermore had to appear at the same place the following Saturday when, according to an annual custom, linen was to be distributed to the men, women, and children; to wit, for every man, as much as needed for a pair of trousers; for the women, enough for a skirt to reach about the knees, and likewise for the children. This was my work which kept me busy for several days.

---

234 Cornelis Marinus, Captain of the frigate *Nassau* that arrived in 1671 is referred to here. He officiated as Commander of Berbice between 1671 and 1683 (?), see P.M. Netscher, op.cit., 1888, p. 391.

But another, and more important task, I was given when, 3 weeks later, our ship with its cargoes from the plantations returned to the fort to do the same thing there; on this occasion, apart from the other duties, I went on board with the Chief at least twice a day in order to oversee that the Colony might not be disadvantaged. [15]

Meanwhile, we received news from some Indians who had come from downriver that an English ship had arrived in the river. Immediately, some Indians as well as three Christians were sent towards them, to see how things stood, although we were not at war with that nation at the time. On their return, they brought with them the Master of the English ship who was in need of fresh water. According to the story of the same, it was by only 2 days that we both had put to sea, but he had been quite hindered by storm and tempest and, which is strange, at the same time when we drifted along in the calms, in the vicinity of the Canaries, he had experienced, almost on the same latitude, such bad weather he had no other thought than that man and mouse would have perished in it. Between five and six bottles of seq [dry white wine], brought for our Master, as well as the promise of a barrel of ale, secured him permission to bring his ship into fresh water. Meanwhile the Master remained with us at the fort, and was well received until he got the message that all was clear; when being conveyed by some of our people to his ship, having been treated delightfully, he gave them the promised barrel of ale. Yet this proved an apple of discord and might almost have caused great mischief. The Chief had the said ale brought on board our ship in order to, when one would feast according to an old custom with the Lords Planters prior to the return of the same [vessel], be consumed while merrymaking; wishing to show special courtesy to the Parson of the Colony and to a certain other gentleman, he sent a boy to draw a jug of this English beer for their wives; very unfortunately, it was brought to the house of the said gentleman. His wife, more drawn to it than she ought to be and getting a taste of the beer, drank it all down without giving the Parson's lady her share of it. The latter, greatly upset about this, used some expressions [16] which were not exactly in line with the limits of politeness. The other then responded, so that an awful fight quickly began, and because each thought to be disadvantaged, they complained to their husbands; a serious dispute nearly arose among them and it would have turned out more serious if the Chief had not instructed me to try to satisfy the women and men. I had the luck to be heard and to achieve objective for which I was thanked by all the Lords Planters because, both being men of importance, it was about to happen that this little spark, had it not been extinguished in time, might have discomposed the entire colony. Nevertheless, the merrymaking we had when the ship was ready to set sail, soon made us forget this unpleasantness. On that day, we feasted free from all disturbances and on the following [day] we did likewise at the fort. As the Lords Planters were unwilling to leave before [they finished] the ale, of which a small part had caused far greater strife than the whole, it was drunk in bliss and rejoicing down to the very last drop.

Two days later, I boarded a canoe, covered with a thatch of leaves, along with the Chief in order to go to the river mouth where the ship lay ready for departure. That evening I lay down to sleep on land for the first time, in the forest, with the hammock securely tied to two trees. Meanwhile, the Chief stayed in the canoe lying on the cushions. Just before I wanted to rest, our slaves had built a small 'pleisterhuisje', named thus among Christians and Indians[235] for me at the location where the hammock was to hung. It counted four posts, somewhat higher at the front than at the the back, covered with a thatch made of unusually large leaves often between 4 and 5 feet long and *c.* 2 feet broad. Neither sun nor rain can do it any harm. Because the leaves lie that thickly, one upon the other, the rays of Sun cannot penetrate. One sees such shelters along the entire river and one [17] has them built instantly wherever one wishes. For an Indian, like the tortoise, is at home everywhere. The next day we arrived at the ship, which was anchored about a quarter of an hour away from the mouth [of the river] in the sea. Here I prepared the last despatches and, during the 2 days we stayed there, had the pleasure of sailing with the Indians to the beach and to go out shooting in the forest. Eventually the ship went out to sea, and I returned with the Chief to the fort, after having spent again the night in a shelter.

Two or three days after our return to the fort, the Chief was addressed by a certain planter from the Canje District who had made our Lords Directors believe some fantastic things, concerning the great advantages he would have been able to make with a fair amount of merchandise in the Bourum River.[236] The Chief was already briefed on the case and, notwithstanding all his caution, had a better understanding about it, as was proven by the subsequent events.[237] In the meantime, great deliberation was needed; and I did not like the case. However, it had to go through with it, and I received orders to get ready some merchandise with which this braggart betook himself in our boat on a journey to the said river. Though, how badly that undertaking turned out, we will inform the reader of in the following chapters.

CHAPTER IV.

Ignorance of the Indians in counting. Tediousness of their speeches. Discipline amongst the children. Hatred of theft. Religion. Description of the Indian men and women. Marriage customs, and merrymaking.

While I was busy preparing the said merchandise, some Indians came to the fort with their [18] wares which my interpreter sent off; in accordance with his notes I wrote down the shares. They are ignorant people where counting is concerned as I have noted on so many different occasions. Because, when they come to sell a

235 According to W.E. Roth, a 'pleisterhuisje', or rest-house, is a temporary shelter consisting of thatched leaves. It is called a 'benab' in Guyana and may come in various sizes and shapes.

236 According to W.E. Roth, the name of the Bourum or Pomeroon River is derived from *bourum*, the Arawak term for sand fly. To this day this river is notorious for its sand flies, mosquitoes, and other insect pests.

237 Van Berkel's phrasing is extremely vague and seems to have been constructed in order to evade any accusation of representing the Chief as responsible for the Canje expedition, which was sensitive in view of the animosity between Essequibo and Berbice. Pomeroon was considered a part of the Essequibo jurisdiction.

set of thirty balls of paint, called oriane,[238] they do not know how to count them in succession. They put five balls together, according to the number of fingers of the hand, and then again five others. Observing this for the first time, I asked my interpreter the reason of it; he told me they do not count beyond five. When they likewise wish to count to ten, they show all the fingers the number twenty is signified by means of the fingers and the toes. The wild Indians are even more ignorant, and expressed great amazement when they saw me writing because they could not understand one can share his thoughts with another, who is absent, in this manner.

The Indians here are very tedious when speeching. For something we could relate in half a quarter of an hour, they need at least half a day. In the meantime, due to all this wordiness, they exercise patience by never interrupting eachother; the listener, if he wants to say anything at all to the speaker, is sufficiently satisfied only to say "wa", meaning "good" in our language. Once, while everyone was lying in his hammock, I heard a little girl singing; continually hearing the same words without any change, I asked my interpreter the meaning of this song which was repeated so many times. He replied it meant nothing else than: "Little daddy, little daddy; my little eyes, my little eyes, when I have died." This had lasted nearly half an hour when the mother snarled at her: "If your father was here, he would say something else"; he would have been insulted by the expression "Little daddy".

Regarding the discipline with children, they are never beaten, whatever they may have done, but they are punished for faults and disobedience, so that they may be careful for the future. [19]

Theft is extremely hated among them, and is never committed except through great laziness because they have neither a chest nor a box and consequently would not well know where to hide the stolen [goods]. Even the women have nothing to store their ornaments in except for a small box or basket they call *pagale*.[239]

Religion has absolutely no place there. They also make no difference in days or seasons. But let us talk also about the exterior of these people. The Indians are of an ordinary stature, reddish in colour, and black hair which, when they are raised to the dignity of Captain, is cut off up to the ears. Otherwise, it generally hangs to the shoulders. In the middle partition of the nose a hole contains a small silver plate with the size of a double 'stuiver'[240] hangs between the mouth and the nose; it

---

238 Oriane, or annatto: The seeds of the *Bixa orellana* fruits were processed with oil in order to produce balls of dyestuff. These balls were wrapped in leaves and sold by the Indians to the Dutch. Having put the annatto in barrels, the Dutch shipped 100 barrels a year from Berbice to the Netherlands according to Van Berkel. In the coastal Guianas, annatto was a very important product of the early trade during the late 16th and early 17th century as was tobacco, cotton and hardwood. From *c.*1650 on the production of sugar by means of African slave labour started to develop in the Guianas, notably in Surinam, under the command of Willoughby and to a far lesser degree in Berbice, Essequibo, Cayenne and Approuague. Here the Dutch started only a small number of plantations, see M. van den Bel & L. Hulsman, *Une colonie néerlandaise sur l'Approuague*, 2013. The trade for annatto with the Amerindians remained an important aspect of trade in the Berbice and Essequibo colonies.

239 *Pagale*: a type of basket consisting of two comparatively deep rectangular trays, one of which is slightly larger in order to slip over the other for which it acts as a cover, very much after the style of a lady's holdall dress basket.

240 A double 'stuiver' is a small silver coin worth 2 *stuiver*. The Dutch guilder consisted of 20 *stuiver*.

is lifted when drinking so that it should not be in the way. They pull the hair out of the beard and eyebrows wishing to have no hair on any part of their body. From time to time, the body is smeared with red paint, a colour which finds great favour in their eyes. The beads they highly prize, rarely serve the men as adornments except on a small number occasions of merrymaking. Around the middle of the body, they carry a small band into which their knife is stuck. The lap covering their modesty is likewise stuck under it from front to back, and hangs beyond a ½ ell down over the buttocks. The head is encircled with a small band to which all kinds of feathers are attached, though this is in general found among young Indians.

There are also Indians called 'Acquewyen' [Akawaio]. They live higher up in the country, and in the mountains; from where they very rarely come down to the fort, but do often come to a place called *Markaay*, the trading place highest up [on the river]. They are far more jealous than the other Indians; for which reason they likewise look after their women more carefully. In the vicinity of the said trading place, the land begins to gradually become higher; the river continues up there [20] for between *c.* 5 and 6 miles.[241] The highlands, the source of the river and the many cliffs with the marks of the Spaniards who first discovered the coast and explored the entire river can still be seen here.[242]

When the Indians go to war they prepare all kinds of arrows, among them those that poisonous that only a few of those wounded by them recover. They also have arrows with iron and bone tips, with barbs, etc., which they know how to cut that suitably with their knives. They shoot all their arrows through the air with such accuracy they know how to let them hit the body of whatever they were aiming at.

The Indian women are also of a moderate stature, and, although not pretty, are nevertheless uncommonly proud. Their most prominent ornaments consist of *orewebbe*,[243] a certain kind of bone, which is grinded down flat to about the

241 A Dutch mile measures *c.* 5.5 km.

242 Whether these rock carvings, or petroglyphs, were made by the Spaniards, as Van Berkel suggests, remains unknown. In Guyana, however, we find two kinds of petroglyphs, made by both Spaniards and Amerindians, see N. Horstman's map kept at the *Bibliothèque nationale* in Paris (CPL GE DD-2987 (9612). Along the upper Essequibo River it clearly features a lake situated between the Upper Rupununi and Mahó Rivers (a branch of the Parima River entering into the Rio Negro). Horstman drew this map, entitled *Carte de la Route de Nicolas Horstman, natif d'Hildesheim en Westphalie depuis Rio Esquibe jusqu'à Rio Negro*, after his journey from the mouth of the Essequibo to the mouth of the Amazon River, see H. Bolingbroke, *A Voyage to the Demerary, containing a statistical account of the Settlements there, and of those of the Essequibo, the Berbice, and other contiguous Rivers of Guyana*, Norwich: Richard Philips, 1807, pp. 154-155. The naturalist Charles Marie de la Condamine apparently took this map to France, see C.M. de la Condamine, *Relation abrégée d'un voyage fait dans l'intérieur de l'Amérique méridionale, depuis la Côte de la Mer du Sud, jusqu'aux Côtes du Brésil & de la Guyane, en descendant la Rivière des Amazones* [...], Maestricht: Jean-Edme Dufour & Philippe Roux, 1778, pp. 127-128. A partial reproduction of this map is published in Vol. 1 of *Storm van s' Gravesande* by Harris & Villiers, 1911, pp. 167-174. Horstman's journey was preceeded by two journeys from Paramaribo to Parimé *c.* 20 years earlier, see J.W. Yzerman, Twee reizen van Paramaribo, een naar de Parima in 1718 en een naar de Boven-Corantijn in 1720, *Tijdschrift Koninklijk Nederlands Aardrijkskundig Genootschap* 28, 1911; L. Hulsman, *Routes of the Guianas*, 2011.

243 *Orewebbe*: shell adornments, probably as seen among present-day Akawaio, are bracelets made of the *uruabi* shell. See also R.A. Gassón, Quirípia and Mostacillas: The Evolution of Shell Beads as a Medium of Exchange in Northern South America, *Ethnohistory* 47(3-4), 2000.

thickness of a 'rijksdaalder',[244] and the circumference of a 'bezemstuiver'.[245] I have seen women or daughters, who I believe, carried between 15 and 18 pounds of these small bones round their necks. They also wear short bunches of bones in the ears to which ends copper plates are attached, albeit not within a third as large and thin in comparison. From both sides under the arms, after the manner of bandoliers, they sling all kinds of [string] beads; the green and yellow ones are held in the highest esteem, and a set of between twelve and sixteen strings is sufficient to win the finest women at his will. These bead ornaments are also wound around their arms in three places; to wit, on the wrist, above the elbows, and on the shoulders. A lap,[246] artfully made of the same beads, covers their modesty. Below the knee one sees similar adornments; when placed above the ankle it resembles a kind of sock, about three fingers broad. They never take this off until it is well-worn. When death has taken a kinsman [21] they take off their trinkets and go about stark naked for a short time; this is the way of mourning the deceased. The old women do not adorn themselves anymore, and likewise do not worry about covering their shame, going entirely naked with long pending breasts which sway in front of their body. Many would possibly imagine that in times of mourning, the eyes should be better employed to roam elsewhere, but that is not the case. The young womenfolk are accustomed to keep their legs close together so that, whatever their position,, one can see nothing at all, not even the least signs of being indisposed; when, according to their custom, they sit on the ground, they know how to place the leg neatly under the body, with the result that, even when stooping down, the eye cannot be offended. Every morning they go in the water and even take the sucklings in order to accustom them to this from infancy, because everyone can swim. They often colour their faces with red paint and, just like the men, completely remove their eyebrows where they then put a streak of brown paint mixed with gum. A small number has a part of the body painted with water, now the upper, then the lower part, etc. This water dries up as black ink[247] and is that resistant, even if someone washes himself daily, it will not fade in 3 weeks.

That is all that can be said about their outward appearance and standard ornaments. Concerning their occupation and service in the household, the Indian women have to make bread, attend to the gardens, chew bread for the drinks, and grate *karsy* [cassava] on a stone grater. If a husband has hunted or shot something, it is their work to prepare the hunted or shot catch and to serve it. Be it a hare, rabbit, hog, deer, etc., its hair is burnt off, the guts washed and the meat placed on a *berbekot*.[248] This is an Indian grid consisting of small wooden sticks measuring 2 feet high. On it they place their food, flesh and fish, without salting it, [22]; being

244 Up to the 19th century *rijksdaalder*, or rixdaalder, and the *gulden*, or guilder, were merely monetary units and not real coins. Van Berkel probably refers to the 'real de ocho'; a rixdaalder equals 48 *stuiver* and a guilder 20 *stuiver*. A *stuiver* equals 16 *penningen* (pennies).

245 Bezemstuiver: a *stuiver* with a bundle of seven arrows representing the Seven United Provinces of the Dutch Republic. This bundle resembles a broom, hence the nickname of this coin.

246 Lap: a loincloth, or *camisa*.

247 Water charged with black ink is 'lana' (*Genipa americana*), according to W.E. Roth, op. cit., 1948, p. 23.

248 A barbecue.

half roasted, they crumble it into the pepperpot to eat on the spot or to keep for more convenient times because the pepperpot is the only recourse. They are not familiar with banqueting and commit no excess with food. The best I ever came across amongst them was a piece of hare; otherwise, crabs, apes, monkeys, *ytories*,[249] anteaters, yes, even crocodiles. Rarely does one come across birds and fish.

Although the Indians have neither police nor laws, they nevertheless marry as civilized nations do, in the following way. When the youngsters have reached a mutual understanding, and the parents of both sides agree with the marriage, the blood relations [relatives] come together; a kinsmen takes the word, recommending the groom not to go with any other [women], to take care of his wife, to be diligent, to make a bread garden, to go fishing and shooting for his kitchen daily, to help catch crabs, etc. The bride must have nothing to do with anyone else, show due respect and loyalty to her husband, serve him food and drink every time he gets home, and not to no longer play with children, etc. As a matter of fact, they are correct in recommending the latter to her, because the girls marry at the age of 11 or 12 years, when one rarely finds them with the composure marriage requires. With regard to the men: if they were as laborious as is exhorted to them, they would have food and drink in abundance because the land is full of game, birds, and fish; but their inborn laziness causes them to be content with the pepperpot for days accompanied by a drink of *payewar*, or *beltiery*; of which beverages we shall have opportunity to speak later.[250]

Their way of playing or merrymaking is also noteworthy. On a certain occasion, we had dispatched a message to amuse ourselves a bit. It consisted of a cord with several knots tied into it, according to the number of days, [23] until one has fixed the moment of merrymaking. The Indians, who receive it, cut a knot off it every morning; when the last one is cut off, they set off; between about forty or fifty, young and old, men and women arrived. The beverage prepared for the festivity, or revel, is called 'graaf'[251]; it is made of syrup and water, which, in the space of 3 days, has sufficiently fermented to get drunk. On a given signal, the Indians immediately started dancing, singing, and playing a certain kind of fife which emitted a strange noise. Having observed the preparation of peat in this country, one can imagine a round dance, whereby one does not hold each other, with a huge fire in the middle.[252] All are painted each in such manner one fancies most, albeit often with black gum, but the eyebrows with brown and the cheeks with red paint. And truly, this diversity of colours shows something to the eye, which is not unpleasant. The hair is also cleverly decorated and plaited, mingled with strings of beads, from which ends hang small images and plates that swing along the naked backs. These dances continue till daybreak when everybody goes off to

249 The Creole term for the howler monkey (*Alouatta* sp.) also called 'baboon'.

250 A good compilation provided by the Dutch historian Jan Jacob Hartsinck, *Beschrijving van Guiana*, 1770, pp. 24-25, of various kinds of cassava, sweet potato and maize beverages is presented here by Van Berkel.

251 Graaf: fermented sugar-cane juice which planters sold to the Amerindians; *warrap* is the present-day Lokono term.

252 The side-way action of *turf trappen*, or preparing peat for combustion, is actually rather appropriate when considering the similar (slow) movements of Amerindian ring or row-dancing.

tie his hammock and sleep for a while. In the meantime, I found the old saying to be true here: a drunken woman is an open door, because no sooner were their brains muddled with drink; the evening fell and all the hideouts became boxes for couples, after which they would stealthily rejoin the dance as if nothing had happened.

On Saturdays, I have often seen the Blacks dancing too. They play on a hollow piece of wood, resembling a pump, with an opening above and below, onto which a piece of leather is nailed. They make such amazing movements to the sound of this instrument one cannot refrain from laughing; he who knows how to twist his body into the strangest positions, is the best dancer. [24]

CHAPTER V.

The author is ordered to go to Essequibo. Method of burning the remainders of small bones of the deceased Captains. Cowardice of an Indian Captain. Description of the village Ouden Amen together with the Indian war houses. Arrival of the author at a house of the West India Company of Zealand. Return to Berbice. Description of an Indian village. Return to the fort.

While one was now impatiently waiting what the planter from the Canje District, whom we have mentioned at the end of the third chapter, had done on the River Pomeroon, there comes an Indian with a letter from Essequibo of which the contents said that he as well as ship and cargo had been taken into custody. One summoned the Lords Planters to deliberate what one should do in this confused state of affairs. After long consideration, I was deemed the most suitable [person] to go there as envoy. I had little fancy for it, yet knowing I could not well shove the burden off my shoulders; I wrote a Commission, which was signed by the Chief and all the Councillors, and sealed with the seal of the Colony of Berbice. I had only 2 days time to prepare myself for the journey; which passed, and meanwhile having brought everything to proper order, I went off and took the road at about noon, but could not proceed further that day than the plantation called *den Berg*, inhabited by Master de Feer, which is situated *c.* 3 hours above the fort when travelling with the flood tide. Here, I was well received and my [25] sojourn spent merrymaking. I had taken six Indians with me to carry the baggage. As I had to spend the night there, they came and to ask my permission to in the meantime go to a village called Abary. I asked my interpreter for the reason, he replied that at the said place, *c.* 3 or 4 weeks ago, a Captain had come to die; his bones, on account of his bravery, had been preserved, according to custom, which were now to be burnt. These little bones from various cut-off limbs, being fingers, toes, etc. which, after the flesh has been scraped off, are hung up for 3 or 4 weeks in the roof of the house to dry. This is the only [part] what is preserved that long, whereas everything else the deceased has left (e.g., axe, hatchet, knife, hoe, etc.) is at the same time thrown in the grave as he is, because they imagine he will have use for them during the journey. When one wants to burn the said bones, man and maid are invited to attend the ceremony. There is then an abundance of a drink called *bassia* by the Indians and *pernou* by us. The curiosity, as I had been told of all the circumstances of this affair by my interpreter, impelled me to accompany them there and see as an eyewitness what I could hardly believe from hearsay. My Indians immediately took up their position in the row consisting of about forty persons; and this row was surrounded by another row, somewhat larger. Each one had in his hand something like a long whip, with which they struck one another, turn by turn, a terrible blow on the legs. The one to be beaten stands in the middle of the row; and having endured the flogging, steps in the place of the one who has given it to him. This takes place amidst terrible shouting and screaming, as if they were challenging eachother, one saying "*Bockja watilly*" ("I am a man") and the other "*Dackje wathia*" ("I am also a man"); he who cannot endure this whipping until the following morning is declared a coward, and never dares to enter [26] any company. The one, who has a moment of time, meanwhile goes for a drink, because there is such a quantity of drink it cannot be consumed. During this valorous performance, the wives have their thing to do, too; to wit, they utter dismal wails and lamentations, exclaiming in the midst of their sobbing and sighing, "Who is now going to plant bread, go hunting and fishing, catch crab, etc. for the widow, their sister?" (as they even call Christians their brothers and sisters). Meanwhile they place the small bones of the deceased in the fire, to be reduced to ashes; which the women also must look after; while the men greet one another determinedly outside the house with lashes of the whip, by the flickering of several fires which serve as torches. This is how greatly valour is honoured by this nation. Meanwhile, they reveal themselves to be faint-hearted enough with regard to their enemies, at least to Christians, of which we will forward an example here.

In this same village of Abary lived an Indian Captain who was commonly known to the Christians as "Kakkebaretje" [Shit Hat]. It happened in the year 1665, when we were at war with England, that certain pirates got hold of the River Essequibo without any resistance.[253] This good result prompted them likewise to try a venture on the Berbice River; believing they would meet with the same cowardice over there.[254] The news travelled fast enough to the fort, on which account one immediately prepared to resist. Meantime a few Indians had arrived there to barter their wares. The English showed up on the river in a bark with eight to ten pieces [of cannon] and shot through the roof of the fort. The Indian[s], who could not bear this thundering in their ears, did not know where to save themselves out of fear and crept here and there in the bushes where they deemed themselves safe. The Christians [Dutch] who bravely fired back from their side, tried to stop them; but it was in vain. Accidentally, Captain Shit Hat [27] who apparently wanted to show some courage had remained with the Christians in the fort; yet, inside him something different took place: allowing himself to be wholly overcome by fear, and not knowing where to hide best, he crept into an

253 The colonies of Essequibo and Pomeroon were attacked by an English fleet under the command of Major John Scott whom Francis Willoughby had sent from Barbados, see P.M. Netscher, op. cit., 1888, pp. 76-77.

254 Van Berkel's account reverses the sequence presented by P.M. Netscher, op. cit., 1888, p. 76; see also J.J. Hartsinck, *Beschrijving van Guiana*, 1770, p. 28. A pamphlet published in 1676 mentions sixty Dutch in Berbice whom 500 Arawak assisted when the English attacked. Anonymous, *Een vertoogh*, 1676, pp. 66-67.

empty sugar cauldron standing in the store, which he fouled not a little. The fray lasted about half an hour, after which the English retreated; some people started to look for Captain Shit Hat, whom they finally found in such a position in the cauldron, still trembling with fear. This event caused a great laughter; nobody did not come and visit this courageous war hero. Meanwhile, notwithstanding this extreme cowardice, he had no sooner returned to his companions or he related to them with great bravado and swagger how fearlessly he had fought beside the Christians against the English, adding that the former were hugely indebted to him as the fort had not been taken by their enemies; he reproached them with their own effeminacy, for not having sufficient courage to listen to the thunder coming from the cannons, etc.

But let us return to the house of the mourning. After spending a long time watching the scourging with the whips, and other pleasantry that was performed, I returned during the night, by the light of a small wax candle so as not to get lost in the bush, and arrived at the plantation at about 11 or 12 o'clock; not being able to get my brave Indians with me, who wished to attend till the end of the ceremony. These folk cannot be driven by force. They are engaged by Christians to undertake journeys, to carry goods, and to convey them by day and night; for which they are paid on their return; but they do not stand under the bond as slaves, and wish not to be forced. At about 8 o'clock in the morning my Indians came back again, that whipped one was not able to put a thumb between the knees and the ankles that did not show any [28] bloody smears. There would still have been time to resume the journey, but the Indians being drunk, and not having slept, I had to remain there that day. While having our meal, the young lady of the plantation asked me which victuals I had taken with me, as I would not find much among the Indians. Saying I had more or less provided myself, and that, at the worst, I should easily be able to improvise for a day or three. She then had a dozen turkey eggs boiled for me, a little too hard, along with a piece of meat and a small leg of chicken. I imagined the Indian villages to be just like those of ours in the homeland where one can always get food by paying for it, assuming I should meet one every 2 to 3 hours, but I was greatly deceived by this thought. The next morning we set off, but scarcely had lost sight of the plantation or we found ourselves at a rather deep creek which stretched at least 30 roods [wide]. The baggage was sent ahead and finally followed by me, carried by the Indians. At about noon we arrived a forest in which, having advanced good distance, the baggage was put down from the neck, and a place was chosen to rest a while and to eat. I opened the basket and went for the eggs with a good appetite, while the Indians improvised with somewhat worse food. After staying 1 hour, we resumed our journey, and at about 4 o'clock reached a village called Ouden Amen. Immediately I searched for something to eat that night and, in the meantime, spared our provisions but could find nothing that pleased me. Here, I began to reflect on how concerned the Lady of the plantation had been, and what a great service she had rendered in supplying me with the basket; that had to stand bravely again by the evening because I was quite hungry. After the meal I went to my hammock, but the crying of the children, and the snoring of the Indians, each of whom certainly boasted about their courage, when enduring the flogging displayed at the village of Abary, [29] drove the sleep from my eyes for a long while, but I repaired the damage by resting quite late in the morning. Then the woman of the house came with a *wyda* of thick *payewats*, a little basket with bread, and the pepperpot, for our breakfast; for this as well as for the lodging I gave her, when we departed again, a small bunch of beads counting between fourteen and sixteen little strings which she accepted with great joy and thanks. She would also have fancied other kinds of goods, but as there was nothing to my liking, I closed the *pagale* and wished her well.

This village of Ouden Amen is situated on a delightful spot in a grove; the between sixteen and eighteen houses are built in such a manner one must pass through lanes of trees to get from one to the other. Amongst the same, some were inhabited by four, yes, even five or six households. The house, in which we had slept at night, was one of those that the Indians defend themselves from hostile attacks; likewise such hostilities were practised on various villages during my stay out there. It was between *c.* 120 and 130 feet long and between 30 and 40 feet wide, and encircled by palisades,[255] as thick as an ordinary spar, from place to place with a few openings to shoot through; with which they use bow and arrow, not knowing how to defend themselves in any other manner. I saw likewise therein nothing in the world but bows and arrows. These houses, which have to be maintained by the inhabitants of the villages collectively, are thatched with leaves of an uncommon size which are sewn together firmly below; with various bundles rolled into one another, they are taken up to be further fixed with bands, utilised by them as ropes, in such a way, that in case of fire, one can rapidly cut loose the whole roof.[256] The Indians of one and the same village live very peaceably among each other. Strife can barely arise, because everyone hunts, fishes, and shoots according to his liking. No land or forest is [30] forbidden, no waters are leased out, etc. Meanwhile there is little or nothing to be gained; thus they have but the present to care for, without any worry about the future.

After breakfast, we took to the road again, now marching through forest, now across fields, now through thicket, etc. At about an hour after noon we arrived at a village where there was only one house without any people in it. The Indians however call it a village and say that some folk had once lived there. They still go there to pick their bread and then lodge in this house.[257] We stopped here for over 1 hour to eat and to rest; towards the evening, after about a 4-hour journey, we reached a village of which I have forgotten the name. We stayed here with a Captain called Tomenaq; the Indians having respect for Christians immediately concede a

---

255 W.E. Roth, op. cit., 1922, p. 289 mentions only one example of a palisaded structure (a Macusi central house). Apparently, this type of archicture is the result of warfare between Europeans and Indians which was to be abandoned during late colonial times. See also Whitehead, op. cit., 1988, pp. 58-59.

256 Such thatching was still made removable when specific leaves were used, e.g., *durabanno* leaves are fixed on frames, which may be removed from old buildings to then cover new ones, W.E. Roth, op. cit., 1948, p. 31.

257 Abandoned villages are still part of the Amerindian habitat and often visited to collect fruit or remember the interred. See W. Balée, The Culture of Amazonian Forests, *Advances in Economic Botany* 7, 1989.

part of their house to them. The weariness took away all my appetite for eating, but on the contrary, the Indians who had carried such a load on their shoulders and whose legs were in such miserable condition, seemed to know nothing of it. I then gave orders to make a fire next to the hammock, according to custom, and lay down to rest; nevertheless, the hunger, as I had eaten nothing in the evening, woke me up at midnight. I went to sit by the fire and ate the food and drink that was left there, after which I returned to my bunk. In the morning, the woman brought me breakfast again, consisting of the usual Indian fare; to wit, a *wyda* [in margin: it is the top of a calabash] with *payewar*, that thick by chewing as pap, a small basket with bread, and the pepperpot to moisten the bread in. Now, we were still 3 solid hours from the River called Demerara, belonging to the West India Company of Zealand. We had fifteen to sixteen men stationed here in order to trade with the Indians for the dye, called oriane [annatto]. We then resumed our journey, continually travelling through groves, high and low, to the landing place where we found [31] a large horn. On blowing it, which our people heard, we were picked up with a vessel. The house where our people were put up was made of a certain kind of timber, called *mannekole* which has many fibres and can easily be split.[258] This wood is mostly used by the Christians because it can easily be worked. The provision basket was now empty, and I found nothing here to eat. We now looked now at each other very sadly; all of us, without exception, had to unfortunately put up [with the misery] until next day when the Commander of that group himself would go to the Indians and deal for some food and drink; as he had already lived for 15 or 16 years amongst them, this could not be refused to him. At this moment it fortunately happened that a hare was caught; which are so delicate there that they put the best homeland veal to shame. It was straight away put on the fire. In the meantime also some fish was brought, which a few [people] had caught; and by the Indians some bread, besides a 'commodyen'[259] or large pot with drink, called *pernou*. With hungry teeth we quickly set to eat and the joy caused by the *pernou* lasted until late in the evening when we went to rest. I had in mind to resume my journey to Essequibo by water the next day, but towards the evening an express arrived, despatched overland to Berbice, to bring the news that the planter from Canje, together with his ship, had been released, but that the cargo remained in charge of the Commander of Essequibo. I then ordered my Indians to be prepared for the next day in order to guide me back to Berbice. On that day we had be very abstemious, the reason being that very little was caught when hunting and fishing. The next day, just as we were starting to return, and we had procured some food through the help of the Indians, an Indian woman came and brought me a small fish, just like a little silverfish, *c.* 4 inches long, roasted according to the country's manner, and a piece of bread [32] with it. I would have kissed her as a sign of gratitude. I have never enjoyed an entire codfish in the homeland more than this small fish. At about midday we all stepped into the 'coriaar' [korjaal or canoe].

---

258 The mannekole (G.): palm tree or *Euterpe oleracea*.

259 Commodyen, or 'great pot', a term still preserved in Guyana when referring to the Takwari, or Kumuti Mountain, named after its resemblance to this clay vessel, see W.E. Roth, op. cit., 1948, p. 33.

These small vessels are made from a tree, usually between 16 and 17 feet long and 3 feet wide. One rarely sees them larger. On it we arrived at the village where Captain Tomenaq lived, at whose house we stayed again. I had a good appetite and accordingly started to check out everything, but found nothing else than chickens; of one I cut off the neck, which I paid for with a knife, and immediately plucked and cooked it, and sat down to eat it with some pepper.

This village is not less entertaining than Ouden Amen. It seems almost impossible that nature has arranged everything in such manner. One does not go from one house to another or one sees very pleasant views as well as sights the genius of man has succeeded in organizing. The houses stand on sandy ground close to the forest where one has nothing but clayey ground. I counted seventeen, large and small. There was also a warrior house, just as in the village Ouden Amen, but it was decaying, because the Christians lived so close in the vicinity upon whose care and vigilance the Indians trust. They are also by nature neither careful nor laborious in any way; one thus leads a miserable life, where otherwise one could live in luxury, because the country is fertile enough; if sufficient work is dedicated to it, it would yield all sorts of necessities in abundance. But an Indian plants nothing else around his house than a cotton tree or a tree that yields oriane, because the women are of such a temperament they always have some of this paint in their *pagale*, or basket, in order to colour their cheeks. With other necessities which would be of better use, they are not accustomed to bother. [33] In the morning, as soon as the day broke, we were already at breakfast; 1 or 1 ½ hour after that, we resumed our journey. The first resting place was at the empty house of which we have spoken about before, where we stayed about a half hour. In the afternoon, at 3 o'clock, we found ourselves in a forest, which from far and near appeared equally delightful. Here we rested awhile again next to a small stream and eventually arrived a half hour before evening at Ouden Amen. A chicken I cornered, although somewhat soberly prepared, again provided me with an excellent delicacy. I would also have liked a piece or two for my people, and would have given a double price for it; but the Indians, and particularly the women are that mean they sometimes do not want to miss six times its value, and the Christians must watch out not to make an enemy of them. Amongst themselves, on the contrary, they give away everything even if a stranger-Indian spends 2 months in the house of one or other and that is no problem.[260]

The next morning after breakfast, consumed in the usual fashion, and having paid with a little bunch of beads, we continued the journey, and with such glee, since we, so to speak, already began to scent the stable, that we found ourselves at about 2 o'clock in the afternoon at the plantation *den Berg*; where, having again made clear good cheer, to forget the difficulties of the journey, I stepped with my Indians into a vessel and was conveyed to the fort where we arrived at nightfall. [34]

---

260 Perhaps not observed by Van Berkel, however, reciprocity is of vital importance in Amerindian societies.

CHAPTER VI.

The author receives orders to go to Essequibo for a second time. Preparations for the journey. Strange way of roasting fish. Arrival at the house in Demerara and departure from there. Shape of the 1,000 leg trees. Arrival at the Essequibo River and description of the same. Arrival at fort Essequibo and excellent reception there. Description of the same. Banquet on a plantation. Return expedition to the fort on Berbice.

After having made such difficult journey, I was received in a very kindly way by the Chief, though little I thought that I would have to undertake a second expedition over there; meanwhile, however, it was necessary: one saw no other chance of obtaining the cargo again. I then received instructions to despatch letters to the Lords Councillors stating they should present themselves at the fort the next day in order to consider which measures should be taken to have matters once more straightened out. When this reserved time had passed, the case was discussed. The Commander of Canje, who through his imprudence had messed up things, was present; still seeking to justify his action with some stubbornness, the Lords Councillors told him they had been in this country many years before his arrival; that he should have given them full details [of the affair], and that they would have denied permission with good reason. Notwithstanding, while hoping everything would be set straight, if a capable person were to be sent there, the discussion was suspended; as I had been [35] there once already, I was unanimously appointed to go there a second time. I did not have much to object, except that I must be better provisioned; since there was nothing to find amongst the Indians during the trip. They told me I could have everythingconsidered necessary for the journey without any limitations. But truly, one who had to prepare for such an expedition in the homeland would have reason to be very displeased, but it was the best there was over there. I had only 2 days to get everything ready, but as the equipment was not voluminous, it was speedily prepared. In the meantime, our Parson, just as I was engaged in telling him about the preceding expedition, insinuated he wanted to join our party, but judging it improper for him to ask permission, he saw no opportunity of satisfying his curiosity regarding this matter. Delighted he had made this proposal, I said to him I knew means to arrange for him to be asked; next, having agreed, I went to the fort and lay down in my hammock. A moment later, the Chief came up and asked me if I was asleep. I answered, "No", but that I was thinking about the journey I had to undertake. "It will be all right," said the Commander, "don't worry, and even if it fails, there is only *c.* 600 guilders lost". I do not doubt either if I shall be able to justify it; as the Directors had been informed about it. Let us wash away the trouble from the heart [minds]. While drinking, I said: "Something has just occurred to me, of which Your Honour will certainly approve. The Parson is a clever man; if he is willing to try this expedition with me, one would expect good results. The difficulty was he might refuse. I said I would check him out, and if I came upstairs with him that he might then be assured of his permission. This was put into practice and when coming up with me, [36] the Commander received us in the most friendly manner. Then he prepared himself to accompany me on the journey for the next day, being a Monday. The provisions consisted of raw smoked bacon, cooked eggs, and a large bottle of brandy. Meanwhile three more Christians asked the Commander if they might go, too, in order to make the embassy more considerable; as I was willing, this was permitted, albeit on the condition they would have to bring their own Indians to carry their goods. Our baggage was embarked with the tide, together with ten Indians, and having thereupon taken leave of the Chief we were taken to the plantation *den Berg*. Here, the Indians divided the goods they should carry.[261] In the meantime, as reflecting there might not be much to eat among our people at the house at Demerara, I judged it advisable to send two Indians ahead in order to let them know of my arrival, together with orders they should for Thursday set apart a canoe with a tent cover under which two or three people could sit, and also that I must have twelve to fourteen oarsmen. Some 2 hours after their departure, having set off at day break, we said goodbye to our friends, our company now increased to a sixth man, to wit, the brother-in-law of the Parson who lived on the plantation *den Berg*. Towards midday we halted in the forest at a beautiful creek of which we have spoken before. It was an image of a small caravan travelling through the wilderness. I had two eggs distributed to each Christian and a sip of brandy to drink. The Indians had two baskets, or quakes, of bread for which I had given them salt; thirst was quenched by means of water from the creek, after which we continued the journey;,some 2 hours on this side of Ouden Amen, the Indians asked through the interpreter if they might halt here, not because they were weary of the loads, but [37] they wanted some fish. I asked the interpreter if they were bereft of their senses to propose catching fish in a place where one would rather expect, for various reasons, quadruped animals, because it was a stretch of land, flat and even, which one could scarcely look over. And even if they should catch fish, I could not understand how one would make fire, as no combustive material was present. My interpreter objected that I did need not to worry if they caught fish there, adding they would also make fire. The Parson and I sat down in the grass to wait patiently for what the Indians would do; having been absent for barely a small hour, the returned with a huge quantity of a certain kind of fish, called *louwkiddy* by the Indians and shaped just like the eelpout of the homeland; if we could have prepared the same with sauce, it would have tasted exactly the same which causes me to believe it is the same fish. One also finds a kind of fish in the shape of a perch; yet the taste differs somewhat, and they are so full of bones that they can hardly be eaten. But let us return to our Indians. When the said fish (caught in a small stream of water which, as we afterwards went to see, had no exit) was cleaned, an Indian set fire to a cotton wick. The others meanwhile plucked some grass and set it on fire by blowing. This was thrown on the other grass which burned more and more; thus they heated the fish, and finally got it done. The Parson and I tried it, found them of a tolerable taste; yet prepared in this manner, they could not really please us as to satisfy our hunger with; because, on the other hand, the desire being not sufficiently strong to incite us. We therefore left them to the Indians who ate them with an extraordinary avidity. Now, each one of them

261 "Here, I divided the loads" in stead of the Indians, see W.E. Roth, op. cit., 1948, p. 38.

took his load on the shoulders, and [we] walked on again until we reached the village of Ouden Amen where we intended to spend [38] the night. We again lodged in the warrior house, which was spacious enough for between 100 and 200 men. Here I was first told that I had *zieken* in my feet, which the call Indians *mebyky*.[262] I did not believe it because I always wore stockings, and consequently imagined I could not be subject to this complaint. Meanwhile, I found out afterwards that which I, not willing to show my feet, had taken for weariness was indeed the complaint for which one had warned me and which will be discussed later in more detail. In the morning, the pepperpot appeared together with a small basket of bread, and *payewar* to drink for which we paid with a batch of beads; we proceeded on our way. At about 11 o'clock we halted in a forest alongside a creek, where, except for a few, we had to resort to the last eggs. In the meantime the bacon, of which we had not yet eaten a mouthful, had gone missing; one of our people said that, during the night, two or three dogs had been there, which he had seen eating but had thought they had something else under their paws. We looked sadly at each other; the loss could not be repaired. We had still a fair way to go, with dry bread and salt only. Yet it was done and could not be helped; the steward should have taken better care of the quake. Taking heart again, we went on to the solitary house where we once more halted; by the evening we reached the village, which we call Naby, where Captain Tomenaq lived. Here we had our nights rest; next, having eaten and paid for breakfast, we continued, but before reaching the landing place, the Parson proposed we ought to eat the remainder first in order to ease the Indians; for he maintained we could carry it better in our bodies than on their shoulders. We then made another halt, and ate the remainder of our food and drink; after which, with fresh courage, we set off again to we reach [39] the landing place at about 11 o'clock in the morning, and next the house in Demerara. Here I found everything to be prepared according the instructions I had sent ahead through the despatched Indians, and ordered the baggage, together with a supply of fresh water, the supplies of bread and salt still being sufficient, to be placed in the canoe; while, in the meantime, we waited for the ebb, and an Indian was despatched with a letter to the fort in Berbice, relating the misfortune the dogs had brought on us concerning the bacon, as well as the abstemious condition in which we found ourselves, with the request that the Commander kindly send a bottle of brandy together with two or three pieces of bacon to the house of Tomenaq, so that we might be able to make use of it on our return. Once all this was ordered, I got an Indian woman to wash my feet to see if there were any prickles in them. She found seven chigoes or *mebyky*, of which we will speak later. At 3 o'clock in the afternoon the journey was resumed, floating down the river with the ebb. This Demerara River is very pleasant and of about the same width as the Berbice River; moreover, provided on either side with high trees, but few or no savannahs or pastures. At about 8 o'clock in the evening we reached the landing place where we went ashore in order to take a night's rest during the flood tide. Immediately, the Indians cut some wood and made fire as is customary in this country. In the

262 Mebyky: sand flies, or jiggers.

morning, before dawn, we continued the journey and found ourselves near the sea that evening, at about the distance of a half hour from the river. Here we had to make camp again to set off along the coast with the ebb the next day. Yet the greatest difficulty was to get on land; because one had to climb over a certain kind of tree called "thousand-legs". These trees grow on the edge of the water, about between 5 and 6 roods from the mainland. They shoot out their branches to between 1½ and 2 fathoms, and then again take root in the ground; so they appear like a [40] long series of arches. Here, climbing over them is dangerous; being slippery due to slime and mud, one hardly knows where to get a safe grip. Meanwhile, daily practice makes that perfect the Indians will climb over them much more easily by night than the Christians by day. We passed them, however, without any accident; after which, having taken a sober meal, my interpreter said he wanted to go fishing for a while with the line. This seemed strange to me as it was very dark and I imagined he, owing to the slipperiness of the said trees, would give the other Indians the duty of catching him. Meanwhile, after a short half hour, he returned with a fish with the size of an ordinary cod named *loulouw* by the Indians.[263] We had already forgotten the interpreter and were already asleep, but recognizing his good catch, everybody jumped out of his hammock; apparently one would have swallowed the fish alive. They also scarcely permitted themselves time to cook it; within 1 hour, nothing but bones was to be seen. The next morning, we resumed our journey with the ebb, continually remaining between *c.* 2 and 3 feet of water, as one did not dare to go farther out to sea. Scarcely had we reached half way when the Indians said they saw boats. This startled us very much since we imagined they might well be Caribs, the deadly enemies of the Arawak and of us; in which case they would certainly have saved themselves by fleeing and would have abandoned us. We gave them courage and told them through the interpreter we would fight for them. But it was our luck it did not come to this, for they do not let themselves to be persuaded with such words; for, in a real situation they do as they like. The fear of cruelties committed on the vanquished makes them choose to flee, if it is in any degree possible; indeed, these [cruelties] are terrible; as we will inform in due course when speaking of their wars, [41] to the readers. In the meantime we advanced slowly; having got somewhat closer, our Indians shouted they saw Christians; now all trouble and anxiety ceased in one moment. We counted four canoes and in the same several Christians and Indians; the latter were busy catching fish with bow and arrow. They were from Essequibo and sold to me, against the value of 5 or 6 pence, a good quantity of *quereman*,[264] a delicate fish. Our Bucks hurried on in order to enter the river of Essequibo so that the pot might go on the fire; for, those poor people had not eaten much since Thursday and it was now already Saturday. Finally, we arrived in the mouth of the said river where, only if it was still ebb, could we paddle to land. Immediately, a fire was lit here, the

263 *Piratinga* sp., see W.E. Roth, op. cit., 1948, p. 42.
264 *Mugil* sp., ibid., p. 43.

fish cut up and, according to the custom of the country, cooked with *atty* or peppers. Everyone satisfied himself completely; after which we continued again with the flood till late in the evening when we looked out for a good landing place.

This Essequibo River is *c.* 3 miles wide at its entrance but without depth in proportion; its greatest depth, at high water, is not above between 10 and 11 feet. The mouth is obstructed by many shallows of sandbanks, together with three islands overgrown with trees; a multitude [of islands] is also to be counted within the river, altogether covered with trees. Landing is here easier than I have ever seen elsewhere, being sandy ground from the beginning; which I have never seen in any river. However, there is clay ground on the main land, just as on other rivers. It remains, on the whole, wide and pleasant in appearance by reason of the trees on the said islands, together with the groves which are very delightful to the sight. The fort is situated *c.*12 hours from the sea on an island; a little above which on the slope of the forest, stone cliffs and a greater depth are found. This much about the most important features of this river. [42]

In the morning, at daybreak, we set off again with the tide and finally came up to the fort, where everyone were already standing and looking at us, as if one expected an embassy, of which our vessel furnished with a tent was a fit token. We had ourselves put ashore at a suitable place. The Commander, named Hendrik Rol, came to welcome me and the Parson, with the sword in hand, and lead us through a double row of soldiers amidst the discharge of their muskets. Higher up we were received by the secretary, and another three shots with the light cannon were fired. Truly, these honours took our breath away; we imagined ourselves to be a few European monarchs making a public entrance somewhere. Then, we were brought into the Commanders room where I wanted to open my commission; yet he begged friendly if I would like to wait 4 days and first to rest awhile. The other Christians of my retinue were lodged among the soldiers. In the meantime a strong drink was fetched from above, besides a jug of wine, presented to the Commander to entertain us. At night, we sat at an excellent [table] and were treated to five courses, roasted and boiled; next, with a well filled body, we lay down to rest and slept until 9 o'clock in the morning, when my Indians came to ask permission to visit their friends for a few days. I gave them a cord (of which we have given the explanation elsewhere) for a period of 8 days. Then I went to inspect everything; which was quickly done, because the fort Essequibo lies on a small island, not larger than one can throw a stone across lengthways. The fort itself has a quadrangular shape; at the lower part, the magazine and above this: three halls in which the soldiers are housed, a room for the Commander, and one for the secretary, which also serves to store merchandise. The island has many rocks. Around the fort one usually goes hunting [43] albeit there is no other game than that which swims over, this being abundant enough. Just before midday, when I had finished my tour, a Christian arrived from the plantation of Master de Graaf (who had had the kindness to forward the said wine to the Commander for our arrival) with the request if the Commander, as well as his guests, would be pleased to pay him a visit the next day, when a good meal would be prepared. It was accepted without many compliments; the next day we stepped at flood tide into the corial, a suitable vessel to carry us to the said Master's plantation, situated *c.*1 hour above the fort. Here we found everything just as well regulated as if we had been in the homeland. The entertainment was also excellent and consisted of five kinds of roast, such as deer meat, fowl, turkeys, ducks, and pigeons; together with three courses, soup of deer, hare, and turkey meat. The drink was mom-beer from Dordrecht,[265] wine, and brandy; with which we kept up the merrymaking until the evening, thus returning full and happy to the fort. There were altogether three plantations, that of Master de Graaf being the largest, with between twenty-eight and thirty slaves. The other two could not boast more than twelve to fourteen each. One lives the life of a prince, as far as plenty of food and drink is concerned, but he who is of a sociable character and likes to be around people does not want to go there. And indeed, besides this defect, tropical countries have, in larger part, not all of the conveniences which one imagines from the tales told by various people. The scorching rays of the sun are difficult enough to bear; the lack of many things which are necessary for existence produces a certain disagreement which one cannot quite get rid of. But let us return to our matter. Having sufficiently rested ourselves, it being already Friday, I begged the Commander we needed to discuss the affairs [44] that were the reason why they had sent me here. The proposal was that we should abandon the Demerara River and never do any more trading there; then they would appraise the seized cargo and pay for it with *Balsam copeiva*, commonly called "maraan". This balsam is obtained by the Indians near the River Aernocque [Orinoco] at the mouth of which fort Trinidad lies, belonging to the King of Spain. It drips from a certain kind of tree which is cut with a hatchet and to which a calabash is attached in order to collect the liquid, gradually flowing from the crevice. It represents a wholesome remedy for gravel, [kidney] stone, and fresh wounds. My commission did not extend that far; the conference was accordingly suspended on the condition I would return with further instructions. I then begged to allowed to return in 2 days; which was permitted, but first the Parson had to do service on the Sunday by baptizing two children; which he did, of course. This was the reason why we stayed there until Monday about noon, when reasonably well provisioned and gun saluted, we started the journey back; after crossing the sea, we arrived with the rising flood at the mouth of the Demerara River. Here, I got the Indians to catch some crabs to serve us on the journey over water. These crabs, also caught in quantities at the cliffs in the Essequibo River, are called 'sweetwater crabs' and are much tastier than those caught at sea, albeit not quite as large. Then, we returned once more to our people in Demerara where we were very welcome, because we had kept numerous crabs. We remained her until the following day at noon, when, after being brought to the landing, we stayed at Naby village in Captain Tomenaq's house; here, to our uncommon joy, we found provisions of bacon and brandy with which we had some refreshing pleasure in the evening. The next morning at dawn, we set off [45] on again and reached Ouden Amen village by evening; when, having spent the night, we travelled on

265 A thick, strong and hops-free beer named after its legendary first brewer, the German Christiaan Mumme. Here Van Berkel refers to the Dutch variety brewed in Dordrecht.

again in the morning to arrive at the plantation *den Berg* at about 4 o'clock in the afternoon: from there further on the next day to the fort where we were received friendly by the Chief.

CHAPTER VII.

Third expedition of the author to Essequibo. Frightful method of appointing an Indian to the captaincy. Arrival at fort Essequibo. Settlement of the dispute concerning the merchandise mentioned, and agreement with the Essequibo Commander settled. Return to the fort of Berbice.

After I had made a detailed report of my actions to the Commander, a meeting with the Councillors of the Colony was again convened, which would rather not have abandoned the Demerara River; but considering the lawfulness of their possession, they resolved that I would be once more provided with a new commission, and given full authority in order to settle with those of the Company, as I would consider best advisable. I had 2 weeks to take a rest and prepare everything required for the next expedition, on which the Parson again wanted to keep me company. Then we left together with various Indians on a Friday once again to plantation *den Berg* where we spent the night. The next day we proceeded to the village of Ouden Amen, where we were again asked if we were willing to stay over on Sunday as an Indian was going to be made Captain.[266] The journey was [46] not that hurried so

Figure 12: 'Strange way how an Indian was made Captaine'. Print in A. van Berkel, Amerikaansche Voyagien, 1695.

266 The plantation *Den Berg* apparently had a strong relationship with the village of *Ouden Amen*. The people at this plantation were well informed of the events in this Amerindian village.

we could have some entertainment; therefore very curious to see with our own eyes this ceremony, of which strange things had been told, we were easily persuaded to do so. On the Sunday morning we went over to the place where the ceremony was held, a private house of an Indian. Immediately, our hammocks were tied up, because one finds no stool, bench, nor table there; Indians always squatt down. There was a quantity of *pernouw*, a kind of beverage, of which everybody may drink as much as he pleases on this occasion. It is distributed by one of the prettiest daughters who keeps three or four fingers inside the calabash and the thumb outside; in that way she offers the Christians as well as the Indians drinks, without anyone being allowed to touch it with hand or finger, except when one has had enough, and pushes the calabash away. The larger the company, the larger number of girls who hand around the drink; in want of these, women likewise take on [this task]. At about noon, while the girls and women were still busy satisfying the needs of the guests as to drinks, the Indian appeared who was to be raised to the dignity of Captain. He was led by three Captains who, with curious gestures, encouraged him in bravery; reaching the middle of the house, he remained standing and raised his arms above his head. In the meantime, the said three Captains got ready, each holding a *maquary*, a kind of plaited whip, *c.* 5 feet long, thick at the lower side, and tapering off at the top. Here they took turns at lashing the poor Indian that brutally on the body hardly any flesh remained on his armpit to his stomach, all torn to shreds in a terrible manner. One could hear the cracking of the whips from outside the house; yet the patient did not betray the slightest sign of pain. Shortly after, now [47] as good as flayed, he was laid upon a wooden grid, called *berbekot* by the Indians, and covered with leaves. Under this grid a small fire was kindled, which produced more smoke than flame. Meanwhile, a few leaves raised now and then raised to see if there was any danger of his fainting; when this noticed after a short time they took him off the *berbekot*, poured about a bucket full of water over his face; when he had regained consciousness, they encouraged him with strange gestures. Now, his broken skin was again greeted by each of the said Captains with eight or nine whip lashes; he now looked like a beggar whose rags and tatters were hanging off him. This ceremony must take place again after 2 or 3 weeks, before he can be raised to the dignity of Captain; on which occasion, if he has a wife, she will also get two or three lashes, so that she may also participate in the glory of her husband; though she does not receive more than two or three lashes, she immediately runs off. After all the tortures mentioned, the patient is brought back to his quarters: a small rectangular room, partitioned off in the house, just large enough to put his hammock in. In the meantime the drinking went on steadily, and the women appeared very happy with such courageous husbands who would never fear to die when taking vengeance on their enemies; singing songs to the glory of their same heroic deeds. When speaking of their war expeditions, we shall have an opportunity of treating there what deeds they have to fullfil in order to obtain the dignity of a captaincy. As to the man we have just discussed, he had in a certain act of war beaten an old woman half dead; having thrown her in the water and martyrized her with a thousand torments, she was finally, under unspeakable torture, put to death. This is what their bravery consists of, to wit, to endure blows and perform the most gruesome cruelties [48] in the world. Otherwise they are ignorant cowards who, on the firing of cannon or musketry, scarcely know where they should hide themselves; just as we have already given an example of.

At dawn the next morning we set off again to eventually reach, after covering 11 miles, our old Captain Tomenaq; from there we proceeded the next day to the Demerara River. Here we rested until Friday when we again boarded a vessel covered with a good tent; with which, sailing along the beach, we entered the Essequibo River the next day and arrived at the fort; where we were again received in the same manner, as on the previous trip, by Master de Graaf with full courtesy. After a sojourn of a few days, during which we spent time hunting and by means of other amusements, I negotiated with the Commander about our seized merchandise, which, after we had come to a cordial arrangement with one another, was appraised and, within a certain time, to be paid for with *Balsam Copeiva*, for which we were held responsible when abandoning the Demerara River. Mutual documents concerning this matter were drawn and signed; next, on the Tuesday following, we travelled with the Commander of Essequibo to Demerara in order to effect the agreement with my arrival, and have our people withdrawn from there. We spent 4 days travelling before reaching the house in the Demerara; where, having slept that night, all of us were brought to the landing place at noon the next day; the merchandise and boxes of the people were shipped to Berbice by water after which we parted from one another in friendship. The night's rest was then again taken at Naby village, at the house of Captain Tomenaq. Here we again found provision consisting of victuals and drink, sent there by our Commander at my request. I commandeered fourteen men to [49] be ready in the morning and to make their way by passing through Ouden Amen. The four of us passed by a village called *Woeroenje* [Wironi], located a good day's going from the village of Naby. I have never trodden a more delightful road. The groves contain trees growing in such regular manner it is as if they had been planted by hand. In the village of *Woeroenje* we had three men posted to trade with the Indians. They received us with food and drink in abundance; the next day a corial was prepared, with which we reached the plantation, called de Mierenberg, located *c.* 8 hours by water from the fort of Berbice. I found this way much easier, yet wishing to again spend a night on plantation *den Berg*, where I had always enjoyed a very friendly welcome, we proceeded again on foot and within 3 hours found ourselves at the said plantation, from which we left the next day at about noon; after sailing 2 hours we arrived once more at the fort.

CHAPTER VIII.

Arrival of some Indians at the fort who are about to undertake a war expedition. Things prepared for the same. Terrible treatment of prisoners, etc.

Shortly after my last return from Essequibo, and after I had been thanked by the Governor as well as the Lords Councillors for my efforts, (because little lost was on the Demerara River as it had to be occupied by a large force in order not to be expelled by those from Essequibo) some Indians arrived at the fort; [50] to inform us, as was their custom, that they intended to wage war in 28 days against their enemies living on the Corantyne River, at 7 miles south of the Berbice River. It is astonishing how much they exert themselves on this occasion to prepare their fleet, consisting of about between sixteen and eighteen canoes, because it is the laziest nation to be encountered. In the homeland a similar number of warships would be manufactured in the same time. When they set their minds on march against their foes, they send a few men to various villages and the Captains residing there. Everybody whom they wish takes a card, made of small reeds, from which each morning one is cut off. It is, as we said elsewhere, their method of reckoning time. Immediately the young men start to work, each seeking to gain the highest honour; however, to tell the truth, it goes rather slowly, because they work barely between 1 and 2 hours per day on their boats, spending most of the time rejoicing over the imaginary result of the future expedition. Now, when the canoes are ready and provided with all requirements, they celebrate an entire day and then go to the place of rendezvous. Here the Captains deliberate with one another about their undertaking; once the decision is made, the same is immediately made public to everybody, even the women are not excluded, nobody knows of treason or traitors. Now, all the heroes gather around the fort; one to borrow a gun, the other for powder, a third one for bullets, etc., all of which, without anything asked in return, is given to them the greatest gift consists of three charges of powder and as many bullets. They make ridiculous gesticulations and postures on this occasion in order to show us how they will beat up their enemies and make slaves of their daughters; thus, as the saying goes, selling the [51] skin before they have caught the bear. In each canoe, too, two or three women are seated whose duty is to make the drink, and to serve the men. The entire expedition usually lasts between 20 and 22 days. In two ebb tides they arrive at the coast; meanwhile, this usually takes between 2 and 3 days, because each time they see for example a little bird, they snap their fingers and they tell each other something about it. When they gradually arrive all together at the seaside, another war council is held; then the entire fleet puts to sea, advancing *c.* 3 miles a day. Yet when they find themselves in the river of their enemies, they only travel by night, taking advantage of the moon in this manner. During the day, they hide themselves deep in the forest, and conceal their canoes under some cut-off green branches, which they know how to arrange that naturally the keenest eye can be deceived, so that their arrival may not be noted. Meanwhile, one goes out scouting at night, [to see] if one can find some foes in which case one hurries back to give the information to the fleet. Next all the vessels are brought in action; the Indians go on land and everything proceeds that silently the enemies are overpowered before they have time to save themselves by fleeing. But, as far as this silence is concerned, it only lasts until they have surrounded their enemies, because they then make a horrible noise and put to death everything they come across in this first fury. When they consider themselves complete victors, and resistance is no longer of any avail, they start to take prisoners. Those who in the meantime can escape may consider themselves very lucky. The womanfolk they capture who are neither young nor pretty, such as they judge them suitable to gratify their lusts upon although they will nevertheless remain slaves, are put to death straight away, but if they are somewhat handsome, they are given into custody to other women, to wit those who came [52] with them. As to the children, either boys or girls, they will live according to their fancy. If they are pleasant of countenance, they may expect a hard domestic service, yet they stay alive, but if they captured many of children, a few are killed to be cooked for eating. But unfortunate is he, man or bachelor, who, finding no chance for escape or of fighting to the death, happens to be caught alive in the hands his enemies, because one cannot imagine any cruelties they do not apply in order to tyrannise him and to end his life in a horrible way. Yet, as they cannot always outwit their enemies in this manner, they ride higher up the river and, after the canoes are landed, try to surprise some other village. This often occurs at dawn and with a noise that echoes through the air. But since the luck of war will not always serve equally well, it also happens that they meet with such a resistance they are obliged to seek flight head over heels and to withdraw from the river. In this case, to wit, when they reach home again with nothing done [empty-handed], drink is made; while squatting, they say that they have pain in the stomach, and drink that much they have to vomit, after which they apparently become quite well again. See thus their way of waging war and expect now how they treat their prisoners.

The fleet, of which we have just spoken, brought with her on her return two youngsters from the enemy who were surprised. It travelled by night silently past the fort and had the same that well looked after, there was not the slightest chance of escape. These unfortunate ones, who had thus been captured during a war expedition, were confined and shackled for *c.* 3 weeks; during which time they

Figure 13: 'Terrible gestures inflicted upon the prisoner who had been taken during a raid'. Print in A. van Berkel, Amerikaansche Voyagien, 1695.

were provided with good food and drink. Meanwhile, they keep themselves busy, finding a distraction in this dreadful situation, by making a *pagale*, or small basket, used as a box [53] in that country. The prisoners are guarded by night; when one of them is going to be burnt, the women prepare a large quantity of drink called *pernou*, of which we have spoken elsewhere and the qualities of which we will later on deal with elaborately. On the day before he will die, I have seen with my own eyes on more than one occasion that they receive them elegantly with food and drink so that he might yet go heartily to death. In the afternoon, as a humiliation, they take him from one house to another; on this occasion he may unexpectedly receive a blow on the head, so that the blood drips down, while snarling at him: "Your friends have done just the same to ours." At sunset, a Captain asks if he can still see the sun; next, having answered "Yes," the Captain says: "You shall never see it again." This is his condemnation. I have seen one put to death who, proud enough not to faint by any threats or fear of subsequent torture, replied to the Captain, who passed sentence on him, with a heroic and disdainful face: "It is true, fate is at present against me, but my friends will likewise come to your people at some time, and demand a reckoning for the torture you are about to inflict on me. Life is not so attractive to me or I can easily leave it, though I am troubled about having to die without being able to take vengeance for my death, etc." During the evening they give him food and drink as much as he desires; everyone brings him something. Now they tie his hands behind his back and, to each foot, a long rope. In the meantime those invited have gathered there, each provided with a few *maquarys*, a kind of torch smeared with a certain substance which looks like pitch, so that it may burn better. In the evening at about 7 o'clock, one starts making fires around and in the house; after which the prisoner is placed in the middle of his enemies and the oldest Captain causes a boisterous upheaval, screaming loudly: "Your people have caught my friends [54], and treated them likewise." Next he stabs the burning *maquary* into his skin; after which everyone, who can but reach him, attacks him. One stabs him in the face, the other about the male genitals, a third in other most tender spots, while at the same time he is dragged hither and thither by the said ropes. Meanwhile, if he begins to faint due to this torture, they give him a short pause from time to time, in order to make his torments longer, because they want to have as much satisfaction as possible. In between, they drink again with eachother, just as if they were good friends; the sufferer thus somewhat refreshed, the work starts again. This lasts until the morning, about a short hour before sunrise, because then they have to make an end to it, which is done by a Captain who crashes the miserable prisoner's head with a wooden sword. Now, everybody attacks him with a knife, one cuts a piece from the buttock, another from the thigh, a third rips up another spot. In short, everybody gets what he can. The cut-off flesh, once boiled, is put into the pepperpot and eaten as good food. I have spoken to two Christians who had tried it and declared it tasted very nice. The bones are buried in the earth, except for a few small ones out of which they know how to make flutes. During this bustle, the women are seated and sing; the singing consists of repeating the tortures, suffered by some of their own friends who had fallen into enemy hands, together with the praises of their valiant men who, in the way described, took vengeance for their deaths. It is a horrible thing to see; besides that, the smell of the flesh which is burnt incessantly with the *maquerys* and the seething fat that gushes from it, is able to make a Christian not only vomit due to disgust, but also even nearly suffocate him. In the meantime, one does marvel, as to all these tortures, at the courage of the prisoners that is so extraordinarily great that they can thus let themselves [55] die in the most horrible and painful manner without showing the least cowardice, comforting themselves that, at some time, they will be avenged by their friends.

CHAPTER IX.

The author takes another trip to the Essequibo. Danger of shipwreck. Arrival at the fort of Essequibo. Return from there. Strange way of Indian women with regard to the birth of twins. Return at the Berbice.

The time allowed for those on the Essequibo to pay for our seized goods, about which we have spoken towards the end of Chapter VII, having expired, I received orders to go there once more and to provision the bark for that purpose with all necessities. On the day before departure, according to custom, we had a fine merrymaking; after which we embarked and set sail, but scarcely 2 hours had elapsed, during which we steadily had to tack, when the boom unfortunately broke. The steersman of the ship, of whom we have spoken before, who on this occasion replaced the Master, had to return to the fort in order to retrieve a new boom, while I remained on board waiting for him. The other day he returned and brought with him, besides the boom, a large jar of wine, deliciously prepared with egg yolks and spices. Meanwhile, the number of people on our bark had increased by one young son; this had happened that quietly hardly anyone had had knowledge of it. An Indian slave had served as midwife.[267] I sent [56] the woman in labour, an Indian woman to whom our hunter had conferred the kindness of making her pregnant, a pot of negus; next I was notified she had enjoyed it very much, yet it was for once and forever, because the taste of the wine was much too good to be given away to these ugly coloured people. The other day, towards the evening, we reached the sea, ran into it at 9 o'clock and sailed all night with a tolerable breeze. In the morning we set eyes on the River *Majeyke* [Mahaica], and shortly after noon the Demerara River. But while we thus sailed ahead with reasonable speed, the bark struck, at 4 o'clock not far from the Essequibo, a sandbank where we were stuck for about half an hour, steadily bumping up and down; the water came in from all sides and gave us trouble enough to keep her above water while every man bailed out the boat. And hardly had we surmounted this danger or we were roughly hurled upon another sandbank; we thought nothing else than that the bark would explode to splinters,; truly, if the trough of a wave had not carried us from there, we would have run the greatest risk of shipwreck. Now we had to make quarter to pump and bail by which means we finally arrived at night in the River

267 Indian slave: Van Berkel applies the term for a male slave, however, when referring to a slave woman.

Essequibo where the anchor was cast to the ground. Because no cooking could be done here, we were forced to comfort ourselves, like the commoners, with a piece of raw pickled bacon; however, with this distinction that the steersman and I took on a good glass of brandy. At about 10 o'clock, we had stopped two or three bad leaks; which gave great security. With the floodtide we sailed on to arrive at the fort on the next one [tide] following, where honorary gun salutes were exchanged from both sides. Now I stepped ashore with the steersman, where we had a very friendly reception and treatment from the Commander; after a sojourn of 2 days, the business discussed, and the payment received, I ordered those on the bark to return [57] again. Because it was in such a bad condition, I preferred to take my old road. After between 6 and 7 days I took leave of the Commander accompanied on my journey by a certain friend who had something to do in Demerara, taking little or no provisions with us; because my fellow traveller convinced me it was unnecessary for us to burden ourselves as we would find everything in abundance at a nearby village where a feast of the Indians would be taking place. But instead, we found ourselves wretchedly deceived, because when we arrived at this village which was very pretty and consisted of about twenty houses, we did not observe the slightest sign of the said feast, as it had been suspended for some reason. We once again had to do according to the country's custom, sufficiently sober, and totally not to my liking. On the morning of the next day, just as we intended to leave, they showed us an Indian woman, moderately handsome in face and figure; about a month or a month and a half earlier, having two fully grown children into the world at the same time, she had killed one of them with her own hands and put it in the ground. Because they consider twins unnatural in a human being, and do not wish to be on a par, so they say, with dogs and other similar proliferous animals in this matter. I looked at her attentively and as well as at the surviving child; how young it still might be, according to the countries custom, it was rummaging in the sand close to her dwelling, as not that much trouble with children is taken with children over there, as in the homeland and elsewhere. We resumed our way; having experienced no more adventures of interest during the remainder of this return journey, I will only tell the reader I returned to our fort safe and sound, albeit with very little satisfaction. [58]

CHAPTER X.

Arrival of a ship from the homeland. Quarrel between the old Chief and the Parson. Burning of a trading house by the Carib Indians. Expedition of the Commander and the author to that place, etc.

There was now a general desire for a ship from the homeland, since no tidings from there had been received for a long time. Finally, one appeared, and with the same [came] a new Commander or Chief. With whom, after we had spent a few days feasting and merrymaking, in accordance with old custom, I found myself obliged to go to the plantations again in order to see how things stood over there. In the meantime, while we were busy with this, a quarrel arose between the old Chief and the Parson; the latter, being the weaker, received orders against all right and reason, that as soon as we returned he was to prepare to return home, together with his wife and children. The old Chief was a vindictive man who, for a long while, had tried to get the good Parson into trouble, yet he could find no opportunity to do so. Now, an accident had occurred during the feasting, which he lept at and had several attestations made in exchange for a drink of brandy, in which the truth was ravished in a shocking manner. I had warned my friend very often as I had for quite some time expected that at a certain moment he would trip him up; yet it seems he could not avoid this misfortune. Meanwhile, as I wanted to help him in advice and deed, I secretly provided him with a letter to the Church Council of the French community at Flushing; with which, as I afterwards [59] learnt, all the attestations of the old Commander were annulled. But how friendly he treated him [the Parson] during the voyage (because they both departed shortly afterwards on the mentioned ship, albeit one in a much better quality than the other) the reader can easily guess. I conducted them as far as the sea, and thanked the Commander when we said goodbye for the kind reception I had always enjoyed from him. This was indeed true, though I could not however help objecting I took it much to heart that the Parson had to go with him; and that, like myself, many would have liked to see that he could have stayed. The Commander objected to this with some reasons filled with calmness and hypocrisy, but if he had known I had given the mentioned letter to the pious teacher, we would not have parted as such good friends. His foolish hatred was so great he want to exert all means to accomplish that the parson should be forbidden his pulpit. Yet, to the satisfaction of many honourable folk, his mission failed; for this he subsequently, as will be told in the following chapter, intended revenging himself on me.

Shortly after the departure of the old Chief with the said ship to the homeland, news came from the Canje River that the Carib Indians of the Corantyne River (who are the enemies of the Arawaks, by which name those of the Berbice are signified) had burnt the house we had there; that our people had been forced to save themselves by fleeing; although they had further done little damage and killed no one, or taken any prisoners, because they had been discovered in time by three Indians. Consider now the courage of these folk. The our garrison consisted of seven men, who, warned by the said Indians, fled and posted themselves in the neighbouring village. The Caribs, who were not so much after our people as well as after their [60] enemies, also came to attack this village with a terrible noise, but seeing that these seven Christians had joined the Indians, they let their courage drop, and returned without doing anything, albeit they were more than three times as strong. Receiving this message, the Commander dispatched a cord of a few days to the neighbouring Indians in order to put out a tender for the construction of a new house, for which we would visit the place. Three days prior to our departure we sent three Christians ahead in order to arrange that we would be able to find food and drinks as well as suitable accommodation on the way. Next two horses took the Commander and me there; although rushed on rather well it nonetheless took us 4 hours to bring us to the water place. Three Negroes had gone 2 hours ahead in order to prepare grass for the horses. Two others, besides six Indians to carry the luggage, remained with us. The path was delightful, consisting of fields and groves, everywhere flat land without any hills or dales. We had to go through the water with the horses twice; having further arrived at the Canje River, we found a vessel there with which we were brought to the place where it was judged the house ought to be built. Here we saw a large party of Indians, coming from all sides; many out of curiosity to see the new Commander and others to become engaged in construction work. Everything there was well regulated according to the custom of the country, and food and drinks enough. The ground furnished us with a table and some large green leaves served as table cloths and towels. The brandy was kept hidden from the Indians, but we had taken three jars of kill-devil with us to give them.[268] It has the power of making you drunk, of which we shall speak later. In the evening, several had to go to sleep already; others were that much taken by it they spent most of the night talking and [61] joking, which prevented me enjoying the sweetness of the rest, etc. The other day, in the morning, an agreement was made between us and the Indians to the effect that within 5 days they would finish deliver the house, surrounded by palisades and with portholes. One might thus not be taken by surprise anymore in the future. Now, so that they might work extra diligently, they were presented with the remainder of the kill-devil; after which, having taken leave, we returned in the same manner.

CHAPTER XI.

Arrival of a ship from the homeland. Grudge of the former Chief against the author. Strange adventure of an Indian. Dreadful accident of two Negroes, etc.

It now lasted a considerable time before a ship arrived again from the homeland on which account the table began to be mighty lean, because our wine and brandy, very necessary things in the country here for the preservation of health, were almost consumed. Finally one received the news that a boat had arrived at the mouth of the river. Immediately, the bark was sent there; though we learnt very soon, to our heartfelt sorrow, it had not brought as many provisions as we would wanted to have, and which we surely needed. The reason was partly that it had taken its cargo at Hamburg, and partly that a certain grudge against the most notable [persons] of the colony, the Captain being the one who had been my first Chief, a vindictive man, who seemed to have apparently forgotten the mischief done, but he never forgot. However, little did I think I was reckoned among the number of his enemies, as I came to learn sufficiently well not much later. The [62] ship, in the meantime, sailed upwards, and having cast her anchor in front of the fort, I received orders from the Commander to welcome the Captain. I then sailed to his boat and with very friendly manners, yet with a dissembled heart, was invited into the cabin. Immediately I was served smoked meat, butter, cheese, and white biscuit. While eating, the wine was not spared too. But after exchanging some

268 Van Berkel applies the term *stoop*, a Dutch liquid measure of *c.* 2.4 liter.

glasses, the hypocrisy could no longer be sustained; the merrymaking changed into a sudden silence very soon, then to a mumbling, and eventually into an outburst about why I had changed a beautiful fine hammock, which the Commander of Essequibo had given me to hand over to him, for another but worse one? It was quite true; but I had learned from his example that "he who serves the altar has to live from it."[269] On that occasion, I had also rendered him services which could have been paid for by no hammock, even if it had been much finer. Yet this was only to lead up to the text [point]; because having then objected with an ironical smile, whether he had not always lived with me as if I had been his own child, I had answered him "Yes", asking me what had then prompted me, without his knowledge, to deliver such a letter to the Parson. I told him I would discuss the matter with him afterwards, that I had come to welcome him in the name of the Chief, and not "to pick up old cows out of ditches"; that I had to return to the shore again and wished to part in friendship. He understood very well what I meant; had a large bumper brought into the cabin, and drank to my health, without rapping about any other troubles. As soon as I had set foot on land, I informed the Commander about my meeting; who told me he knew him better than I did, and that he only wished he could find a chance of thwarting him as he [63] should have done much earlier. This smouldered for some days, but was never extinguished, because when one morning when walking together with the Captain to the plantation, called Mierenberg, he again brought up the case of the Parson. I said to him curtly, that I had acted according to [my] conscience; that he really showed not to have had much intercourse with such people; that even the best could make a mistake; that it was unreasonable to wish to damage a person's prospects because he had been drunk once; that one must not indulge one's passion so much, etc. He became very angry, bit his lip and held his tongue; yet confirmed with his facial expressions he would like very much to have his revenge on me. Two or three days later we returned together with the Chief to the fort, from where we several times went to the ship to makemerry, but I never went there alone, despite the friendly invitations; because I had been warned by one of my friends, to whom he had confided this secret as he believed there were some disagreements between us, that he wanted me to play a bad trick through Jan Hagel, of which he afterwards would falsely not have known. Nevertheless although I considered myself sufficiently safe under the protection of the Chief, I tried to conciliate myself with the old Commander, with which purpose I talked the matter over with him. He behaved himself very strangely and said that, far from having any ill feelings towards me, he was, on the contrary, one of my best friends, and that he would prove himself to be so in every forthcoming occasion. But as to how far these words were intended, became clear on several encounters, during which he could never restrain himself that much or even the most stupid person would have noticed that something lurked in his heart which he did not dare utter openly. I kept quiet accordingly, and avoided his presence as much I could. Meanwhile the

---

269 1 Corinthians 9:13: 'Don't you know that those who serve in the temple get their food from the temple, and that those who serve at the altar share in what is offered on the altar?'

time for departure was drawing near. According to custom, we were merrymaking together with the Lords Planters on the ship, which had by now descended the river and had reached the mouth of the river; [64] next, the day following, it put out to sea, without the old Commander, during his whole period of his stay on the Berbice River, being able to find an opportunity to take revenge on me.

Not much later, just as we had once again arrived at the fort, something very remarkable occurred. A certain Indian, who had gone to the forest to cut wood, was surprised from behind by a tiger; with a first blow, it tore off a considerable piece of flesh from the thickest part of his thigh, just below the buttock; resuming the attack, it stuck its claws in his back. The Indian, overcome with astonishment, dropped his axe; but, however thinking of his defence, managed to twist round so as to come face to face with the enemy, notwithstanding he was receiving wounds all over due to the claws and teeth of this voracious animal. Now he took heart; while the tiger was standing over him with his front paws and it jaws fixed to his left arm, he seized with his right hand the knife which the Indians carry on a cord around their body; he stuck it up to the hilt in its stomach, after which the wound was wider, bringing the tiger dead to the ground. For sure, it was the right moment, because, weakened by the loss of his blood, he was found by some Indians who had gone into the forest shortly afterwards, lying not far from the dead tiger, the bloody knife still in his hand. Sensing he was alive, they brought him to the fort; here, through the care of our physician, he was restored to his former health and strength. I have seen this brave Indian for a long time afterwards; still carrying the scars inflicted by his enemy just as vividly as if they were freshly.

Hardly 1 week after this event, news was brought to us that two Negroes from the plantation, called *Mierenberg*, while busy stirring sugar, and I do nott know if through carelessness or accident (one could never get a correct version of it) had fallen into [65] the cauldron. Next, I was sent off with our surgeon and found both said Negroes still alive, yet they were in such a pitiful state I could not look at such a sad event without tears. The bodies appeared as being flayed; the holes burnt into it by the seething sugar were that abundant one could not place a flat hand to cover an entire spot. The surgeon covered them entirely, so to speak, in bandages, though there was hardly any use for a third one. They died after the second [bandaging] in the greatest agony; one that raging one had to tie his hands and feet; because he tore everything to pieces and struck out at all he could reach. In the meantime, on the plantation the people took little notice of it. They ate and drank, there was joy. Since the Negroes, according to all appearances, had to die anyway, they did not trouble themselves if they suffered much or hardly any pain. So little are these poor people valued by the Christians who ought to have a greater charity and pity.

This is the largest part of my experiences until now at the Berbice River. At present, as nothing much of concern took place for some time, I will now entertain the reader by presenting him with various extraordinary things concerning the condition of the country, the manner of living of the Indians, the vegetables and tree fruits, the animals, birds, fish, and what relates to this, and a few curious matters which an attentive reader deserves. [66]

CHAPTER XII.

The outline of the country. Description of a specific sort of Indians, called Warau. Obligingness of the Indians for the Christians. Other notable peculiarities concerning Indian men and women, etc.

As far as the country's features concern, it often consists of forests; the trees in various places stand hardly half a mile from the sea, along which the land stretches to the South and North. The front land is submerged at the flood but not very far. Higher up it rises gradually, and is not subjected to inundation. The Christians catch many deer near the seacoast, though the Indians do not take the trouble of doing so, and content themselves with some crabs. On the edge of the forest live a certain kind of Indians, called Warau. They live there much safer than anyone on the river, because it is impossible to reach their houses for the reason that the roads are made of thick spars, standing tall, between 10 and 11 feet high from the ground, and in such a strange order that no man in the world who can walk over them by day as they do by night. The other Indians, of whatever nation they may be, also hesitate, because he who tumbles off, falls naked onto the thorns of which the woods are full. These roads stretch near and far, until they get on the higher land which is sandy and where some stream or another runs its course in order to get fresh water. They never wage war with the Arawaks, however, they are killed by the Caribs, if they are caught, but this rarely happens. Their language [67] differs about as much from one another as Walloon and French; the Waraus understand the Arawak well, but the Arawaks do not completely [understand] the Waraus. They do not bother with sowing or mowing, and just live from fishing and hunting for the Christians. When the time [season] is right for catching the *jarouw*, (a fish about the size of a stout roach, between 7 and 8 inches long, though not that white) they inform the Christians about it, and suggest a rendezvous place for the vessels. Now, those from the fort and the plantations go there in order to attend the catching of the fish; which is done with a piece of basket, manufactured for that purpose, with which the Waraus stop up the creeks or streams coming from above. The said fish are caught there in such abundance the Christians can hardly pickle them properly; once the guts are taken out and the head cut off, it [is] put in the salt in the same way as the herring. The payment for this service is done with axes, knives, and similar things; with which they again buy their necessities from the other Indians. The Warau women do not appear to be that noble and beautiful as those of the Arawaks; their ornaments consist of beaded strings, strung crossways over the body, yet they do appear quite white; the men are rather jealous but nevertheless more impudent, most of them walking around without a lap in front of their privates; this lap is hoisted up around the head in front of the stomach and securely tied around the body. Their posture is either standing or squatting even when they come across a bench, because the continuous habit has made this manner of sitting that agreeable to them they care for no other. Furthermore they are tremendously lazy, just as the Arawaks, who also will only go hunting or shooting if they are forced to do so by necessity. We have spoken elsewhere of this matter comprehensively to which we shall now add a few more singularities.

Notwithstanding their extreme laziness, they are however [68] very willing for the Christians who send them wherever they desire and have them perform various services for them. When we had them bring a letter to the Demerara River or Essequibo, the payment was a knife which costs 3 halfpence in the homeland. They are neither fastidious nor dainty, and eat various foods to which other nations would have an aversion; because I have seen more than once that they ate rotten eggs that gave such a stench one had to keep one's nose closed. When one has gone out hunting with them, they always take the clippings of the game, guts, paunch, etc., which they cook with *atty*, and consider it a delicacy. Religion is unknown to them; the one day is not an exception from the others. They also have neither laws nor police and do not know of any authority or inferiority. However, there is a Captain whom the Christians call Prince. He has the most power yet, and therefore every 2 years receives a red robe and a hat with which he also often appears at the fort. Manslaughter occurs very rarely; if an Indian happens to kill anyone, he can satisfy all punishment by giving the widow or children a male or female slave instead. Childbirth, which is such a troublesome affair among European nations, is quite easy here. Immediately after delivery, the woman who gave birth runs to the river to wash herself and her infant; who furthermore, without knowing anything of binders or swaddling clothes, is carried around for between 2 and 3 weeks by the mother in a hammock, manufactured for that purpose, hanging from the right shoulder on to the left side of the back; after this period she merely puts it down on the sand, letting it creep and crawl there until such time as it gradually obtains the strength to stand upright and learns to walk. And, the children there do not know about howling and crying as in the homeland, and crawl with greater patience along the ground; whereas ours, comfortably and well wrapped up, are lying in their cradle. Notwithstanding the little care for the children, I have never seen [69] lame or cripples ones, except for one with a paralysed hand, as well as one with a limp, but never one with a squint. They have a deadly enmity towards lice. When women catch them off eachother, they sit four, five, or six behind the other; as many as they get, they kill between the teeth; saying, when asked for the reason, it is but payment for when biting them.

I had meant to add here a description of their manner of waging war; but considering I have spoken about it in two different places and that I could not say much more about it, at least as far as concerning the essentials, I have thought it better to omit it, and not to lengthen the matter by relating one and the same thing twice.

CHAPTER XIII.

Bread of the Indians and in what manner it is prepared. Description of the vegetables and fruit trees. Various drinks among the Indians, and even used by the Europeans, etc.

Having thus discussed the principal characteristics of the land and its inhabitants, we will now continue to speak of everything the same produces for the support and comfort of human life, and first of all of bread, the most necessary of all things required.

The bread served as recourse in this country, and which is also used comfortably as such, is made of the root of a tree, called *carsaay*.[270] This tree usually grows to the height of 8, 9 or 10 feet, and is almost similar to the leaf of an ash tree. When one plants it, the ground is somewhat turned over, just [70] as one does when planting sugar. After that, a few pieces of wood [branches] of this tree are put in the ground, from which the tree then shoots; the other sprigs that shot out from the same, albeit not that luxuriant, are cut off. The root is rather tough and is such that the bread is made of, as said above; for which purpose the same, after its skin is scraped off, is grated on a manufactured stone for such purpose; the gratings were put into a press, *c.* 4 feet long, and plaited very tightly with fine reed. Now the women sit on it and press the overlying cover or board back through the weight of their body so that the juice pours out from below through a certain opening. This [juice] is caught in a pot and boiled with *atty* or pepper, because when eaten or drunk without boiling it is a great poison, as we found out when a few of our pigs swallowed it accidently and immediately died; otherwise it is sweet as sugar, and pleasantly enough of taste. So, when it is completely pressed out, it is put into a round-shaped iron pan and baked softer or harder, according to the use to which they want to put it; in order to make [alcoholic] drinks it must be baked much harder, until burnt; for food on the other hand, more softly. It is good and tasty bread; which I personally like better than the ordinary ship's biscuit; Once it is made, it can remain good for 2 years, without salt, but to bite it must the teeth must be good.

This is the way the Indians know to make bread. The other foods, such as meat and fish will be discussed subsequently, after we shall have spoken about the vegetable and fruit trees, the various drinks, etc.

Among the various vegetables which grow in the bountiful nature of this land, one also finds a kind of small beans which do not need to fall short to white Dutch beans. They grow there in abundance, yet they are always planted and split by the Christians. [71]

The small beans that grow wild have the size of the split pea beans at home and hairy on the pod.[271] This hairiness which is very short and finer than hair is the best chervil herb to be found in the world. If one takes a little of it on the finger, and touches someone with it this, causes an intolerable itching that lasts longer than half an hour and is that painful one cannot for an instance take the hand off the touched part. However, if these beans are good on the inside, I do not know. They run like ramping trees but are much smaller leafed.

270 Carsaay: cassava.

271 *Ormosia coccinea* is known among the Amerindians of Demerara as *barakara*. Its red seeds are highly toxic, inedible and often found in necklaces; see W.E. Roth, op. cit., 1948, p. 73.

Artichokes, brought over there, thrive reasonably well. If Dutch butter could be that easily obtained, much more use would be made of them. At present celery is also fairly popular.

Pumpkins and cucumbers, of the same sort as in the homeland, are to be had the whole year round.

Purslane grows everywhere in the wild, and is likewise very healthy.

Yams and potatoes, indigenous vegetables, are found in great quantity, both white and red. They are flowery and, if cooked like beetroot, tasty when eaten like a salad, especially if mixed with vegetables such as purslane, mustard leaves, etc. These yams and potatoes are, when grated, often mixed with annatto by the Indians. A drink is made of it, too. They grow like cucumbers; however, the leaves are much smaller.

As to grapes, they grow excellently there. We had a vineyard behind the fort; our garden produced ripe grapes three times a year.

Sugar cane thrives luxuriantly and in abundance. It can bear fruit during three successive years, however, in the fourth [year] it is unsuitable, as it comes up very dry and gives no juice. It stands 12 months before it is cut.

Tobacco, although not used as food, must however have its place here. It grows as much as can [72] be consumed, but is not as good as that from Virginia, being heavier to smoke.

Extremely good tree fruits grow likewise; some are that tasty the Dutch ones cannot be compared to them. Of this kind are the water melons, albeit not so called as they grow in water (because the trees stand on land just like any other) but because they are very watery and cool however this does not prevent one from eating as much as one likes without any inconvenience. On the outside they are green, but reddish on the inside, like apple blossoms.

Orange trees are unusually large. Near the fort is an alleyway of them, measuring between 80 and 100 roods long, surrounded by another alleyway of lemon trees, very pleasant to walk under on account of the shade and the pleasant scent, because they are always blossoming; they carry green and ripe apples [fruit]. They have the size of an ordinary apple in the homeland, with a good taste and smell. The lemons are smaller, about a sugar pear, though very juicy. Every year, we had pressed about ten to twelve barrels of juice which went towards the homeland.

Palmyt trees also grow extremely good. This [palm] tree has a heart which, eaten raw in the hand, is as tasty as a nut, and when stewed has a smell resembling cabbage. Its wood is very hard, and would possibly serve some purpose, but one has insufficient knowledge of the properties of things out here.

The guava is also a pleasant fruit. It grows in the savannahs, or pastures, on small trees measuring two or three fingers thick and tastes, when stewed, almost like quince pears. Eaten in the hand, it is equally of taste, but a little astringent. The colour is yellow, and the size of a small apple in the homeland.

One also finds a kind of fruit called cashew apples. They grow on tree like an ordinary apple tree. They are red on the outside and oblong; they [73] are somewhat astringent when eaten and are considered good for the stool [laxative].[272]

One also observes a sort of apple, called yet apple.[273] On the outside they resemble a fir cone; of the size of an ordinary apple; instead of a core, [they] have a very large stone. Around it, as thick as the back of a stout knife, is a certain yellow flour; it has the characteristic, when one eats eight or ten of these apples, the body is coloured that yellow, even the shirts carry stains. This fruit grows on a tree of ordinary size, with a leaf resembling that of a pear tree.

Figs are very tasty here; coloured like apple blossom, with the size of an ordinary pear. They hang on the tree almost all year round.

Another certain small tree, about [the size] of a cherry tree, carries a strange kind of nuts called 'schijtnootjes'.[274] They grow in a husk, which as they ripen turns black; [they] are very tasty, almost like a hazelnut; though better, and not that hard. But they must be eaten with care; because, in case one does not properly remove a certain membrane found in the middle of the kernel, they will cause nausea, dizziness in the head, and a horrible stool, which makes the sufferer run with its trousers in his hands. Otherwise, they do not bring on any pain; they often deceive newcomers.

Except for all above-mentioned fruit trees, one can also indulge in pineapples, bananas, bacoves, etc., all of these fruits have an excellent taste to be obtained in abundance.

The marmalade is likewise a tasty fruit, growing on trees of ordinary size, between two shells almost like broad beans although not as thick but just as wide.[275] This fruit is yellow on the outside, reddish on the inside, and tastes like something candied. [74]

The *atty*, or Spanish pepper, grows on a small tree like a currant, yet with a very thin stem. In order to make these small trees grow, the seed is boiled and as such put in the ground.

One could possibly bring up [for discussion] some other vegetable and fruit trees; but these are indeed the most important ones. Regarding drinks, they count many different sorts but altogether to be spoiled.

First of all, the *beltiry* made of cassava bread, masticated by old women and mixed with large quantity of their spittle. These chewed lumps to soaked with about three times as much cassava bread until the time has come it has conglomerated into a thick pap; after which they arrange it neatly in between leaves; now, when a beverage is to be made of it, they take out a handful and mix it with water. When drinking it, one keeps the teeth closed together, so that the lumps may stay in front of them.

---

272 The *cashew* or *cajú* (*Anacardium* sp.).

273 The descripition of this nut refers to the fruits of the Ité palm (*Mauritia flexuosa*); however its leaf is described incorrectly, see W.E. Roth, op. cit., 1948, p. 75.

274 *Jathropha curcas Linn.* A literal translation of the Dutch *schijtnootjes* leaves us with the much revealing 'small shit nuts', see W.E. Roth, op. cit., p. 76.

275 Presumably marmalade the Creole call *waiki* made of the *inga* sp., or sugar peas, see W.E. Roth, op. cit., p. 76.

Payewar is prepared in almost the same way, though it must stand one night, after which it takes on a sharp [sour-like] taste which is not unpleasant. For us, the drink was strained through a bread press in which the lumps stayed behind.

Pernouw, or *bassia,* is likewise made of chewed and unchewed cassava bread; albeit the latter [unchewed bread] must be burnt harder on this occasion and be mixed with it in greater quantity. This compote [mixture] is also put through the press and stands to work for between 3 and 4 days, and produces good yeast. This good beverage has the colour and the taste of beer, though it is not that clear, and has the convenience of making you nicely drunk for *c.* 2 pennies.[276]

Commany is mostly made on the Essequibo, notably from chewings [and] here in this country used for various drinks, and from hard baked cassava bread, [which is] laid aside for a while to grow mouldy, until it has obtained all kinds of colours. Mixed with burnt cassava cakes, and soaked in lukewarm water, it makes a kind of morning drink, very [75] suitable to inebriate yourself; though its taste somewhat nasty.

Cassyry is a drink, made from red yams and potatoes, mastication, and cassava bread. It is also put through a press, then stands for between 2 and 3 days in order to ferment; it then almost has the colour and strength of 'Graafsche' wine; is very good and tasty to drink.

CHAPTER XIV.

Various kinds of trees found along the Berbice River.

Besides the various fruit trees of which we have already spoken, there are still various other sorts of trees, which do not carry fruit, but also have their use though, such as the cedar, cotton, oriane, crab, and many other trees.

Cedar trees grow there in abundance, and are, when sawed into planks, serve to make boxes. Some of them are that thick the planks have a width of *c.* 3 feet.

Another timber is useful, called ironwood or sinkwood, for the reason that when put in water it sinks to the bottom due to its weight.[277] It is very good for making things with which force has to be used.

Letterwood is also to be found there; though it grows mostly in Essequibo, and costs about as much to chop it as it is worth.[278]

Cotton trees are scattered here and there throughout the country in multitudes; but [they] often stand, however, near the Indian houses, although they, because of their inborn laziness, do not make use of them at all, what one could make of it in return.

---

276 David Pietersz de Vries compares *casari* with Haarlem beer from Holland and *pernou* with Bremen beer from Northern Germany, respectively, D. Pietersz de Vries, *Korte Historiael,* 1911, pp. 190, 197.

277 Perhaps Syderoxylon, many (non-timber) tropical hardwoods sinks to the bottom of the river, W.E. Roth, op. cit., 1948, p. 78. The Dutch applied the term Yzerhout as a generic indication of very heavy wood from various trees in America, Africa and Asia; for Surinam, see J. Fermin, *Nieuwe algemeene beschryving,* 1770, pp. 221-222.

278 Letterwood: *letterhout* (Dutch) or speckled wood (*Brosimum guianense* is a synonym of *Piratinera guianensis*).

Around the Indian houses one also sees a certain [76] kind of trees, as large as a low-standing apple tree with the leaves of a pear. This one carries fruit all year round, called oriane,[279] and is recognized here as well as at home as a good dye. The seed resembles the teasels used by wool carders; set with prickles, with a reddish colour, though these prickles are much softer [flexible] than those of the said teasels. Within the seed, which appears whitish, one sees eight to ten pellets of dye, smaller than a white pea. These are gathered by the Indians and mixed with grated yams or potatoes together with some crab oil, so that it may be "freed" of the maggot, which destroys the dye's power.

The crab trees grow everywhere in the forests.[280] The seed, or nut, has the size of a chestnut. Aside from the good dye derived from it, it yields crab, once pounded and placed in the sun, a type of oil found to be very good for the gout, because the affected limbs, smeared with it in front of an oak wood fire,are freed from pain within a few moments. The crab tree nuts are for that purpose also entirely boiled and pounded; then, once dried and pounded, placed in the sun, which will draw out well the said oil in a larger quantity; though it is not that substantially and powerfully [drawn in this manner].

There are also several kinds of trees from which gums should be extracted from. I have held seven or eight in my hand, but without knowing which use they had.

Gitte-gamba should be in abundance there,[281] if the Indians were not too lazy to make openings [cuts] in the trees and collect it. One might express an object here to me that the Christians ought to be doing so; but they have, for more than one reason, no chance to do so.

I do not doubt there would also be Medicinalia, but one has not paid sufficient attention to such matters.

The holes of the trees, over here and over there in the forests, also supply a fair quantity of honey which is sold by the Indians, [77] particularly by the Warouwen, in small amounts just as they take it out of the trees; however, the wax is naturally black. We had our candles made from it. Now and then the wax is also sold in [the shape of] rolls or plaques, on which occasion the Indians themselves keep the honey.

To put it shortly, the land would be good and fertile, if it were inhabited by other people than Indians.

CHAPTER XV.

Various kinds of animals, birds, and fish in the Berbice River, as well as the strange peculiarities of some of the same.

---

279 Oriane: *Bixa orellana* which produces annatto; see note 248.

280 Crab trees: crabwood, or *Carapa guianensis*; nowadays, its oil is usually extracted from the seeds or incisions made in the bark of a living tree. The smell alone prevents it from being more generally utilised by Europeans, see W.E. Roth, op. cit., 1948, p. 79.

281 Gitte-gamba: the rubber tree (*Hevea brasiliensis*), see W.E. Roth, op. cit., 1948, p. 79.

Aside from all the things required for human life, or provide some use or comfort for it, of which we have spoken before, on the Berbice River there is also no lack of cattle, birds, etc., with which we propose to deal in this Chapter. We will first of all speak about the animals which serve as food for the people, then about the other kinds, and so on till we will get to the birds, fish, etc. Giving preference to roasted game, the first place will be taken in by the stags and deer. They are there in abundance, but not always [easily] shot due to their unusual shyness. Many times have have I seen there twenty to twenty-five together, but if they find themselves higher in the wind, one cannot get them within shot. Many are caught in the water, into which they are driven in order to capture them with less trouble. They are very good at swimming and give those, who tried to catch them, to wit if one does not want to kill them immediately, most often as much work as entertainment due to their resisting. We usually counted [78] there at the fort one or two a week, and sometimes even more, according to the opportunity that presented itself and our willingness to make an effort [to catch them]. The Indians cannot appreciate its taste as much as the Christians do; because I once bought a whole deer for a knife costing 2 pence. The flesh is somewhat dry. Remarkably one must cut off the nose of a stag or deer as soon as it is dead; otherwise it would stink within 2 or 3 hours. The cut-off nose also gives off such a nasty stench itself that one has to throw it away immediately.

Hares are in abundance, too, but with another appearance than in the homeland.[282] The back is brown, mottled with white spots; the stomach is white; the paws and ears are short, so that they do not resemble other hares at all. The taste is very delicate, yet not like a hare; the meat is very tender and as white as veal meat. One soaks them in hot water, scrapes off the hair, and prepares them with the skin if one wants to roast or to stew them.

One also sees rabbits in abundance, yet they are not as nice as the homeland ones, but they just as plain [of colour].[283] The meat is much drier, and therefore not that tasty. The head alone slightly resembles our rabbits except, however, for the ears; just like the paws, they are very short. The hair is generally greyish. They also live in the forests, and are hunted, like the hares, with dogs.

Not less plentiful one can find there wild hogs;[284] but they are rarely caught upon dry or high land; since they mostly dwell near the river. In the month of April they make a rush which the Warouwen take note of. Next some boats are prepared at the fort and the plantations, well provided with salt; which are conveyed to the spot where the hunt is to take place, where the Indians post themselves here and there with bow and arrow in hand. The hogs run one behind the other, and thus offer the opportunity to shoot them more easily [79]; however the first of the group is never shot, only the second or third. If they wounded, wherever the arrow may have hit them, the Indians merely let them run on, until they fall dead to the ground due to the loss of blood. Then, to wit, when the whole group has passed;

---

282 Hare: the lowland, or spotted, paca (*Cuniculus paca*), or *labba* in Guyana.

283 Rabbits: probably small rodents, or *accouries*, e.g. *agouti* (*Dacyprocta agouti*) and *acouchi* (*Myoprocta acouchi*).

284 Wild hogs: either the *Tayassu pecari* (*pingo* in Guyana) or the *Tayassu tajacu* (*pakira* in Guyana).

when those taken down have been tracked, they are brought to the Christians who set to work; they burn off the hair, cut all the bones out and lay the flesh [cut] into pieces, well salted, in the casks. It is very good meat, I have but never eaten any fancier as from a young fresh hog or from the hares of which I have just spoken. Nature seems to have worked perversely concerning these animals, because whereas in all others the navel sits below the stomach, it is on their back, as can be seen on the hogs sent to Flushing alive. They are not as big as in other places; the largest usually weighs *c.* 60 pounds.

On many occasions, tame pigs have been sent from the homeland out here for further breeding, but they became that extremely fat they could not raise their young. However, no food was ever given to them, but they knew how to get it from the surrounding forests.

Cows run wild in abundance. They used to be tame, but because of the people's neglect, [they] have found their way into the forests where they have become wild. One shoots them only in the leg; for the reason that, owing to their wildness, one cannot slaughter them. I have never seen any fat on them. The kidney fat is also very sparse. In the beginning, when I first came to the Berbice River, one was shot every 14 days; but afterwards it got out of fashion. Under my second Chief, about every 3 or 4 weeks, we would often drive a number of them into a circle of poles made for the purpose, from which we then took away the calves which we put in an enclosure, but their tameness seemed to have entirely disappeared, because [80] once they came out into the open, they went off into the forest.

Various kinds of dogs that run along the road, just as in the homeland, are found there amongst the Indians; [they] are trained from early age for alls kinds of hunting and are held in high esteem by them. They know how to keep a hog at bay, and how to avoid, with special agility, the snap of its teeth. Whenever a dog is after game, the hunter knows by means of the dog's noise, of which kind it is, because just as different as the hunt is, the sound the dogs make is, too. They are much pestered with bush worms that grow in between the skin [and] flesh and at the beginning are very small; but when having reached the size of a finger joint, they are squeezed out of the dog.

Tigers are there fairly plentiful;[285] albeit one seldom hears they attack the people, as there is plenty cattle into which they can slash their rapacious claws. Yet is has certainly occurred, as in the example we have mentioned before. One observes them measuring between 5 and 6 feet long. However, a kind of small tiger is called cat tiger, possibly because they are much larger than a stout cat. So far on quadruped animals. But if there is an abundance of any animal, it is of monkeys; when traveling along the river, one sees such a number on tree branches the newly arrived cannot be amazed enough. There are various kinds, to wit howlers, *ytoerybalijs*, pilots, bakers, hobgoblins, deadhead monkeys, etc.

The howlers are so called because during the evening and night they make a sound like someone who howls or gargles.

---

285 As to 'tiger', this Creole and general term is applied to all felines in the Guianas.

The *ytoerybalijs* resemble old wrinkled grannies, with no hair on their chaps. They are all ugly and have quite a repulsive appearance.[286]

The pilots have long attractive beards under the chin and show a certain air of elegance.[287] [81]

The bakers are so called because the front paws continuously move in such a way as if someone is kneading dough.[288]

The hobgoblins have possibly obtained that name because of their agile jumps through the trees. For, one sees them now here, now there, with such rapidity, too, that the eye can barely follow them.

The deadhead's are very small and attractive animals.[289] They usually sit on larger monkeys which, when hungry, continue to bite until taken to some fruit trees, where they can get food.

All these kinds of monkeys serve the Indians for food. As for me, I could find little taste in it, probably because they were not well prepared. I have tasted one that was barbecued or roasted in the Indian manner. It is done, as we have said elsewhere, on a wooden grid, standing *c.* 2 feet high above the ground. On it the food is placed; when covered with leaves on top, over a slow fire, roasted until done. However, all the food, thus prepared, tastes mighty dry. There was also a monkey, of which they had burnt off the hair very recently causing the skin to look horrible.

Tortoises live there on land; I have never seen one in water. They are found in the forests and taken by the Indians for sale; [they] have the length, to wit the largest, of between 12 and 15 thumbs [inches]; and width and thickness in proportion. When one wants to have them as food, the lower shell is chopped off, and everything is cut out. Prepared as a soup, it is a very good meal. The upper and lower shells roasted in front of a fire, present a small banquet. The liver quite resembles that of a ray, and surpasses the same in its delicacy.

---

286 According to W.E. Roth, op. cit., 1948, p. 84, the Arawak name for the howler monkey, or baboon, is *ituri*; see also M. F. Patte, *La langue arawak de Guyane. Présentation historique et dictionnaires arawak-français et français-arawak.* In: Collection Didactiques, Paris: IRD Editions, 2011, p. 95. Roth adds that the suffix *–balli* conveys the idea of resemblance, or similarity, to a howler monkey; hence, this is a monkey that resembles a howler monkey.

287 Perhaps the *bisa* (Sr.), bearded saki or black saki (*Chiropotes satanas*).

288 Perhaps the *sagoewonki* (Sr.) (*Sanguinus midas*).

289 Probably the squirrel monkey (Saimiri *sciureus*).

Not less tasty of flesh are the anteaters, a sort of animal with a long body and a long hairy tail, short of paws, brown of hair, and having the size as one can see at the Anatomy Museum in Leyden.[290] They are so called, because with their sharp [narrow] and long tongue, they can get ants out of their holes. [82]

Among the water animals one can also see crocodiles but not in abundance. Never have we been offered more than one living [specimen] for sale. It was rolled up, *c.*3½ feet long; once killed, [it is] prepared in two ways; though it tasted of neither fish nor flesh. Meanwhile, I can, however, say this: whether it be neither fish nor flesh, the same was as white as chalk and very delicate. In all my travels through the land I have never seen more than one crocodile. I had a shot at it, but did not get it, as the bullet bounced off the scales.

Higher up on the river, sea cows are now and again dound;[291] I cannot say much about them, as I have never seen them. Nevertheless, I have eaten the meat; prepared by the Indians; which, if worked in a better way, would not have been unpalatable.

The smaller animals, not easily classified as one species, must also find a place here. Amongst them one sees a number of lizards, altogether of a beautiful green colour, that in the sun renders a brilliancy not surpassed by any birds' feathers. They are very agile and quick at running.

Iguanas are also plentiful there. The colour and shape of this kind of animal looks rather like that of lizards, but larger with exclusion of the tail, *c.*1½ foot long. They generally lay thirty eggs, only coated by a membrane. I have eaten them many times and found them very tasty.

Grasshoppers I have never seen that large. Amongst others, I saw one at Master de Graaf's [plantation] in Essequibo that had been stuffed as a curiosa because of it unusual size. I measured it, and found it to measure over 5 thumbs long.

Of no lesser stout appearance according to its proportions are ants, more than ½ a thumb long. They do no damage, as far as known for certain. Meanwhile, it occurs every 7 or 8 years that the root of the *carsavy*, tobacco, and other fruits, [83] is eaten away; this is ascribed to ants, however, not with complete certainty. I have witnessed enough of such years there and saw for example that a soldier stood

---

290 Anteater: this anteater was given to the Leyden Anatomie Hall by count Joan Maurice of Nassau-Siegen (1604-1679), Governor General of Dutch Brasil (1637-1644). See: F. Schuyl, A Catalogue of all the cheifest Rarities in the Publick Anatomie-Hall, of the University of Leyden, Leiden: Diewertje van der Boxe, 1727, p. 6, no. 49). It was probably imported from Brazil during the 1640s. It is catalogued here as 'A Formican Vorans or Pismire eater'. See J. Nieuhof, *Gedenkweerdige Brasiliaense Zee- en Lantreize, behelzende al het geen op dezelve is voorgevallen, beneffens een bondige beschrijving van gantsch Neerlants Brasil* [...], Amsterdam: Voor de Weduwe van Jacob van Meurs, 1682, p. 28. After an inquiry at the Leiden *Anatomisch laboratorium*, it was stated that this specific anteater was no longer procured. The earliest specimen was acquired in 1835. The present editors are indebted to Dennis Nieweg and Tim Huisman for providing this information. Curiously, Roth translated that anteaters are 'tenacious of life' meaning they have a long (lasting) life. However, Van Berkel reports they have 'a long (stretched) body', see W.E. Roth, op. cit., 1948, p. 85.

291 Sea cows, or manatee (*Trichechus manatus*), of which there were not many left in the vicinity of the plantations when Van Berkel visited the Berbice River; they apparently dwelt upstream and probably depleted in the lower part of this river.

guard for 2 hours to earn one pipe of tobacco, because the root of the tobacco was eaten [by the ants] and had then dried up.

Cockroaches are found only in the houses of the Christians. They are brown with a very flat body; besides they are able of creeping through the cracks in boxes and trunks; yet they do no damage, except to linen and wool. They mostly come out during the evening, and [they] have wings, like certain kinds of beetles in the homeland. The largest measured *c.*1 thumb.

Spiders are large and small. I have had two which, when stuffed, occupied more space than the palm of a hand. The body alone had the size of half a 'rijksdaalder'. They are black, hairy and have teeth; though, whether they are poisonous, as some people want to claim, I do not know. In fact I have never heard they did any harm. One usually finds them up in the roofs of the Negroes houses.

Toads are to be seen a lot, and of an unusual size. These are poisonous, and must also be avoided carefully.

There are many rats too; but they come from the ships, either by swimming or by some other means.

Snakes come in various sorts, and sizes. The most prominent are the rattlesnakes, so called because of the rattle at the end of the tail; when they go their way, it makes a certain cracking sound that indeed resembles a rattle. It consists of various caps; for every year one cap is counted. I have had a specimen with nine caps; as soon as it had barely moved, it rattled terribly. They are very poisonous, and their stings or bites are not curable except by cauterising, or by vomiting after eating human excrement. Other kinds of snakes are not that poisonous. I have seen a skin, or hide, measuring 8 inches wide, and about as many feet long; notwithstanding its size, this snake however had not been very poisonous. [84] There are also many water snakes, principally in the Canje River, yet they do no harm, and are eaten by the Indians and Negroes, even the poisonous ones. I have nothing to say about the taste as I had never had the curiosity or rather courage enough to try it. During all my travels by water and land, I have never met with any vermin; although the snakes seek the coolness at night here and there on the trails.

Foul on the Berbice River is also plentiful, and of various kinds: chickens, turkeys, tame ducks, partridges, etc., of each of which we shall speak separately.

I have seen a lot of poultry in various places throughout the land; though they are not as large as in the homeland or quite that tasty.

On the other hand, turkeys are much fatter and heavier. I have tasted one that weighed more than 24 pounds; the lard or fat of the breast measured more than two fingers thick. They are bred by the Christians, and fed with milie [maize] or Turkish wheat, which grows in abundance over there.

Field poultry, or partridges, are seen in abundance too; though they are not held in great esteem; because someone seldom takes the trouble to fire a shot at them.

A kind of bird is about as large as chicken, [having] the upper part of the body black and, below it, a white stomach and a fairly long tail. They are called *pauyssen*[292]; many are shot, because they are very delicate. If one wants to go out [and hunt them], one must go before daybreak, because they are very shy. They reveal themselves by their whistling; which when heard by the hunter, he goes to the tree, puts out the candle and waits for dawn. He now comes to shoot the bird;which, despite falling down, still runs a short time at such speed the shooter can barely follow it.

Wild pigeons are plenty to shoot, if one will only take the trouble to travel along the river. There are also tame pigeons, which are rather easily bred. [85]

Down in the river lives a bird with the size of a small chicken. No painter could paint with his pencil a more beautiful colour red.[293] They are somewhat shy; yet, I believe, not tasty, for they prey upon fish.

Among the water birds one also finds here tame ducks and water snipes.[294] So far concerning the former; one sees about the same kind as in the homeland; yet they do not go in the water often, and are also of a better taste. However, another kind is bred here, with large red nostrils on its beaks of which I have seen a similar one at Honselaarsdijk.[295] Most of the time they keep out of the water and are good to eat when properly prepared. This kind also flies around aplenty in the wild, especially around the seashore where we frequently went for them, when there for the occasion.

There are water snipes in such abundance that I managed to shoot sixty with one shot;[296] yet there was nobody who wanted to lend a hand at plucking them. They are most often found downstream.

Around the seashore, in the pastures, one sees a kind of bird not unlike storks, as far as shape and size is concerned; but their feathers are more mottled with colours.

The sight of another small bird, as brilliant as a golden beetle, is said by the Indians to mean no good at all, but the Christians do not put much faith in that.

Parrots are there in great numbers, and procurable at a small price. But I do not know why, for the Indians never come to market with young birds. They bring plenty of old ones, sometimes more than desired. One calls them 'stropvogels', because they are caught with a noose in the following way. The Indian, knowing the trees where the parrots usually reside, covers his entire body with green leaves, just as the stick to which the noose is attached. He knows [86] how to let it drop precisely over its head; when drawing the stick towards him, the catch is always certain. However one can never teach this kind of parrots to talk. Those, valued in

---

292 The *pauyssen* may be translated as *powissi* (Sr.), or *hoco* (*Crax elector*).

293 The red ibis (*Eudocimus ruber*).

294 Presumably (domesticated) Muscovy ducks (*Cairina moschata*).

295 Honselaarsdijk is the name of the country house built between 1621 and 1647 for Frederick Hendrick, the youngest son of William of Orange. The monumental building was demolished in 1815 with the exception of an annex and part of the garden.

296 Similar high numbers have also been recorded for the Franco-Dutch hunting party of Chambaut and David Pietersz de Vries on the Counamama River who managed to shoot '33 teelingen' in a single shot. See: D. Pietersz de Vries, *Kort Historiael*, 1911, p. 203; a *teeling* or *taling* is a 'teal'.

the homeland are taken by Indians when traveling by water to the Rio Aarnocque [Orinoco], near the Island of Trinidad, belonging to the King of Spain, and are taken as chicks from the nest.

Parakeets are also seen in abundance [and] have a very beautiful green colour; but I have never heard them talk, neither have I seen chicks. They scream loudly enough; though it is their natural talk, which cannot be changed.

There are two kinds of ravens, both in abundance.[297] The first have a blue breast,and yellow or orange kind of feathers; the second have yellow and blue wings. One also teaches them to speak; but they are not that easily to be taught as parrots. They cannot be confined or kept, because they bite the woodwork to pieces.

Swallows are there the whole year round in abundance.

Bats (if you want to include these animals among birds) occur in large numbers tooa. These awful creatures often feed on human blood; one has the most distress when one goes to sleep in a hammock with bare legs; because then the toes must suffer trouble, for they know how to suck blood from them. It happened to me once or twice; in such matter I can speak from experience. They are very agile; because having bitten for a first time, they fly away to see if the one who has been bitten is waking up. If not, they come and sit on the toes, and suck themselves thick with blood. In such manner, the blood of the chicks of our tame pigeons were sucked by the bats; next we found many of them dead, but when we learnt why their breeding was hindered, we soon took precautions for the future.

There are even more other birds; but having mentioned the most important ones, we will now continue to speak of the various kinds of fish. Whereas we have had a wide [87] arrange of animals and birds, of these there is not as much; the lovers of this kind of food are warned not to come thither to crave their appetite. Nevertheless there is something, and this matter must be included here as part of our tale.

First of all, a kind of fish that fairly resembles the homeland bream, albeit whiter, almost as a bleak.It is very tasty and good, albeit somewhat bony; thus one is required to eat them with care. The Indians frequently shoot them with bow and arrow; that, which is to be wondered at, in places where the Christians, how careful they may look, cannot see [this] fish. The name is *kartabak*.[298]

Another fish is marked like a perch, but that bony it is not eaten much.

Soldiers catch a small fish, of about the size of a small bleak, and not bony, with hooks.

Wanted to dish up a meal of fish, we ordered the Indians around the fort to halt at a creek; next, they subsequently went in it at low water, and stirred with a certain kind of wood, defying the nature of the fish, [they put] down to the bottom, upon

297 Parrots of the genus *Ara* sp., or *ara* (Sr.).
298 The *Characidae* sp., or *paku* (Sr.).

which numerous surfaced, so that we, keeping the most tasty ones, often gave quite half of it to the people.[299]

A few other kinds of fish are not worthwhile and do not deserve to be bothered with.

Crabs, considering them fish too, are there in abundance, large, and very tasty. One catches them at the seashore, at places where the forests are flooded. The ground is clayey here, and usually full of [sink] holes and puts, from where they are taken out by hand at a depth of 1½ feet during low water. The Indians eat them just as they are, but the Christians usually boil them half done, then take off the flesh which comes out easily and stew them further, providing a delicate fare. [88]

CHAPTER XVI.

Various kinds of diseases on the Berbice River.

Just as all countries commonly have their own kinds of disease, the Berbice River, too, is not an exception hereto; in addition, the Christians are also subject to those of the homeland, except possibly the pest, which I have never heard mention. As to the other, I have seen so many examples I could not doubt them. Sometimes, however, there is a difference, as for example in children pox [chicken pox], a disease to which all the children, both Christians and Indians, are receptive; for if any one above 15 years of age is affected, one must be cured in the homeland in the same way as the Spanish pox, to wit with [foot] stoves, pock-drinks, etc., receiving in the meantime too much food to die and almost too little to live.

'Persing' is a sort of disease, accompanied by a troublesome stool, to which one has to force himself. It is caused by eating too much unripe fruit, or by the excessive use of 'graap',[300] a drink made of syrup, and harmful in that it produces this complaint. Brandy is the most precious what one can have over there. But I cannot imagine why a drink of kill-devil is not given twice a day to the population, because, except that it could be done without considerable loss to the Lords Directors a better health could be maintained, as far as this disease is concerned,.

A worse complaint is *mebiky*, called *zieke* in Dutch; a sort of matter or something else, which I do not know to name, very common in the houses of the Indians and as large as the point of a pin. It encroaches [89] the flesh somewhere and continuously grows to the size of an ordinary white pea. I once have had seven removed from my feet at the same time. They are pale have a hard shell which

299 The sap of the 'Haiari' or Hiarra liana (*Lonchocarpus* sp.), an Arawak term, suffocates the fish which are captured in pools or small river branches. See also Richard Schomburgk Travels, 1922, p. 271; C. Moretti & P. Grenand, Les nivrés ou plantes ichtyotoxiques de la Guyane française, *Journal of Ethnopharmacology* 6, 1982, p. 143; M-F. Patte, *La langue arawak de Guyane*, 2011, p. 92. See also J. Farabee, *The Central Arawaks*, 1918, p. 63; J.J. Hartsinck, *Beschrijving van Guiana*, 1770, p. 79; C. Leigh, Capitaine Charles Leigh his voyage to Guiana and plantation there. In: *Hakluytus Posthumus or Purchas His Pilgrimes. Contayning a History of the World in Sea Voyages and Lande Travells by Englishmen and others*, Samuel Purchas (ed.), Vol. 16, Glasgow: James MacLehose & Sons, 1906, p. 313.

300 Graaf: *warrap* according to W.E. Roth, op. cit., 1948, p. 93. See also note 260.

once broken appears as a thick matter inside which, when cut, snaps just like lice. The holes, from which these *mebikijs* have been taken, are stops with the tobacco ash. If they do not heal by this, one runs the risk they will become pock holes out of which, in the course of time, the pox will come out. This often happens here, nonetheless one takes the trouble to go and get them [out] with the womenfolk. Though one has not here much trouble here to cure the pox as in the homeland; for ,the herbs here are green and consequently more potent.

Another kind of disease is called 'landziekte' [dropsy].[301] It is caused by sheer laziness, and not giving the body any exercise, because, as it very hot over here, the heat creates indolence and sleepiness; there are those who lie in their hammocks all day long. It is a very troublesome complaint and accompanied by great headaches, severe giddiness, paleness of the face and many other inconveniences.

CHAPTER XVII.

Happy state of the planters. Situation of the plantations. Planting and harvesting of the sugar-cane, as well as the preparation of the sugar. Strange kinds of trees. Punishment of the slaves, who want to run away, etc.

From all that has been said before, it can be measured, with which ease and unease one can live on the Berbice River. But we have not yet spoken of the plantations; [90] it is there that one leads a princely life, little mixed with trouble, but, on the contrary, accompanied by all the delights, which can be enjoyed in this land. If only the conviviality, an inseparable characteristic of human nature, would not be lacking, one need not visit another country to spend one's [remaining] days in rest and peace, with few cares, and no troubles to worry about.

During my stay, there were five plantations, including the fort's head plantation, which yearly produced a fair quantity of sugar; the most important (next to the oriane, of which is *c.* 100 barrels is shipped) merchandise traded here. They are all located on the riverside, yet not equally attractive or equally easy to access. The plantations, called *den Berg* and *Mierenberg*, are situated fairly high up; with a wealthy pasture around them and a lovely view of the forest at the rear. The two others, on the contrary, are on places where a large and long stretch of forest has been felled, but at a lower level, and on clay ground; therefore, when it has rained heavily, [and] the rain reaches over there, it [the ground] is useless. In the savannahs, or pastures, on the other hand, one has sandy ground; subsequently the roads [are] always useable, along which one can travel from the two first-mentioned plantations towards various villages in the land.

The slaves are also much healthier on the dry grounds, when compared with those living on the clay grounds; yet when regarding the victuals, they are produced on both grounds. But the opportunity for keeping cows is very different: whereas

---

301 Landziekte (lit. land disease): a kind of oedema also known as dropsy. It is also identified as malaria in northeastern Brazil, see B.R. Ferreira Miranda, *Gente de Geurra: Origem, cotidiano e resistência dos soldados do exército da Companhia das Indias Ocidentais no Brasil (1630-1654)*, PhD Dissertation University Leiden, 2011, p. 203.

Figure 14: An anteater. Print in J.J. Nieuhof, Gedenkweerdige Brasiliaense Zee- en Lantreize [...], 1682.

on the plantations situated on the pastures they run in and out on their own account, but have to be driven through the forest on the others and in the same way have to be taken back home. Moreover, one lives there in an excellent way; because one takes care in having all things on the plantation, such as chickens, turkeys, tame ducks, all sorts of greens, and everything else one needs [91] for necessities and pleasure. The cows supply fresh milk daily, of which butter is also made; the Indians, who serve the Lords Planters for a small consideration, hunt many kinds of tasty game for them. The others, who dwell in the surrounding villages, provide them with everything they may get a hold of, etc.

And since we are describing the plantations here, we must not forget to speak about the preparation of the sugar, and what it further concerns; a matter appropriate to arouse the curiosity of the attentive readers. See here, how, from the beginning till the end, the whole thing happens.

First of all, the fields destined for planting sugar cane, are ploughed; cleared of weeds, cut into furrows at equal distances from each another; the plants are placed in these furrows in such a manner, the upper tops touch eachother. The holes require more additional earth during the summer than in the winter; because the penetrating heat of the sun may not scorch the small roots. The more the moisture dampens the cane, the sooner it grows. Within 10, or at the utmost, 12 months, it will attain complete ripeness. January and August, the last winter month, are the most suitable for planting; because the earth, soaked in fresh rains, let the roots shoot easier. The ripened cane, cut at the proper time, sometimes remains lying on the field until the following year.[302] In the meantime grows new cane grows, which frequently reaches the mill at the same time as the old one. But if it stands longer than 2 years, the sweet sap disappears and the cane itself gradually dies. The young plants in this land can only bear fruit for 3 years in succession and must be planted anew in the fourth year. Sometimes, when the scorching sunshine is not followed by rain, the cane dies due to a drought and is burnt during the winter, so that new cane will grow from under the ashes. When the water inundates the fields too long [92], the tender plants are sometimes drowned. They are also suffocated if they are too much overgrown with weeds; therefore the ground is weeded four times a year, until such time that the cane can stand the weed. Furthermore, one cuts off the ripened cane at the lowest knob as well as the leaves from the cane, after which it is bound in bushels and brought to the mill. This one consists of three strong wooden axis [rollers], encased with thick iron hoops in between which the cane is crushed. The rollers, through which the sweet juice flows, as well as the trough into which it trickles, must be cleaned twice every 24 hours. The cane, stuck from behind in between the first roller, is turned towards the second, so that the remaining juice can be pressed out. The bruised cane serves as food [fuel] for the flames. The pressed juice runs through wooden gutters into large copper kettles, under which the fires are kept burning with an incredible amount of wood. When it boils too hard, one pours water below, so that it consumes less. Meanwhile the scum is ladled off, which is food and drink for the cattle. Now they pour it into the second kettle, where it is boiled again, and [subsequently] the dirt is being skimmed off by the slaves with a skim spoon. Meanwhile one puts, for further purification, lye into the bubbling fluid, which is finally filtered through cloth.[303] The dregs that remain sticking to the cloth, mixed with water, provides a kind of beverage from which one can drink a good drunk [graap *sic*]. From the large kettles the fluid flows into the small one, where it is boiled a third time; it is continually stirred until it acquires the thickness of syrup and eventually of sugar. It must be reckoned among the secrets of nature, that, while the sugar boils in the small kettles, oil should be added by drops; which, if it happened when boiled in the large kettles, the fluid would not congeal into sugar. Again, if lye was poured into the small kettles, as in the large ones, the fluid in it would be instantly spoiled; just as when lemon juice or something sour is put in. Thus, when it has obtained a fair [93] consistency, it is poured into wooden troughs, which are broad and square at the top, but gradually taper towards the bottom to the size of a penny; a hole here, which, for the time being, remains stopped with a plug, until the sugar has become

302 This is a rather strange observation or conclusion: the fresh cut sugar cane has to be transported as quickly as possible to the factory in order to obtain the best juice.

303 Five cauldrons or boilers are often applied in the destilation proces. Hereto, in boiler 2, ash and quick lime (calcium oxide) are added. The cloth mentioned is of a crude quality and is called *stramien* in Dutch. See: J.H. Reisig, *De Suikerraffinadeur, of volledige beschrijving van het suiker, deszelfs aankweking, bereiding en verzending...* Dordrecht: A. Blussé en zoon, 1793.

cold and solid. Now, one takes out the plug and lets the sugar trickle down through the hole; it is then cooped into barrels, and shipped away.

Here we must finally add that the hoops of these barrels are made from the wood of a certain tree, called *meby* in Indian. These shoot neither leaf nor bud, and only have a few drooping branches, of which the thickest serve for making the said hoops.

The thinnest branches have another use, to wit punishing the misdeeds of the slaves, and especially when one understands they want to run away; on which occasion, they are pitifully beaten with them, so that not only the blood runs down the black skin, but entire pieces of skin are torn off. And, notwithstanding this punishment, if they want to run away more often, as happens occurs, the sinews at the heels are slit, thus impeding fast running. [94]

CHAPTER XVIII.

News of the war between the Kings of France and England against the United Provinces brought to the Berbice River.[304] Mutiny of the soldiers against the Governor who is thrown into prison. The author is appointed night watch, who is harassed by a fleet of Caribs, and forced to forsake his Post. Danger of being thrown into chains, which he escapes through wit.

After having thus spoken of all the most important characterics of the land, I will return to the story of my exceptional experiences, as well as what may have some relation to it.

In the month of June of the year 1673, we received tidings about Essequibo, by means of a vessel that arrived there from Holland, telling how the *d'Eendracht,* sent to us according to the old custom, had captured an English ship coming from the East Indies and had sailed with the same to Bergen in Norway, and from there to Elbe. We had received no tidings for 17 months, and subsequently imagined that the ship we were expecting must have been wrecked. But little did we think that the Kings of France and England had come together, and declared war against the United Provinces. At the same time we also learned of the surrender of so many cities and forts, which, within a few days' time, were dragged away by the enemy's forces, like by a powerful stream; next, we did not doubt, but the entire land would have already bowed under the yoke of the conquerors, [95] or after all be in such a pitiful state we could not expect anything from it, because our letters were already 4 months old. In this troublesome situation, it was decided by the Commander, to

304 The year 1672 is known in Holland as *Rampjaar,* or 'Year of Disaster' when following the outbreak of the Third-Anglo Dutch War and the Franco-Dutch War, the Republic of the Seven United Provinces was attacked by the mighty monarchies of England and France, as well as by the prince-elector, Archbishop of Cologne, and finally by the prince-bishop of Munster (the former two in their capacities as heads of the temporal possessions of the Archdiocese of Cologne and the diocese of Munster respectively). The invasions prompted the Orangists to call for the restauration of the position of Stadholder. The young Prince of Orange (b. 1650) became Stadthouder William III (1672-1702). His political opponent, statesman Johan de Witt (1625-1672) and his brother Cornelis de Witt (1623-1672) were killed by an Orangist mob in The Hague. The role of the new Stadtholder in this sad event remains unclear. Also in 1672 a disastrous sea flood inundated many parts of Zeeland and Holland, killing thousands of people.

continue with the utmost frugality, in particular about the lard and meat; as we did not know, when we would be relieved with supplies; but we had little hope for that. When the rations, making a virtue out of a necessity, were reduced, the soldiers, releasing the reins of their stupid instincts, began to grumble to such an extent that they, instigated by one Dirk Roosekrans of Flushing, a Constaple [head gunner], whose name is to be mentioned here to an everlasting shame, shouted, in the month of November, with a loud voice: "More food, and another Chief." I had already heard this muttering for some time, and had warned the Commander on various occasions, that it could not continue [like this] and that the people had turned against him in such a way, that one had good reason to fear a bad outcome. The Commander then declared to me he had done as he could justify himself before God and his Masters; that he would love to give more to the population but, whilst one could expect the enemy every day and there were more that eighty mouths at the fort, that the same [fort], if one did not curtail the rations somewhat, would be very difficult to defend. Indeed, our entire provisions consisted of four barrels of lard, and three of meat; barely enough, if one had given them the whole lot, to provide that many men for 14 days with food. Supplies were not to be expected and the people knew well there was no more in the store. Nevertheless the said Dirk Roozekrans knew to instigate them to such a degree they boldly made clear that another Commander should be appointed. This was promised as well as that the Lords Councillors would satisfy them. The latter assembled on Sunday morning before 9 o'clock at the fort. We were mightily embarrassed to conduct the business in such a way the people might be appeased. The decision made was [96] that the oldest Councillor should soothe them with soft speeches, but in vain. Their fury carried them that far that a few of the gang forced themselves into the room; the Commander was apprehended and thrown into the prison below. This insult aroused our compassion; accordingly we demanded he would be sent to a plantation or to the Essequibo until a ship arrived. But the raging crowd was not to be diverted. The Chief had misbehaved in many matters, and, if set free, he might desert to the enemy; together with a hundred other similar idle remarks. Soon, a new Commander was to be chosen from the Lords Councillors. This one, fearing a similar fate as his predecessor, of whom he was not at best of terms with, gave plenty [victuals]; thus we saw ourselves without lard and meat within a few days. It was then, one could hold out very well with bread and salt for a while; not to be sad about the time; custom was second nature, etc. In the meantime, many visited the imprisoned Commander; for whom, just as the wild rabble that listens only to lust and not to reason, even those, who had been most embittered towards him, started to gain respect again; if it had lasted longer, I doubt not, he would have been restored. Meanwhile it was decided by the Council that a night watch would be send out on the seacoast;[305] just as had been done in the last days of the captive Chief's; to wit, since one had received the news of the war. Every [member] of the Lords Councillors should take his turn to be in charge and would be relieved

305 *Brandwacht* literally means 'watch to prevent fire and plunder'; here it is the ship serving as a signal station in order to observe any approaching enemy ships.

after a sojourn of 14 days. I took down the minutes of what had passed. The second turn was mine. I was given four Christians, three Negroes, and five Indians in a small canoe, in which the imprisoned Chief had made a chest in order to keep the flintlocks dry. We went through the forest of *Marepaan*, right in view of the sea, *c.*1 hour within the river, between 13 and 14 miles below the fort. Fourteen days passed, and 2 more, without that I was [97] relieved; however, I did not dare to leave my post, so resolved to send one of my Christians with an Indian towards the fort to see what was going on and why I was not relieved. But it was Christmas, the new Commander merry It seemed I had been forgotten. Meanwhile, the following night, at about 2 o'clock, the man, who stood guard woke me, saying he saw a canoe. At once, I [got] out of my hammock and saw them too; because, notwithstanding the foggy sky, the moon provided that much light one could distinguish the objects from quite far off. I had called two or three [men] one time, but got no answer, and therefore gave orders to fire next to them. Next all my men woke up and presented themselves. In the meantime, the hostile canoe (because they were Indians from the Corantyne River, enemies of ours) slowly returned to their fleet, of which we had no knowledge yet. I commanded everyone to check their rifles, to knock the powder of the pan, and to put on some fresh; and distributed to each a few more bullets. Now we got into the canoe, and arranged in order: me, with another Zealander behind me and two Flemings in front, who were given orders to warn me at the first sight. After *c.* ½ an hour of paddling, we got sight of the Caribs (this is how we named the Corantyne people), and went slightly closer in order to count how strong they were. One counted twenty-seven and the other twenty-eight; in each canoe, when reckoned altogether, are at least twenty-four Indians. We were in a tight spot! Nevertheless, as the cowardice of the Indians was not unknown to me, as well as that three Christians were as good as thirty of the bravest among their men, we ran our canoe back to land where we took in all our baggage; next we four Christians held council and after having promised each other to live and die together, and to stand tall until the last drop of blood, we prepared to defend ourselves. Meanwhile [98] our Indians and Negroes made sufficiently clear they did not fancy this kind of work,without a doubt, if there would be any physical fighting, they would immediately jump into the water, swim towards land and run into the forest; for this is their only refuge on this kind of occasions,. At the same time we feared that the enemy fleet, favoured by the cover of the forest, might want to hinder us or fight us over the passage way. We had set out into the middle of the River with the tide, so that we could observe both sides of us, yet we encountered no enemy. In this manner we arrived at the end of the long reach,[306] so called because it requires a journey of more than 1 hour. Here I found a few Christians accompanied by a few Indians, who had been sent to relieve me. Now, I wanted to know, why they had not sent twenty to twenty-five of that ilk along to serve as scouts to here and there discover the enemies, because after 14 days, one could have paid each at the highest with a 2 pence knife. But everybody searches at his utmost in order to gain the favour of

306 A reach (*rak* in Dutch) is the straight part at the end of a river.

the Lords Directors, and, by keeping the costs low, to remain in favour. While we were waiting here for the next tide, the others had something to state to my men, which I was not allowed to hear. Suspecting some mischief here and thus separated from each other, I called upon the person whom I most trusted of my Christian men and asked him if he wanted to tell me this news, whether it were good or bad. It entailed that I was to be treated in the same manner as the imprisoned Commander, as soon as we were back at the fort again. Glad to know what to be prepared for, yet, also trying to find out who intended to play this trick on me, I asked the same friend again if he could enlighten me about this. He began to grin and said, if I could guess, he would then reveal the man to me. The first time was a hit, as I knew full well [99] who were my friends or enemies. It was a certain carouser, stationed at a place called Maikony,[307] to whom I had dispatched many cargoes for which I had very seldom seen returns. For all these goods sent to him I had a receipt, signed by his own hand, about which I had often warned him he would not be able to justify his policy in the homeland and that I, according to my duty, was forced to account for it in the (near) future. In the meantime we went steadily along on the tide and again arrived at the fort in the evening at about 7 o'clock. Soon, I went to see the new Commander to give him an account of what had happened during my night watch, but he was busy banqueting and too much occupied in conversation to pay attention to such trifles. I observed the situation, went stealthily to my room, opened my chest, took out the books and handed the same to a trusty friend through the window in order to safeguard them in his own [chest]. This happened without anyone knowing it, except that it was spotted by a certain young woman who, not being my enemy, immediately came to me and said that such a thing, if the people would learn of it, would be taken very wrong. I objected that I had nothing to do with the people, closed the box and joined the company, after whose departure the Chief, now feigning to be able to talk freely, warned me that I should not go in my chest, and that he warned me as a friend. I asked him the reason. He excused himself by saying he did not know of any reason; but that the people wanted to put me in chains. I gave him the answer I had given to the young woman, but now knowing what to do, I immediately went up to the very person, who had hatched the whole game, and asked him, what reason he had to put the people up against me. He denied it stoutly and strongly, and swore he had never had the slightest idea of doing so. I told him he should come with me into the galley and that I would convince him there with his own hand. Here [100] I showed him the account and threw it into the fire. You see, this is how I presented him the apple of discord with a laugh. Indeed, so it was; and with it the entire storm vanished.

307 Maikony is probably an Amerindian village whereas the stationed rake is probably a *legger* or *factoor*, the delegate at a trading post of the Berbice colony. See also the outpost at the 'Rivier Majecoene' at the Berbice map of S. H. Sanders (NL-HaNA_4.VELH_576A). See Figure 15.

CHAPTER XIX.

Arrival of two ships. Strike of the imprisoned Commander and appointment of a new one. Arrival of a new secretary in place of the author. Departure of the same. Appearance of a peace-fire. Meeting of three ships. Arrival of the author before Flushing, etc.

While the things were in this state, in the month of January 1674, we received tidings from the fort concerning the arrival of two ships, which caused unusual happiness, testified by the firing of three cannon shots. The large boat was immediately to be sent down [river] in order to ascertain the truth. In the meantime the said ships went upstream and dropped their anchors on the ground in front of the fort, after which the Commander was sent on board to welcome the Captains, and I presented myself first to the Flagman who had been my first Chief; secondly to the other Commander, who had formerly been his steersman and Lieutenant, and had now come here to occupy the post of Commander for the space of 1 year [interim]. I was very courteously received on both ships and brought back to land in the Admiral's sloop; where the next day the two other Captains were presented; next, after the Lords Councillors were summoned, it was decided in their meeting to immediately release the imprisoned Commander immediately, then the commission [101] of the new Commander was read, and eventually the day spent merrymaking.

With the said two ships a new secretary arrived, too: because as my time had expired, and because I was not inclined to stay longer in that position on the Berbice River, I had long ago asked that the Directors would choose to appoint a suitable person to succeed me in my position. I immediately started to instruct this person concerning that which he had to observe while performing his duties; however, without letting him take care of anything, retaining the management to myself until the time of my departure.

In the meantime, after between *c.* 3 and 4 weeks, the Captain who had carried the flag, having had his ship cleaned in the river, and taken in some sugar and dye, in order to go to sea with ballast (because he was fitted out for privateering, with twenty-six pieces of ordnance and 124 men) started to prepare for his departure; therefore, a meeting having been convened, it was indeed decided (notwithstanding the order carried by the Lords Directors; for, the imprisoned Commander would depart as Captain with the second to the homeland) he should travel as a passenger, and would stay in his cabin, and also that the Lieutenant should command the second ship as a Captain, on which a place had been ordered for me. This being arranged in such manner, they went out to sea *c.* 7 or 8 days later in order to go cruising [privateering] off the coast of Barbados.

Meanwhile, preparations were also made for the departure of our ship; at the end of the month of February, having delivered the merchandise, or cargoes, to the new secretary, I used the remaining time to enjoy myself in visiting the Lords Planters who presented me with chickens, tame ducks, turkeys, etc., as provisions for my voyage. On the 15 March the [102] ship left for the mouth of the river, though I still had certain special affaires to settle; not before 18 March, accompanied by the

Chief and the gentlemen Beekman and Heyn, my most important friends, I was brought on board with a canoe. On 22 March [1674], in the morning at daybreak, we went out to sea; the ship was named *d'Eendracht*, and the Captain Adriaan de Vyver, and having arrived at between 6 and 8 fathoms of water, the anchor was cast to the ground. Now the large bark, or boat was moored next to us in order to deliver the remainder of the cargo to us together with some provisions for the journey. Now, the last meal was shared and our farewell drinks; next once three guns were fired from both sides, the final ones by us, to thank the friends, the anchor was weighed and we set sail; by evening the land was already out of sight. We had generally good weather, but for some winds now and then mixed for *c.* 2 hours with *travado* [storms]. These are sudden strong winds which toss the ships as if they would be torn to pieces, but usually do not last very long. But on the latitude of the Island of Bermudas we were hit by a heavy storm which imposed itself from midday at about 12 (o'clock) until about 11 o'clock late at night with terrible violence. During most of that time, as one could neither talk nor stand, I laid in my bunk; but I was fetched out of it at about 8 or 9 o'clock in the evening by the Captain, who told me there was something to see, which often is not seen by people who have sailed the seas for 20 years. It was a light, like a candle; it showed itself on top of the wing of the great mast and is named a "Peace fire" [Saint Elmo's fire] by the Dutch, and regarded by the old seamen as a sign that the storm is at its summit. Indeed, the wind diminished hand over hand; the next day in the morning the weather was completely calm; however, the sea was still very troubled, and rolled along in huge waves. Thus we sailed for 9 weeks and 2 [103] days, without having observed land or ships; I might well have said with Ovid:

Quocunque aspicio, nihil est nisi Pontus et æther.[308]

But on the said second day in the late afternoon, a sail was seen towards which we immediately set course. A half an hour later we discovered two more ships with the first; we then prepared everything to stand tall. We counted twenty-eight pieces and eighty-four heads altogether, among them two women; though we were laden 14 feet deep, which would have been not a little inconvenient for us, if it had come to the pinch. In the evening at 9 o'clock we came within reach of the cannons of one another. We showed the Prince's flag [and] the three others the Burgundy Cross or the Spanish flag.[309] Next the sails were brought to the wind and the skippers of the Spanish ships were sent to board us, to show their passes. They came from Bilbao and travelling to Greenland. Yet our Captain, not sufficiently satisfied with these, had the ships searched to see if they were carrying any 'non-free' goods, but one found nothing else than whaling equipment. They

308 Here Van Berkel refers to the description of Tomis by Ovid. The latter was banned to Tomis on the Black Sea: *quocunque aspicio nihil est, nisi Pontus et aer/ fluctibus hic tumidus, nubibus ille minax* wich may be translated as 'In whatever direction I look, there is nothing except sea and air, one swollen with waves, the other menacing with clouds', Tristia 1.2: 23-24.

309 The *Prinsenvlag,* or Prince's flag, counted three red, white, and blue horizontal stripes. The flag with the Burgondy Cross, or the Spanish flag, was, until 1785, coloured white with a red knotted cross.

announced to us we were at peace with England, and that we would be in sight of *Fero* in the morning. Indeed, we found ourselves, having parted that evening, in sight of that island the next day, being Saturday; on Sunday we watered there close under with little wind, so therefore used this occasion to careen our ship and clean it , so that it might sail better. On the same evening we set sail again, and in the morning, at daybreak, we sailed past various fishermen from whom we received a fresh quantity of cod, for which we gave them a few knick knacks in return. On following Tuesday, we came in sight of a French privateer to windward. We made for him, but he immediately raised all sails and threw everything on deck overboard. [104] In the meantime we could not gain on him sufficiently by tacking, for he was too high [in the wind] and our freight was too heavy; next we changed course after chasing him for 1½ hour. About 2 or 3 days later, a roqual [fin fish] came near us, with which we passed a merry time. Finally, after a few days of sailing and tacking, we found ourselves near Texel, where we had orders to run in; but since four warships were busy leaving, we tacked to the island of Schouwe. Here we dropped anchor to wait for a suitable tide. The next morning we set sail again and arrived before Flushing at about midday, where for the final time, we cast it to the ground; having thus spent 11 weeks minus 2 days *en route*.

THE END

[105]

AMERICAN VOYAGES
SECOND PART.
Containing A
VOYAGE to SURINAM
Situated in the Northern Part of the
Landscape
GUIANA.

[106] blanco

[107]

VOYAGE to SURINAM

CHAPTER I.

Desire of the author to go once more to foreign countries. Gets, through a specific happening, the opportunity to do so. Is appointed manager of a plantation in Surinam. Sets sail. Arrival in the River Surinam, etc.

The craving to go once more to foreign countries was, despite the inconveniences one often has to suffer there, not extinguished in such a way that I wanted to have seized another opportunity to undertake a new journey. Meanwhile, I would like to confess that the Berbice River was not the place to which my affection would stretch. The loneliness was there too great; being a lover of society and people all my life, I had seen, during my previous voyage, enough lifeless things, not to wage a second trip there, although the opportunity was proposed there to me on more than one occasion. Because I had served the Lords Directors not that badly or their house always stood open for me. In the meantime, just as you cannot get what you want most of the time nor that you do not always have the strength to follow your own inclinations, I had been kept waiting for so long I had given up all hope, and had started to organise things to change my way of life seriously; when quite unexpectedly an opportunity arose to satisfy my desire. A certain gentleman, who had a beautiful plantation in Surinam, received, in addition to a few of his relatives, an inheritance of rather fair importance, which, if he [108] wanted to have it rightly divided, urged him to personally come over to Zealand. He made this journey, but had barely set foot on land or he learnt there had been that much selfishness that the division and distribution was not going to be done easily. Indeed, as everyone was obstinate or at least that there were litigious people, the work was rapidly taken to court; the refuge of unrighteous people who by this means tried to appropriate more than they rightfully deserve. The winter, already in progress, when the said Gentleman arrived, ran its course without having much advanced [on the matter]; therefore not knowing when one could expect the end of it, and the plantation in Surinam could not remain without a supervisor to oversee it, he started enquiring for a suitable person; having, for this purpose, turned to the Lords Directors, I was proposed to him, and the next morning I was summoned to discuss the matter later on that very evening. The conditions were that reasonable that, after a few words, they wished me luck with managing the plantation. And, as there was a ship loading at that moment, called the *Juff. Sophia*,[310] carrying several small cannons, which was bound to go there for a few private persons, I received instructions to get myself prepared. The contract held good for 4 years, which I considered to be a handsome time, and I made as many preparations as if I would have ended my life in that colony. Meanwhile the ship had been loaded and when the ship owners had been feasting one or two times together on board, the skipper, called Cornelis Blom, received instructions to set sail to sea with the first good wind. This happened on 17 April 1680. The weather was all to be desired for; the wind favourable; the company good (because there were, besides myself, another three passengers in the ship, all fine fellows living in Surinam); in sum, if it had not been the steady motion of the waves, reminding us that we were on the fields of Neptune, we might have described our voyage as a gentle [109] transfer from one country to the other. In this way we reached the latitude of the Canaries, where we met with the trade winds a few days later; fortunately we took them somewhat high. Because afterwards, during foggy weather, we fell away several miles; this should have otherwise given us great difficulty in coming up again. Finally, having been at sea for between 9 and 10 weeks, without any remarkable encounters, we cast anchor in the mouth of the Surinam River on 23 June [1680].

CHAPTER II.

Situation of the River Surinam. Fish in the same. Wonderful peculiarity of the torpedo fish. Quantity of waterfalls, etc.

The river is located at between 6 and 5½ degrees latitude North of the Line [Equator].[311] At the entrance, it has several sandbanks, however, at high water 3 fathoms deep, and at spring tides even deeper. The width at the mouth is *c.*1 mile, which it usually retains until the place where it divides into two curved arms [branches], of which one stretches towards the East, the Commewijne, and the other, shooting towards the West, is called the Surinam. These branches, alongside which

---

310 Many Dutch ships are called *Juffrouw* or, abbreviated, *Juffr.* meaning housewife, the term used for married women of the Dutch middle-class.

311 After a few adaptions, brought together in Chapter I, the publisher of Van Berkel's *American Voyages*, takes up G. Warren's Chapter I *Of the River*, merely assigning a new chapter number, viz. Chapter II. Again some lines were added to Warren's first chapter (or rather, to its translation). In it, Chapter I reads: 'Which is in Six, of Five and a half Degrees of Northerly Latitude, barr'd with Sand at the Entrance: but yet, Three Fathom deep at High-Water; and in Spring Tides more. 'T is about a League over at the Mouth, of which breadth, or but very little narrower, it holds five Leagues, up to a small Village, call'd the *Fort*; and then, by degrees, in two Leagues farther, decreases a Mile, and so continues as far as hath been discover'd. It hath a Channel on either side, to the *East*, and *West*, but the first is reputed best, in which, Vessels of 300 Tons have sailed neer 20 Leagues up to the Metropolis or chief Town of the Colony, called *Toorarica*, consisting of about One hundred Dwelling Houses, and a Chappel. Before the Town is a very fair Bay or Harbour, large enough to contain an Hundred Sail of Ships. 'T is on both sides Woody, unless here [p. 2] and there a Plantation be open to it; and so perfect a *Meander*, that in a matter of fifteen Leagues sailing, a Ships steers all points of the Compass'; G. Warren, op. cit., 1667, pp. 1-2.

stretch a multitude of plantations, and from which, when crossing the savannahs or pastures in fine weather, one can reach the other within half a day one, are each *c.*½ mile wide, and that deep they can be sailed by the largest ships for *c.* 30 miles up the river; furthermore, they are beset with forest on both sides. At *c.* 2 miles from the mouth of the river, directly along the Surinam River, one constructed a stone fort called Parimari- [110] bo, as well as a village counting between fifty and sixty houses; somewhat higher up, on a branch of the same river, a strong house has been built during the government of the Lords van Sommelsdijk. Still higher up, on the same river, 'Zandpunt' [Sandy Point] is located, a village of Christians, consisting of between twenty-five and thirty houses and a church. Above this village there is a place called Jew's Quarter, because many Jews live there. Here are the best plantations of the entire colony. It was formerly the furthest settlement but the sister of the Lords of Sommelsdijk, having arrived in the year 1684 together with her company of Labadists, has founded a plantation even higher up, bearing the name of their sect. At the confluence of the two river branches, the Commewijne and Surinam, the 'Krabbebosch' [Crab Forest] is located, drowned land, which cannot house a fort; otherwise both rivers could have been defended there. But at the [confluence] of the Commewijne and the Cottica, a branch of the same mouth of the entire river, a fort of fair strength is to be seen. Along these branches many plantations are founded, too, though as far as between *c.* 15 and 16 miles as well as various [plantations] along a certain creek, called Piereka, coming out

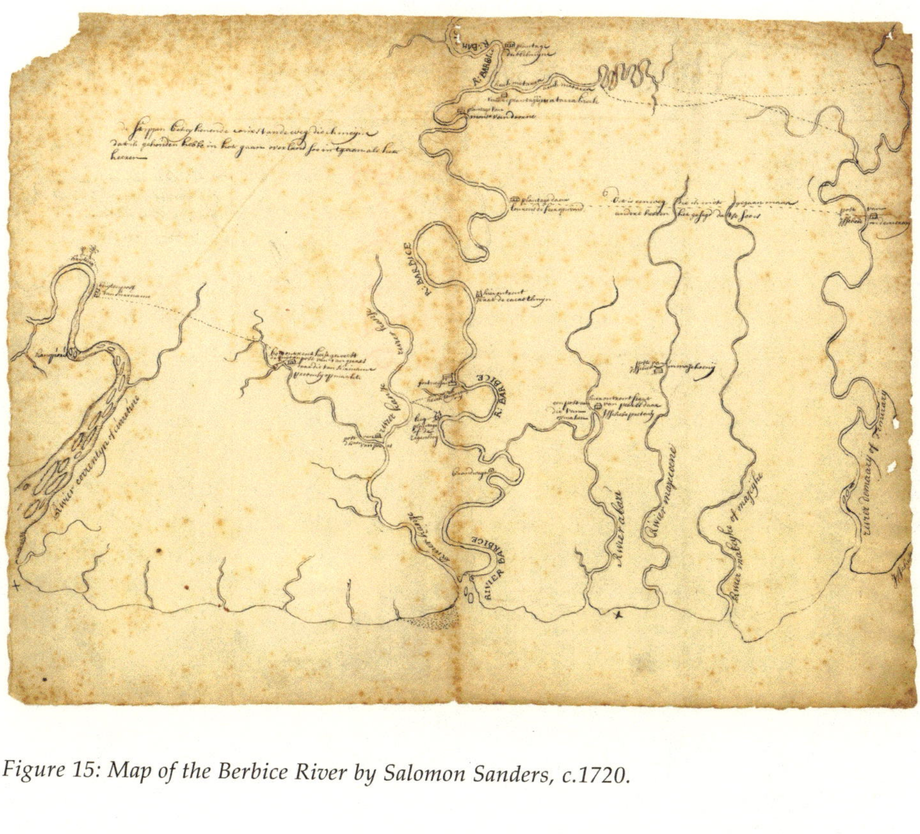

Figure 15: Map of the Berbice River by Salomon Sanders, c.1720.

of the Cottica into the Commewijne. Still there are more creeks alongside which plantations are also located, too long to mention them all here, and which cannot be depicted intelligibly for the reader.

This is the situation of the river which is also very rich in fish; it is well provided with an inmeasurable quantity of large fish, and also of others that are not quite edible; they are, however, rare and worthy of observation, such as, amongst others, the swordfish, which is so called because of a bone that grows out of its snout, and resembles a sword or rather a saw, of which I have seen that must measured *c.* 1 ell long. There is, however, another kind of fish, called *manaty*, which feeds alongside the river on bushes or leaves of such. She is suckled by her young like a cow, and tastes more like meat than [111] like fish. The third kind of fish I shall merely name here, because it is that strange it would be worth the trouble to describe it separately. Its name is torpedo, or in English numb eel, that is to say, a numbing eel or 'paling'; when alive it touches any creature or, when brought into contact with it, gives to all limbs of the same such numbness and paralysis they are insensible for a long time and cannot be used; it is credible that various people drowned who were unlucky when swimming across the river to be touched by one of these fish. They do the same thing, when they are but touched with the end of a long stick, or whenever a man holds the hand of another who has been numbed. We witnessed this when such a fish was caught and thrown on land and a dog that sniffed at it took it in his mouth and suddenly fell to the ground. The dog's Master, seeing this, went towards it and thought of taking it away but he was immediately numbed in all his limbs, without being able to move at all. Another man who stood next to him, and who wanted to drag him away, was also affected by it; it lasted that long that this eel escaped; then they all totally recovered and could turn and move themselves as before.

The plantations are found *c.* 30 miles up along the river; it appears that the colony will not extend her boundaries further on account of various cataracts, or waterfalls, on both sides of the same, where the passage of the river, because of the water that falls with force from the edges of the boulders being the best way of bringing all necessaries higher up, is at once rendered unusable. Because if there was only one single waterfall, means would be found in time to deal with it, but now a few [falls] occur about every 5 or 6 miles, and that for as high up in the land as already [112] known. It happened once that a few Indians, who had come from above and had murdered an English woman and plundered the house in which she was staying, were tracked down in the vicinity of these waterfalls. For this, several men were engaged who were supplied with the only the best; having carried their vessel overland, passing seven or eight of these waterfalls, they eventually had to turn back, without doing anything because they did not see any Indians at all. Now when, on their return, a few of them agreed to go down these falls with their vessels, some of them were smashed to pieces, and the others barely escaped with their lives. Such waterfalls are common in all rivers upon this coast and prevents one from discovering this rich country properly.

CHAPTER III.

On the climate or temperature of the country, together with some peculiarities that concern this matter.

From November till in July it is but moderately hot here, caused by the clouds that hang overhead, and by the abundant rain which falls and then refreshes the soil as well because of the continuous blowing of the northeastern wind which cools the air not a little. During the other 5 months, when no rain falls, and one comes to miss the sweet shadow of the clouds, it is already very hot here, and that is not only from the reflection or the rebound of the sunbeams on the often sandy soil, but also from the sun itself which is then that close; indeed the heat would be hardly bearable, were it not somewhat moderated by the aforesaid [113] coolness. Because this land is so close to the Line, day and night by and large quite the same or do not differ more than 1 hour, because the sun never rises earlier or later or sets half an hour before or half an hour after 6 o'clock. The unchangeable warmth causes this land to be much more pleasant for old than for young people. Because it seems as if the country smiles at them, and rejuvenates their years; for those who were formerly lame, weary and weak, become youthful and full of life again here. The young people on the contrary lose much of their strength here, and come to fall away earlier than in northern countries, although Surinam is otherwise sufficiently healthy enough for moderately sound people. The diseases most common here are cold and hot fevers, yaws,[312] and the 'water' called land disease [dropsy] there.[313] At first, the people were mightily troubled with it; but I believe it was more due to bad housing and miserable food than the intemperateness of the country. Yaws is almost one and the same disease as the Spanish Pox;[314] one catches it only too easily through intercourse with the Indian women, who seem to be infected with it naturally; just as this disease, too, which was first brought to us by the Spaniards, is at present not considered strange at all in any part of Europe. It is produced by a not well attended sore, because the country is by nature that opposed to such things it causes change into this miserable and almost incurable disease. The water disease or land disease has come, in my opinion, to the population by means of unhealthy and poor food, of which the poor servants had to do with, through the lack of good Lords and Masters in that sorry country, because I noticed there that

---

312 Yaws is a chronic infection. Occuring widely in Africa, Asia and Iberian America, it is caused by a bacterium that affects the skin, cartilage and bones, spreading to all who come in contact with it. Yaws results in skin lesions which increase if not treated properly. H. Benjamins & J. Snelleman (eds), *Encyclopaedie van Nederlandsch West-Indië*, Den Haag/Leiden: Martinus Nijhoff/E.J. Brill, 1914-1917, suggests *Framboesia tropica* referring to Warren, op. cit., 1669, p. 7.

313 Water… land-disease: see note 301.

314 Spanish pox: 'French-Pox', see G. Warren, op. cit., 1667, p. 4. The 'French disease' was first described after a French invasion of Naples in *c.*1495. This term was adopted by the English. However, a strong hypothesis has it that the Spaniards introduced syphilis from the Americas to Europe, Hence the term 'Spanish pox' which their enemies, i.e., the French and Dutch applied. Therefore, the Dutch translation of Warren, *Een onpartydige beschrijvinge*, speaks of the 'sieckte die ons eerst door de Spanjaerts toegebracht is' ('the disease first inflicted upon us by the Spaniards'). Needless to say, the Spaniards preferred the description 'French pox'.

scarcely anybody else has been suffering from this than this sort of people. Because the unhealthy food does not give nothing but heavy blood and drugged spirits; that is why these people do not take any pleasure for themselves, but waste away; therefore they finally do not have sufficient strength to expel the evil fancies and moods, which such [114] melancholic people develop more and more; thus they often die and perish, if the disease is not attended to from the start.

The land next to the river mouth is low, woody, and full of swamps, or drowned [inundated] places. Thirty miles higher up, it is high and mountainous, with in between large and open fields or plains which here and there are that grown with small bushes, it appears they were small islands in a green sea. It is an excellent pleasure to see the wonderful and delightful works of nature in the small beasts, that, in comical postures, jump from one branch of these evergreen trees to another, on which a continuous shooting and falling of the leaves is to be seen. Because as soon as one falls, another takes its place. In the meantime, the trees are never deprived of their summer livery. On some, one will always find blossoms and some fruits of which a few are still unripe, whilst the rest is riper than others. None of the human senses has more pleasure in these forests than the sense of smell, because the trees there diffuse their spicy scent far around in the air; thus the seasick people are hughly refreshed thereby.

It is also wonderful to observe the varied worms this hot and humid land produces. I have seen a white spot, which at first was not larger than a pin's head; on a fresh soft outgrowth of a root of a large tree, it grew within 2 or 3 days into a kind of somerbird, or 'pepel' [butterfly], with beautiful black and saffron colour speckled wings. I have found others, which were not yet fully grown but stuck that firmly onto the bark of the tree, as if they were grown to it. There is another kind, called the camel fly because of its long neck of which I do not know how it is produced; but when it has lived a while, it falls to the ground, roots, and changes [115] into a plant.[315] Without doubt this will appear to be incredible, but I can confirm it is as true as the manifold changes of the silkworm.[316]

315 On the camel fly: 'It is a belief among certain of the present-day Creoles that "walking-leaf" and "stick" insects thus change into plants.' See footnote in W.E. Roth, op. cit., 1948, p. 119.

316 Warren states: 'This I relate, not from any certian Knowledge of my own, but I was encouraged to insert it, from the Information of the Honourable *William Byam*, Lord General of *Guiana*, and Governour of *Surinam*, who, I am sure is too much a Gentleman to be the Author of a Lye. Many more Observations of this Nature no doubt I might have made, if the vanity of my years would have suffered me to mind it. The Gouvernment is Monarchical, an Imitation of ours, by a Gouvernour, Council, and Assembly; the Laws of *England* are also theirs, to which are added some by Constitutions, no less obliging, proper to the Conveniences of that Country'. G. Warren, op. cit., 1667, p. 6. This sentence has been copied in the Dutch translation, but was omitted by the publisher of *American Voyages*.

CHAPTER IV.

On the Food.

This consists of yams, plantains, and cassava instead of bread. The first is a root which bears a cluster as hops do. It becomes ripe within 8 months and when boiled or roasted, it is dry and crumbly. As far as its taste is concerned, there is not much to say, because I could never find much taste in it. Plantains are the fruit of a tree which requires about a year before it is fully grown. It is quite the same as the husk or shell of a bean, but larger. Forty or fifty hang in a bunch, but the tree never bears more than one. One picks them before they become very ripe, and [are] boiled or roasted. According to my feelings this kind of bread is no better than the former. The last, namely cassava, which can properly be called bread is [made] of a kind of root as thick as a man's leg but of various shapes. From it sprouts a tree with the height of 8 feet. The root is pulled out when the tree is 1 year old, and is replanted with the sticks [cuttings] of the tree, which one puts into the earth. The root is taken out and scraped; the juice, which is an evil poison, is pressed out of it. Afterwards it is dried and pounded; of this meal round cakes are baked on hot stones which are half a thumb thick. It is nice when they are freshly baked but when 1 day old, there is little taste to it. From this cassava the Indians make various kinds of strong drink, of which a certain kind, called *perrinoe*, is indeed good, slightly resembling [116] our strongest March beers which are 1 year old.[317] We have described in the chapter dealing with the drinks on the Berbice River, how this beverage is manufactured and therefore will not repeat it here.[318]

Meat and fish have to be continuously brought here from New England, Virginia, and other places. Although the forests and rivers are sufficient in providing everything but the constant rain and the floods prevent that the fish can be caught in such a quantity, as one would certainly like to have them. Although there is nevertheless by day that much to obtain that nobody who is willing to take the trouble has any reason to complain about the lack of it. The fish there are very tasty but one, which is somewhat tasty; one will quickly notice, how much better the meat is in our Netherlands than out here, because the same kind of beasts kept over there have, in these hot countries, very poor meat which has no taste, except for the pigs, which are much fatter and of better taste here than in the homeland.

317 In order to have enough stock in the summer, several German breweries produced extra strong, preservable beer in March. This routine apparently existed in England, too, for 'March-beer', see G. Warren, op. cit., 1667, p. 7.

318 The section omitted from Warren's Dutch translation reads in the English original: 'But the relation of their manner of Brewing it, will, I believe, Rebate the edge of any one's desire here, which, perhaps, might be otherwise sharp enough to taste it; First, they take *Cassader*-bread bak'd for that purpose very black, which the oldest Women, and snotty Nose Children chaw in their Mouths, and with as much Spittle as they can, throw into a Jar of Water, so letting it stand a while, then strain the Bread from it, and with some Chaw'd Potatoes set it a working, which becomes fit to drink in few days. The English [8] Planters make their Cool Drink of the Juice of Sugar-Canes, and Water boyl'd together, a most pleasant Liquor, and suppos'd wholsom'. G. Warren, op. cit., 1667, p. 7. See note 286 on *pernouw* and *bassia*, and the text in A. van Berkel, op. cit., 1695, p. 53 and 74.

At a certain time of the year tortoises or turtles, too, are caught on the seacoast, not of those whose shell is that expensive and costly; but they do weigh between *c.* 200 and 300 pounds. The females are considered best and often have quite a small barrel full of eggs in their stomach, of which each is as large as a hen's egg but not that good. These eggs they lay, when crawling out of the water, in the sand where they cover them with the same, and thus let them incubate through the heat of the sun. The salted flesh of the turtles can be eaten in times of great need; for hunger, it is said, sweetens raw beans, but when fresh, it is prized highly by some as excellent food. Although I do not fancy them a lot, though the taste is not that unpleasant, yet it always burdened the stomach which for something new is of the weakest. However, it cannot represent anything else but coarse and slimy food because it goes bad that easily; it immediately begins to stink, when one leaves it [117] unsalted for only 2 hours after the animal is killed. Sheep cannot be bred here at all, because it seems these animals thrive better in a cold and dry country than in a hot and damp one. Oxen and cows thrive well, notably on the seacoast, but at the moment there are not that many yet that the butchers would have much to do; however, there would be an infinite number of swine if the bats, which bite off their nipples, did not prevent it.[319]

CHAPTER V.

On the birds and animals.

I believe there is not a more beautiful or better kind of birds to be found in the world, than in this region. Only the nightingale with its lovely little warble is wanting; because it seems that this country is all too sad and rough for such a sweet guest. The birds, which are here, make no other note or common tune than that which one can only be terrified by, because one howls, another screeches, the third groans and weeps, but all together they sound as if it was music out of hell. Thus then what is missing in the sweetness of the voice, of which one does not fatten, is made up for by other things which are good and excellent for man's life and pleasure, because over here the ducks, teal, arrow tails [widgeon], plovers, or wild doves, snipes, pheasants, partridges, etc., which are much larger and quite as good as those in the homeland, are plentiful everywhere. Here the parrots are more common than crows in the Netherlands. And on the seacoast lives a certain bird whose name I do not remember,[320] which is that large that, whenever a few of them are together and at some distance from us, one would think there would be, marching soberly, a company of soldiers along the sand, because their feathers of

319 Roth translated here: 'Oxen and cows thrive well, especially on the sea-coast: but they are not so particularly plentiful there that the butchers have much <u>salting</u> to do.' However, Van Berkel stated that they are not abundant yet, W.E. Roth, op. cit., 1948, p. 121.

320 According to Roth, Warren's original text refers to flamingoes (*Phoenicopteris rubber*), see W.E. Roth, op. cit., 1948, p. 122. These tall pinkish birds are common in the continental Antilles but may reach the Orinoco delta; see S. Hilty, *Birds of Venezuela* (2nd Edition), New Jersey: Princeton University Press, 2003, p. 205. On the other hand, the description better suits the smaller scarlet ibis (*Eudocimus ruber*) which frequents the seacoast of the Guianas.

scarlet paint which can be imitated [118] by no art, are that brilliant they almost blind the eyes of those who look at them. There is yet another kind of bird which surpasses them in beauty, although they differ hugely from the other in size, [being] no greater than a wild bee or bumblebee. Turning up here and there in the forests, they show such multitude of the most beautiful lively colours it is impossible to describe it. One calls them honey birds,[321] because they mostly obtain their food from the flowers. Moreover, a certain kind of blackbird hangs is nests upon the utmost end of the branches of trees, out of fear of thievish monkeys, which would otherwise destroy the same.[322] I should have included here something about the bats, but as one still disputes as to whether they are birds or beasts, I shall postpone the it's description until dealing with the noxious animals, thinking it would serve better to discuss them there. In the meantime, Surinam is well provided with all sorts of bats; thus, if it would praise this country, one would be able to say that the stars in the skies were more readily to be counted than the various sorts of these monsters. But I will not abuse the patience of the reader longer and provide a short description of the most prominent animals which enter my mind: deer,[323] hares,[324] rabbits,[325] armadillos, hogs, buffaloes,[326] anteaters, jaguars, etc. Baboons,[327] quottoes, apes, marmosets, cuscharees, sloths live in the trees, as do many others of which I have forgotten the names. The deer are almost like ours in the homeland. The hares resemble a suckling pig more than any other animal I have seen. They are brown and smooth-haired, speckled with white and larger than the hares in the homeland, to which they have no resemblance except for the mouth. It is an extremely good meat and much better than any quadruped animal known to us in the Netherlands. The rabbits are red-haired, not of that good a taste, [119] also smaller than the hares which they otherwise resemble in shape. The armadillos are of two kinds, one large and the other somewhat smaller.[328] Of the larger ones I have seen specimens weighing 80 pounds. They have short legs and three claws on their feet; a head like the pigs, no teeth, and a small mouth. They are covered with scales except for the head and the stomach which no pike or lance can pierce, unless it could be hit in between the joints of the scales. They bore themselves in the ground with their snout and paws; it would be a very good food, if they would not have had such a strong smell of musk. There are three kinds of hogs of which one, like an otter, lives mostly in the water.[329] These are highly prized, but I have never had

---

321 The *honingvogel*, or *kolibrie* in Dutch, refers to the hummingbird (*Trochilidae*).

322 The well-known blackbird that builds hanging nests in the Guianas is the very noisy blue-eyed caciques with a yellow or red tail (*Cacicus* sp.).

323 Deer: of which there is a small species, *kuriaku* (Sr.) (*Mazuma gouazoubira*); and, a larger: the *redidia* (Sr.) (*Mazama americana*) as well as the savannah deer, or *sabanadia* (Sr.) (*Odocileus virginianus*)

324 Hares: *paca* (Sr.), *labba* (G.) (*Agouti paca*).

325 Rabbits: *konkoni, aguti* (Sr.) or *agouti, agauti* (*Dasyprocta leporina*).

326 Buffaloes: here the tapir or *bofro* (Sr.) (*Tapirus terrestris*) is referred to.

327 G. Warren, op. cit., 1669, p. 12, mentions *meerkatten* (mongoose). G. Warren, op. cit., 1667, p. 11 gives 'baboons'. Mongoose and baboons do not inhabit the Americas. Howler monkeys (*Alouatta* sp.) are referred to here.

328 Armadillos: the small nine-banded armadillo (*Dasypus novemcinctus*); a larger armadillo (*Dasypus kappleri*) and the giant species (*Priodontes maximus*) inhabit the Guianas.

329 The capybara (*Hydochaeris hydrochaeris*).

the luck to see one. The two other kinds are called *pakkyra* and *pinko*.[330] The first has a navel on its back, is coloured grey, and but moderately good food. The *pinko* is not as large as our hogs and just as good. The buffalo is said to be as large as one of our 2-year old cattle and just as good food too. I cannot describe this kind of animals in more detail because they never came on my path, as long as I lived out here; likewise I have learnt they very rarely come as far down as where I resided.

The anteater is of the size of a common pig,[331] coloured dark grey, with a long hairy tail like a fox or squirrel, with which it covers its whole body against the rain. It has a small head, but its snout is *c.*1 foot long measured from the eye; furthermore no teeth, its tongue is long and fine: it can stick it out to the length of *c.*1 foot. It puts it in the nests of the ants which must necessarily stick to it; thus slings them into its crop or stomach, having no other food as these small animals. It is a strong animal, notably in the foremost part of its body. It has sharp claws, the width of 1½ inch, with which it can do serious harm, [120] but the best is: it moves slowly so that one can easily escape from it. Its flesh is not the best or the sweetest, but when one is very hungry, one has to swallow it.

There are three kinds of tigers: black, speckled [spotted] and red.[332] The first is regarded as the cruelest, but is rarely seen in inhabited places. The spotted, I believe, are misnamed because they are rather leopards than tigers; they do most damage to the people by destroying their cattle and poultry, such as chickens, geese, and such. They are that strong that one of them will jump over a garden [fence] of between 5 and 6 feet high with a pig in its mouth. For example, one of them came to the populated places and having killed a 2-year old cow dragged it to more than a quarter of an hour away into the forest. Yet, they will not attack anybody by day, unless they are very hungry or wounded; I have never heard of more than two or three people being torn apart, ever since the foundation of this colony. One of them was a [hunter],[333] a lively fellow, who had always wished he might once find a tiger; he had frequently lamented had never had the luck to encounter one of these beasts during all his hunting. At last it happened one night when he was lying in his hammock with the doors open that a tiger came there, seized him, and carried him off into the forest for 2 hours. He called in vain for help, although an English woman next door in a closed house heard him, and encouraged herself by firing a musket from the window. But those who have had to do with these animals know that a tiger will not drop its prey on the slightest noise. The next day they found the man whose head and shoulders were eaten off. It is noteworthy that there are not that many tigers in those regions as before, partly because they have gone further into the forests, and partly because many have been caught by hunters. A certain Jan Miller told [121] me how very courageous he had been, having all in all killed no less than between twelve and fourteen of them with

330 Pakkyra: *pakira* (Sr.) (*Tayassu tajacu*); pinko: *pingo* (Sr.) (*Tayassu pecari*).

331 Anteater or antbear: the giant anteater or *tamanuwa* (Sr.) (*Myrmecophaga tridacta*).

332 The black panther (*Felis yaguarondi*), the jaguar (*Panthera onca*), and the puma (*Felis concolor*).

333 The Dutch edition of Van Berkel (1695) gives 'Huysman', duly copied from Warren's Dutch translation, op. cit., 1669, p. 12; G. Warren, op. cit., 1667, p. 12, gives 'Huntsman'. In *American Voyages*, this error in the Dutch translation of 1669 is simply copied and *Huysman* ('houseman' or the surname Huysman) is used instead of 'huntsman'.

a gun or spear, having escaped miraculously with his life and hurt very badly by others. There are not that much red tigers as others, and these are not as cruel as the previously mentioned ones.

In the forests, a quantity of land turtles is to be found, which are not three-quarter larger than those on the seacoast.[334] Their shell is that hard and strong a loaded cart could cross over it without breaking or cracking it; they protect themselves with it, being otherwise defenceless against all her enemies, except for men and tigers. Men open the turtle houses with an axe; the tigers turn them over and then devour their flesh. They eat everything that comes in their way; the habitants are accustomed to lock a number of them up in a slum in order to make use of them when it suits; considered not the worst fare in these regions.

Moreover, porcupines correspond almost to hedgehogs, but are somewhat larger and armed all over with white and black spines like the quills of a pen, 2 hands long and sharp as needles; nature has taught them to shoot these with wonderful dexterity from all sides at those who would want to catch them.[335]

The monkeys and 'meerkatten' are already known in the homeland,[336] and everywhere, so there is no need to describe them in particular; but there is one thing about the meerkats in these regions I believe is different from all others, and which I cannot pass by without mentioning in this place. To wit, at a certain hour by day as well as by night, they produce such a horrible screech with their hollow throats that if you are not used to hearing it, you can probably not think of something more strange and awful; this shrieking is heard further than 2 miles from the place where these beasts hide out. [122]

The marmoset is a pretty little animal of a yellow and green colour,[337] much smaller than an ape; yet it commandeers and, to some extent, rules all these rope dancers, by riding on their backs and jumping with them from one tree to another, spurring them on here, there, and upwards; they bite them in the ears, the latter not knowing how either to reach it, restrain it. or is pushed "out of the saddle".

The quotto has various black shades but larger than an ape; it has a long tail with which it swings from one tree branch to another.[338] They have a red face, the hair hanging over the forehead making it look like an old hag. Its scream has a sharp, marvellous sound.

The cuscary is black, smaller than a marmoset, and entirely shaped like a lion.[339]

---

334 The land tortoises (*Chelonoidis* sp.) and sea turtles (*Dermochelys coriacea, Chelonia mydas, Lepidochelys olivacea*).

335 Porcupines: *gindyamaka* (Sr.) *(Coendoe prehensilis)* or *koni gindyamaka* (Sr.) (*Coendoe melanurus*).

336 Monkeys and 'meerkatten': the real 'meerkat' is from Africa. Van Berkel probably meant the baboon or opossum (*Chironectes minimus*). Other South American animals to be considered as 'meerkatten' are coati (*Nasua nasua*), ayra (*Eira Barbara*) or 'bush dogs' (*Procyon cancrivorus, Speothos venaticus*).

337 The marmoset (*Callitrichidae*).

338 The red-faced spider monkey or Guana spider monkey (*Ateles paniscus*) also known as *kwatta* (Dutch) and *quata* (Sr.).

339 Cuscary: the red-handed tamarin monkey or *Saguinus midas* (*Callitrichidae*) also known as *sagoewonki* (Sr.).

The sloth is a creature thus named because of its dull and slovenly nature.[340] It is somewhat larger than a baboon[341] and has a skin of various colours; furthermore that lazy no blow or push will make him go faster than it is used to; one can imagine it cannot be considered one of the quickest, because it takes a 1-day journey to climb a tree from which it descends only when no more food left on it; then it comes down again with great dignity and pomp; next it climbs again up another [tree], where it spends his leisure time (of which, however, little remains, if one takes into account the time spent eating and sleeping) whistling a tune which however is not very pleasant to listen to.

Several other kinds of birds and animals do not enter my mind at all. I am also certain that even if the most diligent observer stayed in those regions during 7 years, he would still find some other creatures he had not seen before, to merit his attention. [123]

CHAPTER VI.

On the fruits.

The fruits of the country are oranges, lemons, limes, pomcitrons, watermelons and muskmelons, together with certain grapes. All of which do not grow there naturally, but have been brought from outside and are cultivated that good; they thrive and prosper as well as in other places. The native fruits are: plantains or potatoes, bananas, semmerimars, guavas, pines, and an abundance of wild stuff which, when transplanted, might perhaps not be that despised as at present. I have already told something about the plantains. Bananas are nearly the same, since there not much difference between them, only that the latter is as good or better than the former, although I find no special taste in either. The semmerimars grow on a rather tall tree.[342] They look quite like peaches, are woolly on the outside, and cannot be eaten before they go bad and rot; then they taste of marmalade or quince. The guava is about as large as a medlar, yellow, and full of seeds.[343] It is indeed one of the nicest fruits to be found; when ripe, it tastes like the red currant. They grow in the savannahs or pastures.

The pineapple, or ananas, is quite the prince of all fruits. They are very large, in the round quite 8 inches thick and 1 foot long. Green on the outside and yellow on the inside, they are juicy and full of cavities like a honey comb. At the top it has a small handsome crown of leaves, announcing as it were the vanguard which it takes regarding all other fruits: it rightly possesses it, because it is by far the best of those

---

340 The two sloth species are: the larger grey coloured with three forehand nails (*Bradypus tridactilus*) and the smaller with two forehand nails (*Choloepus didactylus*).

341 G.Warren, *An Impartial Description*, p. 14 mentions 'Baboon'. In the Dutch translation of Warren and Van Berkel we read *meerkat*. See note 337.

342 Semmerimars: G. Warren, op. cit., 1669, p. 15 'semmerintarre'; no match found, possibly sapodillas (*Manilkara* sp.); Warren compares the taste of this fruit with the marmalade of the quince (Cydonia oblonga). In the Dutch translation of Warren and in *American Voyages*, *queen* is perhaps a corruption of the Dutch *kwee*.

343 Guava: *Psidium guajava L.*; the *Psidium guinense* is a common kind.

[124] which I have ever seen or tasted. It grows on a small shrub *c.* 4 feet high. The stalk comes out from the root, just like that of an artichoke. If the small crown is cut off and planted in the ground, it produces a fresh fruit within 10 months.

CHAPTER VII.

On the commodities and merchandise of this country.

The commodities of this country with which one carries out merchandising are: sugar, speckled wood, or speckled timber, cottons, tobacco, various gums, and wood for dyeing.

Sugar is manufactured in considerable quantity and mostly considered 10% better than sugar from Barbados.

Speckled wood is also abundant enough; formerly sold in England for the same price as sugar, but once such a quantity of it was brought over, it has fairly diminished [in price].

Cotton does not thrive here that well here as in Barbados and other islands, possibly because too much rain falls here, and because they are all located too far from the sea, from which a salt-like dew arises which drives caterpillars and other noxious worms away from the trees.

Tobacco grows here very well; however, it is not as good as the one from Virginia. And I believe that hitherto no more is planted than the colony requires for its own use, because everybody there, men, women, and children, love some pipe smoking.

One has not especially tried indigo.

Rum is a distilled fluid from the juice of sugar cane, generally again as strong as brandy; therefore it is called 'kill-devil' in New England or 'devil's death'; a can of 2 'stoopen' is sold over there for 12 pounds of sugar.[344] [125]

Molasses consists of sugar from which it drips when the sugar is poured into pots.

The best known gums amongst our druggists are *montagne* and *gummi semnia*. They are both readily obtainable; without doubt several others are better, which in time will be brought to light by experience.

Cassia fistula is also in abundance there; and there is also a kind of balsam which drips from a tree.[345] None is believed to be better for fresh wounds than this one.

There is likewise no lack of any kind of timber for dyeing; with which a fair trade could be carried out.

---

344 Stoop: *c.* 2.4 liters; G. Warren, op. cit., 1667, p. 17, uses the old English gallon of *c.* 4.6 liters; the Dutch translation of Warren also mentions the measure of *stoop*. See also note 268.

345 Cassia fistula: *Bursaceae* sp., have dripping gums also known as copal.

CHAPTER VIII.

On the population.

The number of households for some time hardly counted between 400 and 500; yet, at present there are many more amongst the same *c.* 300 estates, which bring no small profit to their Masters, considering the decent rents which can be drawn within a few years from a small capital; when the work is but prudently managed, which, barring accidents, should be much greater than from a larger population, and from a country where more effort is done.[346]

The season for felling timber is between April and August. At the end of which it is left lying around on the ground to dry, until the month of September; then it is set on fire, and the ashes serve for manure. Indian corn and sugarcane are planted in the valleys; yams and other foods on higher ground. The corn grows [126] on a stem-like cane, generally 6 or 7 feet high. It bears only two ears on each stem, but the grain is as large as a pea and ripens in 4 months. One has two crops in a year; the corn gives at the least 500 for one. The sugar cane is suited to be broken or cut when 1 year old, and *c.* 6 feet high and as thick as a man's arm near the hand. Its top resembles a flag which is cut or broken off, and pressed in a mill. The juice is heated in copper boilers to a proper thickness and then poured into wooden containers with a wide, square upper part but gradually tapering at the lower part to the size of a penny; here a hole which is kept closed by means of a small piece of wood, until the sugar has become cold and solid; then one pulls out the wooden plug, and lets the syrup produced by the sugar descend through the hole; when it is thus stored for some time, the contents is finally removed from the containers into hogsheads, and shipped.[347]

CHAPTER IX.

On the Negroes and slaves.

These are mostly brought from Guinea in Africa and sold as dogs. Likewise they are no more minded in their work with which they are occupied the whole week; at which they are kept with the greatest paucity imaginable, severely punished for the least faults they commit; that lasts up to Saturday afternoon when they are allowed to take care of their own gardens and plantations; because they do not have

346 This is a good example of the small and rare adaptations made by the publisher of *American Voyages*: the fifty plantations in Warren's description have been adapted and changed into 300. 'Chap. VII. *Of the Plantations*, Which are in all about five hundred, whereof Forty or Fifty have *sugar-works*, yielding no small profil to the Owners, for a slight Disbursement, considering how brave a Revenue, if prudently manag'd, may be rais'd [18] from it in a few years: far larger (if no Contingency divert the ordinary Course of things) than is usually produc'd from a greater foundation, and more Continu'd Industry in *England*.' G. Warren, op. cit., 1667, pp. 17-18.

347 A hogshead could measure between 52 and 117 imperial gallons (*c.* 237-530 liters). The barrels were also used for dry goods, such as sugar. In *c.*1770, a Dutch oxhoofd of sugar contained between 650 and 700 pound (1 pound equals 494 grams), i.e., between 321 and 345 kg.

anything else from which they could live, except what their Masters provide them once or twice a year with some smelly salt fish, [127] or some roasted meat from a cow or horse that has come to die of itself. Their lodging consists of a hard plank and their blanket of their own black skin.

Because of this great misery they are sometimes driven by depression to do desperate things in order to free themselves; when they fear to be caught, [they] kill themselves; or, with the hope of forgiveness, brought back to their Masters, and punished there as an example and [to instil] fear; they will show their resolution or even more their obstinacy, courageously courageously the greatest tortures that can be inflicted upon them. It is a mixture of various nations, which always live together in contention and strife; therefore no conspiracy or confederacy can hatch amongst them without being immediately exposed by those who for some reason do not favour treason, because a few of their enemies are taking part in it, though they are mostly traitors and bloodthirsty by nature and do not have any religion at all, notwithstanding that several among them are baptized. However, many have the old sentiment of Pythagoras, concerning the transmigration of the soul from one body to another; and, that they, at the time of death, will be reborn and return to their Fatherland, [and] will live forth in the world in continuous change. These presumptions often make them sigh and wish for their death, since they have no hope of being freed from their dreadful enslavement in any other way.

CHAPTER X.

On the poisonous and noxious beasts and worms.

It is to be believed that the frightful heat of the Country, and the small number of inhabitants are the cause of the infestation of that many kinds of worms and [128] noxious beasts, with which man is harassed there and often imperilled with. Those most known include: snakes, crocodiles, scorpions, bats, ants, mosquitoes, toads, and frogs.

Concerning snakes, it is certain, that [specimens] are killed measuring 30 feet long and thick in proportion to the length. It is for the best there is not that great a danger from these frightful beasts; because they are absolutely non-venomous; likewise, when they are not hungry, by no means snappy. They are in fact water snakes, although they sometimes come to feed on land. They catch their food by speed, not by quick running or rolling, because I have never heard of anyone who would have been that foolish as to hurt himself by an accident, which one can so easily avoid as that of these snakes. But another kind is smaller and in large numbers, which one may well take caution of, because amongst them, there are those that poisonous nothing surpasses them; we have had the sad experience during two or three journeys, that not only the people hurt by them died of it a short while after, but that the flesh of the legs of those they had bitten, fell off in pieces within 24 hours. There are snakes which are very beautiful with spotted living paint [colours]; but under these beautiful colours lies the deadliest poison.

Others are knotted, have horns on their long tail, and tusks on the palate of the jaw which measures 2 inches broad and long.

There are not very large nor very many crocodiles, too. I need not describe them, because their stuffed skins can be found in almost all apothecaries' shops and elsewhere.

The scorpions are black and quite like a lobster. They often take shelter in dry wood and corn. Their sting is in the tail; whoever they sting with it, will have the greatest pain in the world for a few hours; but it [129] does not affect life. The common cure is taken from the creature itself, because one crushes the same and puts it upon the wound.

The bats are noxious creatures for man and beasts; because they suck the blood of both, and do it that dexterously one does not feel it until it is too late. It is said that various people have been forced to leave their homes in order to retain the small amount of blood they had left. In flight, they appear to be as large as doves; as I have already related, they are thus the only reason why pigs cannot be bred in greater numbers in that country.

The ants are quite small creatures and however, that innumerable and harmful that Surinam has hardly anything more troublesome than these small animals. The sandy soils, especially, are full of them; the poor people to whom such land has fallen to their share, and who have had no help of servants in order to exterminate them, are forced to leave their lands, and search for better places.

The muskyta [mosquitoes] is a sort of gnat, of which one can have no rest at nights, bitten that much by them; immediately large pimples arise from the flesh. One is mostly harassed with these vermin in the lowlands and on the seacoast, where the sea runs up and down over the land; in such a way the fishermen, in order to be able to sleep at night, must cover the entire body with mud, except for the eyes and mouth.

Toads and frogs, the horror of the womenfolk, are here in all places, just as in Egypt, both in the houses as well as in the fields; after a rain shower has fallen, they make such a loud sound you can scarcely hear yourself; some have such a frightful sound one can safely compare them with the moans or groans of a person who is about to die.

Now, this is the worst that can be said about Surinam, [130] because the country is otherwise so blessed by God and has so many virtues, that these hardships cannot be compared with it. For the same, complete and infallible remedies and cures have been discovered; for the remainder, solutions will be found in time to come.

CHAPTER XI.

Circumstantial account of all the most important peculiarities, which belong to the household, manner of living, etc., of the Indians.

It is said that faint-hearted people are often treacherous. Various nations interact with the people of this colony and trade, but the original inhabitants of the country are *Charibes*, or cannibals, who are quite the most numerous of those who occupy these lands; they have spread themselves mostly onto all the islands in the vicinity, and across the mainland along the Amazon River to the Orinoque. They are fully and entirely naked, except that they, for decency's sake, wear a lap; but the women, who have had one or two children, take them off. Their skin is of an orange-yellow paint [colour], their hair black and without curls. It would be a happy people, regarding the things of this world, if they knew their own luck; because nature has provided them in such manner with all necessary things they need little trouble to turn the same things to their use. The womenfolk are in general lustful; there are amongst them those who are that beautiful of face, body, and limbs that whenever the best and versatile sculptors would see them, they would not oppose to it. Their shame especially of virgins, before strangers, gives to all their other perfections, which are that [131] openly exposed such an attractive grace and charm that those who have contact with them, have to practice no less than Joseph's Chastity, in order to not arouse forbidden lust. They have been that innocent until now that, besides all the other friendliness with which they allure the menfolk, they have not learnt the sweetest and purest pleasure of kissing; but as they now have intercourse with Europeans, and [they] are by nature quick witted and eager to learn, it will be conceivable that they will indeed learn it in time. They have two kinds of houses. One for the night, a construction with a roof that almost touches the ground. The other one serves to stay in during the day. These are somewhat higher and wider, in order to shelter from the hot rays of the sun; they are open on all sides, so that the cool wind can make its way through. Their household goods consist of nicely painted earthen pots and dishes; their table linen consists of the leaves of trees. Their beds or hammocks are made of cotton, more or less square like the quilt of a bed, with boards at each end through which the hammock is stretched out stiff and square. Their bread and drink come from their cassava gardens; the forests and rivers continuously provide them with meat and fish. In order to look more attractive, they paint themselves neatly applying a red colour, *anatto*, which grows on small trees in husks, and with the sap of various trees. They pierce the nose, lips, and ears, to adorn them with glass pendants, pieces of copper, and other trifles earned from the Hollanders for their labour.[348] They load the neck, arms and legs with beads, scales of fish, or with any odd items they can get hold of. They have no other government or law than that of the household; along with that, entire

348 G. Warren, op. cit., 1667, p. 24 mentions 'English' instead of 'Hollanders'.

generations [lineages][349] live together as in the times of the time-honoured patriarchs, and the eldest son always follows his father's footsteps. Nevertheless they count excellent men who [132] are their Captains or headmen who lead them in the battle, and this valour is being tested by flogging them passionately with rods; if they can stand that, without screaming or making any other noticeable movement, then they are regarded as brave persons, and are revered when compared to the others who have less courage. The heads of the lineages usually have three or four wives, whereas the others have but one; one may call them altogether with reason servants rather than housewives because they must be autonomously around their husband, as the lowest [female] servant with us around her Master or Mistress. The man will very rarely tax his shoulders with any freight or burden, but always passes it on his wife's shoulders; they have such respect for their husband they always wait upon him at the table, and will not eat, until he has done. When the woman has given birth, she immediately resumes her work just as before.[350] Their language does not sound strange, but one can scarcely learn it, because it counts that many words meaning various things and which one cannot distinguish otherwise than by means of the various pronunciations. When an expedition is decided on, the general or supreme Captain sends a stick to all the villages and to all households to be gathered in council, in which there are as many notches, as there are days remaining to come together at the meeting place; of these notches they cut out one every day, till the time has passed and only in this manner they can all know that the time has passed; because their numbering or ciphering, does not extend beyond twenty and they have no names for the remainder; likewise they indicate these twenty with their fingers and toes, hereby sometimes doubling or tripling the same number. What goes beyond that, their ciphering art is at an end; then they burst out with their 'Ounsa awara' that is to say: 'as much as there is hair on our head.' They go out to sea in painted *canoas,* or boats, made of one piece; it is a [133] tree hollowed out like a trough and is that large one can altogether carry two or three charges [4 or 6 tons] of goods. Their weapons are bows with poison arrows and short sticks consisting of speckled wood.[351] For their protection, some carry bucklers or shields which are handsomely made and encarved with figures. They do not keep order in fighting and do not attack at night unless they see a real advantage in it. The men they manage to capture are put to death with the greatest cruelty faint-hearted people can think of with regard to their enemies they have in their power. The children and women they enslave are sold for trifles. Once they

349 Ibid. on 'Kindred'. Generations, i.e., families of the same lineage or kinship.

350 Roth translated: 'The woman who has been confined immediately resumes her work just as before.' However, Van Berkel wrote that this woman resumed work immediately after having given birth, W.E. Roth, op. cit., 1948, p. 139. Again, publisher Johan ten Hoorn has left out a complete section from Warren. We read: '(…) when a Woman is delivered of her first Child, she presently goes about her business as before, and the husband fains himself distemper'd, and is hang'd up to the Ridge of the House in his Homacko, where he continues certain dayes dieted with the Bread and Water of Affliction, then, being taken down, is stung with *Ants* (a punishment they usually inflict upon their Women, Dogs, or Children, when they are foolish, for that's the term they usually put upon any disdemeanours) and a lusty drinking Bout is made at the Conclusion of the Ceremony', G. Warren, op. cit., 1667, p. 25.

351 See W.E. Roth, op. cit., 1924, pp. 171-173 on the war club or 'casse-tête'.

attacked the French in Surinam, and also tried this with the English when they first arrived there; but they were treated in such manner by the latter they still regret their foolishness. Today, now the colony has become strong, they do not dare to return but at least behave courteously. Very vindictive amongst themselves they will revenge the suffering inflicted upon them at some time or another; but always in a treacherous manner and not daring to see their man face to face. I have never been able to observe if they have had any religion or religiousness; although they sometimes talk of a Captain of the clouds, they do not serve him or any other. They have some knowledge of the devil and call him *yarakin*;[352] the imposters of the people, who they call *peies* and who occupy the place of priests, or 'popes', among them, convince them they have great intimacy with him. Whether this is indeed the case, or not, I am unable to say. It always serves them in order to make them look better amongst the rest who imagine that death, disease, and all kinds of accidents, come directly from the devil. They also have a small scrap of knowledge of another life; where reward and punishment would be for the good and evil committed in this life; but they are cleverer, as [134] they would like to know what kind of reward and punishment it will be and where it will happen. The image they have concerning the intimacy between of the *peies* with the devil and the knowledge which they might have obtained from herbs and medicines causes them to use the same as physicians. But they do not have to boast about their professions or art too highly, because if one of them is called to an ill person nothing can be availed. If, when performing his exorcisms and magic, the patient passes away, the surviving friends reward the physician with death for his trouble, if he does not hasten to get away. They burn the corpse along with and everything else the deceased owned while alive; everything,they cannot burn, such as ironwork and the like, they will destroy in some other way so that the dead may at least not lack anything in the other life. If he had owned had any male or female slaves they are killed too, so that they may wait upon their Master. The burial is celebrated with a feast with drinking and toasting as well as comical, disorderly dancing, which is very customary amongst them; whilst the wives, who are relatives of the deceased, sit next to the corpse, crying plaintively over the loss of their friends and kinsmen.[353]

Thus regarding the most noteworthy things about the manners and customs of the natives. Let us now turn to other matters. [135]

---

352 Roth added in a footnote that 'Yarakin is the present-day Yurokon or evil spirits of the Caribs', W.E. Roth, op. cit., 1948, p. 140. For further information on *yurokon* and *piai* men, see W.E. Roth, op. cit., 1915.

353 The publisher of *American Voyages* omitted an entire section from Warren's text in order to include a new chapter on actual events. We read: 'Hast, and an unfaithful Memory, made me omit an Observation, in my opinion, very remarkable, and for which, I want a greater reason than my own, to give me satisfaction. I have said the Warmth and Moisture causes a constant Verdancy and Flourishing of Plants in *Surinam*, holding true not only in all Trees natural to that Country, but also in Transplanted Vines which bear there twice a [p. 28] year; yet this Exception I observed in an *European* Apple-Tree, which, notwithstanding the equality of Seasons, always shed its Leaves, and continu'd bare after the usual manner in its Native Soil all our Winter Months, and grew green again in Spring: But how it comes to pass, that the Heat and Moisture of that Climate should not Cause in that Tree an Assimilation with the rest (as well those transplanted as natural to that Country, since they say the spirit of Nature is universally diffusive) I leave the *Virtuosi* to dispute. FINIS. G. Warren', G. Warren, op. cit., 1667, pp. 27-28.

CHAPTER XII.

Death of Lord of Sommelsdijck, Governor of Surinam. Unsuccessful attack of the French on this colony. Misfortune that befell Lord of Châtillon on that occasion. Departure of the author from Surinam, and return to Middelburg.

After the reader has thus been given a description of the most important subjects to be noted on the colony of Surinam, I shall return to other matters which happened there in my time, because the contract I had signed with my Director, once expired and subsequently renewed, I can speak with a sufficient accuracy not only about the death of Lord of Sommelsdijck, Governor of the colony, as I have witnessed it with my own eyes,[354] but also the attack of the French on Surinam, during the government of Master Scherpenhuizen; with which I shall finish my voyages.

It was already for a long time that the soldiers of the garrison, on whom indeed a too hard and slave-like labour had been imposed, had complained about the bad rations; their complaints finally burst out that far that they all of them, instigated by certain scoundrels, declared they would not do another hand's turn, unless better provided with victuals. The Adjutant, who commanded them, seeing it was serious, promised to go to the Governor and to speak for them which he indeed did, but this one, instead of giving him a smooth reply, grabbed a cane and drove him, with many a bad word, out of his room. Then he returned to the people and told of his experience in which they placed no belief and they rushed [136] altogether to the Governor's house. In the meantime, they met the Commander Verboom, a man, as much loved by everybody as Lord of Sommelsdijck was hated, because of his unfriendliness and severity. He immediately asked them, with kind words, the reason of their discontent and having learnt it, promised to arrange better victuals for them and begged them to now return to their homes. The soldiers obeyed, but arriving the next day at the place of work, and getting no answers, they took the decision to do justice themselves and to obtain by force that which they had not been able to achieve by humble request. Immediately each one [went] for his rifle and while cursing dreadfully, they all [went] together to the Governor's house. At this sight he was now more than ever urged by the Commander Verboom, and by the terrible threats of the soldiers who did not want to listen to anymore speeches to grant the request of the militia. But instead of evading the storm, the Governor rushed out, with sword in hand, through the door towards the mutineers, of whom he meant to split one's head. This one, seeing he was targeted, discharged his rifle, and fired a bullet in the Governor's thigh, causing him to fall directly to the ground, where he was subsequently finished off instantly with forty-seven wounds, without uttering a single word. In this mayhem, Commander Verboom, although the soldiers shouted out to him to keep out of the way, received a bullet in the stomach from which he died 9 days later. This happened on 19 July in the year 1688, a day still in the memory of many, because the mutineers, not satisfied with this, marched on; took possession of the fort; strengthened themselves up to

354 Notably Roth omits this phrase on Van Berkel being present, W.E. Roth, op. cit., 1948, p. 142.

between 140 and 150 men; appointed officers of their own choice in place of the fort's officers; overpowered two ships on the river; furnished them [the ships] with necessities from the warehouse; extorted 3500 guilders from the civilians, after disarming them; made all preparations [137] for their departure. The country's political Councillors in attempt to bring matters back to order with kindness, let them know that those who wished to remain would be acquitted. Between forty and fifty acknowledged this. The others boarded the ship, but surrendered when the entire colony came together; they were promised that only the guilty would be punished. Indeed, eight scoundrels were hanged, three broken on the wheel, and the remainder acquitted.

Between 9 and 10 months later, when we were again involved in an open war with the King of France, several French men-of-war in the West Indies seized the island of St. Christopher,[355] belonging to the English; they intending shortly after the arrival of Master van Scherpenhuizen, the incoming Governor, to treat Surinam in the same way; this is what happened. On 6 May in the year 1689, the garrison was warned by the sentinel of Motte Creek, 2 miles lower down, that a French King's fleet consisting of ten sails was moving towards the river. Next the Governor ordered all the Captains to join up with their companies at the fort. Meanwhile the enemy sailed up the river, allowing a bombing ship, one of ten, to fire at the fort overpowering the country's bark the *Wapen van Amsterdam*, which was anchored as a guardpost. On 7 May, the garrison got their ships ashore, being six [vessels] as well as two fire-ships strong; they divided themselves at the required posts, seventy-eight men under Captain Swart, eighty-four Jews under Captain Samuel Nassi, and sixty-nine Soldiers under Captain Lucas Codri, all well armed and of good disposition; all the more since the fortifications, owing to the good care of Master van Vredenburg, Commander of the colony, were almost in the desired condition. On 8 May, the French bombing ship fired its guns, very heavily at night, but weaker during the day, at the fort and the six ships, but the enemy fleet remained out of reach of the Dutch guns. During the following night, the French sent out spies [138]; who, once discovered, retreated quickly and due to the darkness could not be followed. On 9 May, the enemy prepared to storm the fort and fired a few bombs in order to hinder the Dutch, who marched out to receive them, but without result. In the evening the bombing ship approached the fort, followed by the other ships. The sentinel reported they found themselves in a half moon within a pistol shot of the fort. The weather was dark. Two of them fired first, but, notwithstanding their steady fruitless bombing and throwing grenades, they were greeted with more than 3,000 cannon balls during 2 hours, it caused them to cut the anchors and steal away on the ebb. The garrison received four to six wounded, though of little importance; the next day they saw two of the five enemy anchors afloat, as well as several men without heads, legs and hands, and further signs of the French loss. On the [10 May][356] the bombing ship which in all had thrown between 140 and 150 bombs, often weighing *c.*100 pounds, at the fort

355 The French conquered Saint Christophe, or Saint Kitts, in 1689 during the Nine Years' War, or the War of the Grand Alliance (1688-1697), which General Codrington retaliated a year later.

356 *American Voyages* mentions 18 May which evidently must be 10 May 1689.

and the ships, but not one inside [the fort], returned again below the fort, but was soon driven back by the heavy cannonading. The enemy ships retreated too. On 12 May, the French still stood in sight of the fort; drifted down the river during the night; the next day, seeing there was nothing much to do, set off out to sea.

Pitiful was the accident, which befell the Lord of Châtillon,[357] son of Lord of Sommelsdijck during this event. He was in command of a battery, which was steadily shooting upon the French; wanting to discharge a cannon himself for the second time, it took fire prematurely, blew two fingers off his right and three off the left hand, scorched his face, and wounded him painfully.

Between 3 and 4 weeks after this incident, my sojourn in Surinam came to an end; because my Director having joined me there about a month earlier, [139] ordered me to get ready for my return voyage to the homeland; on which journey, as nothing noteworthy happened to me, I will only say that, having been *en route* between 6 and 7 weeks, I stepped ashore on 6 August of the year 1689 at Middelburg in Zealand.

THE END.

357 See note 66.

Dutch text of 1695

[i]

AMERIKAANSCHE VOYAGIEN
NAAR
RIO de BERBICE en SURINAME
Siet Fol. 64

[ii] [blanco]

[iii]

AMERIKAANSCHE
VOYAGIEN,
Behelzende een Reis na
RIO de BERBICE,
Gelegen op het vaste Land van GUIANA,
Aan de Wilde-Kust van AMERICA,
Mitsgaders een andere na de Colonie van
SURINAME,
Gelegen in het Noorder Deel van het gemelde
Landschap GUIANA.
Ondermengd met alle de byzonderheden noopende de Zeden,
Gewoonten, en Levenswijs der Inboorlingen, Boom-en Aard-
gewassen, Waaren en Koopmanschappen, en andere
aanmerkelijke zaaken.
BESCHREVEN DOOR
ADRIAAN van BERKEL
Vercierd met kopere Plaaten.

TOT AMSTERDAM,
By JOHAN ten HOORN, Boekverkooper tegen over
het Oude Heeren Logement, in de Historischryver 1695.

[iv] [blanco]

[v]

AAN DEN LEEZER

Nooit zou ik gedacht hebben om deze mijne Americaansche Voyagien in 't licht te geven; en ongetwijfeld zouden ze wel met my ten grave zijn gedaald, indien niet de gestadige aanprikkelingen van goede Vrienden, met de welken ik menigmaal van deze mijne jeugdige Tochten had gesproken, my eindelijk het besluit hadden doen nemen van aan de Wereld mede te deelen, 't geen tot dus lang in mijne herssenen begraven was geweest. 't Is het gemeen zeggen der Auteuren, dat ze tot het uitgeven van hunne Werken gedwongen zijn geworden, om kwansuis een zekere soort van zedigheid te vertoonen: Doch ik kan met waarheid zeggen, dat het zich in deze gelegentheid met my zodanig heeft toegedragen. 'k Heb al over lang geweeten, hoe weinig eers men met dusdanigen arbeid kan behalen, en derhalven niet veel lust gehad om onder het [vi] getal der Boekmakers gerekend te worden: Maar men praatte my deze swaarigheid uit het hoofd, en trachte my aan te wyzen, dat ik groot nut zou doen met een beschrijving van Landen uit te geven, daar tot noch toe niemand of had gesproken. Inderdaad, 't is een groote slofheid, de gantsche Wereld, om zo te zeggen, te beschrijven, en niet te reppen van twee Colonien, daar zich zo veele lieden van onze Landaart onthouden; van dewelken men licht genoeg zou hebben konnen krygen, om zonder genoodzaakt te weezen zelven op de plaatsen te zijn, ten minsten een schets 'er af te geven. Ondertusschen heeft men dit verwaarloosd, en, na het schijnt, de moeite voor my overgelaten om de hand aan dit Tafereel te steeken. 'k Heb mijne vlijt aangewend, op dat het zelve zich eenigsints behaaglijk voor d'oogen zou vertoonen, doch daarom echter de waarheid nooit in het minste deel verkort. Deze is mijn voornaamste oogmerk geweest; [vii] en indien ik geen swarigheid had gemaakt van 'er zo los over heen te stappen, als veele Reizigers gedaan hebben, 'k zou den Lezers de vreemste dingen der Wereld hebben konnen verhaalen, insonderheid wegens *Rio de Berbice*, als minder bevaaren, dan *Suriname*. Doch de waarheid, gansch naakt, heeft altijd meerder bekoorlijkheden voor my gehad, dan de leugen opgetooid met alle de cieraaden waar mede men haar behagelijk tracht te maken. Hier durf en mag ik mijne Leezers af verzekeren, en dat ik, mijns weten, in het gantsche Werk niets en heb gezegt, 't geen ik niet ten allen tyde met het getuigenis van anderen zou konnen bevestigen. Ontbreeken 'er nu cierlijke vertellingen en zeldsame voorvallen aan; zo denkt, dat het geen Roman, maar een ware beschrijving van zaaken is; waar af men overtuigd zal weezen, wanneer men anderen van dezelve dingen zal hebben hooren spreeken. Hier mede stel ik my gerust tegens aller laster, en wensch den onzydigen Leezer wel te vaaren.

[viii]

OP DE VOYAGIEN van ADRIAAN van BERKEL

Hier ziet gy Leser, door *van Berkel* op 't papier;
De staat en handel van de wilde Amerikanen.
's Lands vrugtbaarheid en dracht, haar zeden en manier
Van godsdienst, trou en dood, rivieren, bosschen, banen.
Dus wort van *Hem* vertoont als in een tafereel,
Wat wonderen dat geschiên in 's werelds ander deel.
J. Schriek.

[1]

REIS
Na
RIO de BERBICE
Gelegen op het vaste Land van
GUIANA,
Aan de wilde Kust van
AMERICA

I. HOOFDSTUK

Den Auteur word aengenomen om na Rio de Berbice te gaan. Steekt, door storm terugh gedreven, tot verscheydene malen in Zee. Eigenschap van de Passaad-winden. Manier van de Zeeswynen of Bruinvisschen te vangen. Aanmerckinge omtrent de selven. Beschryving van de Haayen, Bonitos, en vliegende Visschen. Beschryving van een Hoos. Gevaarlijkheid van de Hoozen. Hoozen van een andere soort, Pypen geheeten. Komst in de Rivier van Berbice.

Aangeprikkeld door een edelmoedige begeerte om vreemde gewesten en Landen te bezichtigen, vond ik gelegentheid om mijne lust voor een gedeelte hier in te voldoen; alzo de Heeren *van Ree* en *van Peere*, Patronen der Revier en Colonie de *Berbice*, een Schip lieten uitrusten, 't geen sig eerstdaags derwaarts stond te begeven. De voorspraak van goe- [2] de Vrienden bragt zo veel te weeg, dat ik voor Koopman en Secretaris op het selve wierd aengenomen. Na dat ik dan mijne Equipagie voor af na *Vlissingen* had gesonden, begaf ick my op den 24 october des jaars 1670 in persoon mede derwaarts; alwaar vier weeken lange nae een goede wind gewacht hebbende, ende selve eindelijk beginnende te waayen, liet ik my aan boord voeren. Hier vond ik alles tot de tocht gereed, en den vier en twintichsten November staken wy met een Ooste wind in Zee; zijnde het schip, 't geen sestien stukken kanon voerde, genaamd het Fregat *Nassau*, en de Capitein *Cornelis Marinus*: maar des andren daags, zo als wy *Grevelingen* in 't gezicht hadden, keerde de wind, en wy met de selve weder na *Zeeland*. Doch eer wy de haven konden bereycken, maakte d'ongewoonte van de Zee, hoewel wy maar met een labber koeltje wierden voort gedreven, zulk een veranderingh in mijn ligchaem, en keerde alles sodanig het onderste boven, dat ik, wat moeite ik ook aenwendde om het te wederhouden, alle de spijs en dranck door den zelven weg, waar langs ze genuttigd waren, weder uitgaf. En deze moeijelijkheid verzeld zijnde met een sware hoofd pijne en vreemde duyselingen, vond ik my gantsch onpasselijke; doch echter kort daar nae, stekende de neus in de wind, en siende de Zee in 't aanzicht, weder t'eenemaal hersteld.

Na verloop van acht dagen bekwamen wy weer goede wind; weshalven men het anker begon te lichten: maar zo als wy nu haast klaar waren, kwam ons een Oost-Indischvaarder voor de boeg, die ons Galjoen kneusde, zulks dat wy, om de schade te herstellen, tot des anderendaags moesten blyven leggen. Den volgenden dag was het, zeilen by: en wy liepen op den namiddag ook weder in Zee. 's Avondts riepen eenige Gasten, die onder in 't Schip waren, dat wy zonken, op welk geroep ik, gantsch onwetende van dese streeken, en derhalven in een doodelijke verbaestheid, hervoor kwam stuiven: maar Jan Hagel, ziende hoe seer de schrik my had ingenomen, lachte om mijne onnoselheid, seggende, dat het was om dat de Kluysen niet gestopt waren. Ik ging dan weer na de kooy, vry wat [3] geruster als ik er uit was gekomen, en sliep des nachts sonder eenige verhinderinge.'s Anderendaags, so als wy in 't Canaal by *Bevesier* waren gekomen, keerde de wind weder, wakkerde hand over hand, en liet sich des nachts met sulk een geweld gevoelen, dat het Schip uit malkander scheen te willen slingeren. Maar rampsaliger lot trefte den Oost-Indischvaarder, daar ik so even af gesproken heb. Hy stiet op een Zandbank, de *Gom* of *Gonje* geheeten, borst van een; en haalde in 't kort de neus onder: doch, op den Stuurman na, wierd al het Volck, en het meeste gedeelte der Goederen geborgen. Een ander Schip, komende van *Bilboa*, en geladen met Spaensche Wol en veertig duysent stukken van Achten, kwam by dese gelegentheid van gelijken te vergaan. Wy sagen het by ons leggen, eer wy gingen schaffen, en toen wy gegeeten hadden, sei de Ketelwacht, dat het gesonken was: doch dat het Volk sich altemaal gebergd had op een Schip, 't geen aan ly van hen lag. Wat ons belangt, wy moesten het na den storm, die ons tusschen *Douvres* en *Calais* bracht, door tegenwind weder te rug setten, en kwamen op het vijde etmaal weer voor *Vlissingen*; alwaar mijn Hospes, daar ik nu tweemael huysvesting had gehad, my met groote blijdschap verwelkomde; also hy meende, dat wy verongelukt waren, ter oorsaak dat 'er omtrent *Zeeland* ook een Schip was gebleven.

Twee dagen daar na waaide de wind weder uit den oosten; weshalven wy des namiddags voor de darde maal onder zeil staken. Wij voorderden toen so sterk, dat wy in de Dagwacht de Vuuren van Engelandts Voorland sagen: en toen ik uit de slaap kwam, bevonden wy ons in 't gesicht van Bevesier, daar wy te vooren van den storm waren overvallen. De koude, die ons tot noch toe vry wat lastig was geweest, begon nu daglijks te minderen; en de goede wind, die toenmaals bleef duuren, deed ons onse Reis dapper spoeden, en bracht ons tot omtrent op de hoogte van de *Canarische Eilanden*: maar hier ging ze leggen, en liet ons voor een wijl in stilte heen drijven.

Ondertusschen kregen wy kort daar na verandering: want zijnde in 't gesicht van het Eiland *Madera* gekomen, wierd [4] my gesegt, dat wy de Passaad hadden aangetroffen, tot groote blijdschap van al het Scheepsvolk. Dese winden waayen altijd uit een selven hoek, tusschen 't Noorden en 't Oosten; en behoeft men als dan sich met het Want en Zeilen niet veel te bemoeyen. Ten anderen, gelijk ze getemperd zijn, maatigen sy de hette van de *Zon*, welke sonder dat onverdraagelijk sou wesen. Men vind ze gemeenlijk omtrent de hoogte van het gemelde Eiland; en als men ze aangetroffen heeft, voordert men doorgaans 40 a 50 mylen in een etmael; sonder dat men byna de beweging van 't Schip, noch het stampen van de Zee gevoelt.

Middelerwijl hadden wy over dag het vermaak van de Vischvangst: want wy sagen byna alle dagen een seer groote menigte van allerhande Visschen, insonderheid Zee-swijnen of Bruinvisschen, welke met gantsche benden rondom het Schip swommen. De vangst geschiedde op de volgende wijs. Daar stonden op eenige plaatsen van het Schip, en voornamentlijk voorin, ettelijke Matroosen, ieder met een Harpoen in de hand, aen welkers eind een touw, van dikte omtrent als een pink, vast was. Als nu de Bruinvisschen voorby hen heenswommen, smeeten sy 'er den Harpoen met sulk een geweld in, dat sy ze by wijlen door en doorboorden. Sy lieten hem in de wond steken, houdende hem altijd by het touw, 't gene sy soo lang lieten schieten, tot dat de Visch, verswakt door het verlies van haar bloet, sich sonder eenige tegenweer liet inpalmen, en binnen boord halen. Daar wierden 'er ettelijken op dese manier gevangen. Sy waren vier of vijf voet lang, en dik na proportie. Dese Visch word te recht Zeeswijn geheeten, also ze seer wel na een Varken of Swijn gelijkt, niet alleenlijk wegens het Vleesch en 't Spek, maar ook noch wegens de gedaante van binnen en van buiten. 't Vleesch heeft echter gantsch geen lekkerheid, en smaakt wat traanachtich.

't Is een gemeen gevoelen by veele lieden, welke nooit Zeeswijnen gesien hebben, dat het bloed van dese Dieren niet warm is: maar ik heb het tegendeel ondervonden, en kan 'er met volkomene sekerheid af spreeken. Want hebbende 'er een den buik doen opsnyden, had ik de nieuwsgierigheid van de hand in het ingewand te steeken, en vond [5] het bloed byna so warm als het van een Varken. Oock kon ik niet twijfelen of ze ademden, wanneer ik hunne longen so bekwaam sag tot de ademing als die der Dieren welke buiten 't water leeven. Zy hebben geen kieuwen, als d'andere Visschen, maar slechts twee gaten aan de zyden des hoofds, om de lucht te scheppen: en gewisselijk is het hierom dat ze van tyd to tijd het hoofd, en by wylen het gantsche lichaem, buiten 't water beuren, en altyd na de windzyde swemmen: waar van daan het oock komt, dat, als de Matroosen geduurende een stilte Zeeswijnen na eenige kant sien heen loopen, sy aanstondes seggen, dat de wind van die kant moet komen. Behalven de Bruinvisschen of Zeeswijnen, vingen wy ook noch veele Haayen. Dese Visschen zijn een soort van Zeehonden, hebbende een heel breed en plat hoofd, en een seer diepe keel, ter oorsaak van het onderste kaakebeen 't geen veel korter is al het bovenste; sulks dat, als ze byten willen, sy genoodsaakt zijn op de zyde, en somtijdts selfs op den rug te gaan leggen. Een weinigje beneden het hoofd is hunne huid een soort van Segrein, waar af de korlen seer groot zijn, met ses openingen aan elke zyde, welke sich toesluiten door het middel van sekere seer dunne vellen, die hen voor kieuwen of wammen verstrekken. 't Zijn de gulsigste Dieren van allen die men kan noemen: want hoewel ze drie of vier maal achter malkander aan den hoek gevangen worden, en den bek gantsch in bloed hebben, komen sy 'er echter altijd met deselve gretigheid weder aan, tot dat ze gevangen zijn, of het aas weg hebben. Wijders, als ze iemand vat hebben gekregen, is 't met hem gedaan: want ze laaten nooit los. d'Oorsaak van dese ongemeene gretigheid is de grootte van hunne lever. Sy hebben drie ryen tanden, waar af d'eene omgekromd, en d'anderen recht en van verscheidene gedaantens zijn. De derde ry is van driehoekigen, voor dun, en boven saagswijse toelopende. Sy zijn altijd verseld van sekere kleine Visschen, welke hunne stoet uitmaken, en zo onaffscheidelijk aan hen gehegt zijn, dat ze sich liever met hen willen laten vangen, als hen verlaten. Men noemt ze hunne Stuur- [6] lieden of Lootsen; dewijl men beweert, dat ze hen tot leidsmannen verstrekken, om hen te brengen ter plaatsen daar aas te vinden is. Sy eeten d'overblijfselen van de vangst, en houden sich gehecht op de huid der Haayen, door het middel van een kraakachtig velletje van ovale gedaante, 't geen sy op het hoofd hebben, en dat met sleuven loopt.

Wy vonden ook hier omtrent een menigte van *Bonitos*, d'onversoenlijke vyanden der vliegende Visschen, daar ze gestadig jagt op maken. Dese Visch is van grootte als de kloekste Vaderlandsche Karpers, doch veel dikker; wyders sonder schobben, met een zilverachtich vel, en den rug getekent met lange dondere en vergulde strepen. De *Bonitos* zijn gemakkelijk te vangen: want gelijk ze geweldig heet zijn op de vliegende Visschen, bedient men sich van der selver gedaante, gemaakt van vederen, welke aan het eind van een lijn vast gemaakt word. Dit vederwerk doet men op het water voor hen heen en weder huppelen; daar ze terstond, bedroogen door de gelijkenis, met sulk een happigheid na springen, dat er dikwijls, alleenlijk met twee of drie lijnen, in minder als een uur dartig of veertig gevangen worden. De Smaak is goed.

Wat de vliegende Visschen belangt, wy sagen 'er verscheidene schoolen af sich in de vlucht opheffen, ter hoogte van omtrent acht of tien voeten, en 50 of 60 treden ver vliegen eer ze weder in 't water vielen om hunne vlerken nat te maaken, en nieuwe krachten tegens de *Bonitos* te nemen, welke hen somtijdts in 't nedervallen betrapppen, of uit het water springen om hen in de vlucht te vangen. Behalven de *Bonitos*, hebben de vliegende Visschen noch een anderen vyand, zijnde een seker soort van Vogelen, welke, als ze uit het water opvliegen om sich voor de *Bonitos* te bergen op hen nederschieten. Onse Konstapel bracht my de eerste vliegende Visch, welke, door een der gemelde Vogelen van

naby vervolgd, in ons Schip was komen nedervallen. Sy was van gedaante, van koleur, en van grootte als een Haring, de rug een weinigje dikker, en het voorste van 't hoofd rondachtig gelijk een Zeebraassem, met vlerken bo- [7] ven de wammen, seer wel na die der Vleermuysen gelykende.

Wy seilden aldus voort tot den seventienden Januarij des jaars 1671 zijnde een Sondag, wanneer sich omtrent den middage een groote swarte wolk vertoonde, daar sich kort 'er na een gedeelt van afsonderde; en gelijk dit afgesonderde gedeelte door een geweldige wind wierd voortgedreven, veranderde het allengskens van gedaante, en nam die van een lange kolom aan, welke van de lucht af tot op d'oppervlakte der Zee nederdaalde. Wy, Kajuitsgasten, die nooit op Zee waren geweest, sagen dit verschijnsel, 't geen ver genoeg van ons was om 'er niet bevreesd voor te wesen, met verwondering aan, en verstonden van den Stuurman, die 'er met ons over zat te redeneeren, dat dese verschijnsels of Hoosen seer gevaarlijk zijn, niet alleen (wanneer men genoodsaakt is 'er in te zeilen, en dat ze door de reeën en masten van het Schip doorgesneeden worden) ter oorsaak van het water 't geen alsdan in het Schip komt te vallen; maar ook noch wegens het schielijk geweld en uytstekende swaarte van de dwarlwind, daar het door weg word gevoerd, en die bekwaam is om de grootste Schepen hunne masten t'ontrukken, en hen ook selfs in 't gevaar van vergaan te brengen. En dewijl hunne ontmoeting so gevaarlijk is, stelt men alles in 't werk wat men kan om ze te vermyden. Ondertusschen doet men ze dikwils sonder eenige uitwerking nederstorten; te weten, wanneer men de beweging van de wind, met de gebuurige lucht door Kanon-en Musketschooten te verdunnen, kom te verbreken: by welke gelegentheid het water, wijlde het als dan niet meer ondersteund word, in seer grooten overvloed nedervalt, en de gantsche Hoos aanstonds komt te verdwijnen. Dese Hoosen, hoewel ze sich van verre klein, en als kolommen van ses of seven voeten diametres, vertoonen, hebben echter een veel grooter uitgestrektheid: en onse Stuurman versekerde ons, dat hy 'er onder het bereik van een pistool van meer als hondert voeten inden omtrek gesien had.

Doch siet men op Zee een andere soort van Hoosen, bye eenigen *Pypen* genaamd ter oorsaak van hunne lange gedaante: [8] doch desen zijn niet gevaarlijk, en vertoonen sich alleenlijk in het benedenste gedeelte van de lucht; verschijnende met Zonnen op- en ondergang, ontrent deselve plaats daer de Zon als dan is. 't Zijn lange en dikke wolken, omringd van andere heldere en doorschijnende wolken. Sy vallen niet neder, maar verwarren sich altemaal naderhand door malkander, en verdwijnen allengskens; in plaats dat de Hoosen met geweld voortgedreven worden, langen tijd duuren, en altijd met regen en dwarlwinden verzeld zijn, welke de Zee doen kooken, en met schuim bedekken.

Den selven dag, te weten, den seventienden Januarij sag men de Zee geweldig branden, even of ze met vuur bedekt was geweest: weshalven wy onbevarenen, op het minste gesicht van ongewoone dingen of verwonderd of verbaasd, den Capitein en Stuurman na d'oorsaak vraagden; welke ons seiden, dat wy in twee a drie dagen wel land mochten sien. 't Lood kwam ook voor den dag, en wierd de diepte op drie en veertig vademen waters bevonden, de tweedemaal meer, en de darde reis veertig. Thans riep de Capitein, dat de Stuurman twee streeken sou loeven; en des anderen daags, omtrent den middag, sagen wy land, 't geen sich donkerachtig opdeed, en, nader by gekomen zijnde, bevonden wierd de *Duivels-Eilanden* te weesen. Dien dag, namentlijk Maandag, gelijk ook Dingsdag, zeilden wy over land; een manier van spreken, by de Zeelieden gebruikelijk, die daar mee betekenen willen, dat men te hoog is, en voor de wind na het land toe loopt. 's Namiddags (na dat wy de Rivier *Suriname*, mitsgaders *Coppename* en *Suramkeka* gepasseert waren) wierd het anker in de grond geworpen, en de Rivier de *Correntijn*, behoorende onder *Suriname*, gesien. Ik, die de Zee niet gewoon was, verlangde nu uit al mijn hert om het vaste land onder de voeten te hebben; doch moest geduld nemen tot dat wy aan de *Rio de Berbice*, seven uuren van daar gelegen, gekomen souden wesen. 's Anderendaags wierd het anker gelicht, om bekwaamelijk met het hoog water binnen de Rivier te loopen; 't geen, na het vijf weeken over de reis besig geweest, en de darde maal op een Woonsdag namiddag in Zee gelo- [9] pen te zijn, op een Woensdags avond geschiedde, wordende het anker ene mijl binnen de Rivier uitgeworpen.

II. HOOFDSTUK

Den Auteur vaart de Rivier van Berbice op. Treed te land. Bedriegt sich door het eeten van Atty. Keert weder aan boord. Word na het Fort afgevaardigd. Drank van Kaauwsel van Wyven gemaakt. Vermaakelijkheid der Rivier van Berbice. Komst aan het Fort.

Dien avond, soo als wy in de Rivier waren gekomen, gelijk in 't voorgaande Hoofdstuk gesegt is, konden wy niet veel sien, als d'aangename groene Bosschen, war uit van tij tot tijd, en by wylen ook wel gestadig, een seer verward geluid van Aapen, en ander gedierte wierd gehoord. 's Morgens, met het krieken van den dag, stond ik al in de mars, om te sien hoe sich het Land opdeed; van waar my dogt dat de dofheid, op Zee bekomen, door een aangenaem gesicht der groene bomen en versche lucht, t'eenemael verdreven wierd. Omtrent negen uuren wierd het anker opgewonden; en wy dreeven met de vloed vast langhsaem voort. Daar was weinig wind; weshalven wy niet boven drie a vier mylen voorderden: wanneer wy het anker weder moesten laten vallen. Thans vernamen wy eenige Indiaanen, gemeenlijk *Bokjes* geheeten. Eenigen van het Scheepsvolk, die 'er meer geweest waren versochten met de Boot na land te mogen vaaren, om *Palmyt* te kappen; 't geen toegelaaten wierd. Ik, nieuwsgierig om dit slag van Menschen te sien, voer mede: en aan land komende, vond ick 'er Mannen, Vrouwen, Kinderen, altemaal moedernaakt, uitgesondert het geen haar sy hunne schamelheid mee bedekken, en daar wy hier na af sullen spreeken. Ondertusschen, terwijl ik dese Menschen met verwon- [10] dering stond aan te kyken, viel mijn oog op een swarte pot met roode Peper, een pottazie die tot allen tyde by hen gebruikt word. Gelijk de Vreemdelingen gemeenlijk groote nieuwsgierigheid hebben, en dikwils vry meer als van nooden is, kreeg ik aanstonds lust om 'er af te proven; nam een stuk van hun brood, en doopte het 'er in. Maar dit gesnoep bekwam my niet wel: want naauwelijks was het brood door de keel, of de mond begon my sodanig te branden, als of ze in vuur had gestaan. Ik vraagde derhalven aan de geenen, dier er meer hadden geweest, wat dit voor kost was; en bekwam tot antwoord, dat ze *Atty* geheeten wierd, en tot de gemeenste spijs der Indianen verstrekt, die 'er meestentijd hun maal mee deeden: gelijk wy hier na breeder sullen verhalen.

Ondertusschen naderden wy vast boschwaart, alwaar een stuk wegs langs ongebaande paden in zijnde gevoorderd, wierd 'er door ons Volk *Palmyt* gehakt; waar af wy insgelijks hier na sullen spreeken. Thans keerden wy weder na de Rivier, traden in de Boot, en deeden ons na het Schip voeren. Hier wierden wy besocht door eenige Indianen, met Vrouwen en Kinderen. Ettelijken van ons Scheepsvolk, die 'er meermaals waren geweest, en iets van de Taal kenden, begonden 'er mee te spreeken, en met eenige snuisteringen handel te dryven. Ondertusschen, terwijl d'Indianen noch aan boord waren, wierd 'er geroepen: een Zeil. 't Was de groote Boot van het Fort, die na Zee ging om te visschen. Onse Capitein seinde ze aan boord; en aldus bekwamen wy kondschap hoe het aldaar geschapen stond. Sekere Vriend, die 'er noch eens was geweest, kreeg, benevens my, order om met de selve na het Fort te zeilen, en, wanneer wy aldaar gekomen souden wesen, brieven na de Plantazien te stuuren, ten einde onse komst bekend te maken. Wy stapten dan over, lichten het anker, en gaven malkander een eerschoot. Omtrent twee uuren voort zijn de gedreeven, kreeg ik door de hette grooten dorst, en vraagde derhalven aan den Schipper, of hy ook iets te drinken had. Drinken genoeg, gaf my dese ten antwoord: en hier op aen een Neger, die den dienst van Kok waarnam, last gegeven [11] hebbende om my daar af te versorgen, waste dese sijne swarte handen; ging schoon water tappen; en kreeg ene hand vol van eenig goed, 't geen niet kwalijck na bry geleek, uit een Kweek. Dit vreef hy door de handen tot dat het water wit wierd; goot het in een Kalebas, daar te lande voor Bekers gebruikelijk; en reikte het my toe. Ik, sonder iets te vragen, sette de Kalebas aan den mond, en haalde daar wel een goede pint uit. Onder 't drinken sei de Schipper, dat ik de tanden wat van malkander moest houden, op dat de drank te gemakkelijker konde doorschieten.

Ik bevond het ook in der daad also: want zijnde dese drank als een soort van bry, schiet het dunne door, en de krummelen blyven voor de tanden sitten. Midlerwijl kon de Schipper sich niet onthouden van te meesmuilen; waer af de reden willende weten, vraegde hy my, of ik wel wist wat ik gedronken had? 'k Zei neen; maar dat, vermits ik geweldig door den dorst geprangd was geweest, my de drank, ze mocht dan weesen wat ze wilde, redelijk en wel had gesmaeckt. 't Is kaeuwsel van Wijven, sey de Schipper, daer men sich, by gebrek van beter, hier te Lande mee moet behelpen. Ondertusschen dreeven wy al soetjes voort; by welke gelegentheyt ik het vermaek had van de Rivier op mijn gemak te beschouwen. Sy is doorgaens seer lustig, en geeft door hare hooge groene boomen een heel aengenaem gesicht, verseld door een gestadig gekrieoel van Aapen, Meerkatten, Bavianen, Papegaeyen, enz., welke laetsten ons van tijd tot tijd met gantsche schoolen over 't hoofd vloogen, en een geschreeuw maekten, dat men naeuwlijks een kanonschoot sou hebben konnen hooren. Toen wy omtrent op twee uuren na aen het Fort waren gekomen, wierden riemen te boord gelegt, dewijl wy anders noch de naeste vloed souden hebben moeten afwachten. Midlerwijl, alsoo den avond op hand begon te schieten, en dat derhalven mijn gesicht niet meer door d'aengenaemheid der voorwerpen verlustigd kon worden, lei ik my te rust: maer ik had niet lang geslapen, of wierd gewekt, vermits wy ons voor het Fort bevonden. Twee uuren te voren hadden wy ons Kanon gelost, om de komst van ons Schip bekend te maken; 't geen daer ter plaet- [12] se gemakkelijk gehoord kan worden, ter oorsaak dat de Rivier met groote bochten loopt, en de nadering aen het selve aldus voor een wijl verachtert. Wy stapten dan over in de kleine Boot; wierden na land gevoerd; en kwamen des nachts tusschen een Vrydag en Saturdag op het Fort, *Nassau* geheeten, alwaer men een groote blijdschap over onse komst vertoonde, en wy van het Opperhoofd met alle bedenkelijke minnelijkheid ontfangen wierden; van wien ons, na dat wy eenige vermakelijke redenvoeringen met malkanderen hadden gehouden, ieder een hangmat wierd aengewesen, om 'er het overige van de nacht in door te brengen.

III. HOOFDSTUK

Brieven door den Auteur na de Plantazien gesonden. Schoone Dreef van Oranje-en Limoenboomen. Komst van het Schip voor 't Fort. Aanstelling van een nieuwen Commandeur, of Opperhoofd. Vertrek van het Schip na de Plantazien. Den Auteur gaat derwaarts om te inventariseeren. Doet het selfde aan het Fort. Uitdeeling van Linnen aan de Slaven. 't Schip met sijne laading weder voor het Fort. Komst van een Engelsch Schip in de Rivier. Geschil over een pul Ael tusschen Vrouwen ontstaan. Den Auteur gaat na den mond van de Rivier. Vreemde soort van Pleisterhuisjes. Vertrek van het Schip. Onderneming van een handel in de Rivier Bourum.

Hoewel ik redelijke vaek had, kon ik die nagt echter weinig slapen, also ik nooit in een hangmat had gelegen. Ook wist ik, dewijl ik 'er niet na had gevraegd, de manier van leggen niet: want in dat soort van hangmatten, die acht, tien, en ook wel twaelf voeten [13] wijd zijn, legt men over dwars. Zo haast dan als het dag was, stond ik op, en maakte mijne Brieven gereed, welke aanstondts na de Plantazien wierden gezonden. Thans kreeg ik lust om te zien waar ik was. Alles stond my wel aan. Niet ver van het Fort vertoont een Dreef van Oranjeboomen, waar af ieder zo groot is als een gemeene Lindeboom in 't Vaderland, en aen de welken altijd blossem, groene en rijpe Appelen in overvloed gezien worden. Deze Dreef is omheind met Limoenboemen, die in schoonheid voor d'Oranjeboomen niet gehoeven te wijken, en gezamentlijke met de zelven een seer lustig gezicht en aangename reuk geven. Hier ging ik een uur of anderhalf wandelen; waar na weder in het Fort gekomen zijnde, wier my mijne kamer aangewezen, welke ik groot en ruim genoeg bevond voor 't geen dat ik 'er te verrichten zou hebben. Omtrent den middag kwam ons Schip voor het Fort; waar op aanstondts van wederzijde eenige kanonschooten wierden gedaan: en traden vervolgens de Passagiers altemaal te land, gevolgd door den Capitein, die de laatste was, en gekomen om het Opperhoofd af te lossen, wiens plaats hy voortaan stond te bekleeden.

Ondertusschen vervoegden zich de Heeren Planters, welke Raaden van de Colonie zijn, hebbende de Brieven, daar wy hier voor eenige melding af hebben gedaan, ontfangen, des Saturdags nachts en Zondags morgens aan het Fort; en wierd door den Predikant een fraaye Predikatie gedaan: waar na zich ieder na zijne rang aan tafel ging zetten. Daar was deftig opgedischt: maar naauwelijks waren wy een half quartier gezeten geweest, of ik moest opstaan; alzo ik zeer misselijk wierd. In de lucht komende, braekte ik een weinig; waar door ik groote pijn in 't hoofd kreeg. Ik ging dan in een hangmat leggen; doch wierd door den Lieutenant, of tweede Persoon, daar uit gehaald, die my sei, dat ik niet moest leggen, maar het op de been houden, of dat ik anders aan de Land-ziekte kon raaken. Ik stond dan weder op; nam mijne plaats aan de tafel, at noch iets onder het storten van een braven beker; en bevond my een uur of twee daar na geheel hersteld. 's Namiddags wierd de [14] klok geluid, en vervolgens in de tegentwoordigheid van alle de Raaden de nieuwe Commandeur, of Opperhoofd, dien zijne Commissie door my wierd voorgeleezen, voorgesteld: waar na het overige van den dag, en ook zelfs een goet gedeelte van de nacht, in vrolijkheid wierd doorgebracht.

's Anderendaags morgens wierd 'er een aanvang met het lossen van ons Schip gemaakt, en eenige kisten en vaatjes aan Land gebracht, welke ik onder mijne bewaring moest hebben, mitsgaders eenige andere goederen voor de Bedienden van het Fort. Vervolgens ging het Schip na boven, na de Plantazien. Het Opperhoofd en ik volgden met een Kanoo vol naakte Indiaanen, alzo wy op de zelven moesten gaan inventariseeren, en de Slaaven monsteren, om te weten hoe veel 'er gestorven en geboren waren. Hier had ik op d'eerste Plantazie, een bezigheid van drie a vier uuren; waar na wy treffelijk met eeten en drinken onthaald wierden. Over-al daar wy kwamen, was de wijn al ontsteken; weshalven wy des nachts het byten van de Musschieten niet veel en voelden. Kort om, 't was een Heeren leven; en ik wenschte wel, dat het wat langer had mogen duuren.

Na dat wy hier eenige dagen mee hadden toegebracht, keerden wy weder na het Fort, daar het zelfde voor eerst omtrent de Koopmanschappen, en vervolgens omtrent de Slaven, wierd gedaan; welke wijders Saturdags daar aan volgende ter zelve plaatse moesten komen, wanneer men volgens de Jaarlijksche gewoonte, Linnen voor Mannen, Vrouwen, en Kinderen zou uitdeelen, te weeten, voor ieder Man zo veel als hy tot een broek van nooden had, de Wijven tot een rok die omtrent de kniën gelijk hangt; en de Kinderen op de zelve wijs. Dit was mijn werk, en gaf my voor ettelijke dagen bezigheid.

Maar een andere, en gewichtiger, kreeg ik, wanneer drie weeken daar na ons Schip, 't geen aan de Plantazien zijne laading had ingenomen, weder voor het Fort kwam om het zelfde ook aldaar te doen; by welke gelegentheid, behalven d'andre bezigheden, ik met het Opperhoofd ten minsten twee maalen daegs aan boort ging, om de bezorgen dat de Colonie niet benadeeld mocht worden. [15]

Midlerwijl ontfingen wy bericht van eenige Indianen, die van beneden kwamen, dat 'er een Engelsch Schip in de Rivier was gekomen. Aanstondts wierden ettelijke Indianen, benevens drie Christenen, derwaarts gezonden, ten einde te zien hoedanig het hier mee geschapen mocht wezen, hoewel wy toenmaals met die Natie niet in oorlog waren. Dezen, terug gekomen, brachten den Schipper van het Engelsch Schip mede, die verlegen was om varsch water. 't Scheelde, volgens het verhaal van den zelven, geen twee dagen, dat wy te gelijk in zee waren gesteken; maar hy was door storm en onweer vry wat verhinderd geweest: en, 't geen vreemd is, ter zelve tijd als wy omtrent de Canarische Eilanden eenige dagen in stilte hadden leggen drijven, had hy by na op de zelve hoogte zulk een kwaad wëer gehad, dat hy geen andere gedachte maakte of hy zou 'er met man en muis gesneuveld hebben. Vyf a ses bouteljes Sek, voor den Schipper medegebracht, benevens belofte van een ton Ael, verkreegen hem het verlof van met zijn Schip tot in het varsche water te mogen komen. Ondertusschen bleef de Schipper by ons op het Fort, en wierd wel onthaald, tot dat hy bericht kreeg dat alles klaar was; wanneer door eenigen van ons Volk aan zijn boord gebracht zijnde, gaf hy hen, na dat ze heerlijk getracteerd waren, de beloofde ton Ael mede. Doch het was een appel van tweedracht, en die by naer een groot onheil te weeg gebracht zou hebben. Het Opperhoofd liet de gemelde Ael aan boord van ons Schip brengen, om, wanneer men na ouder gewoonte met de Heeren Planters voor het vertrek op het zelve stond te gastereeren, onder de vrolijkheid genuttigd te worden: en willende noch een zonderlinge beleefdheid aan den Predikant van de Colonie, en aen zekeren andere Heer, betoonen, liet hy een pul van dit Engelsch Bier door een Jongen voor hunne Vrouwen weg dragen; en wierd tot alle ongeluk de Ael ten huise van den gemelden Heer gebracht. Zijne Vrouw, natgieriger als ze wel behoorde te wezen, en smaak in het Bier krijgende, dronk het gantsch en al uit, zonder aan de Vrouw van den Predikant haar portie uit te deelen. Deze hier over geweldig te onvreede, liet zich sommige woorden [16] ontvallen, die met de beleefheid niet al te wel over een kwamen. d'Andere daar weër tegen aan; zulks dat 'er in 't kort een vervaarlijk geweld ontstond: en gelijk ieder, meenende verongelijkt te weezen, aan haren Man klachtig viel, rees 'er ook wel haast een swaar geschil onder dezen, en zou tot arger uitgeborsten hebben, indien het Opperhoofd my geen order had gegeven om te trachten en de Vrouwen, en de Mannen, te bevreeedigen. 'k Had het geluk van gehoor te krijgen, en mijn oogmerk te bereiken; waar over ik door alle de Heeren Planters wierd bedankt: want gelijk ze beyden Persoonen van aanzien waren, stond het geschapen, dat dit kleine vonkje, indien het niet by-tijdts gedempt was geworden, de gantsche Colonie in brand gezet zou hebben. Doch de vrolijkheid, welke wy hadden toen het Schip onder zeil meende te steken deed deze ongeneugte welhaast vergeeten. Wy banketteerden dien dag helder uit de borst, en des anderendaags wierd het zelve op het Fort gedaan: Want de Heeren Planters wilden niet scheiden voor dat de Ael, waar af een klein gedeelte veel meer geweld had gemaakt als het geheel deed, in vreugde en gejoel tot de laatste droppel toe uitgedronken was.

Twee dagen daar na trad ik met het Opperhoofd in een Kanoo, overdekt met een tent van bladeren, ten einde ons na den mond van de Rivier, daar het Schip zeilree lag, te vervoegen. Dien avond lei ik my voor d'eerstemaal aan land, in 't Bosch, met de hangmat aan twee boomen vast gemaakt, te slapen. Het Opperhoofd bleef ondertusschen in de Kanoo op kussens leggen. Even voor dat ik my te rust wilde begeven, hadden onze Slaven een Pleisterhuisje, onder de Christenen en Indianen alzo geheten, voor my opgerecht, ter plaatse daar de hangmat gespannen moest worden. 't zijn vier stijlen, de voorsten wat hooger als d'achtersten, overdekt met ene dak van bladeren, ongemeen groot, zijnde doorgaans vier a vyf voet lang en wel twee voet breed. Zon noch regen kan hier hinder doen: Want de bladeren leggen zo dicht op en over malkander, dat 'er de straalen van dat groot Licht niet door konnen dringen. Dusdanige Pleisterhuisjens ziet men langs de gantsche Rivier; en men [17] laat ze in een oogenblik oprechten waar men wil: Want een Indiaan is gelijk de Schildpad, overal t'huis. 's Anderendaags kwamen wy aan het Schip, 't geen omtrent een quartier uurs van den mond der Zee af lag. Hier maakte ik de laatste depesches gereed, en nam, in twee etmalen dat wy 'er ons onthielden, het vermaak van met d'Indianen na strand te vaaren, en in 't Bosch uit schieten te gaan. Eindelijk stak het Schip in Zee; en ik keerde met het Opperhoofd, na de nacht nochmaals in een Pleisterhuisje doorgebracht te hebben, weder na het Fort.

Twee a drie dagen na dat wy weder aan het Fort waren gekomen, wierd het Opperhoofd aangesproken door een zekeren Planter uit het Gouvernement van *Canje*, die onze Heeren Patroonen wonderlyke dingen had weeten wijs te maken, wegens de groote progressen welken hy met een tamelijk Cargesoen in de Rivier *Bourum* zou konnen doen. Het Opperhoofd was er alreedts af verwittigd, en had 'er, niet tegenstaande alle zijne voorzichtigheid, veel grooter gevoelen af, als het naderhand wel quam uit te vallen. Ondertusschen was 'er groot overleg toe van nooden; en ik verstond my de zaak niet. 't Most 'er echter mee door; en ik kreeg order om eenige Koopmanschappen gereed te maken, waar mede deze Windbuil met onze Boot zich na de gemelde Rivier op reis begaf: Doch hoe slecht die onderneming kwam af te loopen, zullen wy den Leezer in 't gevolg mede deelen.

IV. HOOFDSTUK.

Onnozelheid der Indianen in het tellen. Langwyligheid in hunne redenvoeringen. Tucht omtrent de Kinderen. Haating van Diefstal. Godsdienst. Beschrijving van d'Indiaansche Mannen en Vrouwen. Manier van te Trouwen, en Vrolijck wezen.

Terwijl ik bezig was met de gemelde Koopmanschappen gereet te maken, kwamen 'er eenige Indianen met hunne [18] waren aan het Fort, welke mijn Tolk afvaardigde, en uit zijne notulen stelde ik de partyen te boek. 't Zijn onnozele menschen omtrent het tellen, gelijk ik in de verscheidene dusdanige gelegentheden heb aangemerkt: Want als ze met een party van dartig bollen verw, *Oriane* genaamt, te markt komen, weeten zy die niet achtervolgens te tellen. Zy leggen vijf bollen by malkander, volgens 't getal van de vingeren der hand, en dan weder vyf anderen. Toen ik dit d'eerstemaal zag, vraagde ik 'er aan mijnen Tolk de reden af; die my zei, dat hun getal zich niet verder uytstrekte als tot vijf. Als ze ook tien willen wijzen, toonen ze alle de vingeren; en twintigh word door de vingeren ende de teenen beduid. De wilde Indianen zijn noch ruim zo onnozel, en betoonden een groote verwondering wanneer ze my zagen schrijven: Want zy konden niet begrijpen, dat men op deze manier zijne gedachten aan een ander, die afweezig is, kan mede deelen.

d'Indianen hier te lande zijn zeer langwijlen in hunne redenvoeringen. 't Geen wy in een half quartier uurs zouden verhaalen, daar hebben zy ten minsten een halven dag toe van nooden. Ondertusschen gebruiken zy by alle deze langwijligheid het geduld van nooit in malkanders redenen te vallen: en den aanhoorder, zo hy al iets wil zeggen, vernoegt zich met den spreeker te gemoet te voeren *wa*, 't geen in onze taal *wel* betekent. 'k Heb eens, zoals wy elk in zijne hangmat lagen, een Meisje hooren zingen; en hoorende gestadig de zelve woorden, zonder eenige verandering, vraagde ik aan mijnen Tolk, wat dit gezang, 't geen zo meenigmaal herhaald wierd, doch behelsde. Niet anders, gaf hy my ten antwoord, als *klein Vadertje, klein Vadertje: mijn oogjes, mijn oogjes als ik gestorven ben*. Dit had wel een half uur geduurd, wanneer de Moeder haar toegraauwde: *Dat je Vader hier was, hy zouje wat anders zeggen*. Want de Man zou met den naam van klein Vadertje geaffronteerd geweest zijn.

Wat de tucht omtrent de Kinderen belangt, zy slaan de zelven nooit, wat zy ook begaan mogen hebben, maar bestraffen wel de fouten en mislagen, op dat zy 'er zich in 't toekomende voor mogen hoeden [19].

Diefstal word onder hen zeer gehaat, en nooit begaan als uit groote luiheid: Want wy hebben kist noch kas, en zouden derhalven het gestolen niet wel weten te verbergen. Zelfs hebben de Vrouwen niets om hunn Cieraden in te bergen, als alleenlijk een Doosje of Korfje, 't geen zy *Pagale* noemen.

Godtsdienst heeft 'er gantsch geen plaats. Ook maken ze geen onderscheid in dagen of tijden. Maar om ook van het uitwendige dezer menschen te spreeken. D'Indianen zijn van een gemeene gestalte, roodachtig van koleur, en Swart van hair; 't geen wanneer ze tot de waardigheid van Capiteyn worden verheven, tot aan de ooren afgesneeden word. Anders hangt het gemeenlijk tot de Schouders. In 't middenschot van de neus hebben zy een gat, daar een zilver plaatje, van grootte als een dubbelde stuiver, vast word gemaakt, 't geen hen tusschen den mond en de neus hangt, en in het drinken, op dat het hen tot geen beletsel zijn, opgelicht, werd. Zy trekken het hair uit de baerd en de wijnbraauwen; willende gantsch geen ruigte aan eenig gedeelte van hun lichaam lijden. Dit word van tijd tot tijd met roode verw bestreeken; welke koleur een groote bevalligheid in hunne oogen heeft. 't Koraal, zo hoog by hen geacht, ziet men van de Mannen weinig tot cieraad gebruiken, 't en zy in sommige gelegetheden van vrolijkheid. Midden om het lijf hebben zy een bandtje, daar hun mes insteekt. De lap, om hunne schamelheid mee te dekken, word hier ook van voor en achter doorgesteken, en hangt ruim een half el over de billen nederwaarts. 't Hoofd word omvangen met een bandtje, daar velerhande soort van vederen aan vast zijn: doch dit vind men meest by de jonge Indiaanen.

Men heeft er ook een soort van Indiaanen *Aquewyen* genaamd. Deze woonen hooger op in het land, en in 't gebergte; van waar ze zeer zelden omtrent het Fort komen, maar wel op een plaats *Markaay* geheten, zijnde de hoogste handel plaats. Zy vallen veel jalourser als d'andere Indiaanen; weshalven zy de Vrouwen ook zorgvuldiger bewaren. Omtrent de gemelde Handel-plaats begint het land allengskens hooger te worden; en loopt de Rivier daar noch [20] ongevaar vyf a zes uuren boven. Hier heeft men het Gebergte, en den oorspronk der Rivier, mitsgaders veel Steenklippen, waar op als noch de merken der Spanjaarden, die de kust eerst ontdekt, en de gantsche Rivier doorgesnuffeld hebben, gezien worden.

Als d'Indiaanen ten Oorlog zullen gaan, bereiden ze veelerhande soorte van Pijlen, waar onder eenigen zo vergiftig, dat 'er weinige, die 'er mee gekwetst zijn, van opkomen. Ook hebben zy 'er met ijzere en beene punten, met weerhaaken, enz. welken zy 'er met hunne messen zodanig toe bekwaam weten te maken. Zy schieten alle hunne Pijlen in de hoogte, met zulk een nette raaming, dat zy ze den geen daar ze 't op gemunt hebbe, in 't lijf weten te doen vallen.

d'Indiaansche Vrouwen zijn insgelijke van een matelijke gestalte, en, hoewel niet schoon, echter ongemeen hovaardig. Hunne voornaamste Cieraden bestaan in *Orewebbe*, zijnde een zeker soort van been, 't geen plat geslepen word, omtrent ter dikte van een Ryksdaalder, en in de rondte als een bezemstuiver. 'k Heb Vrouwen of Dochters gezien, die ik geloof dat vyftien a achtien pond van deze beentjes om den hals hadden. Ook draagen zy 'er korte trosjes af in d'ooren, aan welker einde koper-plaatjes hangen: doch deze zijn op drie deelen na zo groot niet, en dun na advenant. Van wederzyde onder de armen, op de wijs van bandeliers, slingeren veelerhande soorten van Koraal, waar af de groenen en de geelen voor de besten gehouden worden, en een trosje van twaalf a zestien strengetjes genoeg is om het best Vrouwmensch tot zijne wil te krijgen. Deze Cieraden van Koraal hebben zy ook op drie plaatsen om d'armen gewonden, te weten aan de hand, boven den elboog, en aan de schouders. Een lap, op een zeer geestige wijs van het zelve Koraal gemaakt, bedekt hen de schamelheid. Onder de knie ziet men het zelve Cieraad, gelijk ook boven den enkel, daar het zich als een soort van een kous, omtrent drie vingeren breed, vertoont. Deze verlaaten zy niet, voor dat ze t'enemaal versleeten is. Als de dood iemand van hunne Bloed verwanten heeft weggerukt, [21] leggen zy hunne Kleinoodien af, en gaan voor een korten tijd gantsch naakt; zijnde dit de manier van over d'afgestorven rouw te draagen. d'Ouwe Wijven vercieren zich niet meer, en draagen ook zelfs geen zorg om de schamelheid te bedekken, gaande t'enemaal naakt, met lange hangende borsten, die hen voor het lijf heen slingeren. Veele zouden zich mogelijk inbeelden, dat men in den rouw tijd d'oogen wel elders sou konnen laten weiden: maar 't is mis. De jonge Vrouwlieden zijn zo gewoon de beenen geslooten te houden, dat, in wat gestalte zy zich ook voegen, men 'er niets ter wereld af kan zien, zelfs ook niet de minste tekenen wanneer ze onpasselijk zijn: ende als ze, volgens hunne gewoonte, op de grond nederzetten, weeten ze 't eene been op een aardige manier onder 't lijf te leggen; invoegen dat, al bukken ze ook voor over, het oog niet geargerd kan worden. Alle morgens gaan ze in 't water, en neemen 'er ook zelfs de zuigende kinderen mee, om het hen van jongs aan gewoon te maken: want alles wat 'er is kan Swemmen. Zy beschilderen zich dikwijls het aanzicht met roode verw, en trekken, even als de Mannen, de wynbraauwen schoon uit, daar ze dan een streek van bruine veruw, met gom gemengd, geven. Sommigen laten zich met water een gedeelte van 't lijf beschilderen, nu het bovenlijf, dan het onderlijf, enz. dit water droogt inkt Swart op, en is zo bestandig, dat, al gaat iemand zich ook dagelijks wassen, het in de tijd van drie weeken niet af zal gaan.

Ziet daar wat d'uiterlijke gedaante en gewoonlijke cieraden belangt. Noopende hunne bezigheden en diensten in de huishouding: d'Indiaansche Vrouwen moeten brood maken, de Tuin schoon houden, brood tot den drank kaauwen, en *Karsy* raspen, 't geen op een steene rasp gedaan word. Indien den man iets gejaagd, of geschooten heeft, is het hun werk het gejaagde of geschootene te bereiden, en op te disschen. Is 't een Haas, Konijn, Varken, Hert, enz. word 'er het hair afgebrand, 't ingewand gewasschen, en het vleesch op een *berbekot* gelegt. 't Is een Indiaansche Rooster, van houte stokjes, omtrent twee voet hoog. Hier leggen zy hunne spijs op, vleesch en visch, zonder te zouten; [22] en half gaar gebraaden zijnde, kruimelen zy ze in de Peperpot, 't zy om terstond te eeten, of tot een ongelegener tijd te bewaren: want de Peperpot is d'eenigste toevlucht. Zy weeten van geen banketteren, of overdaad in spijs bedrijven. 't Best, 't geen ik ooit by hen heb gevonden, was een stuk van een Haas: anders Krabben, Aapen, Baviaanen, *Ytoeriës*, Miereeters, ja zelfs Krokedillen. Vogels vind men 'er niet, en Visch zelden.

Hoewel d'Indiaanen noch Politie, noch Wetten hebben, trouwen ze echter onder malkander zo wel als de geciviliseerde Natien : 't geen zich aldus toedraagt. Wanneer de jonge Lieden zich onderling verstaan, en dat de wederzijdsche Ouders met het huwlijk te vrede zijn, komen de Bloedverwanten by een, waar na een van 't geslacht het woord neemende, recommandeert hy den Bruidegom by geene andere te loopen, zorg voor zijn Wijf te draagen, naarstig te weezen om een Broodtuin te maken, dagelijks voor zijne keuken uit Visschen en schieten te gaan, Krabben te helpen haalen, enz. en aan de Bruid, dat ze met niemand anders te doen moet hebben, haaren man de behoorlijke getrouwdheiden en eerbiedigheid bewijzen, hem t'elkens als hy t'huis komt spijs en drank voorzetten, met de kinderen niet meer speelen, Etc. In-der-daad, zy hebben gelijk in haar dit laatste aan te beveelen: want de Dochters trouwen 'er ter ouderdom van elf of twaalf jaren, wanner men 'er noch zelden zo veel bezadigdheid in weet te vinden, als het huwelijk wel vereischt. En noopende de Mannen; indien ze zo werksaam waren, als hen wel word voorgehouden, zouden ze spijs en drank in overvloed hebben; want het land is vol van wildbraad, Gevogelte, en Visch: maar hunne aangeboorene luiheid doet hen zich dagen lang met de Peperpot behelpen, verzeld met een dronk *Payewar* of *Beltiery*; van welke dranken wy hier na gelegentheid zullen hebben om te spreeken.

Hunne speeltijden, of vrolijkheden, zijn ook aanmerkens waardig. Wij hadden op zekren tijd, om ons wat te verlustigen, een kaart afgezonden. 't Is een touwetje, met ettelijke knoopen 'er in gelegt, na het getal der dagen [23] waar tegen men de vrolijkheid heeft beraamd. d 'Indiaanen, die het ontfangen snijen 'er alle morgens een knoopje af; en het laatste afgesneeden sijnde, begeven ze zich op weg. Daar kwamen 'er omtrent veertig a vijftig, Jong en Oud, Mans- en Vrouwspersoonen. De drank, die tot de vrolijkheid, of joeling, bereid was, word *Graaf* geheeten, en is gemaakt van Siroop en Water, 't geen in den tijd van drie dagen genoeg gegest heeft om 'er zich dronken in te drinken. Op een geven teken vielen d'Indiaanen aanstondts aan 't dansen, zingen, en speelen; gebruikende daar toe een zeker soort van Dwarsfluyten, welke een vreemd geluit van zich geven. Die hier te land Turf heeft zien trappen, verbeelt zich een ronde dans, daar men malkander niet vast houd, met een groot vuur in 't midden. Zy zijn altemaal beschilderd, ieder op zodanig een wijs als hy de bevalligste oordeelt, doch meestendeel met swarte gom, de wijnbraauwen met bruine, en de wangen met roode verw. En waarlijk, deze verscheidenheid van koleuren vertoont iets aan het oog, 't geen niet onaangenaam is. 't Hair word ook geestig gehuld en gevlochten, vermengt met strengen koraal, aan welker einden beeldtjes en plaatjes hangen, welke hen langs den naakten rug slingeren. Dit dansen duurt tot aan den dag, wanneer ieder zijne hangmat gaat ophangen, en een poos slapen. Ondertusschen bevond ik hier het spreekwoord waarachtig, dat een dronke Vrouw een opene deur is: want niet zo haast waren de herssenen door den drank beneveld, en den avond gevallen, of alle schuilhoeken wierden paarhokken; waar na ze zich stilletjes weder aan den dans voegden, even of 'er niets was omgegaan.

Saturdags heb ik ook de Zwarten dikwijls zien dansen. Dezen speelen op een hol stuk houts, even als een pomp, hebbende een gat onder en boven, daar een lap leer op is gespijkerd. Op 't geluid van dit instrument maaken ze zulke wonderbaarlijke figuuren, dat men zich niet van lagchen kan onthouden; en die het ligchaam in de vreemste postuuren weet te draaijen, is de beste danser. [24]

V. HOOFDSTUK.

Den Auteur krijgt ordre om na Ysekepe te gaan. Manier van d'overgehoudene Beentjes der afgestorvene Capiteinen te verbranden. Flaauwhertigheid van een Indiaanschen Capitein. Beschrijving van het Dorp Ouden Amen, mitsgader van der Indiaanen Oorlogs Huisen. Komst van den Auteur aan een Huis der Westindische Compagnie van Zeeland. Wedertocht na Berbice. Beschrijving van een Indiaansch Dorp. Wederkomst aan het Fort.

Terwijl men nu met ongeduld verwachte, wat de Planter uit het Gouvernement van *Canje*, daar wy aan het eind van het darde Hoofdstuk af hebben gesproken, in de Rivier *Boirrum* zou uitgerecht hebben, komt 'er een Indiaan met een Brief van *Ysekepe*, waar af den inhoud behelsde, dat hy met Boot en Cargesoen in verzekering was genomen. Hier was goed raad duur. Men ontbood de Heeren Planters, om te raadpleegen wat men in dezen verwarden staat van zaaken zou doen. Na lang overleg, wierd ik de bekwaamste geoordeeld om als Gezant derwaarts te gaan. 'k Had 'er weinig lust toe; doch weetende dat ik den last niet wel van den hals zou hebben konnen schuiven, vervaardigde ik een Commissie, die door het Opperhoofd en alle de Raaden ondertekend, en met het Zegel van de Colonie *Berbice*, gezegeld wierd. 'k Had maar twee dagen tijd, om my tot de reis gereed te maken; welke verstreeken, en ondertusschen alles in behoorlijke order gebracht zijnde, begaf ik my omtrent den middag op weg, doch kon dien dag niet verder komen als op de Plantazie, genaamd, *den Berg*, bewoond door *Mons[ieu]*[r] *de Feer*, zijnde met de vloed op te vaaren omtrent twee uuren boven het Fort gelegen. Hier wierd ik wel onthaald, en het [25] verblijf met vrolijkheid doorgebracht. 'k Had zes Indiaanen meegenomen, om de Bagazie te draagen. Dezen lieten aan my verzoeken, dewijl ik doch den nacht daar moest blijven, of ze ondertusschen wel na een zeker Dorp, *Abary* geheeten, mochten gaan. Ik vraagde mijnen Tolk na de reden, die my ten antwoord gaf, dat 'er ter gemelde plaatse over drie a vier weeken een Capitein was komen te sterven, van wien, om zijne dapperheid, volgens gewoonte eenige beentjes waren gehouden, welk nu verbrand zouden worden. Deze beentjes van deze of geene afgesneden ledemaaten, 't zijn vingers, toonen, enz. welke, na dat 'er het vleesch schoon afgeschrapt is, drie a vier weeken boven in het dak van 't huis te droogen worden gehangen. Dit is het eenigste, 't geen ze zo lang behouden, wordende anders alles, 't geen den overleeden heeft nagelaten, als bijl, kapmes, mes, houweel, Etc. Te gelijk met hem in het graf gesmeten: alzo ze zich inbeelden, dat hy het op de reis van nooden zal hebben. Als men nu de gemelde beentjes zal verbranden, word man en Maagd genoedigd om deze plechtigheid by te woonen. Hier is dan overvloed van drank, by d'Indiaanen *Bassia*, en by ons *Pernou* geheeten. De nieuwsgierigheid, alzo ik my de saak met alle omstandigheden door mijnen Tolk had doen verhaalen, drong my aan om mede derwaarts te gaan, en als ooggetuige te zien, 't geen ik van hooren, naauwelijks kon gelooven. Mijne Indiaanen voegden zich aanstondts in de ry, bestaande uit omtrent veertig Persoonen; en dez ry was omvangen van een andere, ruim zo sterk. Ieder had iets in de hand gelijk een lange sweep, daar ze malkander beurt om beurt een vervaarlijke slag mee om de beenen geven. Die geslagen zal worden, staat in 't midden van de ry; en den slag verduurd hebbende, treed hy, in de plaats van den geenen die ze hem gegeven heeft. Dit geschied onder een afgrijselijk geroep en geschreeuw, als of ze malkander tarten, zeggende den een *Bockja watilly* (ik ben een man) en den ander *Dackje wathia* (ik ben ook een man) en die dit streelen niet tot des anderendaags morgens kan verdraagen, word als een lafhertige uitgekreeten, en durft nooit in eenig [26] gezelschap komen. Die een oogenblik tijd heeft, gaat ondertusschen eens drinken: want daar is zulk een meenigte van drank, dat ze niet geconsumeerd kan worden. Onder deze dappere actie hebben de Wijven mede het hunne te doen, te weeten, zy maaken een naar geschrey en gejammer, roepende midlerwijl al snikkende en zuchtende, wie dat nu voor de Weduwe, hunne Zuster, (want zy noemen zelfs de Christenen hunne Broeders en Zusters) Brood zal Planten, uit Jagen en Visschen gaan, Krabben vangen, enz. ondertusschen leggen de beentjes van den overleedenen in het vuur, om tot asch verteerd te worden; daar ook de Wijven op moeten passen; terwijl de Mannen malkander buitens huis zo treffelijk met Sweepslagen begroeten, onder het geflikkere van ettelijke vuuren dien hen tot toortsen verstrekken. Ziet daar, hoe zeer de dapperheid onder deze Natie geëerd word. Ondertusschen betoonen ze zich flaauwhertig genoeg omtrent hunne Vyanden, ten minsten omtrent de Christenen, waar af wy hier een voorbeeld te berde zullen brengen.

Op dit zelve Dorp *Abary* woonde een Indiaansche Capitein, by de de Christenen in de wandeling *Kakkebaretje* geheeten. 't Gebeurde in den Jaare 1665 wanneer wy met *Engeland* in Oorlog waren, dat eenige Roovers de Rivier *Ysekepe* zonder slag of stoot kwamen in te neemen. Dit goed gevolg deed hen ook een onderneeming op *Rio de Berbice* ter hand slaan; geloovende, dat ze aldaar de zelve flaauwhertigheid zouden ontmoeten. De tijding hier af kwam wel haast aan het Fort; weshalven men zich aanstondts tot tegenweer bereide. Ondertusschen waren eenige Indiaanen aldaar gekomen, om hunne Waaren te verhandelen. d'Engelschen vertoonden zich met een Bark van acht a tien stukken op de Rivier, en Schooten door het dak van het Fort heen. d'Indiaan, die dit gedonder in hunne ooren niet konden verdraagen, wisten niet waar ze zich van angst zouden bergen, en kroopen hier en daar in 't kreupelbosch, en elders daar ze zich veilig achten. De Christenen, die van hunne kant mede dapper vuur gaven, trachten hen wel te wederhouden; maar het was te vergeefs. By ongeluk bevond zich daar ook de Capitein *Kakkebaretje*, [27] welke, willende kwanswijs noch eenige moedigheyt betoonen, by de Christenen in het Fort bleef; doch het was 'er van binnen wel anders geschapen: want latende zich gantsch en aldoor de vrees verwinnen, en niet weetende waar hy zich best zou verschuilen, kroop hy in een leedige Suikerketel, die aan het Magazijn stond, welke hy niet weinig bevuijlde. De torn duurde omtrent een half uur; waar na d'Engelsche afgeweeken zijnde, liepen eenigen den Capitein *Kakkebaretje* zoeken, dien zy eindelijke in dusdanig een postuur in de Suikerketel vonden zitten, bevende noch van angst. Over dit geval ontstond een groot gelag; en niemend was 'er die dezen dapperen Krijgsheld niet kwam bezichtigen. Ondertusschen, niet tegenstaande deze uiterste lafhertigheid, was hy niet zo haast weder by zijne Medgezellen gekomen, of hy verhaalde hen met groot pogchen en snorken, hoe kloekmoedig hy benevens de Christenen tegens d'Engelschen had gevochten, met byvoeging, dat zy 't voor een groot gedeelte aan hem verschuldigd waren, dat het Fort niet door hunne Vyanden was ingenomen geworden; verwijtende hen met eenen hunne verwijfdheid, als die niet moedts genoeg hadden om het gedonder van het Kanon te komen aanhoren, enz.

Maar om weder tot het Sterfhuis te keeren. Nadat ik dit slaan met de sweepen, en d'andere grollen die daar uitgerecht wierden, een tijd lang had aangezien, keerde ik des nachts, gelicht met een kleine waskaars om in het Bosch niet te verdwaalen, omtrent elf tot twaalf uuren weder na de Plantazie; konnende mijne dappere Indiaanen niet mee krijgen, welke de plechtigheid tot den einde tot wilden bywoonen. Deze Lieden kan men met geweld niet dwingen. Zy worden, wel door de Christenen aangenomen om de reis te doen, de goederen te draagen, en hen by dag en nacht voort te voeren; waar voor ze ook op de wederkomst betaald worden; maar ze staan niet onder verband als Slaaven, en willen niet gedwongen weezen.'s Morgens omtrent ten acht uuren kwamen mijne Indiaanen weder te rug, sodanig geslagen, dat men tusschen de knien en d'enkels geen duim gezet zou hebben, daar zich geen bloedige streepen [28] vertoonden. 't Waar noch tijdts genoeg geweest om ons op reis te begeeven: maar d'Indiaanen dronken zijnde, en niet geslaapen hebbende, moest ik dien dag daar verblijven. Over de maaltijd vraagde my de Juffer van de Plantazie, of ik wel wat mondkost had mee genomen, alzo ik onder d'Indiaanen niet veel zou vinden. Ik zei, dat ik my eenigsins verzorgd had, en dat, ten kwaadsten genomen, ik my licht een dag of drie zou konnen behelpen. Zy liet dan een doesijn Kalkoen-eyeren voor my kooken, aan de harde kant, en ley 'er een stuk vleesch, en een boutje van een Hoen by. Ik verbeelde my d'Indiaansche Dorpen even als die van ons Vaderland, daar men voor de betaaling altijd spijs kan bekomen, mitsgaders dat ik 'er om de twee a drie uuren een zou ontmoeten: maar dit geloof bedroog my geweldig. 's Anderendaags morgens sloegen wy op weg: maar naauwlijks hadden wy de Plantazie uit het gezicht verlooren, of wy bevonden ons by een Kreek, welke zich ten minsten dartig roeden verstrekte, en tamelijk diep was. De Bagazie wierd voor afgeschikt, en eindelijk van my, door d'Indiaanen gedragen, gevolgd. Omtrent den middag kwamen wy aan een Bosch waar in een goed stukwegs gevoorderd zijnde, wierd de Bagazie van den hals gelegt, en plaats gekoozen om wat te rusten en te eeten. Ik sloot de korf open, en ging met goede appiteyt aan de Eyeren, terwijl d'Indiaanen zich met wat slechter spijs behielpen. Na verblijf van ruim een uir, togen wy weder voort, en kwamen omtrent vier uuren aan een Dorp, *Ouden Amen* geheeten: Aanstondts zocht ik na 't een of 't ander, om dien avond te nuttigen, en onze kost ondertusschen te spaaren; doch kon 'er niets vinden 't geen my behaagde. Hier begon ik dan t'overdenken, hoe bezorgd de Juffrouw van de Plantazie was geweest, en hoe grooten dienst zy my had gedaan met de korf te voorzien; die nu weder tegen den avond, alzo ik goeden honger had, dapper moest aanhouden. Na de maaltijd begaf ik my in mijne hangmat: maar het gehuil van de Kinderen, en het gesnork van d'Indiaanen, die vast ieder om 't zeerst op hunne manhaftigheid, in het verduuren der Sweepslagen op het Dorp *Abary* getoond, roemden, [29] hield my de slaap voor een goede wijl uit d'oogen: doch ik verzette die schade met een braaf gat in de morgenstond te rusten. Thans kwam de Vrouw van de huise met een *wyda* dikke *Payewats*, een korfje met Brood, en de Peperpot, om onzen ontbijt te doen; waar voor, gelijk ook voor de huisvesting, wanneer wy weder vertrokken; ik haar een bosje Koraal van veertien a zestien strengetje vereerde, 't geen zy met groote blijdschap en dankbaarheid aannam. Zy zou ook wel zin ander soort van goed gehad hebben: maar alzo 'er niets en was 't geen my behaagde, sloot ik de *Pagaal*, en wenschte haar welvaren.

Dit Dorp *Ouden Amen* legt op een vermakelijke plaats in een Bosschazie, en heeft zestien a achtien Huisen, welke zodanig gebouwd zijn, dat men door Laanen van geboomte moet heen gaan om van het eene aan het ander te komen. Onder de zelven waren 'er welke door vier, ja vijf en zes Huisgezinnen, bewoond wierden. 't Huis, daar wy des nachts hadden geslapen, was een van de geenen, daar d'Indiaanen zich by vyandelijke overvallen in verweeren; gelijk zodanige vyandelijkheden by mijnen tijd op verscheidene Dorpen zijn gepleegd. 't Had de langte van ongevaar 120 a 130 voet, en de breedte van tusschen de dartig en veertig, en was rondom bezet met pallissaden, zo dik als een gemeene spar, van plaats tot plaats met eenige openingen om daar te konnen schieten; waar toe ze Pijl en Boog gebruiken, zonder dat ze weeten van zich op eenige andere wijs te verdeedigen. 'k Zag 'er ook niets ter wereld in, als eenige Boogen en Pijlen. Deze Huizen, welke van de gezamentlijke Inwoonders der Dorpen onderhouden worden, zijn gedekt met bladeren van een ongemeene grootte, welke onder vast gehegt, en met verscheidene partyen, in malkander gerold, naboven gevoerd, en wijders met banden, by hen voor touw gebruikt, zodanig vast gemaakt worden, dat men, by gelegentheid van brand, het gantsch dak metter haast kan los snijden. d'Indiaanen van een en het zelve Dorp leeven anders zeer vreedsaam onder malkander. Daar kan ook niet wel twist ontstaan: want elk Jaagt, Vischt, en Schiet na zijn welgevallen. Geen land of Bosch is [30] verbooden, geene wateren verpacht, enz. ondertusschen is 'er weinig, of niets, te bekomen; alzo ze maar voor de tegenwoordige nooddruft zorgen, zonder eenige bekommering voor de toekomende te hebben.

Na dat wy den ontbijt genuttigd hadden, begaven wy ons weder op weg, marcherende dan door Bosch, dan door Veld, dan door Kreupelbosch, enz. omtrent een uur namiddag kwamen wy aan een Dorp, daar maar een huis stond, zonder eenig mensch 'er in. d'Indiaanen noement het echter een Dorp, en zeggen, dat 'er wel eer eenig Volk gewoond heeft. Zy gaan 'er noch hun brood plukken, en logeren als dan in dit huis. Wy bleëven daar een goed uur, om te eeten en te rusten; en kwamen wijders tegen den avond, na een weg van omtrent vier uuren afgelegt te hebben, aan een Dorp, waar af my de naam vergeeten is. Hier namen wy huisvesting by een Capitein *Tomenaq* geheeten; hebbende d'Indiaanen die eerbiedigheid voor de Christenen, dat ze hen aanstonds een gedeelte van hun huis inruimen. De vermoeidheid benam my de lust om te eeten: en in tegendeel d'Indiaanen, die zulk een last op de schouderen hadden, en welker beenen zo jammerlijk gesteld waren, scheen 'er niet van te weeten. Ik gaf dan aanstondts order om een vuur nevens de hangmat te stooken, volgens de gewoonte, en leidde my tot de rust: dog den honger, alzo ick des avonts niet gegeten had, wekte my ter middernacht. Ik ging by het vuur zitten, en nuttigde 't geen my noch van spijs en drank overig was, waar na ik my weder te kooy begaf. 's Morgens wierd ons hier weder door de Vrouw den ontbijt gebracht, bestaande in het gewoonlijk Indiaansch tractement, te weeten, een *wyda* met *Payewar*, zo dik van kaauwsel als pap, een bennetje met Brood, en de Peperpot om het Brood in nat te maaken. Nu waren wy noch omtrent drie goede uuren van de Rivier *Tannerary* genaamd, behoorende aan de West-indische Compagnie van Zeeland. Hier hadden wy vyftien a zestien man leggen, om de verw, *Oriane* geheeten, van d'Indiaanen in te handelen.Wy begaven ons dan weder op weg, gaande gestadig door Boschagie, hoog en laag, tot aan de Waterplaats, daar wy een [31] grooten Hoorn vonde. Op het geblaas, 't geen van ons Volk gehoord kon worden, wierden wy met een vaartuig afgehaald. 't Huis, daar de onzen op lagen, was gemaakt van een zeker soort van hout, *Mannekole* geheeten, 't geen heel draadig is, en zich wel laat klieven. Dit hout word by de Christenen meest gebruikt om dat het zeer gemakkelijk te bearbeiden valt. De voorraadkorf was nu leedig, en hier vond ik niet om te eeten. Thans zagen wy malkander zeer droevig aan, en moesten altemaal, niemand verschoond, jammerlijk byleggen, tot des anderendaags, wanneer de Commandant van die Bende zelve na d'Indiaanen ging, en eenige spijs en drank besprak, die hem, alzo hy alreedts vyftien a zestien jaaren onder hen had gewoond niet geweigerd kon worden. Hier by kwam noch het geluk, dat 'er een Haas wierd gevangen; die daar zo delikaat zijn, dat ze het beste Vaderlandsch Kalfsvleesch beschaamen. Hier daatelijk mee te vuur. Onderstusschen wier 'er ook Visch gebracht, welke eenigen hadden weezen vangen; en door d'Indiaanen Brood, benevens een *Commodyen*, of groote pot met drank, *Pernou* geheeten. Men viel dan wel haast met graage tanden aan 't schaffen; en de vrolijkheid, veroorzaakt door de *Pernou*, duurde tot laat in den avond, wanneer men zich te rust schikte.

Ik was in de wil om des anderendaags mijne reis te water na *Ysekepe* voor te zetten: maar tegen den avond kwam 'er een expresse, over land na *Berbice* afgevaardigd, om de tijding te brengen, dat de Planter van *Canje* met de bark ontslaagen was; maar dat het Cargesoen noch onder den Commandant van *Ysekepe* beruste. Ik gaf dan order aan mijne Indiaanen, dat ze zich tegen des anderendaags gereed zouden houden, om my weder na Berbice te geleiden. Dien dag hadden wy ons zeer sober moeten behelpen, ter oorzaak dat 'er met Jagen en Visschen heel weinig was opgedaan. s'Anderendaags, zo als wy op ons vertrek stonden, en ons door de behulpsaamheid der Indiaanen van eenige weinige spijs hadden verzorgd, kwam een Indiaanse Vrouw my een Vischje brengen, even als een bleytje, zijnde omtrent vier duym lang, na 's Landts wyze gebraaden, met een stukje brood [32] toe. Ik zou haar, tot teken van dankbaarheid, wel gekust hebben: en nooit heeft een gansche Kabeljaauw my in het Vaderland zo veel blijdschap aangebracht, als wy nu dit kleine Vischje deed. Omtrent den middag traden wy gezamenlijk in de *Coriaar*. 't Zijn kleine vaartuigen, van een Boom gemaakt, gemeenlijk in zestien a zeventien voet lang en drie voet breed. Men ziet er grooter, doch zelden. Hier kwamen wy mee tot aan het Dorp, daar de Capitein *Tomenaq* woonde, in wiens huis wy weder inkeerden. 'k Had goeden appeteyt, en ging derhalven alles doorsnuffelen, doch vond 'er niets als eenige Hoenderen, waar af ik 'er een den hals afsneed, 't geen ik met een mes betaalde, en aanstondts plukte, kookte, en met wat peper ging zitten op eeten.

Dit Dorp is niet minder vermaakelijk als *Ouden Amen*. 't Schijnt by na onmogelijk, hoe de natuur alles zodanig geschikt heeft. Men gaat niet van 't eene huis na 't ander, of men heeft 'er zeer lustige gezichten, even als perspectiven, welke de vernuftigheid der menschen heeft weeten 't ordineren. Daar de Huizen op staan, is zandgrond; en dat zo dicht aan de Bosschen, daar men niet als kleygrond heeft. Ik telde 'er zeventien, groot en klein. Daar was ook een Krijgshuis, even als in het Dorp *Ouden Amen*: maar het verviel, ter oorzaak dat 'er de Christenen zo dicht omtrent woonden, op welker zorg en wakkerheid d'Indiaanen zich verlaaten. Zij zijn ook van natuure gantsch niet zorgvuldig, noch werksaam; waar uit het dan voorspruit, dat men zich zo bekrompen moet behelpen; daar meen anders in weelde zou konnen leeven: want het land is vruchtbaar genoeg; en indien 'er de behoorlijken arbeid toe aangewend wierd, 't zou allerhander nooddruft in overvloed voortbrengen. Maar een Indiaan plant omtrent zijn huis niet anders als een Katoenboom, of een Boom die *Oriane* voortbrengt: want de Wijven zijn 'er zodanig van aart, dat ze altijd wat van deze verw in hunne *Pagaal*, of korfje hebben, om er de wangen mee te koleuren. Met andere nootzakelijkheden, daar ze meerder nut of zouden ko[m]nen en genieten, zijn ze niet gewoon zich te bekommeren. [33] 's Morgens, zo haast als den dag aanbrak, waren wy al aan den ontbijt; en een uur of anderhalf daar na wierd de reis weder voortgezet. d'Eerste rustplaats was aan het leedige Huis, daar wy hier voor af hebben gesproken, alwaar wy omtrent een half uur vertoefden. s' Namiddags ten drie uuren bevonden wy ons in een Bosch, 't geen zich van verre en naby even vermaakelijk op deed. Hier rusten wy weder wat by een Beekje, en kwamen wijders ongevaar een half uur voor den avond tot *Ouden Amen*. Een Hoen, 't geen ik in 't naauw maakte te krijgen, verstrekte my nu weder, hoewel wat sobertjes toegemaakt, voor een uitsteekende lekkerny. 'k Had 'er ook gaarne een stuk of twee voor mijn Volk willen hebben, en 'er dubbelde betaaling voor geeven; maar d'Indiaanen, en voornamentlijk de Wijven, zijn zo krengig, dat zy ze bewijlen voor een zes dubbelde waardy niet zouden willen missen: en de Christenen moeten zich wachten van hen te vyand te maaken. Voor malkander in tegendeel hebben ze alle dingen over; en al blijft een vreemde Indiaan een maand of twee by den eenen of den anderen t huis leggen, daar word niet op gezien.

's Anderendaags morgens, na den ontbijt op de gewoonlijke manier genuttigd, en met een boschje Koraal betaald te hebben, ging de reis weder aan, en met zulk een luchtigheid, dewijl wy, om zo te spreeken, de kreb nu al begonden te ruiken, dat wy ons des namiddags omtrent ten twee uuren op de Plantazie *den Berg* bevonden; alwaar weder helder goede cier gemaakt hebbende, om de moeyelijkheid van de Reis te vergeeten, trad ik met mijne Indiaanen in een Vaartuig, en deed my na het Fort voeren, daar wy met het vallen van den avond aankwamen. [34]

VI. HOOFDSTUK.

Den Auteur krijgt order om ten tweede maal na Ysekepe te gaan. Bestelling tot de Reis. Vreemde manier van Visch braaden. Komst aan het Huis in Tarnerary, en vertrek van daar. Gedaante van de Duizend Been-boomen. Komst in de River van Ysekepe, en beschrijving van de zelve. Komst aan het Fort Ysekepe, en treffelijk onthaal aldaar. Beschrijving van het zelve. Gastery op een Plantazie. Wedertocht na het Fort van Berbice.

Na een zo moeyelijke Reis afgelegt te hebben, wierd ik heel minnelijk door het Opperhoofd ontfangen: doch weinig dacht ik om een tweede tocht derwaarts te zullen moeten ondernemen; en ondertusschen was het echter noodzakelijk; dewijl men geen andere kans zag om het Cargesoen weder onder handen te krijgen. Ik kreeg dan order om Brieven aan de Heeren Raaden af te vaardigen, behelzende, dat ze zich des anderendaags aan het Fort zouden laten vinden, ten einde middelen te beraamen om alle dingen weder in de rechte plooy te brengen. Dezen ter bestemde tijd verscheenen zijnde, wier de zaak in beraad gelegt. De Commandant van *Canje*, die door zijne onvoorzichtigheid het werk in d'asch had gebrouwen, was 'er tegenwoordig, en zoekende als noch met eenige halsterrigheid de zaak te verdeedigen, wierd hem door de Heeren Raaden te gemoet gevoerd, dat ze lange jaaren voor hem in het Land waren geweest; dat hy 'er ook aan hen volkomene kennis af had behooren te geeven; en dat zy 'er met goede redenen niet toe verstaan zouden hebben. Niettemin, dewijl men hoopte, dat alles noch wel te recht gebracht zou worden, indien 'er een bekwaam Persoon na toe wierd gestuird, staakte men het geschil; en alzo ik een maal derwaarts was [35] geweest, wierd ik eenmondig genoemd om 'er my ook de tweede maal heen te begeeven. 'k Had 'er niet veel tegen in te brengen, als dat ik beter geproviandeerd moest zijn; dewijl 'er onder wege by d'Indiaanen niets en was te vinden. Men zy my, dat ik my van alles, 't geen ik oordeelde tot de Reis van nooden te zullen hebben, zonder eenige verhindering mocht verzorgen. Maar waarlijk, die zich in 't Vaderland alzo tot een tocht gereed moest maaken, zou reden hebben om zeer misnoegd te weezen: maar 't was 'er niet breeder. 'k had maar twee dagen tijdts om alles klaar te maken; doch zijnde de toerusting van geen grooten omslag, bevond ze zich wel haast gereed. Midlerwijl had onze Predikant, zo als ik bezig was met hem de voorgaande tocht te verhaalen, my te kennen gegeven, dat hy wel mee van de party wilde weezen : maar alzo hy oordeelde, dat het hem niet en zou passen zulks te vraagen, zag hy geen gelegentheid om zijn nieuwsgierigheid hier in te voldoen. Ik, verheugde dat hy my deze voorslag deed, sei hem, dat ik wel middel wist om te maaken dat het hem gevraagd zou worden: waar op afgesproken zijnde, vervoegde ik my weder na het Fort, en ging in mijne hangmat leggen. Een oogenblik daar na komt het Opperhoofd boven, en vraagt my, of ik slaap. Ik antwoord neen, maar dat ik in gedachte was wegens de reis, welke ik moest onderneemen. 't Zal alles wel gaan, zei de Commandant, stelt u maar gerust; en komt het al te mislukken, zo is er maar omtrent zes honderd guldens verlooren. Ook twijfel ik niet, of ik zal het wel konnen verantwoorden; dewijl 'er de Patroonen kennis af hebben gehadt. Laat ons de swarigheid eens van het hert spoelen. Onder het drinken zei ik: daar komt my iets te binnen, 't geen zekerlijk by uwe Edelheid goed gevonden zal worden. De Predikant is een gaauw man; en indien hy de tocht met my wilde waagen, men zou 'er een goeden uytslag af mogen verhoopen. De swarigheid was, dat hy het zou weigeren. Ik zei, dat ik hem de pols zou voelen, en als ik met hem boven kwam, dat hy dan van zijne toestemming verzekerd mocht weezen. Dit wierd in 't werk gesteld, en hy nevens my boven gekomen, [36] met alle minlijkheid door den Commandant ontfangen. Hy maakte zich dan gereed, om des anderendaags, zijnde Maandag, met my op reis te gaan. De voorraad bestond in raauw gerookte Spek, gekookte Eyeren, en een brave boutelje met Brandewijn. Midlerwijl verzochten noch drie Christenen aan den Commandant, dat ze mee mochten gaan, ten einde het Gezantschap aanzienlijker te maken; 't geen met mijne bewilleging wierd toegestaan, doch onder voorwaarde dat ze hunne eigene Indiaanen zouden bezorgen, om hunne Goederen te draagen. Met de vloed wierd onze Bagazie ingescheept, benevens tien Indiaanen; en hebbende daar op afscheid van het Opperhoofd genomen, wierden wy na de Plantazie *den Berg* gevoerd. Hier verdeelde d'Indiaanen de Goederen, die zy zouden draagen. Ondertusschen, alzo ik overdacht, dat 'er by ons Volk op het Huis te *Tamerary* niet veel te eeten zou vallen, oordeelde ik het raadsaam twee Indiaanen voor af te schikken, ten einde mijne komst te laaten weeten, benevens order dat ze tegen Donderdag een Canoo gereed zouden houden, overdekt met een tent, daar twee a drie menschen onder konden zitten; mitsgaders dat ik twaalf a veertien scheppers moest hebben. Een uur of twee na het vertrek van dezen, die met het krieken van den morgenstond op weg waren geslagen, namen wy onze afscheid van de Vrienden, zijnde ons gezelschap nu vermeerderd met een zesden Man, te weeten den Swager van den Predikant, die op de Plantazie *den Berg* woonde. Tegen den middag hielden wy halte in het Bosch, by een schoone Kreek daar wy hier voor af hebben gesproken. 't Was een verbeelding van een kleine *Karvaane*, die door de Wildernissen reisde. Ik liet aan ieder Christen twee Eyeren uitdeelen, en een teugje Brandewijn toe drinken. d'Indiaanen hadden twee kerven of kweeken met Brood, daar ik hen Zout toe liet geeven; en wierd de dorst met water uit de kreek gelescht: waar na weder op weg zijnde geslagen, deeden d'Indiaanen ongevaar twee uuren aan deze zijde van *Ouden Amen* door den Tolk aan my verzoeken, dat men aldaar halte mocht houden, niet om dat ze door den last vermoeid waren, maar [37] alzo ze eenige Visch meenden te gaan haalen. Ik vraagde den Tolk, of ze van zinnen beroofd waren, dat ze Visch wilden halen op een plaats daar men met meerder reden viervoetige Dieren verwacht zou hebben: want het was een streek Landts, vlak en effen, die men naauwlijks overzien kon. En als ze nu al Visch mochten bekomen, kon ik niet begrijpen, waar men vuur mee zou maken, dewijl zich geene brandelijke stoffen vertoonden. Mijn Tolk voerde my te gemoet, dat ik daar niet voor bekommerd behoefde te weezen als 'er Visch kwam, dat 'er dan ook wel vuur zou komen. De Predikant en ik gingen in het gras nederzitten, om met geduld af te wachten wat d'Indiaanen zouden uitrechten, dezen naauwlijks een klein uur uitgeweest, kwamen te rug met een brave Zoo van een zekere soort van Visch, by d'Indiaanen *Louwkiddy* geheten, en van gedaante eveneens als de Puitaal in het Vaderland: en indien wy deselve met saus hadden konnen bereiden de smaak, gelijk in 't eeten bevonden, zou ook 't eenemaal eveneens zijn geweest: 't geen my doet gelooven, dat het deselve Visch is. Men heeft 'er ook een soort van Visch van gedaante als Baars; doch de smaak verscheelt eenigsins: en zy is zo harig, dat ze naauwlijks gegeeten kan worden. Maar om weder tot onze Indiaanen te keeren. De gemelde Visch (die gevangen was in een klein Watertje, 't welk, gelijk wy naderhand gingen bezichtigen, geen uitgang had), schoon gemaakt zijnde, sloeg een Indiaan vuur aan een katoene lont. d'Andere plukten ondertusschen Gras, en staken dat door middel van blaazen in brand. Dit smeeten ze in het ander gras, 't geen hand over hand voortbrande: en aldus brachten ze de Visch te vuur, en kregen ze eindelijk gaar. De Predikant en ik proefen 'er van, en vonden ze van een tamelijke smaak: doch op deze wijs toegemaakt, kon ze ons niet genoeg behaagen om 'er den honger mee te verzaden; daar ons ten anderen de nood noch niet sterk genoeg toe aandrong. Wy lieten ze derhalven aan d'Indiaanen, die ze met een zonderlinge gratigheid op aten. Thans nam elk zijne dracht op de schouderen, en stapte weder voort, tot dat wy aan het Dorp *Ouden Amen* waren gekomen, alwaar wy den nacht meenden over [38] te brengen. Wy logerenden weder in het Krijgshuis, daar ruimte genoeg voor een honderd man of twee was. Hier wierd my eerst gezegt, dat ik *Zieken*, by d'Indiaanen *Mebyky* genaamd, in de voeten had. Ik geloofde het niet, ter oorzaak dat ik altijd de kousen aan hield, en dat ik my derhalven inbeelde die kwaal niet onderworpen konnen wezen. Ondertusschen bevond ik naderhand, dat 't geen ik, willende niet na mijne voeten laten zien, voor vermoedigheid had genomen, inderdaad de kwaal was, daar men my voor had gewaarschouwd, en hier na breder afgesproken zal worden. Des morgens kwam de Peperpot voor den dag, mitsgaders een bennetje met brood, en *Payewar* om te drinken; 't geen met een voddery van Koraalen betaald zijnde, begaven wy ons weder op weg. Omtrent elf uuren hielden wy halte in een Bosch, by een Kreek; alwaar, behalve eenige weinigen, de laatste Eyeren moesten aan houden. Midlerwijl wierd het Spek, daar wy noch geen mond aan hadden gezet, gemist: en een van ons Volk wist te zeggen dat 'er des nachts twee a drie Honden waren geweest, welken hy had zien eeten, doch met meening dat ze iets anders onder de kluiven hadden. Hier zag men malkander bedroefd aan; en de schade kon niet hersteld worden. 't Stond ons schoon noch zulk een weg te moeten afleggen, alleenlijk met droog brood en zout. Doch het was geschied, en kon niet verhopen worden: de Bottelier had beter op de *kweek* mogen passen. Wy namen dan weder moed, en gingen voort tot aan het alleen staande Huis, daar wy nochmaals halte hielden: en met den avond brachten wy 't aan Dorp, door ons *Naby* geheeten, daar Capitein *Tomenaq* woonde. Hier hielden wy onze nachtrust; en hebbende vervolgens den ontbijt genuttigd en betaald, gingen wy weer voort: maar eer wy aan de Waterplaats kwamen, sloeg de Predikant voor, dat wy eerst het restantie behoorden op te eeten, om den Indiaan t' ontlasten: want hy liet zich voorstaan, dat wy 't met ons zessen in 't lijf konden draagen, als deze alleen op de schouderen. Men hield dan weder halte, en consumeerde de rest van onze spijs en drank; waar na met een frisschen moed weer voorstappende, kwamen wy 's morgens [39] omtrent ten elf uuren aande Waterplaats, en vervolgens aan het Huis in *Tamerary*. Hier vond ik alles, 't geen ik door de voor uit gezondene Indiaanen had laten weeten, gereed, en gaf order om de Bagazie, benevens een partij schoon water, zijnde van brood en zout noch genoegsaam voorzien, in de Canoo te brengen, terwijl men ondertusschen de ebbe afwachtte, en een Indiaan met een Brief na het Fort in de *Berbice* afgevaardigd wierd, behelzende het ongeluk 't geen de Honden ons omtrent het Speck hadden toegebracht, mistgaders den soberen staat daar wy ons in bevonden, met verzoek dat de Commandant ons een boutelje Brandewijn, benevens twee a drie stukken Spek, aan het Huis van *Tomenaq* beliefde te stuuren, op dat wy 'er ons op onze wederkomste af mochten konnen bedienen. Dit alles besteld zijnde, liet ik door een Indiaansche Vrouw mijne voeten wasschen, met last om te zien of er ook doornen in waren. Zy vond 'er zeven stuks *Zieken*, of *Mebyky* in, waar af wy hier na zullen spreeken. 's Namiddags ten drie uuren ging de reis weder aan, drijvende wy met de ebbe de Rivier af. Deze Rivier van *Tamerary* is zeer plaaizierig, en omtrent van de zelve wijdte als de Rivier van *Berbice*; wijders aan wederzijde voorzien met hooge Boomen, doch weinige of geene *Savaanen*, of Weylanden. 's Avonts omtrent ten acht uuren kwamen wy aan een Waterplaats, daar wy te land traden, om 'er, terwijl de vloed ging, onze nachtrust te neemen. Straks tegen d'Indiaanen aan het hout hakken, en vuur maken, gelijk daar te Lande gebruikelijk is. 's Morgens voor den dag gingen wy weder voort, en bevonden ons tegen den avond omtrent de Zee, blijvende ongevaar ter verte van een half uur binnen de Rivier. Hier moesten wy weder opleggen, om 's anderendaags met de ebbe langs de Zee heen te steeken. Doch de meeste swarigheid was om aan Land te komen; want men moest over een zeker soort van Boomen, *Duizendbeenen* geheeten, heen klimmen. Deze Boomen groeijen aan de kant van 't water, ongevaar vijf a zes roeden van 't vaste land; schieten hunne takken omtrent anderhalve a twee vademen uit; en vatten dan weder wortel in de grond: invoegen dat ze zich als een [40] lange reeks van boogen vertoonen. Hier moet men met gevaar over heen klauteren; want zijnde glad van slijm en slik, weet men naauwelijks waar men zich aen vast zal houden: en Ondertusschen heeft de gewoonte zodanig een Macht dat 'er Indinaanen by nacht veel gemakkelijker over heen klauteren, als de Christenen by dag. Wy geraakten 'er echter altemaal zonder ongeluk over; waar na een sobere maaltijd gehouden hebben, zei my mijn Tolk, dat hy wat met de lijn wilde gaan visschen. 't Docht my vreemd, alzo het heel donker was: en ik beeld my in, dat hy, ter oorzaak van de gladheid der gemelde Boomen, aan d'andere Indiaanen wel werk zou konnen geven om hem te vangen. Midlerwijl kwam hy na een klein half uur weder te rug met een Visch van grootte als een gemeene Kabeljaauw, by d'Indiaanen *Loulouw* genaamd. Wy hadden den Tolk al vergeeten, en ons tot slaapen geleid: maar verstaande zijne goede vangst, sprong ieder ter hangmat uit; en 't liet zich aanzien of men de Visch leevendig verslonden zou hebben. Men gunde zich ook naauwlijks den tijd om ze te kooken; en binnen ene uur zag men 'er niet meer als de graaten af. 's Anderendaags morgens voeren wy me de ebbe weder voort, blijvende gestadig omtrent op twee a drie voeten waters, alzo ze sich niet dieper in Zee durven begeeven. Naauwlijks ware wy ter halver weg gekomen, wanneer d'Indiaanen zeiden, Vaartuigen te zien. Dit ontzettede ons altemaal geweldig; dewijl wy ons inbeelden, dat het wel licht *Caribischen* konden weezen, de doodvyanden van *d'Arrewakken*, of d'onzen; in welk een geval zy zich zeekerlijk met de vlucht gebergd, en ons verlaten zouden hebben. Wy gaven hen moed, en lieten door den Tolk zeggen, dat wy voor hen zouden vechten. Maer het was ons geluk, dat het 'er niet toe kwam: want zy laten zich met deze woorden wel een weinigje paaijen; maar als de nood aan den Man komt, doen zy evenwel hunne zin. De vrees voor de wreedheden, welke op d'overwonnenen gepleegd worden, doet hen, zo 't maar eenigsins mogelijk is, de vlucht kiezen, en in der daad, ze zijn afgrijzelijk; gelijk wy in 't gevolg, wanneer wy van hunne Oorlogen spreeken, [41] aan den Leezer bekend zullen maken. Ondertusschen voeren wy vast langsaam voort; en zijnde wat nader gekomen, riepen onse Indiaanen, dat ze Christenen zagen: waar mede alle bekommering en angst in een oogenblik ophield. Wy telde vier Canoos, en in de zelven ettelijke Christenen en Indiaanen, waar af de laatsten bezig waren met Visch te vangen, 't geen met pijl en boog gedaan word. Zy waren van Ysekepe, en verkochten my voor de waardy van vyf a zes stuyvers een goede Zoo *Quereman*, zijnde een delikaate Visch. Onze *Bokjes* haasten zich om in de Rivier van *Ysekepe* te komen, op dat de pot te vuur mocht gaan: want die arme menschen hadden sedert Donderdag, en 't was nu al Saterdag, niet veel gehad. Eindelijk kwamen wy in den mond van de gemelde Rivier; alwaar, vermits de ebbe noch ging, wy ons aan Land lieten pagaaijen. Straks wierd hier vuur gemaakt, de Visch gesneeden en na 's Landts wijze met *Atty* of peper gekookt. Ieder verzadigde zich nu ten vollen; waar na wy met de vloed weder voort gingen, tot des avonts laat, wanneer wy na een goede Waterplaats lieten om zien.

Deze Rivier van Ysekepe is in haar inkomen omtrent drie mijlen wijd, maar zonder diepte na proportie; hebbende op haar diepst, als het hoog water is, niet boven de tien a elf voeten waters. De mond is met veele droogtens van Zandbanken belemmerd, mitsgaders met drie Eilanden, begroeid met Boomen; waar af 'er ook een meenigte binnen in de Rivier geteld word, altemaal met Boomen bezet. d'Aankomst aan Land is 'er gemakkelijker als ik ooit elders heb gezien, zijnde van den beginne af zandgrond; 't geen ik nergens in eenige Rivier heb ontmoet. Ondertusschen heeft men echter aan het vaste Land kleygrond, gelijk omtrent andere Rivieren. Zy blijft doorgaans wijd, en lustig in 't aanschouwen, ter oorzaak van het Geboomte der gemelde Eilanden, mitsgaders de Bosschazien die zich zeer vermakelijk voor het gezicht op doen. Het Fort legt omtrent twaalf uuren van de Zee, op een Eiland; een weinig boven het welk aan de kant van het Bosch

Steenklippen, en meerder diepten, gevonden worden. Ziet daar, wat het voornaamste dezer Rivier belant. [42]

's Morgens, met het krieken van den dag, zettende 't wy met de vloed weder voort, en kwamen eindelijk aan het Fort, daar men al na ons stond te zien, alzo men 'er een Gezantschap verwachte, waar af ons Vaartuig met een Tent tot een genoegsaam teken verstrekte. Wy lieten ons op een bekwame plaats aan Land zetten. De Commandant *Hendrik Rol* genaamd, kwam my, benevens den Predikant, met de degen in de hand verwelkomen, en deed ons door een dubbelde ry Soldaten heen geleiden, onder het lossen van hunne Musketten. Boven wierden wy ontfangen door den Secretaris, en noch drie schooten met licht Kanon gedaan. Waarlijk, deze eerbewijzingen brachten ons als buyten ons zelven; en wy verbeelden ons, eenige Europische Vorsten te weezen, die ergens een openbaare intreede deeden. Vervolgens wierden wy in de Kamer van den Commandant gebracht alwaar ik mijne Commissie wilde openen; doch hy verzocht my vrindelijk, dat ik 'er noch een dag of vier mee wilde wachten, en eerst wat uitrusten. Mijne andere Stoet van Christenen bleef onder de Soldaaten logeren. Ondertusschen wierd 'er sterke drank van boven gehaald, benevens een pul Wijn, aan de Commandant vereerd om ons te tracteren. Wy zaten 's avonts treffelijk aan, en wierden onthaald met vyf schotelen gebraaden en gezooden; waar na met een dicht ligchaam ons te rust gelegt hebbende, sliepen wy tot 's morgens ten negen uuren: wanneer mijne Indiaanen my verlof kwamen vragen om voor eenige dagen na hunne Vrienden te mogen gaan. Ik gaf hen een Kaart (waar af wy elders d'uitlegging hebben gedaan) mede voor den tijd van acht dagen. Vervolgens ging ik alles bezichtigen; 't geen haast gedaan was: want het Fort *Ysekepe* legt op een Eilandtje, niet grooter als dat men het met een steen over zijne langte kan overgooijen. Het Fort zelve is vier kantig van gedaante, hebbende onder het Magzijn, en boven drie vertrekken, en daar de Soldaten in huis houden, een Kamer voor den Commandant, en een voor den Secretaris, welke met een en dient om de Cargesoenen in te plaatsen. Het Eiland heeft veele Klipsteenen. Rondom het Fort gaat men gemeenlijk jaagen, [43] hoewel 'er geen Wild is als 't geen 'er komt aanswemmen, zijnde dit overvloedig genoeg. Tegen den middag, wanneer ik mijne wandeling had afgelegt, kwam 'er een Christen van de Plantazie van den Heer de *Graaf* (die de goedheid had gehad van de gemelde Wijn tegen onze komst aan den Commandant te stuuren) met verzoek dat de Commandant, benevens zijne Gasten, hem des anderendaags geliefde te komen bezoeken, tegen welken tijd men een goed maal zou bereiden. 't Wierd zonder veele complimenten aangenomen; en wy traden 's anderendaags morgens met de vloed in de *Coriaar*, zijnde ene bekwaam Vaartuig, om na de Plantazie van den gemelden Heer te vaaren, welke omtrent een uur boven het Fort gelegen was. Hier vonden wy alles zo wel gereguleerd, als of wy in 't Vaderland waren geweest. 't Onthaal was ook treffelijk, en bestond in gebraad van vyfderhande soorten, als Hartevleesch, Hoenders, Kalkoenen, Endvogels, en Duiven; mitsgaders drie schotelen, Pottazie van Harte-Haaze-en Kalkoenevleesch. De drank was Dortsche Mom, Wijn, en Brandewijn; waar mede wy de Vrolijkheid tot aan den avond gaande hielden: komende wijders vol en zoet weder aan het Fort. Daar waren in 't geheel drie Plantazies, zijnde die van den Heer *de Graaf* de grootste, en van acht-en-twintig a dartig Slaaven. d'Andere twee konden 'er ieder niet boven de twaalf a veertien uitmaken. Men voert 'er een Prinsen leven, voor zo veel de Spijs en drank belangt: maar die van een gezelligen aart is, en gaarne met menschen verkeert, behoeft zich derwaarts niet te begeeven. En in der daad, behalven dit gebrek, hebben de warme Landen voor een groot gedeelte niet al het gemak, 't geen men 'er zich uit de vertellingen van dezen en geenen wel af verbeeld. De brandende Zonnestraalen vallen lastig genoeg te verdragen; en het mangel van veele dingen, welke tot het leven noodzakelijk zijn, geeft een zekere wanlust, daar men zich niet wel af kan ontslaan. Doch om weder tot onze stoffe te keeren. Na dat wy ons nu genoegsaam hadden uitgerust, zijnde alreedts Vrijdag, verzocht ik den Commandant, dat wy doch eens mochten spreeken van de zaaken, [44] waarom men my derwaarts had afgevaardigd. De pretentie was, dat wy de Rivier *Tamerary* zouden verlaten zonder daar ooit meer in te handelen, en dan zou men het aangehaalde Cargesoen wardeeren, en met *Balsamum Copeira*, in de wandeling Maraan geheeten, betaalen. Deze Balsem word d'Indiaanen gehaald omtrent de Rivier *Aernocque*, aan welkers mond het Fort *Trinidad*, den Koning van Spanjen toebehoorende, gelegen is. Zy druipt uit een seker soort van Boomen, daer met een bijl ingehouwen en wijders een kalbas aangehangen word, om de vocht, zijpelende allengskens uit de kloofs, daar in 't ontfangen. 't Is een heilzame remedie voor 't Graveel, de Steen, en varsche Wonden. Mijne Commissie strekte zo ver niet; weshalven de Conferrentie gestaakt wierd: onder beding, dat ik met nader last derwaarts zou keeren. Ik verzocht dan, binnen ene dag a twee te mogen vertrekken; 't geen my wierd toegestaan: maar de Predikant moest alvoorens des zondags een Predikatie doen, en twee Kinderen Doopen; daar hy zig gemakkelijk toe liet gezeggen. Dit was oorzaak, dat wy 'er tot 's Maandags omtrent den middag bleeven; wanneer, redelijk wel geproviandeerd zijnde, en met eenige schooten begroet, wy de reis weder aannamen; komende na de Zee gepasseerd te zijn, met de voorvloed aan den mond van de Rivier Tamerary. Hier liet ik door d'Indiaanen een party Krabben vangen, om 'er ons op de tocht te water af te bedienen. Deze Krabben, welke ook met meenigte in de Rivier van *Ysekepe*, aan de klippen worden gevangen, werden Zoetwaterkrabben geheeten, en zijn veel smaalijker als die in de Zee gevangen worden, doch niet wel zo groot. Vervolgens kwamen wy weder by ons Volk in *Tamerary*, daar wy zeer welkom waren, ter oorzaak dat wy noch ettelijke Krabben hadden overgehouden. Hier bleven wy tot des anderendaags middags wanneer ons aan de Waterplaats hebbende laten brengen, was onze rust plaats in het Dorp *Naby*, ten huize van de Capitein *Tomenaq*, daar wy tot onser aller ongemeene blijdschap provisie van Spek en Brandewijn vonden, waar mede wy ons dien avond helder vrolijk maakten. 's Anderendaags morgens, met den dageraad, toogen [45] wy weder voort, en kwamen des avondts aan het Dorp *Ouden Amen*; alwaar den nacht overgebracht hebbende, en des morgens weder op zeg zijnde geslagen, vervoegden wy ons 's namiddags omtrent ten vier uuren op de Plantazie *den Berg*, en van daar wijders des anderendaags aan het Fort, alwaar wy minnelijk van den Commandant ontfangen wierden.

VII. HOOFDSTUK.

Darde tocht van den Auteur na Ysekepe. Schrikkelijke manier van een Indiaan tot Capitein te maaken. Komst aan het Fort Ysekepe. Geschil wegens d'aangehaalde Koopmanschappen beslecht, en accoord met den Commandant van Ysekepe geslooten. Wederkomst aan het Fort van Berbice.

Na dat ik een wijdloopig verhaal van mijne verrichting aan den Commandant had gedaan, wierd 'er weder een Vergadering met de Raden van de Colonie belegt, die wel niet gaarne de Rivier van *Tamerary* verlaten zouden hebben; doch overdenkende met wat recht wy die bezaten, resolveerden zy, dat men my nochmaals met een nieuwe Commissie zou voorzien, benevens een volkomene authoriteit om met die van de Compagnie zodanig te accorderen, als ik 't het best raadsaam zou oordeelen. 'k Had twee weeken tijds om my uit te rusten, en alle noodwendigheden tot de aanstaande tocht gereed te maken, op de welke de Predikant my weder gezelschap stond te houden. Wy begaven ons dan, verzeld van ettelijke Indiaanen, op ene Vrijdag weder na de Plantazie *den Berg*, daar wy den nacht overbrachten. 's Anderendaags toogen wy voort tot aan het Dorp *Ouden Amen*: alwaar ons gevraagd wierd, of wy des Zondags over wilden blijven, alzo 'er een Indiaan tot Capitein gemaakt zou worden. De reis was [46] zo haastig niet, of wy konden wel een dag tot ons vermaak neemen: weshalven wy, heel nieuwsgierig om deze plechtigheid, daar ons vreemde dingen af verhaald wierden, met eigene oogen aan te schouwen, ons 'er licht toe lieten beweegen. Zondags morgens vervoegden wy ons dan na de plaats, daar de Ceremonie stond te geschieden, zijnde het Huis van een particulieren Indiaan. Aanstondts wierden onze hangmatten vervaardigd; want men vind 'er stoel, noch bank, noch tafel: zittende d'Indiaanen altijd op de hucken. Men zag 'er een meenigte van *Pernouw*, zijnde een soort van drank, waar af een ieder by deze gelegentheid zo veel mag drinken, als 't hem belieft. De drank word omgedeeld door een van de mooyste jonge Dochters, die drie of vier vingeren in de kalebas, de duim 'er buiten, heeft, en zo wel den Christenen, als den Indiaanen, op die manier te drinken geeft, zonder dat men er niet de hand of vinger mag aanraken, als alleenlijk wanneer men genoeg heeft, en de kalebas van zich afweert. Zo het gezelschap groot is, zijn de Dochters, die den drank omdeelen, ook meerder in getal: en by gebrek van dezen, worden 'er ook wel Vrouwen toe genomen. Omtrent den middag, terwijl de Dochters en Wijven noch al bezig waren met den Gasten hun bekomst van drinken te geeven, verscheen den Indiaan, die tot de waardigheid van Capitein verheven zou worden. Hy wierd geleid door drie Capiteinen, die hem met wonderlijke gebaerden tot dapperheid aanmoedigden; en zijnde in het midden van het Huis gekomen, bleef hy staan, verheffende d'armen boven zijn hoofd. Ondertusschen maakten de gemelde drie Capiteinen zig gereed, hebbende ieder een *Maquary* in de hand, zijnde een soort van een gevlochtende sweep, omtrent vyf voet lang, onder dik, en boven smal toeloopende. Hier sloegen ze, beurt om beurt, den armen Indiaan zo deerlijk mee om het lijf, dat 'er van d'oxelen af tot aan den buik weinig heel vleesch overbleef, zijnde alles op een schrikkelijke wijs aan flarden geslagen. Men kon het geklets van de sweepen tot buiten het huis hooren; en echter toonde de Patient niet het minste teken van pijnlijkheid. Kort hier na, wanneer hy nu [47] zo goed als gevild was, wierd hy op een houte rooster, by d'Indiaanen *Berbekot* geheeten, gelegt, en met bladeren overdekt. Onder deze rooster was een klein vuur gestookt, 't geen meerder rook als vlam van zich gaf. Midlerwijl wierden 'er nu en dan eenige bladeren opgelicht, om te zien of hy ook gevaar liep van te beswijmen: 't geen na een korte wijl bemerkt zijnde, namen zy hem van de *Berbekot* af; gooten hem omtrent een emmer vol water over 't aanzicht; en spraken hem op nieuws, zijnde nu weder tot zich zelven gekomen, met vreemde gebaarden moed in. Thans wierd zijn gebroken huit weer van ieder der gemelde Capiteinen met acht a negen sweepstreeken begroet; zulks dat hy 'er uit zag als een bedelaar, dien de lappen en vellen by hangen. Deze plechtigheid moest na twee a drie weeken weder geschieden, eer hy tot de waardigheid van Capitein verheven kon worden; by welke gelegenheid, zo hy een Vrouw heeft, zy mede een steek twee drei krijgt, op dat zy ook aan de glorie van haren man deelachtig mag weezen: doch zy verwacht geen meer als twee a drie slagen, en loopt aanstonts weg. Na alle de gemelde tormenten, wierd de Patient weder in zijn quartier gebracht, zijnde een klein vierkantig vertrek, in het huis afgeschooten, even zo groot dat 'er zijne hangmat kon hangen. Ondertusschen ging het drinken gestadig zijn gang: en de Wijven vetoonden zich zeer vrolijk, dat ze zulke dapperen Mannen hadden, die niet en zouden schroomen, om wraak van hunne Vyanden te neemen, voor hen in de dood te gaan; zingende liederen tot roem van der zelver Heldendaaden. Wy zullen, wanneer wy van hunne Krijgstochten spreeken, gelegentheid hebben om met eenen te verhandelen, wat daaden zy verricht moeten hebben om de waardigheid van Capitein te konnen bekomen. Wat den geen belange, daar wy zo even af hebben gesprooken, hy had in zeker Oorlogsactie een oude Vrouw half dood geslagen, wijders in het water gesmeeten, haer in het zelve met duizend tormenten gemartilariseerd, en eindelijk met onuitspreekleijke pijnigingen om 't leven gebracht. Ziet daar, waar hunne dapperheid in bestaat, te weeten, in slagen te verduuren, en de gruwelijkste wreedheden [48] der wereld te verrichten. Anders zijn ze lafhertige guilen, die op het losbranden van Kanon, of miskettery, naauwelijks weeten waar ze zich zullen bergen; gelijk wy 'er hier voor ene exempel af hebben verhaald.

Met het krieken van den volgenden dag begaven wy ons weder op de been, en kwamen eindelijk, na een weg van elf mijlen afgelegt te hebben, by onzen ouden Capitein *Tomenaq*, en van daar wyders des anderendaags in *Rio de Tamarary*. Hier rusten wy tot des Vrijdags, wanneer wy ons weder in een Vaartuig, overdekt met een goede tent, inscheepten; met het welk wy, langs de strand heen gevaaren, des anderendaags in de Rivier van *Ysekepe*, en vorders aan het Fort kwamen; alwaar wy op dezelfde manier, als de voorgaande reis, wierden ontfangen, en nochmaals met alle beleefdheid van den Heer de *Graaf* getracteerd. Na eenige dagen vertoevens, geduurende de welken wy den tijd met jaagen en andere vermaakelijkheden doorbrachten: geraakte ik met den Commandant in onderhandeling wegens onze aangehaalde Koopmanschappen; welke, na dat wy inder minne met malkander over een waren gekomen, gewaardeerd wierden, en binnen zekeren tijd met *Balsamum Copeïva* betaald moesten worden: waar en tegen wy gehouden zouden weezen de Rivier van *Tamerary* te verlaten. Hier wierden wederzijdsche Geschriften af gemaakt, en getekend: waar op wy Dingsdags daar aan volgende met den Commandant van *Ysekepe* na *Tamerary* voeren, ten einde met mijne komst het accoord te volbrengen, en ons Volk van daer te doen vertrekken. Vier dagen waren wy onder weg eer wy aan het Huis in *Tamerary* kwamen; alwaar dien nacht geslapen hebbende, lieten wy ons des anderendaags middags altemaal na de Waterplaats brengen, en de Koopmanschappen en Kisten van het Volk te water na *Rio de Berbice* voeren : waar na wy in vriendschap afscheid van malkander namen. De nachtrust wierd vervolgens weder op het Dorp *Naby*, ten Huize van den Capitein *Tomenaq*, genomen. Hier vonden wij weer provisie van kost en drank, door onzen Commandant op mijn verzoek derwaarts gezonden. Ik commandeerde veertien man om [49] zich 's morgens gereed te maken, en hunnen weg over *Ouden Amen* te nemen. Wy met ons vieren namen dien op een Dorp, *Woeroenje* geheeten, een goeden dag gaans van het Dorp Naby gelegen. Nooit heb ik daar te land vermaakelijker weg bewandeld. Men heeft 'er Bosschazien, daar het geboomte zo regulier in staat, als of 't 'er met handen geplant was. In dit Dorp *Woeroenje* hadden wy drie man leggen, om met d'Indiaanen te handelen. Zy onthaalen ons met Spijs en Drank in overvloed, en lieten des anderendaags een *Coriaar* voor ons gereed maken, waar mede wy des middags aan de Plantazie, de *Mierenberg* geheeten, ongevaar acht uuren te water van het Fort van *Berbice* gelegen, kwamen. Ik vond dezen weg vrij gemakkelijker; doch willende nochmaals een nacht op de Plantazie *den Berg*, daar ik altijd een zeer vriendelijk onthaal had genooten, over brengen, stapten wy op onze voeten weder voort, en bevonden ons binnen den tijd van drie uuren op de gemelde Plantazie: van waar des anderendaags omtrent den middag vertrokken zijnde, kwamen wy na twee uuren vaarens weer aan het Fort.

VIII. HOOFDSTUK.

Komst van eenige Indiaanen, die een Krijgstocht zouden gaan onderneemen, aan het Fort. Bereidselen tot dezelve. Schrikkelijke handeling omtrent de Gevangen, enz.

Kort na dat ik de laatstemaal van Ysekepe weder terug was gekomen, en van den Gouverneur beneffens de Heeren Raaden, voor mijne moeite bedankt geworden (want daar was weinig aan de Rivier *Tamerary* verlooren ter oorzaak dat men ze, om door die van *Ysekepe* niet verdreeven te worden, met geweld van Volk moest beleggen) vervoegden zich eenige Indiaanen aan het Fort; [50] welke ons, volgens gewoonte, kwamen bekend maaken, dat ze over acht-en-twintig dagen tegens hunne Vyanden, woonende in de Rivier de *Corentijn*, zeven mijlen bezuiden de Rivier van *Berbice*, ten Oorlog meenden te trekken. 't Is te verwonderen, hoe zeer zy zich by deze gelegentheid uytslooven om hunne Vloot, bestaande uit omtrent zestien a achtien Kanoos, klaar te maken: want het is de luiste Natie, die men ergens kan aantreffen: en men zou in het Vaderland al zo gaauw een diergelijk getal van Oorlogschepen vervaardigen. Als ze zich deze gedachten van tegens hunne Vyanden te willen optrekken in 't hoofd brengen, stuuren ze eenige Manschap uit na verscheidene Dorpen, aan de Capiteinen die zich aldaar onthouden. Al wie men wil, neemt een Kaart, van riedtjes gemaakt, waar van alle morgen een afgesneeden word. 't Is, gelijk wy elders gezegt hebben, hunne tijd rekening. Straks valt de jonge Manschap aan 't arbeiden, zoekende ieder om 't zeerst eer in te leggen; doch het gaat, om de waarheid te zeggen, langzaam genoeg toe: want ze werken pas een uur of twee daags aan hunne Vaartuigen, brengende den meesten tijd door met zich te verheugen wegens het ingebeelde gevolg van de toekomende tocht. Wanneer nu de Kanoos klaar, en van alle noodwendigheden voorzien zijn, maken ze zich een gantsch etmaal vrolijk, en begeven zich wijders na de vergader plaats. Hier raadpleegen de Capiteinen met malkander over hunne onderneeming; en het besluit genomen zijnde, is het zelve terstond aan een ieder openbaar, zelfs ook de Wijven niet uitgezondert: doch men weet 'er van verraad, noch verraders. Thans komen 'er de Helden op afzakken, en leggen altemaal aan 't Fort, den een om een karabijn te leenen, den ander om kruid, een darde om kogels, enz. 't geen alles, zonder dat men 'er iets voor vordert, aan hen gegeven word; en bestaat de grootste gift in drie schooten kruid, en zo veel kogels. Belagchelijk zijn de gebaarden en postuuren, welken zy by deze gelegentheid maken, om ons te beduiden, hoe zy hunne Vyanden zullen slaan, en der zelver Dochters tot Slaavinnen maaken; verkoopende, volgens het spreekwoord, aldus den [51] huid, eer zy den Beer hebben gevangen. In elke Kanoo ziet men ook twee a drie Wijven, welker werk is den drank te maken, en de Mannen te dienen. De gantsche tocht duurt gemeenlijk twintig a twee-en-twintig dagen. In twee ebben komen ze aan de Zeekant; en ondertusschen zijn ze hier gemeenlijk twee a drie dagen mee bezig: want ze zien niet een Vogeltje zitten, of ze knippen op de vingers, en vertellen malkander daar iets af. Als ze nu aldus met horten en stooten gezamenerhand aan de Zeekant zijn gekomen, word 'er weder Krijgsraad gehouden, en vervolgens met de gantsche Vloot in Zee gesteeken, voorderende ieder dag omtrent drie mijlen: doch wanneer ze zich in de Rivier van de Vyanden bevinden, vaaren ze niet als by nacht, neemende ten dien einde de Maan tot hun voordeel. By dag versteeken ze zich diep in de Bosschen, en verbergen de Kanoos, op dat men hunne aannadering niet gewaar moge worden, onder eenige afgehakte groene takken, welken zy zo natuurlijk weeten te schikken, dat 'er het gaauste gezicht mee misleid zou konnen worden. Midlerwijl gaat 'er by nacht een uit verspieden, of hy ook ergens eenigen van hunne Vyanden weet aan te treffen; in welk ene geval hy 'er metter haast kondschap af gaat geven aan de Vloot. Hier op worden alle de Vaartuigen bezorgd: d'Indiaanen treeden te Land; en alles gaat zo stil toe, dat de Vyanden overrompeld zijn, eer ze den tijd hebben om zich met de vlucht te konnen redden. Doch wat deze stilte belangt, die duurt niet langer als tot dat ze hunne Vyanden hebben omcingeld: want als dan maken ze een afgrijzelijk getier en slaan in die eerste woede dood alles wat ze ontmoeten. Maar als ze zich nu volkomen meester zien, en dat de wederstand geen baat meer kan doen, beginnen ze gevangen te maken. Die 't ondertusschen kan ontvluchten, mag zich overgelukkig rekenen. Indien ze Vrouwlieden krijgen, die niet jong en mooy zijn, zulks dat zy ze bekwaam oordeelen om 'er hunne lust mee te konnen boeten, hoewel ze daarom evenwel Slavinnen blijven, die slaan ze aanstonts dood: doch zijn ze wat goelijk, worden ze aan andere Vrouwen, te weten van de geenen die met hen vaaren, in [52] bewaring gegeven. Met de Kinderen, 't zy Jongens of Meisjens, leven ze na dat ze hen aanstaan. Zijn ze bevallig van weezen, mogen ze een harde dienstbaarheid te gemoet zien, doch blijven in 't leven: maar hebben zy 'er wat veel gevangen gekregen, zo worden 'er wel eenigen om koxswil gedood. Maar ongelukkig is hy, 't zy Man of Vryer, die geen kans vindende om 't ontvluchten, of zich dood te vechten, levendig in de handen zijner Vyanden komt te vallen: want daar konnen geene wreedheden bedacht worden, welken zy niet in 't werk stellen om hem te tirannizeren, en op een schrikkelijke wijs aan hun eind te helpen. Doch gelijk ze niet altijd op dese manier hunne Vyanden konnen verkloeken, vaaren ze de Rivier hooger op en de Kanoos bezorgd zijnde, trachten het een of ander Dorp t' overrompelen. Dit geschied al mede met het aanbreeken van den dag, en met een getier dat 'er de lucht af wedergalmt. Maar alzo het geluk van den Oorlog niet alijd even wel wil dienen, gebeurt het ook wel, dat ze zodanig een wederstand vinden, dat ze genoodzaakt zijn hol over bol de vlucht te nemen, en zich uit de Rivier voort te pakken. By deze gelegentheid, te weten als ze onverrichter zaake weder 't huys komen, word er drank gemaakt; en zijnde op hunne hucken gaan neder, zeggen ze, dat ze pijn in de buik hebben, en drinken zo veel dat ze moeten braaken: waar na ze kwansuis weder gesond worden. Ziet daer hunne manier van oorlogen, en verwacht nu hoe ze zich omtrent den gevangenen dragen.

De Vloot, daar wy zo even af hebben gesprooken, bragt op hare wederkomst twee Jongelingen, op de Vyanden onverrompeld mede. Zy voeren by nacht stil voor by het Fort heen, en hadden de zelven zo wel bezorgd, dat 'er niet de minste kans was om t' ontkomen. Deze rampzaligen, die aldus op een Krijgstocht gevangen worden genomen, zitten omtrent drie weeken opgeslooten, en geboeid; geduurende welken tijd zy hen van goede spijs en drank verzorgen. Ondertusschen houden ze zich gemeenlijk bezig, om in deze bekommerlijken staat wat tijd verdrijf te hebben, met een *Pagaal* of bennetje daar te lande voor een doos gebruike- [53] lijk, te maaken. By nacht worden de Gevangen bewaakt; en tegen dat 'er iemand van de zelven verbrand zal worden, bereiden de Vrouwen een menigte van drank, *Pernou* genaamd, waar af wy elders hebben gesproken, en van welkers hoedanigheden wy hier na een omstandige melding zullen doen. Daags voor dat hy zal sterven, heb ik met eigene oogen meer als een maal gezien, ze hem deftig met kost en drank onthaalden, op dat hy doch frisch ter dood mocht gaan. Na den middag word hy als tot een spot van het eene huis in 't ander te zien gebracht, by welke gelegentheid hy wel onverwacht een slag op 't hoofd krijgt, dat 'er het bloed by nederloopt, bijtende hem toe : *uwe Vrienden hebben 't aan de onzen ook wel gedaan.* Als de Zon aan 't ondergaan is, vraagt een Capitein, of hy de Zon wel ziet; waar op *ja* geantwoord hebbende, zegt de Capitein: *gy en zult hem niet weder zien.* Dit is zijn vonnis. 'k Heb 'er een ter dood zien brengen, die moedig genoeg zijnde om zich door geenige dreigementen, of de schrik voor d'aanstaande pijningen te laten verflaauwen, den Capitein, die hem zijn vonnis velde, met een heldachtig en versmaadend gelaat te gemoet voerde: *'t is waar, het lot is tegenwoordig op my gevallen: maar myne Vrienden zullen ook wel 't eeniger tyt by u lieden komen, en rekenschap eisschen van de tormenten die gy my staat aan te doen. Het leven is my niet zo aangenaam, of ik kan het licthelijk verlaten: doch dit moeit my dat ik sterven moet sonder wraak over mijne dood te konnen neeme, etz.* Met den avond geven zy hem te eeten en te drinken, zo veel als hy begeert; brengende een tegelijk het hem al eens toe. Thans binden zy hem de handen achter den rug, en aan ieder voet een lang touw. Ondertusschen hebben zich de genoodigden aldaar vervoegd, elk voorzien met eenige *Maquarijs*, een soort van toortsen, bestrecken met een zekere goed 't geen de hoedanigheid van pek heeft, op dat ze te beter mogen branden. 's Avonts omtrent ten zeven uuren begint men rondom, en binnen 't huis, vuuren te stooken; waar na de gevangen in het midden zijner Vyanden gesteld zijnde, word 'er door den oudsten Capitein een groot misbaar bedreven, schreeuwde luidskeels: *u Volk heeft van myne Vrien-* [54] *den gekregen, en hen zodanig gehandeld.* Hier op stoot hy hem met de brandende *Maquary* in de huid; waar na een ieder, die hem maar kan bereiken, op hem aanvalt. d'Een stoot hem in 't aanzicht, d'ander omtrent de manlijke deelen, een darde op een andere van de gevoeligste plaatsen; terwijl hy ondertusschen met de gemelde touwen gints en herwaarts word gesleurd. Ondertusschen, indien hy door al dit martelen te flaauw begint te worden, geven ze hem van tijd tot tijd een korte verpozing, om zijne tormenten aldus te langduriger temaken: want zy willen 'er een volkomene vernoeging af hebben. Midlerwijl drinken ze weder met malkander, even of ze goede vrienden waren; en de lyder aldus wat verfrischt zijnde, word het werk weer aanvangen. Dit duurt tot aan den morgen, ongevaar een uurtje voor Zonnen-opgang: want als dan moet 'er een eind af gemaakt worden; 't welk geschied door een Capitein, die den rampzaligen gevangen met een houte swaard de kop in slaat. Thans valt 'er een ieder met het mes op aan: den een snijd hem een stuk uit de bil, den ander uit de dy, een darde tornt hem op een andere plaats: kort om, elk past wat te raaken. 't Afgesneeden vleesch word, gekookt zijnde, in de peperpot gedaan, en voor goede spijs gegeten. Ik heb twee Christenen gesproken, die 'er af geproefd hadden, en verklaarden, dat het heel lekker smaakte. 't Gebeente word in d'aarde begraven, behalven eenige beentjes daar ze fluiten af weeten te maken. Onder al dit gedoente zitten de Wijven te zingen; bestaande het gezang in het ophaalen van de tormenten, door eenigen hunner Vrienden, in der Vyanden handen gevallen, geleden, mitsgadders den lof van deze dappere Mannen welke op de gemelde wijze wraak van hunne dood haalen. 't Is een schrikkelijk ding om aan te zien: behalven dat de reuk van het vleesch, 't geen onophoudelijk met de *Maquerys* gebrand word, en daar het ziedende vet tappelings by neer loopt, bekwaam is om een Christen niet alleen een braakdriftige walging aan te brengen, maar ook zelfs by na te doen stikken. Ondertussen moet men zich onder alle deze pynigingen verwonderen over de kloekmoedigheid van de gevangenen, die zo ongemeen groot is, dat ze zich aldus op [55] gruwelijkste en gevoeligste manier ter dood laten brengen, zonder de minste laf-hertigheid te betuigen; troostende zich daar mee, dat ze t'eeniger tijd door hunne Vrienden gewroken zullen worden.

IX. HOOFDSTUK.

Den Auteur doet weder een tocht na Ysekepe. Gevaar van schipbreuk. Komst aan het Fort van Ysekepe. Vertrek van daar. Vreemde manier der Indiaansche Vrouwen omtrent het baaren van Tweelingen. Wederkomst aan de Berbice, enz.

De tijd, aan die van *Ysekepe* tot de betaling van onze aangehaalde Koopmanschappen gegeven, waar af wy omtrent het eind van het zevende Hoofdstuk hebben gesproken, verstreeken zijnde, wierd ik gecommandeerd om noch maals derwaarts te gaan, en de bark ten dien einde van alle noodwendigheden voorzien. Daags voor het vertrek waren wy, volgens gewoonte, helder vrolijk; waar na te scheep zijnde getreeden, wierden de zeilen opgehaald: maar naauwelijks waren 'er twee uuren, geduurende de welken wy gestadig hadden moeten laveeren, verloopen, of wy hadden het ongeluk dat de Gijk quam te breeken. De Stuurman van het Schip, daar wy hier voor af gesproken hebben, die by deze gelegentheid de plaats van Schipper bekleedde, moest derhalven weder na het Fort keeren, om een nieuwe Gijk te haalen; terwijl ik hem ondertusschen aan boord bleef leggen wachten. Hy kwam des anderendaags weder te rug, en bracht, gehalven de Gijk, een groote pul Wijns mede, lekker met dooyers van eyeren en kruid toegemaakt. Ondertusschen was het getal der Menschen van onze bark met een Jongen-zoon vermeerderd geworden, en dit zo stil in zijn werk gegaan, dat 'er by na niemand kennis af had gehad. Een Indiaansche Slaaf had het ampt van Vroedwijf waar genomen. 'k Stuurde aan [56] de Kraamvrouw, zijnde een Indiaanin daar onze Jager de vriendschap aan had gedaan van haar te beswangeren, een pot met kandeel; waar af men my wist te berichten, dat ze haar niet kwalijk was bekomen: doch 't was eens voor al; want de smaak van de Wijn wierd al te goed bevonden om aan die wankoleurige menschen weg geschonken te worden. s'Anderendaags, tegen den avond, kwamen wy aan de Zee; liepen 'er ten negen uuren in; en zeilden de gantsche nacht met tamelijke koelte. s'Morgens kreegen de Rivier *Majeyke* in 't gezicht, en kort na den middag de Rivier *Tamerary*. Maar terwijl wy aldus met redelijke spoed voortzeilden, stiet de bark omtrent ten vier uuren, niet ver van de Rivier *Ysekepe*, op een Zandbank, daar wy ongevaar een half uur op zaten, stootende vast op en neer; zulks dat 'er het water van alle kanten kwam in schieten, en ons moeite genoeg maakte om het met alle man met hoozen boven te houden. En naauwelijks waren wy dit gevaar ontworsteld, of wy wierden zo onzacht op een andere bank neer gezet, dat men niet anders docht, of de bark zou tot spaanderen gestooten hebben: en waarlijk, zo ons niet een holle baar van daar had gevoerd, wy hadden het uiterste gevaar van Schip-breuk geloopen. Thans moesten wy quartier maken, om te pompen en te baalien, waar mede wy eindelijk des avonts in de Rivier *Ysekepe* geraakten, alwaar het anker in de grond wierd gesmeeten. Hier waren wy genoodzaakt, ter oorzaak dat 'er niet gekookt kon worden, ons, benevens Jan hagel, met een stuk raauw Pekelspek te belijden, doch echter met dit onderscheid, dat 'er de Stuurman en ik een goed glas Brandewijn op zetteden. Omtrent ten tien uuren kreeg men twee a drie swaare lekken gestopt; 't geen een groote gerustheid baarde. Met de vloed zeilden wy weder voort, en kwamen met de daar aanvolgende aan het Fort, wanneer van wederzijde eneige eerschooten gewisseld wierden. Thans trad ik met den Stuurman te land, daar wy zeer minnelijk van den Commandant wierden ontfangen, en getracteerd; en hebbende vervolgens na verblijf van een dag of twee wegens de zaak gesproken, en voldoening bekomen, gaf ik order aan die van de bark, dat ze weder terug [57] zouden keeren: want vermits ze zo deerlijk gehavend was, wilde ik liever mijnen ouden weg nemen. Na zes a zeven dagen nam ik afscheid van den Commandant, en tot medenmakker op mijne reis een zekeren Vriend die te *Tamarary* iets te verrichten had. Wy namen weinig of geen Proviand mede; alzo mijn Reis-Broeder my wijs maakte, dat het onnodig was ons daar mede te belaaden ter oorzaak dat wy op een na by gelegen Dorp, alwaar een joeling van Indiaanen zou wezen, alles in overvloed zouden vinden. Maar in plaats van dat, vonden wy ons deerlijk bedroogen: want toen wy aan dit Dorp kwamen, 't geen seer fraay was, en wel uit in de twintig huizen bestond, vernamen wy niet het minste teken van de gemelde joeling, alzo ze, om eenige reden gestaakt was geworden. Wy moesten ons dan weder 's Landtswijze behelpen, sober genoeg, en gantsch niet na mijne zin. 's Anderendaags 's morgens, zo als wy meenden te vertrekken, toonde men ons een Indiaansche Vrouw, redelijk fraay van gelaat en gestalte; welke voor omtrent een maand of anderhalf twee voldraagene Kinderen te gelijk ter wereld gebracht hebbende, het eene met eigene handen had gedood, en in d'aarde gesteeken. Want het dunkt hen een onnatuurlijkheid in een Mensch: en zy willen, zeggen zy, hier in met de Honden, en andere zodanige vruchtbare Dieren, niet gelijk wezen. Ik bezag haar met aandacht, gelijk ook het overgebleven Kind; 't geen, hoe jong het ook noch mocht zijn, na 's Landts manier, dicht by haare Wooning in 't zand lag te vroeten: want daar word zo veel werks niet van de Kinderen gemaakt, als wel in 't Vaderland, en elders. Wy toogen dan weer voort; en hebbende op het overige van deze te rug reis geene wederbaaringen van belang meer, zal ik den Leezer alleenlijk zeggen, dat ik gezond en behouden, hoewel met zeer zeinig vermaak, weder aan ons Fort kwam. [58]

X. HOOFDSTUK.

Komst van een Schip uit het Vaderland. Twist tusschen het oude Opperhoofd en den Predikant. Verbranding van een Handelhuis door de Karibische Indiaanen. Tocht van den Commandant en den Auteur derwaarts, enz.

Nu was 'er een algemeen verlangen na een Schip uit het Vaderland, alzo men in een lange wijl geen tijding van daar had gehad. Eindelijk kwam 'er een opdaagen, en met het zelve een nieuwe Commandant, of Opperhoofd. Met dezen, na dat wy volgens ouder gewoonte eenige dagen met gasterijen en vrolijk wezen hadden doorgebracht, vond ik my gehouden weder na de Plantazien te gaan, ten einde te gaan bezichtigen hoe de zaken aldaar geschapen stonden. Ondertusschen, terwijl wy hier mee bezig waren, kwam 'er twist t'ontstaan tusschen het oude Opperhoofd en den Predikant; die, als de swakste zijnde, zo haast wy weder te rug waren gekomen, tegens alle recht en reden order kreeg om zich, benevens zijne Vrouw en Kinderen, tot zijn vertrek na het Vaderland gereed te maken. d'Oude Commandant was een haatdragende man, die al over lang getracht had den goeden Predikant de voet dwars te zetten: doch hy had 'er geen gelegentheid toe konnen vinden. Nu was 'er by een voorval van vrolijkheid een onstaan; welke by 't hair gegreepen hebbende, liet hy voor een dronk Brandewijn eenige Atestatien maken, waar in de waarheid op een schrikkelijke wijs geweld wierd aangedaan. 'k Had mijnen Vriend, dewijl ik al overlang te gemoet had gezien dat hy hem t'eeniger tijd den voet zou lichten, menigmaal genoeg gewaarschouwd; doch het scheen, dat hy dit ongeluk niet kon vermijden. Midlerwijl, alzo ik hem gaarne met raad en daad wilde helpen, voorzag ik hem heimelijk met een Brief aan de kerkenraad van de Fransche gemeente tot Vlissingen; waar mede gelijk [59] ik naderhand verstond, alle de Attestatien van de ouden Commandant gedood wierden. Maar hoe vriendelijk hem deze ondertusschen op de reis gehandeld heeft (want ze vertrokken kort daar na gezamenerhand met het gemelde Schip, doch den een in vry beter qualiteit als den ander) kan van den Leezer lichtelijk afgemeeten worden. Ik deed hen uitgeleid tot aan de Zee, en bedankte den Commandant, wanneer wy afscheid van malkander namen, voor het goed onthaal, 't geen ik ten allen tijde van hem had genooten. 't Was in der daad waar: doch ik kon echter niet na laten hem te gemoet te voeren, dat het my van herte leed was, dat de Predikant mee moest gaan; en dat meer met my gaarne gezien zouden hebben, dat hy daar had mogen blijven. De Commandant bracht hier eenige redenen tegen in, zo vol van bezadigheid als geveinsdheid: maar indien hy had geweten, dat ik den vroomen Leeraar den gemelden Brief had mede gegeven, wy zouden zulke Vrienden niet gescheiden hebben. Zijn onverstandinge haat was zo groot, dat hy alle middelen in 't werk meende te stellen, om te weeg te brengen, dat den Predikant de Stoel wierd verbooden: doch, tot genoegen van veele eerlijke lieden, mislukte hem zijne onderneeming; waar af hy my naderhand, gelijk in het volgende Hoofdstuk gezegt zal worden, het loon betaald dacht te zetten.

Kort na het vertrek van het oude Opperhoofd met het gemelde Schip na het Vaderland, kwam 'er tijding uit de Rivier *Canje*, dat de Karibische Indiaanen uit de Rivier de *Corentijn* ('t zijn de Vyanden van d'*Arewakken*, met welken naam die van *Berbice* betekend worden) het Huis, 't geen wy aldaar hadden, hadden verbrand; dat ons Volk genootzaakt was geweest zich met de vlucht te borgen; dog dat ze wijders weinig schade hadden gedaan, en niemand gedood, of gevangen genomen, ter oorzaak doch dat ze in tijts door drie Indiaanen ontdekt waren. Doch ziet hier de dapperheid van deze lieden. De bezetting der onzen bestond in zeven man; welke, door de gemelde Indiaanen gewaarschouwd, de vlucht namen, en zich in het naast gelegen Dorp posteerden. De Karibischen, die het niet zo zeer op d'onzen, als wel op hunne [60] Vyanden gemunt hadden, kwamen ook met een afgrijzelijk getier op dit Dorp aanvallen: maar ziende dat deze zeven Christenen zich by d'Indiaanen hadden gevoegd, lieten ze den moed zakken, en keerden, zonder iets t'ondernemen, weder te rug, hoewel ze meer als drie-maal zo sterk waren. Op dit bericht dan stuurde de Commandant een kaart van ettelijke dagen aan de rondom leggende Indiaanen, ten einde hen het oprechten van een nieuw Huis aan te besteeden, waar toe wy de plaats zouden gaan bezichtigen. Drie dagen voor ons vertrek stuurden wy drie Christenen voor uit, om te bezorgen dat wy onderweege spijs en drank, mitsgaders bequaam Huisvesting, mochten vinden. Twee Paarden voerden vervolgens den Commandant en my derwaarts; welke, hoewel ze redelijk weg spoedden, nochtans omtrent vier uuren bezig waren met ons tot aan de Waterplaats te brengen. Drie Negers waren twee uuren voor uitgegaan, om gras voor de Paarden gereed te houden. Twee anderen, benevens zes Indianen om de Bagazie te dragen, hielden zich by ons. De weg was vermaakelijk bestaande in velden en bosschazien, altemaal gelijk Land, zonder eenige heuvelen of dalen. Wy moesten twee maal met de Paarden door het water; en zijnde wijders aan de Rivier *Canje* gekomen, vonden wy 'er een Vaartuig, waar mede wy gebracht wierden ter plaatse daar men oordeelde dat men het Huis behoorde op te rechten. Hier zagen wy een groote partij Indiaanen, van alle kanten derwaarts gevloeid, veele uit nieuwsgierigheid om den nieuwen Commandant te zien, en anderen om zich tot ten arbeid te laten gebruiken. 't Was 'er alles, na 's Landtswijze, wel gereguleerd, en spijs en drank genoeg. De grond verstrekte ons tot een tafel, en eenige groote groene bladeren tot tafelaken en handoeken. De Brandewijn bleef voor d'Indiaanen verborgen: maar wy hadden wel twee stoop *Kilduivel* mee genomen, om hem te beschenken. 't Is een drank, die de kracht heeft van dronken maken, en daar wy hier na af zullen spreeken. Met den avond moesten 'er al ettelijken gaan slaapen: anderen waren 'er zodanig door bevangen, dat ze een groot gedeelte van de nacht met praaten en [61] ginnegabben door brachten, verhinderende my de zoetheid van de rust te genieten, enz. 's Anderendaags morgens wierd 'er een accoord tusschen ons en d'Indiaanen gemaakt, behelzende, dat ze het Huis binnen vyf dagen klaar zouden leveren, rondom bezet met palissaden, en schiet gaten 'er in: op dat men in 't toekomende niet meer overrompeld mocht worden. Thans, op dat ze te yveriger tot den arbeid mochten weezen, wierden ze met het overschot van de *Kilduivel* beschonken; waar na onze afscheid genomen hebbende, keerden wy op dezelve manier weder terug.

XI. HOOFDSTUK.

Aankomst van een Schip uit het Vaderland. Wrok van het oude Opperhoofd tegens den Auteur. Vreemde wedervaaring van een Indiaan. Droevig ongeluk van twee Negers, enz.

Het duurde nu ene geruimen tijd eer dat 'er weder een Schip uit het Vaderland aankwam; weshalven de Tafel geweldig mager begon te worden: want onze Wijn en Brandewijn, zeer noodige dingen hier te lande tot bewaaring van de de gezondheid, waren by na t'eenemaal geconsumeerd. Eindelijk kreeg men evenwel de tijding, dat 'er een aan de mond van de Rivier was gekomen. Straks wierd 'er de Bark na toe gezonden: doch wy verstonden wel haast, tot ons hertelijk leedweezen, dat het zo veel provisie niet had mee gebracht, als wy wel gaarne gezien zouden hebben, en ook wel van nooden hadden. d'Oorzaak was eensdeels om dat het zijne laading te *Hamburg* had ingenomen, en ten anderen een zekere wrok tegens de voornaamsten van de Colonie: zijnde de Capitein de geen die mijn eerste Opperhoofd had geweest, een haatdragend Man, die het aangedaane leed wel uiterlijk scheen te vergeven, doch nooit en vergat. Maar weinig dacht ik, dat ik ook onder het getal van zijne Vyanden te boek stond; gelijk my kort daar na genoegsaam kwam te blijken. Het [62] Schip zeilde ondertusschen opwaao[r]ts; en hebbende het anker voor het Fort laten vallen, kreeg ik order van den Commandant om den Capitein te gaan verwelkomen. Ik voer dan na zijn boord, en wierd met zeer minnelijke gebaerden, doch een geveinsd hert, in de kajuit genoodigd. Straks zettede men my voor gerookt vleesch, boter, kaas, en witte biskuit. Onder het eeten wierd ook de Wijn niet gespaard. Maar toen men eenige glazen met malkander had gewisseld, en dat de geveinsdheid niet langer beslooten gehouden kon worden, veranderde de vrolijkheid wel haast in een schielijk stilswijgen, een mompeling tusschen de tanden, en eindelijk in een uitbarsting van waarom ik een schoone fijne Hangmat, door den Commandant van *Ysekepe* aan my mede gegeven om ze hem, als een vriendelijk geschenk, ter hand te stellen, en een andere, vrij slechter van stof, had verwisseld. 't Was wel waar; maar ik had door zijn voorbeeld geleerd, dat die den Altaar dient 'er af moet leeven. Ook had ik hem by die gelegentheid diensten gedaan, welke met geen Hangmat, al was ze ook noch veel fijnder geweest, betaald konden worden. Doch dit was maar om op den text te komen; want hebbende my vervolgens met een valsche grim lag te gemoet gevoerd, of hy niet altijd met my had geleefd gelijk of ik zijn eigen kind waar geweest, en ik hem daar op geantwoord van ja, vraagde hy my, wat my dan doch bewoogen had, om buiten zijne kennis, zodanig een Brief aan den Predikant mede te geven.Ik zei hem dat wy malkander naderhand over die zaak wel zouden spreeken: dat ik gekomen was om hem uit den naam van het Opperhoofd te verwelkomen, en niet om oude koeyen uit de sloot te haalen: dat ik ook weder na land toe moest, en in vriendschap wenschte te scheiden. Hy begreep de meening heel wel; liet een groote berkemeyer in de kajuit brengen, en dronk my toe, zonder verder van eenige swaarigheid te reppen. Zo haast als ik weer voet aan Land had gezet, verhaalde ik den Commandant mijne wedervaaren; die my zei, dat hy hem beter kende als ik, en dat hy maar wenschte gelegentheid te konnen aantreffen om hem den voet dwars te zetten, alzo hy 't al over lang aan [63] hem had verdiend. Dit smeulde zo eenige dagen, doch wierd niet uitgedoofd: want gaande met malkander op een morgen op de Plantazie, de *Mierenberg*, geheeten, wandelen, haalde hy de zaak van den Predikant weder op. Ik zei hem met korte woorden: dat ik had gedaan na conscientie; dat hy wel betoonde niet veel omgang met zodanige lieden te hebben gehad: dat de beste wel een mislag kon begaan: dat het niet redelijk was een Man, om dat hy eens beschonken was geweest, uit zijn welvaaren te willen helpen: dat men zijne passie zo veel niet moest toegeven, enz. Hy bestierf van kwaadheid, beet op de lip, en sweeg stil; doch gaf my met zijn gezich te genoegsaam te kennen, dat hy 't my gaarne betaald wilde zetten. Twee a drie dagen daar na keerden wy gezamentlijk met den Commandant weder na het Fort; van waar wy ons tot verschiedene malen aan het Schip vervoegden, om vrolijk te wezen: doch nooit ging ik er alleen, hoe minnelijk ik 'er ook toe genoodigd wierd; alzo ik van een mijner vrienden, aan wien hy dit geheim vertrouwde ter oorzaak dat hy waande eenige onlusten onder ons te weezen, wierd gewaarschouwd, dat hy my door jan hagel een kwaade part meende te laten speelen, daar hy dan kwansuis niet af geweeten zou hebben. Niet te min, hoe wel ik my onder de bescherming van het Opperhoofd veilig genoeg achte, trachte ik my echter met den ouden Commandant te verzoenen: ten welken einde ik hem daar over liet aanspreeken. Hy hield zich zeer vreemd, en zei, dat, verre van my een kwaad hert toe te draagen, hy in tegendeel een van mijne beste vrienden was, en dat hy zulks in alle voorvallende gelegentheden zou betoonen. Maar tot hoe verre deze woorden gingen, bleek by verscheidene ontmoetingen, waar in hy zich nooit zo zeer kon bedwingen, of de domste mensch zou wel bemerkt hebben, dat er iets in zijn hert schuilde, 't geen hy niet opentlijk dorst uiten. Ik hield my derhalven stil, en mijdde zijne tegenwoordigheid zo veel als ik kon. Ondertusschen schoot de tijd van het vertrek op de hand. Wy waren dan, gezamentlijk met de Heeren Planters, volgens gewoonte, op het Schip, 't geen nu al tot aan den mond der Rivier was afgezakt, [64] vrolijk; waar na het zelve des anderendaags in zee stak, zonder dat den ouden Commandant geduurende zijn gantsche verblijf aan *Rio de Berbice* gelegentheid had konnen vinden om zijne wraakzucht aan my te boeten.

Kort hier na, en zo als wy ons eerst even weder aan het Fort hadden vervoegd, kwam 'er iets te gebeuren, 't geen zeer aanmerkelijk is. Zekere Indiaan, na het Bosch gegaan om hout te hakken, wierd, zo als hy met zijn werk bezig was, van achteren door een Tijger verrast, die hem met den eersten slag een tamelijk stuk vleesch uit het dikste van de dy, vlak onder de bil, weg scheurde; en hervattede den aanval, sloeg hy hem de klaauwen in de rug. Den Indiaan, door verbaastheid bevangen, liet de bijl vallen; doch denkende echter op zijne verdediging, vrong hy zich zo lang, niet tegenstaande hy door de klaauwen en tanden van dit verslinde beest aller wege gekwetst wierd, dat gy zijnen Vyand van vooren kreeg. Thans greep hy moed; vatte, terwijl de Tijger, staande met de voorste pooten over eind, den bek in den slinker arm had gezet, met de rechter hand het mes, 't geen d'Indiaanen aan een snoer om het lijf draagen; en stiet het hem tot het hegt toe in de buik: waar na de wond met het scherp wijder opscheurende, deed hy het Beest dood ter aarde vallen. En zeker, 't was op zijn pas: want verswakt door het verlies van zijn bloed, vonden hem eenige Indiaanen, kort daar na ten zelven einde na het Bosch gegaan, niet verre van den dooden Tijger leggen, hebbende het bebloede mes nog in de hand. Dezen voelende dat 'er leven in was, brachten hem aan het Fort, daar hy door de zorg van onzen Geneesmeester tot zijne voorige gezondheid en krachten hersteld wierd. 'k Heb dien dapperen Indiaan noch langen tijd daar na gezien; draagende de lidtekenen van zijnen Vyand noch zo levendig, als of ze eerst varsch gezet waren geweest.

Naauwlijks een week na dat dit voorgevallen was, wierd ons de tijding gebracht, dat twee Negers van de Plantazie, de *Mierenberg* geheeten, bezig met het roeren van de Suiker, door ik weet niet welk een onvoorzichtigheid of ongeluk (want men kon 'er nooit het rechte bescheid af krijgen) in de ketel [65] waren gevallen. Ik wierd dan, benevens onzen Chirurgijn, derwaarts gestuurd; daar wy de gemelde negers beiden noch levendig aantroffen: doch ze waren zo deerlijk gesteld, dat ik een zo droevig schouspel niet zonder tranen kon aanschouwen. De lighaam en vertoonden zich doorgaans als gevild; en de gaten, door de ziedende Suiker daar in gebrand, waren zo menigvuldig, dat men geen vlakke hand op een heele plaats kon zetten. De Chirurgijn bewond hen gantschen en al, om zo te spreeken, in de pleisters: doch daar was geen darde verband van nooden. Zy stierven na het tweede in d'uiterste elende; den een zo raazende, dat men hem handen en voeten moest binden; want hy scheurde en stiet alles 't geen hy kon bereiken, aan stukken. Ondertusschen scheen men 'er op de Plantazie niet veel weet van te hebben. Men at en dronk, en was 'er vrolijk. Want dewijl de Negers, volgens alle schijnbaarheden, doch moesten sterven, bekommerde men 'er zich niet mee, of ze veel of weinig pijn leeden. Zo weinig worden die arme menschen by de Christenen, die ene grooter liefdaadigheid en medelyden behoorden te hebben, geacht.

Ziet daar voor het meeste gedeelte mijne wedervaaringen tot noch toe aan *Rio de Berbice*. Tegenwoordig, dewijl 'er in eenigen tijd niets van belang kwam voor te vallen, zal ik den lezer gaan onderhouden met hem eenige byzonderheden voor te stellen, wegens de gelegenheid van het Land, de manier van leven der Indiaanen, d'Aard-en Boomgewassen, het Gedierte, Gevogelte, Visch, en wat daar verder van afhangt, en eenige nieuwsgierigheid omtreent een opmerkenden lezer verdient. [66]

XII. HOOFDSTUK.

Gelegenheid van het Land. Beschrijving van een zekere soort Indiaanen, Warouwen geheeten. Gewilligheid der Indiaanen voor de Christenen. Andere aanmerkelijke byzonderheden noopende d'Indiaansche Mannen en Vrouwen, enz.

Wat de gelegenheid van het Land belangd, het is doorgaans boschachtig; en staat het Geboomte op verscheidene plaatsen naauwlijks ene halfmijl van de Zee, langs de welke het land zich Zuid en Noord heen steekt. Het voorste land loop met de vloed onder, doch niet zeer ver. Hooger op rijst het allengskens opwaarts, en is het overstroomen van het water niet onderworpen. De Chistenen vangen omtrent de Zeekant veele Harten: doch d'Indiaanen willen 'er de moeite niet toe doen, behelpen zich met een Krabbetje. Aan de kant van het Bosch onthoud zich een zeker soort van Indiaanen, *Warouwen* geheeten. Deze woonen daar veel veïliger, als iemand in de Rivier: want het is onmogelik by hunne huizen te komen, ter oorzaak van de wegen, die gemaakt zijn van dikke sparren, staande over eind, tien a elf voet hoog van de grond, en in zulk een vreemde schikking, dat 'er geen mensch ter werelt zo wel by dag over kan loopen, als zy by nacht doen. d'Andere Indiaanen van wat Natie zy mogen weezen, schroomen 'er ook voor: want die 'er af tuimelt, valt met de naakte huid in de doornen, daar de Bosschen vol af zijn. Deze wegen strekken zich kort en lang, tot dat ze aan hooger land komen, 't geen zandig is, en daar d'eene of d'andere spruit langs heen loopt, om zoet water te hebben. Zy gaan nooit met de *Arewakken* ten krijg, en worden evenwel door de Karibischen, indien zy ze betrappen, 't geen echter zelden gebeurt, doodgeslagen. Hunne spraak [67] verscheelt omtrent zo veel van malkander, als het Walsch en Fransch; komende de *Waraouen d'Arewakken* wel verstaan, doch d'*Arewakken* de *Warouwen* niet volkomen. Zy bemoeyen zich met zaayen noch maayen, en geneeren zich niet als met Visschen en jaagen voor de Christenen. Als 't tijd is, dat de *Jarouw* ('t is een Visch van gedaante omtrent als kloeke Voorn, zeven a acht duim lang, doch niet zo blank) gevangen moet worden, gaan zy 'er de Christenen af verwittigen, en stellen de vergader plaats voor de Vaartuigen. Thans vervoegen zich die van het Fort en de Plantazien herwaarts, om de Vischvangst by te woonen; welke geschied met een stuk van een Korf, ten dien einde bereid, waar mede de *Warouwen* de kreeken of spruiten, die van boven komen, toestoppen. De gemelde Visch word 'er in zulk een overvloed gevangen, dat de Christenen te naauwer nood bekwaamelijk konnen inzouten, en, na dat 'er het ingewand uitgenomen en het het hoofd afgesneeden is, op de zelve wijs als de Haring in 't zout gelegt. De betaaling voor dezen dienst geschied met bijlen, messen, en diergelijke dingen; waar voor zy weder hunne noodwendigheden van d'andere Indiaanen koopen. De Wijven van de *Warouwen* komen zo groots en prachtig niet voor den dag, als die der *Arewakken*; bestaande hunne sieraaden in koraale snoeren, kruiswijze om het lijf geslingerd: doch ze vallen wel zo blank, en de Mannen vry jaloerser, en evenwel onbeschaamder, lopende meesten zonder lap voor hunne manlijkheid, welke zy met een bandtje om het hoof tegen de buik ophaalen, en achter om het lijf vast binden. Hun postuur is, of te staan: of op de hucken te zitten, al ontmoeten ze ook zelfs een bank: want de langduurige gewoonte heeft hen deze manier van zitten zo gemakkelijk gemaakt, dat ze zich met geen andere bekreunen. Wyders zijn ze vervaarlijk luy, zo wel als d'*Arewakken*, die mede niet zullen gaan jaagen of schieten, indien zy 'er door de nood niet toe gedwongen worden. Wy hebben elders naamelijk wijdloopig van dezen gesprooken, dar wy hier ter plaats noch eenige byzonderheden zullen byvoegen.

Niet tegenstaande hunne overgroote luiheid, zijn ze echter [68] zeer gewillig voor de Christenen, die hen stuuren werwaarts zy begeeren, en hen veelerhande diensten laten verrichten. Als wy een Brief na *Rio de Tamerary*, of *Ysekepe* lieten brengen, was het loon een Mes, 't geen in het Vaderland anderhalve stuyver kost. Zy zijn noch vies, noch lekker, en eeten verschiedene spijzen, daar andere Natien een afweer af zouden hebben: want ik heb meer als eenmaal gezien, dat ze vuil-gebroeide Eyeren aten, die een stank van zich gaven, dat men de neus moest toe houden. Als men met hen ter jagt is geweest, krijgen ze altijd den afval van het Wild, darmen, pens, enz. 't geen ze met *atty* kooken, en voor ene byzondere lekkerny houden. Godsdienst is by hen onbekend; en word den eenen dag niet van den anderen uitgezonderd. Ook hebben zy noch Wetten, noch Politie, en weten van Overigheid noch Onderdanen. Echter is 'er een Capitein, dien de Christenen Prins noemen. Deze heeft noch wel het meeste gezag, en krijgt ten dien inzichte om de twee jaaren uit het Vaderland een roodsaaye Kleed en een Hoed, waar mede hy ook gemeenlijk aan het Fort verschijnt. Manslag geschied 'er zeer zelden: en zo een Indiaan iemant komt te dooden, kan hy voor alle straf volstaan met aan de Weduwe, of Kinderen, een Slaaf of Slavin in de plaats te geven. Het Kinder-baaren, daar by d'Europische Natien zo veel om te doen is, gaat hier zeer gemakkelijk toe. De Kraamvrouw loopt aanstondts na de verlossing na de Rivier, om zich en haar kind te wasschen; 't geen wyders, zonder dat men 'er weet van Navelbandtjes of Bakeren, door de Moeder twee a drie weeken in een hangmatje, tot dien einde gemaakt, van de rechter schouder na de flinker zyde afhangende op den rug gedragen word: na welken tijd zy het slechts in het zand neer zet, laatende het daar zo lang in vroeten en kruipen, tot dat het allengskens de kracht krijgt om zich over eind te rechten, en te leeren gaan. De Kinderen weeten 'er ook zo van geen huilen en krijten, als in 't Vaderland, en kruipen met meerder geduld langs de grond, daar d'onzen gemakkelijk, en wel warm toegedekt, in de wieg leggen. En niet tegenstaande deze weinige zorg omtrent de Kinderen, het ik 'er [69] nooit lammen of kreupelen gezien, uitgezondert een die een lamme hand had, mitsgaders een die mank ging, doch niemand die scheel zag. Tegens de luizen hebben ze een doodelijke vyandschap. Als de Wyven malkander die afvangen, zitten ze vier, vijf, en zes achter een; en zo meening als 'er gekreegen word, die byten ze tusschen de tanden dood; zeggende na de reden gevraagd zijnde, dat het maar betaaling is wegens dat sy hen gebeeten hebben.

'k Had hier noch een beschrijving noopende hunne manier van Oorlogen meenen by te voegen; doch overdenkende dat ik 'er op twee verscheidene plaatsen af heb gesproken, en dat ik 'er niet veel meer af zou konnen zeggen, immers wat het weezendlijke belangt, heeft het my beter gedacht zulks achter wege te laten, en de stoffe, niet twee-maal een en de zelve zaak te verhalen, niet te verlangen.

XIII. HOOFDSTUK.

Brood der Indiaanen, en op hoedanige wyze het zelve bereid word. Beschrijving der Aard-en Boomgewassen. Verscheidene Dranken by d'Indiaanen, en zelfs ook de Christenen gebruikelijk, enz.

Na aldus de voornaamste byzonderheden van het Land en d'Inwoonders verhandeld te hebben, zullen wy nu gaan spreeken van alles, 't geen het zelve tot onderhoud en gemakkelijkheden van het menschelijk leven voortbrent, en voor eerst van het Brood, als het noodzaakelijkste van alle de dingen die daar toe vereischt worden.

Het Brood, waar mede men zich hier te lande behelpt, en daar men zich ook gemakkelijk mee kan behelpen, word gemaakt van ene wortel van een Boom, *Carsaay* geheeten. Deze Boom groeit gemeenlijk ter hoogte van acht, negen, en tien voeten, en is by na van blad als een Esscheboom. Als men hem plant, word de grond wat omgehakt, even [70] gelijk men doet omtrent het planten van de Suiker. Hier na werden 'er eenige stukken houts van zodanig een Boom in de grond gelegt, daar vervolgens de Boom uit voortspruit; wordende d'andere spruiten, die mede met den zelven zijn opgeschooten, doch niet zo weelig, weg gehakt. De Wortel is tamelijk hard, en het geen daar eigentlijk, gelijk wy hier boven gezegt hebben, het Brood af gemaakt word; ten welken einde de zelve, na dat 'er een vlies afgeschrapt is, op een daar toe bereide steen geraspt, en het raspspel in een pers, omtrent vier voet lang, en zeer dicht van fijne rotting gevlochten, gedaan word. Thans gaan 'er de Wijven op zitten, en drukken het daar opleggende deksel of bord door de swaarte van hun lighaam sodanig weder, dat 'er het nat door een zekere opening onder uit loopt. Dit word in een pot gevangen, en met *atty*, of peper, gekookt: want ongekookt gegeeten, of gedronken, is het een groot vergift; gelijk wy bevonden aan eenigen van onze Varkens, die het by ongeluk hadden geslorbt, en 'er aanstondts af kwamen te sterven anders is het Suiker-zoet, en aangenaam genoeg van smaak. Als het nu wel uitgeparst is, word het in een ronde yzere pan gelegt, en zachter of harder gebakken, na het gebruik 't geen zy 'er af willen maken: want tot drank moet het veel harder, en tot brandens toe, gebakken worden; tot spijs daar en tegen zachter. 't Is een goed, smaakelijk Brood; daar ik, voor my, meer af zou houden, als van de gemeene Scheeps-biskuit; en kan, als het 'er na gemaakt is, wel twee jaren goed blyven, zonder sout: maar het moeten goeden tanden zijn, die het bijten zullen.

Ziet daar, hoe d'Indiaanen Brood weeten te maken. Van d'andere spijzen, als Vleesch en Visch zal in 't gevolg gehandeld worden; na dat wy alvoorens van het Aard-en Boomgewas, de verscheidene Dranken, enz. gesproken zullen hebben.

Onder de veelerhander Aardgewassen, welken de milddadige natuur hier te lande doet voortkomen, vind men ook ene soort van Boontjes, die in smaakelijkheid niet voor de witte Vaderlandsche Boontjes behoeven te wijken. Zy groeyen 'er in overvloed; doch worden door de Christenen geplant, en altijd gepeld. [71]

Daar zijn ook Boontjes, die in 't wild groeyen, van grootte als hier de Pel ert-peulen, wyders ruig boven op de schel. Deze ruigte, die heel kort, en fynder is als hair, is het beste krevelkruid, 't geen ter wereld gevonden kan worden. Men neemt 'er wat af aan de vinger; en strijkende daar mede iemand op eenig gedeelte van zijn ligchaam, veroorzaakts zulks een onverdraagelijke jeukte, die langer als een half uur blijft duuren, en zo smertelijk is, dat men geen oogenblik de hand van d'aangeraakte plaats kan houden. Doch of deze Boontjes van binnen goed zijn om te eeten, weet ik niet. Zy loopen op als Klimboomen, maar zijn veel kleinder van blad.

Artisokken, derwaarts overgevoerd, aarden 'er redelijk wel: maar dat 'er de Hollandsche Boter zo gemakkelijk te bekomen was, men zou 'er veel meer werk af maken. De Saldery komt 'er tegenwoordig ook tamelijk wel voort.

Pompoenen en komkommers, van deselve soort als in 't Vaderland, heeft men 'er het gantsche jaar door.

Postelein groeit 'er op veel plaatsen in 't wild, en is 'er ook zeer gezond.

Jammes en *Petaddes*, Inlandsche Aardgewassen, zijn 'er in groote menigte, witten en rooden. Zy zijn meelachtig, en, gekookt als Bietwortelen, smaakelijk om als een Salade te eeten, voornamentlijk vermengd met groente, als Postelein, Mostertbladeren, enz. Deze *Jammes en Petaddes* worden, geraspt zijnde, van d'Indiaanen veeltijdts onder de Oriane vermengd. Men maakt 'er ook drank af. Zy groeyen gelijk de Komkommers; doch de bladen zijn veel kleinder.

Wat de Druif belangt, die groeyt 'er uitstekend. Wy hadden een Wijngaard achter het Fort, in onzen Hof, die drie-maal 's jaars rijpe Druiven droeg.

Suikerreid wast 'er weelig, en in groote meenigte; kan drie jaaren achter malkander vrucht hebben; doch is op vierde [jaar] onbequaam, als komende heel sober op, en gevende geen nat. Het staat twaalf maanden eer het gekapt word.

De Tabak, hoewel niet tot Spijs gebruikelijk, moet hier echter ook plaats hebben. Zy groeit 'er zo veel, als 'er [72] geconsumeerd kan worden; doch is zo goed niet als die uit *Virginia* komt, zijnde swaarder om te rooken.

De Boomgewassen vallen 'er ook uitstekend goed, en sommigen van de zelvenzo smaakelijk, dat 'er de Vaderlandsche niet by vergeleeken konnen worden. Van deze soort zijn de Water-limoenen, alzo niet geheeten om dat ze in 't water groeijen (want de Boomen staan, even als anderen, op 't Land) maar om dat ze zeer waterachtig en koel zijn; 't geen echter niet belet, dat men 'er zonder eenige bekommering zo veel af mag eeten, als men wil. Zy zijn van buiten groen, doch van binnen roodachtig, gelijk appelbloessem.

d'Oranjeboomen zijn 'er ongemeen groot. Omtrent het Fort is er een dreef af, beslaande de langte van tachtig a honderd roeden, omheinigd met een andere dreef van Limoenboomen, zeer vermaakelijk om onder te wandelen, zo ter oorsaak van de lommer, als om d'aangenaame lucht: want men heeft 'er altijd bloeisel, groene en rijpe Appelen. Zy zijn van grootte als een gemeene Appel in het Vaderland, en zo goed van smaak als van reuk. De Limoenen vallen kleinder, omtrent als een Suikerpeer, doch zeer sappig. Wy lieten 'er jaarlijks wel tien a twaalf vaten af porssen, waar af het Sap na het Vaderland ging.

De *Palmijt-boomen* vallen 'er ook uitsteekend goed. Deze Boom heeft een pit, die raauw uit de hand gegeeten, zo smaakelijk is als een Noot, en gestoofd heel wel na kool sweemt. 't Hout is zeer hard, en zou mogelijk goed zijn tot eenig gebruik: doch men heeft hier te lande geen genoegsaam kennis van d'eigenschap der dingen.

De *Goejavis* is mede een aangenaame vrucht. Zy groeit in de *Savaanen*, of Weylanden, aan Boomtjes van twee a drie duym dik; en smaakt, gestoofd, byna als de kweepeeren. Uit de hand gegeeten, is ze van gelijken smaakelijk, doch trekt een weinig. De koleur is geel, en de grootte ongevaar als die van een kleinen appel in het Vaderland.

Men vind 'er ook een soort van vrucht, *Cajouw-appelen* geheeten. Dezen groeijen aan Boomen als een gemeene Appelboom; zijn van buiten rood, en langwerpig; trekken [73] wat in 't eeten; en worden goed voor den afgang gehouden.

Noch ziet men 'er een soort van Appelen, *Yet-appelen* genaamd. Zy zijn van buiten van gedaante als een Pijnappel; van groote als een gemeene Appel; en hebben, in de plaats van 't klokhuis, een seer grooten steen. Hier legt ter dikte van een rug van een kloek mes, een zekere meelachtigheid om, geel van koleur; welke d'eigentschap heeft, so men een acht of tien van deze Appelen eet, doet het ligchaam zo geel uitslaan, dat 'er ook zelfs de hembden de merktekenen af draagen. Deze vrucht groeit aan een Boom van gemeene grootte, en van blad als een Peerboom.

De Vijgen zijn 'er heel smaakelijk; van koleur als Appelbloisel; van grootte als een gemeene Peer; hangen 'er by na het gantsche jaar door aan den Boom.

Daar is ook noch een zeker klein Boomtje, omtrent als een kers, draagende een vreemd soort van Nooten, Schijtnootjes geheeten. Zy groeijen in een dop, die, als ze rijp zijn swart is; zijn heel smaakelijk, by na als een Hazelnoot; doch beter, en zo hard niet. Maar ze moeten met omzichtigheid gegeten worden: want indien men 'er een zeker vlies, zittende midden in de pit, niet netjes uithaalt, veroorzaaken ze een misselijkheid, duizeling in 't hoofd en een afgrijzelijken afgang, die den lijder ieder oogenblik met de broek in de hand doet loopen. Andersints brengen ze gantsch geen letsel aan; de nieuwelingen worden 'er gemeenlijk mee bedroogen.

Behalven alle de gemelde Boom-gewassen, kan men 'er mede zijne lust boeten aan *Ananassen*, *Benanes*, *Bakoves*, enz. altemaal vruchten van een uitsteekende lekkernij, en die 'er overvloedig te bekomen zijn.

De *Marmelade* is insgelijks een lekkere vrucht, groeijende aan Boomen van gemeene grootte, tusschen twee schellen, by na als die van de Roomsche-boonen, doch niet zo dik, maar wel zo breed. Deze vrucht is van buiten geel, van binnen roodachtig, en smaakt als iets 't geen gekonfijt is. [74] d'*Atty*, of Spaansche Peper, groeit aan een Boomtje als een Aalbes, dochwel zo dun van stam. Om deze Boomtjes te doen voortkomen, word het zaad gekookt, en alzo in de grond gesmeeten.

Mogelijk zou men noch eenige andere Aard- en Boomgewassen ter baan konnen brengen: doch dezen zijn wel de voornaamsten. Wat den Drank belangt, die is 'er van veelerhande soorten, maar altemaal een groot gemors.

Voor eerst dan heeft men 'er de *Beltiry*, welke gemaakt word van *Carsavybrood*, door oude Wijven gekaauwd, en met een groote meenigte van hun speeksel vermengd. Deze gekaauwde brokken worden met omtrent drie-maal zo veel *Carsavybrood* te weeken gelegt tot ter tijd toe dat het zich te samen tot een dikke pap hebbe gezet; waar na zy het tusschen bladeren netjes in ordre geschikt, te bewaren leggen: en als 'er nu drank af gemaakt zal werden, nemen zy 'er een hand vol uit, en mengen het met water. Onder het drinken sluit men de tanden dicht op malkander, op dat 'er de brokken voor mogen blijven.

Payewar word byna op de zelve wijze toebereid, doch moet een nacht staan, waar na het ene zerpe smaak aanneemt, die niet onaangenaam is. Voor ons wierd deze Drank door een Broodpers gegooten, daar de brokken dan in blijven leggen.

Pernouw, of *Bassia*, word insgelijks van gekaauwd en ongekaauw *Carsavy-brood* gemaakt; doch het laatste moet by deze gelegentheid harder gebrand wezen, en 'er in grooter quantiteit onder vermengd worden. Deze Compost word mede door de pers gegooten, staat drie a vier dagen te werken, en brengt goede gest voort. 't Is een goede Drank, die de koleur en smaak van Bier heeft, doch zo helder niet word, en de bekwaamheid om iemand voor een stuiver of twee fraay dronken te maken.

Commany word meest op Ysekepe gemaakt, namentlijk van kaauwsel hier te lande tot allerhande Drank gebruikt, en hard gebakken *Carsavy-brood*, ene tijd lang te beschimmelen gelegt, tot dat het allerley koleur heeft aangenomen. Dit, vermengd met verbrande *Carsavy-koeken*, en in laauw water geweekt, maakt een soort van Morgendrank, heel [75] bekwaam om zich dronken in te drinken; doch ze is wat vies van smaak.

Cassyry is een drank, gemaakt van roode *Jammes* en *Petaddes*, kaauwsel, en *Cassavy-brood*. Zy word insgelijks door de pers gedaan; staat vervolgens twee a drie dagen te gesten; heeft als dan byna de koleur en kracht van Graafsche Wijn; en is heel goed en lekker om te drinken.

XIV. HOOFDSTUK.

Verscheidene soorten van Geboomte, welke aan Rio de Berbice gevonden worden.

Behalven de veelerhande Vruchtboomen, daar wy hier voor af hebben gesproken, zijn 'er noch verscheidene andere soorten van Geboomte, die geen vruchten draagen, doch echter hunne nutheid hebben, als de Ceder-, Katoen-, Oriane-, Krap-, en meer andere Boomen.

Cederboomen wassen 'er in overvloed, en worden, tot planken zijnde gezaagd, gebruikt om kisten van te maken. Eenigen van de zelven zijn zo dik, dat de planken de breedte van wel drie voet hebben.

Noch is 'er bekwaam Hout, Yzer- of Zinkhout geheeten, ter oorzaak dat het, in 't water zijnde gelegt, door zijne swaarte te gronde gaat. 't Is zeer goed om dingen, daar geweld mee gedaan moet worden, af te maken.

Letterhout, is 'er ook te vinden: doch dit groeit meest in *Ysekepe*, en kost omtrent zo veel van hakken, als het waard is.

Katoen-boomen zijn 'er in meenigte hier en daar door het Land verspreid; maar staan echter meest by de Huizen der Indiaanen: hoewel zy 'er, door hunne aangeboorne luiheid, het gebruik niet af maken, 't geen 'er wel af gemaakt zou konnen worden.

Omtrent de Huizen der Indiaanen ziet men ook een zeker [76] soort van Boomen, zo groot als een laagstaande Appelboom, en van blad als een Peer. Deze draagt het heele jaar door een vrucht, Oriane genaamd, en zo hier als in 't Vaderland voor een goede verw bekend. De bolster is van gedaante als de Kaarden, die de Droogscheerders gebruiken; met steekstels bezet; en roodachtig van koleur; doch deze steekels zijn veel slapper, als die van de gemelde Kaarden. Binnen in de bolster, daar ze zich witachtig vertoont, ziet men acht a tien bolletjes verw, kleinder als een witte erwet. Dezen worden door d'Indiaanen vergaderd, en met geraspte *Jammes* of *Petaddes*, daar onder eenige Krap-olie, vermengd; op dat ze voor de worm, die de kracht van de verw verteerd, bevrijd mogen wezen.

De Krapboomen groeyen overal in de Bosschen. De bolster, of Noot, heeft de grootte van een Karstanje. Behalven dat 'er een goede verw af bereid word, levert de Krap, gestampt in de Zon gezet, een soort van Olie, die weer goed voor de Jichtigen bevonden is: want d'aangetaste leden, voor een eijken vuur daar mede gestreeken, gevoelen in weinige oogenblikken verlichting van pijn. De Krapnooten worden ten dien einde ook wel heel gekookt, en als dan, gedroogd en gestampt, in de Zon gezet, die 'er den gemelden Olie wel uit trekt, en in grooter menigte; doch ze is zo deugdsaam en krachtig niet.

Daar zijn ook ettelijke soorten van Boomen, daar Gommen uitgetrokken zouden konnen worden. Ik zelve heb 'er zeven of achterhande gehad; doch zonder te weeten, waar toe ze dienstig waren.

Gitte-gamba zou 'er overvloedig wezen, zo d'Indiaanen niet te luij waren om openingen in de Boomen te maken, en ze te verzamelen. Men zou my hier konnen tegenwerpen, dat de Christenen 't dan behoorden te doen: maar die hebben 'er om meer als een reden geen gelegentheid toe.

Ik twijfel niet, of daar zouden ook wel *Medicinalia* wezen: doch men heeft tot noch toe geen genoegsame opmerking omtrent diergelijke dingen genomen.

De holen van de Boomen hier en daar in de Bosschen leveren ook een tamelijke menigte van Honig, die door d'Indiaanen, [77] voornamentlijk de *Warouwen*, by kleine partijen zo als zy ze uit de Boomen haalen, te koop word gebracht: doch de Was is uit de natuur swart. Wy lieten 'er onze Kaarsen af maken. By wijlen word de Was ook wel alleen by rollen of schijven te koop gebracht; by welke gelegentheid d'Indiaanen zelven den Honig behouden.

Om kort te gaan, het Land zou goed en vruchtbaar wezen, indien het door andere Menschen, als Indiaanen, bewoond wierd.

XV. HOOFDSTUK.

Verscheidene soorten van Gedierte, Vogelen, en Visschen aan Rio de Berbice, benevens de vreemde eigenschappen van eenigen der zelven.

Behalven alle de dingen, welke tot het menschelijk leven noodzakelijk zijn, of er eenig nut of gemak aan by brengen, daar wy hier voor af hebben gesproken, heeft men aan Rio de Berbice ook geen gebrek aan Vee, Gevogelt, enz. waar af voorgenomen hebben in dit Hoofdstuk te handelen, zullen wy voor eerst spreeken van de Dieren, die den Menschen tot spijs verstrekken, vervolgens van d'andere soorten; en zo wijders overtreeden tot de Vogelen, Visschen, Ec. En gevende den voorrang aan het Wildbraad, zal de eerste plaats bekleed worden door de Harten en Reën. Dezen zijn 'er overvloedig, doch niet altijd te schieten, ter oorzaak van hunne ongemeene schuuwheid. 'k Heb 'er meenigmaal twintig a vijf-en-twintig by een gezien: maar indien ze zich boven wind bevinden, kan men ze nooit onder schoot krijgen. Veele werden in het water gevangen, daar men ze na toe drijft om ze met minder moeite te bekomen. Zy zijn zeer sterk in het swemmen, en geven den geenen, die hen trachten te krijgen, door hunne wederstand, te weten als men ze niet aanstondts dood wil hebben, dikwijls zo veel werk als vermaak. Wy hadden [78] 'er aan het Fort gemeenlijk een a twee ter weeck, en somtijdts wel meer, na dat 'er zich de gelegentheid toe op deed, of wij 'er moeiten toe wilden aanwenden. d'Indiaanen moeten 'er zo goede smaak niet in vinden, als de Christenen: want ik heb eens voor een Mes van twee stuivers een gantsche Ree gekocht. 't Vleesch valt wat aan de drooge kant. 't Is aanmerkelijk, dat men een Hart of Ree, zo haast als het gedood is, de neus moet afsnijden: andersins zou het in den tijd van twee a drie uuren stinken. De afgesneeden neus geeft ook zulk een lelijke stank van zich dat men ze aanstondts moet weg werpen.

Haazen zijn 'er ook in groote meenigte, maar van een ander fatsoen als in 't Vaderland. De rug is bruin, vermengd met witte stippelen; de buik wit; en de pooten en ooren kort; zulks dat ze gantsch geen gelijk na andere Hazen hebben. De smaak is zeer delikaat, doch niet haasachtig; zijnde het Vleesch heel mals, en zo blank als Kalfsvleesch. Men broeit ze in heet water, schraapt 'er het hair af, en berid ze met de huid, 't zy dat men ze wil braaden of stooven.

Konijnen ziet men 'er mede in overvloed; doch ze zijn zo aangenaam niet als de Vaderlandsche, hoewel ze wel zo blank vallen. 't Vleesch is veel drooger, en derhalven niet zo smaakelijk. De kop alleen gelijkt iets na onze Konijnen, zo men 'er echter de ooren af uitzondert; welke, even als de pooten, heel kort zijn. 't Hair is doorgaans graauw. Zy onthouden zich mede in de Bosschen, en worden, gelik de Haazen, door de Honden gejaagd.

Niet minder overvloedig vind men 'er de Wilde Varkens: maar ze worden zelden op drooge of hooge landen gevangen; alzo ze zich meest omtrent de Rivier onthouden. In de Maand April hebben ze een loop, die van de *Warouwen* in acht word genomen. Hier op maken zich eneige Vaartuigen van het Fort en de Plantazien gereed, wel voorzien van zout; welke zich vervoegd hebbende ter plaatse daar de jagt zal geschieden, posteeren zich d'Indiaanen hier en daar met pijl en boog in de hand. De Varkens loopen al achter malkander, en geven aldus gelegentheid om hen te gemakkelijker [79] te konnen treffen: doch nooit word de eerste van de Troup geschooten, maar wel de tweede of darde. Als ze gewond zijn, 't zy waar de pijl hen ook geraakt mag hebben, laten d'Indiaanen hen slechts loopen, tot dat ze door het verlies van hun bloed dood ter aarde vallen. Thans, te weeten als de gantsche bende gepasseerd, en het geschooten, op het spoor gevolgd, by de Christenen gebracht is, vallen dezen aan het werk; branden 'er het hair af; snijden 'er alle de beenen uit; en leggen het vleesch by stukken, wel gezouten, in de tonnen. 't Is een zeer goede spijs; maar nooit heb ik aangenamer gegeeten, als van een jong varsch Varken, mitsgaders van de Haazen daar ik zo even af heb gesproken. De natuur schijnt omtrent deze Dieren op een verkeerde manier gewerkt te hebben: want daar alle anderen de navel onder de buik staat, hebben dezen die op den rug, gelik betuigd kan worden met het Varken, 't geen levendig na *Vlissingen* wierd gezonden. Zy vallen zo kloek niet, als wel aan andere oorden; weegende de grootsten gemeenlijk omtrent sestig pond.

Uit het Vaderland zijn 'er ettelijke maalen tamme Varkens na toe gezonden, om voort te teelen, doch ze wierden zo overmatig vet, dat ze hunne Jongen niet konden opbrengen. Echter wierd hen nooit eenige kost voorgesmeeten: maar ze wisten ze uit d'omleggende Bosschen wel te haalen.

Koeyen loopen 'er met meenigte in 't wild. Zy zijn eertijdts tam geweest, doch door verzuim der Menschen in de Bosschen geraakt, daar ze een wilden aart hebben aangenomen. Men schiet ze slechts maar onder de voet; ter oorzaak dat men ze, vermits hunne wildheid, niet en kan slachten. Nooit heb ik 'er eenig Smeer in gezien. Het Niervet is ook heel weinig. In den beginne, toen ik eerst aan *Rio de Berbice* was gekomen, wierd 'er alle veertien dagen een geschooten: maar naderhand raakte het buiten gebruik. By mijn tweede Opperhoofd lieten wy 'er gemeenlijk om de drie a vier weeken een partij in een omring van paalen ten dien eynde gemaakt, drijven, van de welke wy dan de Kalven, afnamen, die wy in een stal zetteden: maar de tammen aart scheen gantsch en al verdweenen te weezen; want [80] zo haast kwamen ze niet in d'opene lucht, of ze liepen boschwaart in.

Honden vind men 'er van verscheidene soorten onder d'Indiaanen by de weg loopen, even als in 't Vaderland; worden van jongs aan op allerley slag van jagt afgerecht; en zyn by hen in groote achting. Zy weeten een Varken staande te houden, en zich met een zonderlinge behendigheid voor het slaan van de tanden te hoeden. Als een Hond achter een Wild is, weet de Jaager aan 't geluid van den Hond, van wat soort het zy: want zo verscheide als de jagt is, zo verscheiden is ook het geluid 't geen de Honden maken. Zy worden veel door Boschwormen gekweld. Dezen groejen tusschen vel en vleesch, en zijn in 't begin zeer klein; maar hebbende grootte van een lid van een vinger gekreegen, duuwt men ze daar uit.

Tijgers zijn 'er tamelijk veel; doch men hoort zelden, dat ze de Menschen aandoen, ter oorzaak dat 'er Vee genoeg is daar ze hunne roofgierige klaauwen in konnen slaan. Evenwel is het wel gebeurd, gelijk wy 'er hier voor een exempel af ter neer gesteld hebben. Men ziet 'er van vyf a zes voet lang. Noch is 'er een soort van kleine Tijgers, Kattetijgers genaamd, mogelijk om dat ze veel grooter zijn als een kloeke Kat. Ziet daar wat eigentlijk het viervoetig Gedierte belangt. Maar zo 'er overvloed van eenig Gedierte is, 't is van Aapen; waar af men 'er, als men langs de Rivier-vaart, zulk een menigte op de takken der Boomen ziet, dat de Nieuwelingen zich 'er niet genoeg over konnen verwonderen. Men heeft 'er van veelerhande soorten, als daar zijn *Grolders*, *Ytoerybalijs*, *Lootsmannen*, *Bakkers*, *Kaboutermannetjes*, *Doodtshoofdjes*, enz.

De *Grolders* worden al zo genaamd om dat ze des avonts en 's nachts een geluid maken als iemand die grolt, of gorgelt.

d'*Ytoerybalijs* zien 'er uit als oude gerimpelde Bessen, hebbende geen hair aan het Bakkes. Dit soort is t'eenemaal lelijk, en gantsch onaangenaam voor het gezicht.

De *Lootsmannen* hebben lange nette baarden onder de kin en vertoonen een zekere soort van deftigheid. [81]

De *Bakkers* worden aldus geheeten om dat ze de voorste pooten gestadig op zodanig een manier beweegen, als iemand die deeg kneed.

De Kaboutermannetjes hebben mogelijk dien naam gekregen van hunne vaardige sprongen door het Geboomte. Dan ziet men ze hier, dan daar: en dat met zulk een geswindheid, dat men 'er het oog naauwlijks op kan houden.

De *Doodshoofjes* zijn zeer kleine en nette Beestjes. Zy zitten gemeenlijk op grooter Aapen; welken zy als ze honger hebben, zo lang bijten, tot dat ze hen op eenige Fruitboomen brengen, daar ze te eeten konnen bekomen.

Alle deze soorten van Aapen verstrekken den Indiaanen tot spijs. Wat my belangt, ik kon 'er weinig smaak in vinden, mogelijk om dat ze niet wel toebereid was. Ik heb 'er van een gegeeten, geberbekot, of op d'Indiaansche manier gebranden. 't Geschied, gelijk wy elders gezegt hebben, op een houte rooster, staande omtrent twee voet hoog van de grond. Hier word de kost op gelegt, en, van boven met bladeren gedekt zijnde, met weinig vuur gaar gebranden. Maar al de Spijs, aldus toebereid, valt geweldig droog. Zo was ook en Aap, daar men slechts alvoorens het hair had afgebrand; 't geen den huid vry wat afzienlijk maakte.

Schildpadden heeft men 'er te land: te water heb ik 'er nooit gezien. Zy worden in de Bosschen gevonden, en door d'Indiaanen te koop gebracht; hebben de langte, en wel verstaan de grootsten, van twaalf a vijftien duimen; en breedte en dikte na proportie. Wanneer men 'er zich tot spijs af wil bedienen, word 'er d'onderste schelp afgehakt, en alzo alles uyt gesneeden. Als potazie toebereid, is 't een heel goed eeten. De bovenste en onderste schelp, voor 't vuur gebranden, is een banketje. De lever gelijkt niet kwalijk na die van een Rog, en overtreft de zelve in lekkernij.

Niet minder smaakelijk van vleesch zijn de Miereneeters, een soort van Gedierte lang van lijf, met een lange hairige staart, kort van pooten, bruin van hair, en van grootte als men tot *Leiden* op d'Anatomie kan zien. Zy worden aldus geheeten, om dat ze met hunne scherpe en lange tong de Mieren uit hunne holen weten te halen. [82]

Onder het Watergedierte ziet men 'er ook Krokodillen, doch in geen overvloed. Nooit is 'er ons meer als een leevendig te koop gebracht. Hy was in malkander gerold, omtrent drie en een halve voet lang; wierd gedood, en op tweederhande manieren toebereid; doch smaakte na visch noch vleesch. Ondertussen kan ik 'er echter dit af zeggen, dat, 't mag dan vleesch of vish weezen, het zelve zo wit als krijt, en zeer delikaat was. In alle mijne Reizen door het Land heb ik nooit meer als een Krokodil gezien. Ik schoot 'er op, doch kreeg hem niet, ter oorzaak dat de kogel op de schelpen afstuitte.

Opwaarts in de Rivier worden ook nu en dan Zeekoejen gevangen; daar ik niet veel af kan zeggen, om dat ik ze nooit en heb gezien. Evenwel heb ik van het vleesch, door d'Indiaanen toebereid, gegeeten; 't geen, indien 'er op een beter manier mee te werk wierd gegaan, niet onsmakelijk zou weezen.

Het kleinder Gedierte, niet wel onder eene soort te brengen, moet hier ook plaats vinden. Onder dezen ziet men 'er een meenigte van Haagdissen, altemaal van een schoon groene koleur, welke in de Zon een glans van zich geeft, die door geene vederen van Gevogelte overtroffen word. Zy zijn zeer rad, en snel van loop.

Liguaanen zijn 'er ook zeer veel. 't Is een soort van Gedierte, wegens koleur en maaksel niet kwalijk na de Hagedissen gelijkende, doch grooter; zijnde, behalen de staart wel anderhalve voet lang. Zy leggen gemeenlijk in de dartig Eyeren, daar maar een vlies om zit. 'k Heb 'er menigmaal afgegeten, en vond ze heel smakelijk.

Sprinkhanen heb ik nooit zo groot gezien. Onder anderen zag ik 'er een by den Heer *de Graaf* in *Ysekepe*, zijnde uit curieusheid wegens d'ongemeene grootte opgezet. Ik mat hem, en bevond de langte over de vijf duim.

Geen minder kloeke gestalte na proportie hebben 'er ook de Mieren, zijnde meer als een halve duim lang. Zy doen voor zo veel men met gewisheid weet, geen schade. Ondertusschen gebeurt het om de zeven of acht jaaren, dat de wortel van de *Carsavy*, Tabak, en andere vruchten weg [83] gegeeten word; en dit schrijft men de Mieren toe, doch echter met geen volkomene zekerheid. 'k Heb 'er genoeg zodanig een jaar beleefd; en zag onder anderen, dat een Soldaat twee uuren lang voor een pijp Tabak op schildwacht stond. Om dat d'wortel van Tabak was afgegeten, en dan verdroogt.

Kakkerlakken vind men 'er niet als in der Christenen Huizen. Zy zijn bruin, en zeer plat van lijf, en derhalven bekwaam om door de reeten in kisten en kasten te kruipen; doch doen geen schade, als aan Linnen en Wolle. Zy komen meest met den avond te voorschijn, en hebben vleugelen, gelijk eenige soorten van Torren in 't Vaderland. De grootsten hebben de langte van omtrent een duim.

Spinnekoppen zijn 'er kleen en groot. Ik heb 'er twee gehad, die, opgezet zijnde, meerder plaats besloegen als de palm van een hand. 't Ligchaam alleen had de groote van een halve Rijksdaalder. Zy zijn swart en ruig, en hebben tanden: doch of er vergift by is, gelijke sommige willen beweeren, weet ik niet. Immers ik heb nooit gehoord, dat ze eenige schade hebben gedaan. Men vind ze gemeenlijk in de daken der Negeren Huizen.

Padden ziet men 'er veel, en van een ongemene groote. Dezen zijn fenijnig, en worden ook met alle zorgvuldigheid vermijd.

Men heeft 'er ook Ratten; doch ze komen uit de Schepen, 't zy met swemmen, of by eenige andere gelegentheid.

Slangen zijn 'er van verscheidene soorten, en grootte. De voornaamsten zijn de Ratelslangen, aldus geheeten van de Ratel die ze achter aan de staart hebben, welke in het voortloopen een zeker gekraak maakt, gelijkende niet kwalijk na de Ratels. Deze Ratel bestaat uit ettelijke doppen; en word voor ieder jaar een dop gerekend.

Ik heb 'er een met negen doppen gehad; die, zo haast als zy zich maar verroerde, een verbaarlijk gerammel maakte. Zy zijn zeer vergitig, en hunne steeken of beeten sijn niet te geneezen, dan met uitbranding, of braaken door het middel van menschendrek te eeten. d'Andere soorten van Slangen vallen zo fenijnig niet. Ik heb een Vel of Huid gezien van acht duim breed, en omtent zo veel voeten lang; waar af niet tegenstaande de grootte, de Slang echter niet fenijnig was geweest. [84] Men heeft 'er ook veele Waterslangen, voornamentlijk in de Rivier van *Canje*; doch ze doen geen kwaad, en worden van d'Indiaanen en Negers gegeten, ook zelfs de fenijnige. Van de smaak weet ik niets te zeggen, alzo ik nooit nieuwsgierigheid, of liver stoutheid, genoeg gehad heb om 'er af te proeven. Onder alle mijne Reize te Water en te Land, heb ik nimmer meer ontmoeting van eenig Ongedierte gehad; hoewel de Slangen by nacht hier en daar op de wegen de koelte zoeken.

't Gevogelt is aan *Rio de Berbice* ook overvloedig, en van veelerhande soorten, als daar zijn *Hoenders*, *Kalkoenen*, *Endvogels*, *Veldhoenders*, *enz.* van welker ieder wy alhier afzonderlijk zullen spreeken.

Hoenders heb ik 'er zeer veel aan verscheidene oorden door het Land gevonden: doch ze vallen zo groot niet, als in het Vaderland; ook niet wel zo smakelijk.

In tegendeel zijn 'er de Kalkoenen veel vetter en swaarder. Ik heb 'er van gegeten, die meer als vier-en-twintig pond kon haalen; zijnde het spek of vet op de borst wel twee vingeren dik. Ze worden by de Christenen voortgeteeld, en met *Milie*, of Turchsche Taruw, die daar in overvloed groeit, gevoed.

Veldhoenders, of Perdrijzen, ziet men 'er ook by menigte; doch zijn 'er in geen groote achting: want zelden wil iemand de moeite nemen van 'er een roer op te lossen.

Men heeft 'er een soort van Vogelen, omtrent zo groot als Hoenders, boven op het lijf swart, onder de buik wit, en redelijk lang van staart. Zy worden *Pauyssen* geheeten, en veel geschooten, om dat ze zeer delikaat zijn. Als men 'er op uit wil gaan, moet het voor den dag geschieden, ter oorzaak dat ze heel schuuw vallen. Zy verklikken zich door hun gefluit; 't geen van den Schutter gehoord zijnde, vervoegt hy zich onder den Boom, doet de kaars uit, en verwacht den dageraad. Thans past hy de Vogel te treffen; die, al valt ze ook neder, noch een wijltje zo snel loopt, dat de Schutter haar naauwlijks kan volgen.

Wilde Duiven vallen 'er meer te schieten, als men maar de moeite wil nemen van langs de Rivier te vaaren. Ook zijn 'er tamme Duiven, die 'er redelijk wel voort teelen. [85]

Beneden in de Rivier heeft men een Vogel, van groote als een klein Hoen. Geen Schilder zou met zijn penceel geen schoonder roode koleur konnen malen. Zy vallen wat schuw; doch, na ik geloof, niet smaakelik, alzo ze op visch aazen.

Onder de Watervogels vind men hier ook de *Endvogels* en *Watersnippen*. Wat d'eersten belangt: men ziet 'er omtrent de zelve soort als in 't Vaderland; doch ze gaan weinig te water, enzijn ook beter van smaak. Noch word 'er een andere soort aangeteeld, hebbende groote roode neuzen op de bekken; welker weergaa ik op *Honslaardijk* heb zien loopen. Zy blijven mede meestentijd uit het water, en zijn, wel toebereid, goed om te eeten. Deze soort vliegt 'er ook veel in 't wild ingezonderheid omtrent de Zeekant; alwaar wy 'er, wanneer wy 'er ons by gelegentheid bevonden, dikwils op uitgingen.

Watersnippen zijn 'er in zulk een overvloed, dat ik 'er met eene schoot in de sestig heb zien treffen: doch niemand was 'er, die 'er een hand aan wilde steeken om ze te plukken. Beneden in de Rivier worden ze het meest gevonden.

Omtrent de Zeekant, in de Weylanden, ziet men een soort van Vogelen, den Oijevaars niet ongelijk, voor zo veel het postuur en de grootte belangt; maar ze zijn bonter van veeren.

't Gezicht van een ander klein Vogeltje, van glans als een goude Tor, word van d'Indiaanen gezegt niets goedts te beteekenen: doch de Christenen slaan 'er weinig geloof aan.

Papegaaijen zijn 'er in groote meenigte, en voor een kleintje te bekomen. Maar waar het by toekomt, weet ik niet: immers d'Indiaanen komen nooit met jonge Vogels ter Markt. Ouden brengen ze genoeg, en somtijds meer als men 'er begeert. Men heet ze *Stropvogels*, ter oorzaak dat ze met een strop worden gevangen; 't geen zich aldus toedraagt. Den Indiaan, weetende de Boomen daar de Papegaaijen zich meestentijd op onthouden, bekleed zich over het gantsche ligchaam met groene bladeren, gelijk ook den stok daar de strop aan hangt. Deze weet hy de Vogel met [86] een behendigheid over het hoofd te laten vallen; en trekkende den stok na zich toe, is de vangst altijd zeker. Maar men kan dit soort van Papegaaijen nooit leeren klappen. De geenen, die in het Vaderland in achting zijn, worden door d'Indiaanen gehaald als ze te water na *Rio Aarnocque* reizen, by het Eiland *Trinidad*, behoorende onder den Koning van *Spanjen*, en jong uit de nesten genomen.

Perkieten ziet men 'er mede in overvloed, van een zeer schoone groene koleur: maar ik heb ze nooit hooren klappen, en 'er ook nooit jongen afgezien. Ze schreeuwen wel luid genoeg; doch het is een recht natuurlijke taal, en die niet afgewend kan worden;

Ravens zijn 'er van tweederley soort, en overvloedig, d'Eersten hebben een blauwe borst, en geele of oranje slag veeren; d'anderen, en geele en blaauwe wieken. Men leert ze ook klappen: maar ze vallen zo mild niet van praat, als de Papegaaijen. Ze konnen niet wel opgeslooten of bewaard worden, vermits ze het houtwerk in stukken bijten.

Swaluwen heeft men 'er het gantsche jaar door in meenigte.

Vleermuizen (zo men deze Dieren anders onder het Gevogelte mag rekenen) zijn 'er ook zeer veel. Deze afschuwelijke Schepselen voeden zich dikwils met der menschen bloed; waar af men de meeste nood heeft, als men zich met bloote beenen in een hangmat te slapen legt: want als dan moeten de toonen last lijden, daar ze het bloed weten uit te zuigen. 't Is my zelfs een maal of twee gebeurd; zulks dat ik 'er met ondervinding af weet te spreeken. Hier omtrent zijn ze zeer behendig; want hebbende voor eerst een beet gedaan, vliegen ze weg, om te zien of de geen, die gebeten is, ook wakker word: zo niet, komen ze op de toon zitten, en zuigen zich dik van bloed. Aldus wierd den jongen van onze tamme Duiven door de Vleermuizen het bloed afgezoogen; waar door wy 'er een meenigte hebben dood gevonden: maar toen men wist, waar de voorttelling door verhinderd wierd, droeg men wel haast zorg voor het toekomende.

Daar zijn noch meer andere Vogelen; doch de voornaamsten genoemde zijnde, zullen wy nu van de verscheidene soorten van Visch gaan spreeken. Maar hebben wy een wijdlustig [87] veld met het Gedierte en Gevogelte gehad, hier doet het zich zo breed niet mee op: en de liefhebbers van deze spijs behoeden niet herwaarts te komen, om 'er hunne lust aan te boeten. Niet te min daar is iets; en dit iets moet ons alhier voor een gedeelte van onze stoffe verstrekken.

Door eerst dan heeft men 'er een soort van Visch, niet kwalijk gelijkende na de Vaderlandsche Braassem, doch blanker, omtrent als Bley. Zy is zeer smaakelijk en goed, doch wat hairig; weshalven men ze wel met omzichtigheid dient te eeten. d'Indiaanen schieten ze veeltijds met pijl en boog, en dat, 't geen te verwonderen is, ter plaatsen daer de Christenen hoe naauw zy 'er ook op letten, Visch konnen zien. De naam is *Kartabak.*

Een andere soort is getekend even als Baars, maar zo hairig, dat ze weinig word gegeeten.

Een Vischje, omtrent als klein Bley, en niet hairig, word van de Soldaten met hoeken gevangen.

Wanneer wy een maaltijd van Visch wilden aanrechten, wierd aan d'Indiaanen omtrent het Fort order gegeven om een Kreek af te stoppen; 't geen gedaan zijnde, gingen zy 'er vervolgens met het laag water in, en roerden met een zeker soor van hout, strijdende met de natuur van de Visch, tot op de grond: waar door 'er zulk een meenigte kwam boven drijven, dat wy, behoudende de smaakelijksten, gemeenlijk wel de helft aan het Volk gaven.

Daar zijn noch wel eenige andere soorten van Visch: maar alzo ze te slecht vallen, verdienen ze niet, dat men 'er zich mee ophoud.

Krabben, om diemede onder de Visch te rekenen, zijn 'er overvloedig, groot, en zeer smaakelijk. Men vangt ze aan de Zeekant, ter plaatsen daar de Bosschen onder loopen. Hier is de grond kleyachtig, en doorgaans vol gaten en putten, daar ze wel ter diepte van anderhalve voet met laag water met de hand uitgehaald worden. d'Indiaanen eeten ze zo als het valt: maar de Christenen kooken ze gemeenlijk half gaar; trekken 'er als dan de Visch uit, die gemakkelijk volgt; en stooven ze voorders: 't geen een delikaat eeten geeft. [88]

XVI. HOOFDSTUK.

Verscheidene soorten van Ziektens aan Rio de Berbice.

Gelijk alle Landen gemeenlijk hunne eigen soorten van Ziektens hebben, is *Rio de Berbice* hier ook niet af uitgezondert; waar en boven de Christenen ook noch die van hun Vaderland onderworpen zijn, uitgenomen mogelijk pest, daar ik nooit af heb hooren melden. Wat d'andere belangt, daar heb ik zo veele exempelen af gezien, dat ik 'er niet aan kon twijfelen. Evenwel is 'er somtijdts eenig onderscheid in, als by voorbeeld in de Kinderpokjes, een ziekte die 'er alle de Kinderen, zo wel de Christene als d'Indiaansche, onderhevig zijn: want zo 'er iemand van boven de vyftien jaaren af aangetast word, moet hy op de zelve manier, als de Spaansch pokkigen in het Vaderland, te weeten met stooven pokdranken, *enz.* genezen werden; krijgende ondertusschen te veel eeten om te sterven, en by na te weinig om 'er het leven mee te konnen behouden.

Persing is een soort van Ziekte, verzeld met een moeijelijk afgang, daar men zich toe moet forceeren. Zy word veroorzaakt door te veel snoeijen, of het overmatig gebruik van *Graap*, zijnde een Drank van Siroop gemaakt, en hier in schadelijk, dat ze deze kwaal verwekt. Brandewijn is het kostelijkste, 't geen men daar kan hebben. Maar ik kan niet bedenken, waarom niet twee maal daags een dronk *Kildivel* aan het Volk word gegeven: want, behalven dat het buiten merkelijke schade van de Heeren Patroonen zou konnen geschieden, zou 'er voor zo veel als deze Ziekte belangt, de gezondheid beter behouden konnen worden.

Eern arger kwaal is de *Mebiky*, in 't Nederduits *Zieke* geheeten; zijnde een soort van stof of iets anders 't geen ik niet weet te noemen, heel gemeen in de Huizen der Indiaanen, zo groot als de punt van een speld. Dit zet zich [89] ergens op het vleesch, en groeit voort tot de grootte van een gemeene witte erwet. Ik liet 'er eens zeven te gelijk uit mijne voeten haalen. Zy zijn bleek en hard van schel; welke gebroken zijnde, vertoont zich van binnen een dik goed, 't geen, als het geknipt word, even eens knapt als luizen. De gaten, daar deze *Mebikijs* uitgehaald werden, stopt men met asch van Tabak: en indien ze daar niet mee genezen, loopt men gevaar dat het pokgaten zullen worden; waar uit dan na verloop van tijd de pokken te voorschijn komen. Dit gebeurt hier dikwijls, zonder dat men de moeite behoeft te nemen van ze by Vrouw volk te gaan haalen. Doch men maakt hier zo veel swarigheid niet om de pokken te geneezen, als wel in 't Vaderland gedaan word: de kruiden zijn 'er groen, en by gevolg krachtiger.

Noch is er een soort van ziekte, die men de *Landziekte* noemt. Deze word veroorzaakt door louter luiheid, en geen beweeging aan het ligchaam te geven: want vermits het 'er geweldig heet is, en dat uit deze hette een vadsigheid en slaperigheid ontstaat, zijn 'er die gantsche dagen in de hangmat leggen. 't Is een zeer moeijelijke kwaal, verzeld met groote pijn in 't hoofd, en swaare duizelingen, bleekheid van gelaat, en meer andere ongemakken.

XVII. HOOFDSTUK.

Gelukkige staat der Planters. Gelegenheid der Plantazien. Planting en haavening van het Suikerried, mitsgaders toebereiding van de Suiker. Vreemde soort van Boomen. Straffe der Slaaven, die weg willen loopen, enz.

Uit alles, 't geen hier voor gezegt is, kan ten naasten by afgemeten worden, met wat gemak en ongemak men aan Rio de Berbice kan leven. Maar wy hebben tot noch toe van de Plantazien niet gesproken; en [90] daar is het dat men een Prinselijk leven voert, weinig vermengd met kommer, en in tegendeel verzeld met alle de vermaakelijkheden en wellusten, welke men hier te lande kan genieten. Indien 'er de gezelligheid, een onafscheidelijke eigenschap van de menschelijke natuur, niet aan ontbreke, men behoefde geen ander gewest te zoeken om zijne dagen in rust en vrede, met weinige zorgen, en onbekommerde nooddrust, door te brengen.

By mijnen tijd waren 'er vijf Plantazien, de Hoofdplantazie van het Fort 'er onder begreepen, welke 's Jaarlijks een schoone partij Suiker uit leverden; het voornaamste (benevens d'*Oriane*, waar af men omtrent honderd vaten overvoert) daar hier koophandel mee gedreven word. Zy zijn altemaal gelegen aan de kant van de Rivier, doch niet even vermaakelijk, en ook niet even bekwaam om 'er af en aan te komen. De Plantazien, *den Berg* en *Mierenberg* geheeten, leggen vrij hoog; hebbende een lustig Weyland in 't rond; en een schoone uitzicht van achteren tegen het Bosch. De twee anderen daar en tegen op plaatsen het Bosch, ten groote streek in de lengte en breedte, gekapt is, doch lager, en op kleygrond; weshalven, wanneer het wat sterk geregend heeft, de regen, welke zich derwaarts strekken, onbruikbaar zijn. Aan de *Savaanen*, of Weylanden, in tegendeel heeft men zandgrond, en dien volgens altijd gebruikelijke wegen; langs de welken men van de twee eerst genoemde Plantazien na verscheidene Dorpen in het Land kan wandelen.

De Slaaven zijn op de drooge gronden ook veel gezonder, als die op de kleygronden woonen: doch noopende de levensmiddelen, die worden zo wel op d'eenen als op d'anderen voortgeteeld. Maar de gelegentheid om Koejen te houden scheelt zeer veel: want daar ze op de Plantazien, gelegen aan Weylanden, zelven uit en inloopen, moeten ze op d'anderen door het Bosch heen gedreeven, en op de zelven wijs weder na huis gevoerd worden. Wijders leeft men 'er op een treffelijke manier; want men draagt zorg om alle dingen op de Plantazien te hebben, Hoenders, Kalkoenen, Endvogels, allerhande Groente, en wat meer tot nooddruft [91] of wellust der Menschen van nooden is. De Koejen leveren er dagelijks varsche Melk, daar ook Boter afgemaakt word: d'Indiaanen die zich voor een kleinigheid tot den dienst der Heeren Planters laten gebruiken, jaagen voor hen veelerhande smaakelijk Wild: d'Anderen, welke zich op de naby gelegene Dorpen onthouden, voorzien hen van alles wat zy konnen bekomen, *enz.*

Maar dewijl wy hier op het stuk van de Plantazien zijn, moeten wy niet vergeten te spreken van de toebereiding der Suiker, en wat daar verder aan behoort; een materie die bekwaam is om de nieuwsgierigheid van opmerkende Lezers te kittelen. Ziet hier dan, hoe zich van den beginne tot het einde daar mee toedraagt.

Voor eerst worden de Velden, verordend tot het Planten van 't Suikerried, omgeploegd; van onkruid gezuiverd, tot vooren, even verre van malkander, gesneeden; en de Planten op zodanig een wijs in deze vooren gepoot, dat d'opperste toppen malkander raaken. De kuilen vereisschen meer aanvullende aarde des Zomers, als in de Wintertijd; op dat de doordringende hette der Zonne de wortels niet verzenge. Hoe meerder vocht het Ried nat maakt, hoe eerder het wast. Binnen tien, of ten uittersten twaalf maanden, krijgt het volkomene rijpheid. January en Augustus, de laatste Wintermaand, zijn de bekwaamsten tot de planting; ter oorzaak dat het aardrijk, door de versche regen geweekt, de wortel te lichter laat voorschieten. 't Gerijpte Ried, ter gezette tijd afgesneden, blijft somtijdts tot het volgende Jaar op 't Veld leggen. Ondertusschen groeit 'er weer nieuw Ried, 't welk veeltijdts te gelijk met het oude ter Molen komt. Doch indien het langer als twee Jaaren staat, verteert de zoete vochtigheid; en het Ried zelve sterft allengskens. De jonge Planten konnen hier te lande maar drie Jaaren achter malkander vrucht hebben; en moeten het vierde Jaar weder nieuwe gepoot worden. Somtijts, by brandende

Zonneschijn, daar geen regen op volgt, gaat het Ried uit door de droogte; 't welk van des Winters afgebrand word, op dat 'er nieuw Ried van onder d'assche voortkome. Wanneer ook het Water de Velden te lang plas [92] zet, verdrinken by wijlen de tedere Planten. Ook werden ze wel door het onkruid, te weelig voortgezet, verstikt, waarom de grond viermaal 's Jaars gewied word, tot ter tijd dat het Ried tegens het onkruid bestandig is. Wijders snijd men het gerijpte Ried af by d'onderste knop, en van het Ried de bladeren; waar na het, in busselen gebonden, ter Molen word gebracht. Deze bestaat uit drie sterke houte Assen, met dikke ijsere hoepels beslagen; tusschen de welken het Ried geklomd word. De Assen, door de welken de zoete vocht vloeit, als ook de Bak waar in ze nederzypelt, moeten tweemaal binnen vierentwintig uuren gezuiverd worden. Het Ried van achteren tusschen d'eerste Asse gesteeken, draait tot de tweede; op dat 'er d'overige vocht uitgedrukt werde. 't Gekneusde Ried dient ten voedsel der vlammen. De geperste vogt loopt door houte gooten in groote kopere ketels, waar onder de vuuren met een ongelooflijke menigte van hout gaande gehouden worden. Als ze te hard zied, giet men 'er water onder, ten einde zy te minder verteert. Ondertusschen word 'er het schuim afgeschept, 't geen eeten en drinken voor het Vee is. Thans gieten zy ze over in de tweede ketel, daar ze weder op nieuws gekookt, en door de Slaaven met een lange schuimspaan de drek 'er af geschept wort. Midlerwijl stort men, tot meerder zuivering, loog in de borrelende vocht, en zijgt ze eindelijk door doeken. De droesem, die aan de doeken blijft hangen, met water gemengd, levert een soort van drank, waar aan men zich braaf dronken kan drinken. Uit de groote Ketels vloeit de vocht in de kleine, alwaar ze ten dardemaal gekookt, en gestadig geroerd word, tot dat ze de dikte van Siroop, en eindelijk van Suiker krijgt. 't Moet onder de verborgenheden der natuur worden gerekend, dat, terwijl de Suiker in de kleine Ketels kookt, olie by druppelen gegooten dient te worden; 't geen indien het geschiedde wanneer ze in de grootte Ketels zied, zou de vocht niet tot Suiker willen stremmen. Wederom, by aldien 'er loog in de kleine Ketels gegooten wierd, gelijk in de groote waar de vocht t'eenemaal bedorven; gelijk ook wanneer het sap van een Citroen, of iets zuurs, 'er onder kwam. Als ze nu aldus haar behoorlijke [93] dikte heeft gekreegen, word ze gegooten in houte bakken, die boven breed en vierkantig zijn, maar allengskens benedenwaarts smalder toeloopen, tot op de grootte van een stuiver aan den Bodem, alwaar een gat is, 't geen zo lang met een prop toegestopt blijft, tot dat de Suiker koud en stijf is geworden. Thans, trekt men 'er de prop uit, en laat de Suiker door het gat neder zijpelen; die vervolgens in vaten gekuipt, en alzo afgescheept word.

Hier moeten wy noch eindelijk byvoegen, dat de hoepels van de Vaten gemaakt worden van het hout van een zekere soort van Boomen, *Meby* in 't Indiaansch geheeten. Deze schieten noch blad, noch bot, en hebben alleenlijk eenige nederwaarts hangende takken, van welk 'er diksten men zich tot het maken van de gemelde hoepels bedient.

De dunste takken hebben een ander gebruik, te weeten omtrent het straffen van de misdaden der Slaaven, en inzonderheid als men verneemt dat ze weg willen loopen; by welke gelegentheid zij 'er deerlijk mee geslagen worden, dat niet alleen het bloed by de swarte huid nederloopt, maar gantsche lappen vel 'er af gerukt worden. En indien ze, niet tegenstaande deze straf meermaalen zulks in de wil krijgen, gelijk bewijlen wel gebeürd, worden hen de zenuwen aan de hielen afgesneden, en aldus het hard loopen belet. [94]

XVIII. HOOFDSTUK.

Tyding van den Oorlog tusschen de Koningen van Vrankrijk en Engeland tegens de Vereenigde Provincie aan Rio de Berbice gebracht. Mutery der Soldaten tegens de Gouverneur, die in de Gevangenis word gesmeeten. Den Auteur op Brandwacht gelegt, die aldaar door een Vloot Caribischen bestookt, en genootzaakt word zijne Post te verlaten. Gevaar van in de Boeyen gesmeeten te werden, 't geen hy door list ontkomt.

Na aldus van alle de voornaamsten byzonderheden des Landts te hebben gesproken zal ik wederkeeren tot het verhaal van mijne byzondere wedervaringen, mitsgaders 't geen daar eenige betrekking toe mag hebben.

In de Maand Juny van den Jare 1673 kreegen wy tijding over *Ysekepe*, met een Scheepje aldaar uit het Vaderland aangekomen, hoe het Schip *d'Eendracht*, volgens ouder gewoonte na ons toegezonden, een Engelsch Schip, komende uit *Oost-Indiën*, had veroverd, en met het zelve na *Bergen in Noorwegen*, en van daar na d'*Elbe* was gezeild. Wy hadden in zeventien Maanden geen tijding gehad, en beelden ons derhalven in, dat het Schip, 't geen wy verwachten, verongelukt moest weesen. Maar weinig dochthen wy, dat de Koningen van *Vrankrijk* en *Engeland* zich te samen hadden verbonden, en den Oorlog tegens de *Vereenigde Provintien* verklaard. Ter zelve tijd verstonden wy ook het overgaan van zo veele Steden en Forten, welke binnen weinig dagen tijdts door de Vyandelijke Wapenen, als door een geweldige stroom, waren weg gesleept; weshalven wy niet en twijfelden, of het gantsche Land zou alreedts onder het jok van den overwinnaars hebben moeten [95] bukken, of immers in zo deerlijken staat zijn, dat wy 'er niets af konden verwachten: want onze Brieven waren by de vier Maanden oud. In deze bekommering wierd by den Commandant beslooten, met d'uiterste spaarzaamheid te werk te gaan, in zonderheid omtrent het Spek en Vleesch; alzo wy niet wisten, wanneer wy met proviand ontzet zouden worden; en dat wy 'er ook zelfs weinig hoop toe hadden. Het ransoen dan aldus, dewijl wy van de nood een deugd moesten maken, verminderd zijnde, begonden de Soldaten, vierende den toom aan hunne domme driften, te morren; tot zo verre dat zy, aangehitst door eenen *Dirk Roosekrans*, van *Vlissingen*, Konstapel, wiens naam hier tot een eeuwige schande gemeld zy, in de maand November luidtskeels uitriepen: *meerder kost, en een andere Opperhoofd*. Ik had dit mompelen al lang gehoord, en den Commandant tot verscheidene malen gewaarschouwd, dat het niet en zou lukken, en dat het Volk zodanig tegens hem was ingenomen, dat men groote reden had om voor een slecht gevolg beducht te wezen. De commandant voerde my hier op te gemoet, dat hy deed 't geen hy voor God en zijne Meesters kon verantwoorden: dat hy gaarne meer aan het Volk wilde geeven: maar dat, dewijl men alle dagen Vijand te verwachten had, en tachtig Eeters in het Fort waren, men het zelve, indien men de Proviand niet wat en rekte, zeer beswaarlijk zou konnen verdeedigen. Inderdaad, onze gantsche Provisie bestond in vier vaten Spek, en drie vaten Vleesch: naauwelijks genoeg, zo men hen den vollen houw had gegeven, om 'er zo veel man veertien dagen af te bestaan. Toevoer was 'er niet te verwachten; en het Volk wist wel, dat 'er niet meer in het Magazijn was. Niet te min wist de gemelde *Dirk Roozekrans* hen zodanig op te hitsen, dat ze rond uit verstonden, dat 'er een andere Commandant zou aangesteld worden. 't Wierd beloofd, gelijk ook dat de Heeren Raaden hen voldoening zouden geven. Dezen vervoegden zich op een Sondag, 's morgens voor negen uuren, in het Fort. Wy waren geweldig verlegen om het werk zodanig te bestieren, dat het Volk tot stilstand gebracht mocht werden. Het besluit was [96] dat d'oudste Raad hen met zachte redenen zou ondergaan: doch te vergeefs. In het woeden ging zelfs zo ver, dat eenigen van den hoop ter kamer kwamen indringen; den Commandant by het lijf greepen; en beneden in het Gevangenhuis smeeten. Deze smaad vond deernis by ons; weshalven wy verzochten, dat hy op een Plantazie, of na *Ysekepe*, verzonden mocht worden, tot ter tijd dat 'er een Schip kwam. Maar de woedende menigte was niet te verzetten. Het Opperhoofd had zich in veele dingen misgaan: en, zo hy op vrye voeten stond, mocht hy by de Vyanden overloopen: met honderd andere diergelijke praatjens. Straks wierd uit een van de Heeren Raden een nieuwe Commandant gekoozen. Deze beducht voor een zelve lot als zijn Voorzaat, daar hy de beste vriend niet af en was, gaf vol op; en aldus zagen wy ons binnen weinige dagen zonder Spek of Vleesch. Toen was 't : men kon 't wel voor een wijl met Brood en Zout harden: niet bedroeft voor den tijd; gewoonte was de tweede natuur, *enz.* Ondertusschen ging men by den gevangen Commandant af en aan; voor wien gelijk het woeste graauw maar na driften, en niet na reden, luistert, zelfs de geenen, die het meest op hem verbitterd waren geweest, weder respect begonden te krijgen; en indien het langer geduurd had, 'k twijfel niet af hy zou hersteld zijn geworden. Ondertusschen wierd in het Raad beslooten, dat men Brandwacht aan de Zeekant zou uitzenden; gelijk in de laatste dagen van den gedetineerden Commandant was gedaan, te weeten, sedert dat men tijding van den Oorlog had gehad. Ieder der Heeren Raaden zou zijne rang, als Hoofd, hier in hebben, en na een verblijf van veertien dagen afgelost worden. Van 't gepasseerde hield ik notulen. De tweede beurt was de mijne. Men gaf my vier Christenen, drie Negers, en vijf Indiaanen in een kleine Kanoo, daar ons gevangen Opperhoofd een Kist in had laten maken, om de Snaphaanen te bergen, of droog te houden. Wij leiden op in 't Bosch *Marepaan*, recht in 't gezicht van de Zee, omtrent een uur binnen de Rivier, dartien a veertien mijl beneden het Fort. Veertien dagen verliepen, en noch twee daar en boven, zonder dat ik afgelost [97] wierd, en echter dorst ik mijne post niet verlaaten: weshalven ik resolveerde een van mijne by hebbende Christenen met een Indiaan na het Fort te zenden, om te zien, waar het aan scheelde, dat men my niet kwam aflossen. Doch het was Kerstmis, de nieuwe Commandant vrolijk; en ik, na 't scheen, vergeeten. Ondertusschen gebeurde het den volgenden nacht, omtrent ten twee uuren, dat de Man, die op schildwacht stond, my wekte; zeggende, dat by een Kanoo zag. Ik terstond uit de hangmat, en zag ze ook; door dien, niet tegenstaande een nevelige lucht, de Maan zo veel lichts gaf, dat men de voorwerpen van redelijk verre kon onderscheiden. Ik liet ene maal twee a drie roepen, en kreeg geen antwoord: weshalven order gaf om 'er besijden heen te schieten. Hier op wierd al mijn Volk wakker, en kwam voor den dag. Ondertusschen ging de Vyandelijke

Kanoo (want het waren Indiaanen van de Rivier *Corentijn*, Vyanden van d'onzen) zachtjes te rug na haare Vloot, daar wy noch geen kennis af hadden. Ik commandeerde ieder na zijn geweer te zien, 't kruit van de pan te smijten, en versch kruid 'er op te doen; en deelde aan elk noch eenige kogelen mede. Thans in de Kanoo gevallen, en ons in order gezet, ik met noch een Zeeuw achter, en voor twee Vlaamingen, met last om my op het eerste gezicht te waarschouwen. Na omtrent een half uur vaarens, kreegen wy de *Caribischen* (aldus worden die van de *Corentijn* by ons genoemd) in 't oog, en lieten 't al wat nader gaan, om te tellen hoe sterk zy waren. d'Een telden 'er zeven-en-twintig, en d'andere acht-en-twintig: en in ieder Kanoo door malkander gerekend, zijn ten minsten vier-en-twintig Indiaanen. Dit stond ons schoon. Niet te min, gelijk my de bloohertigheid der Indiaansche natien niet onbekend was, als mede dat drie Christenen zo goed waren als dartig van de dappersten onder hen lieden, liepen wy met onze Kanoo weder na land, daar wy al onze Bagazie in namen: waar na met ons vier Christenen raad gehouden, en malkander beloofd hebbende te samen te leven en te sterven, en tot den laatsten droppel bloedts stand te houden, maakten wy ons tot tegenweer gereed. Ondertusschen lieten [98] onze Indiaanen en Negers genoegsaam blijken, dat ze geen zin dit werk hadden; en buiten twijfel, zo men hand gemeen was geraakt, zouden ze aanstondts in het water gesprongen, na Land geswommen, en in 't Bosch geloopen hebben: want dit is by dusdanige gelegentheden hunne eenigste toevlucht. Midlerwijl waren wy beducht, dat de Vyandelijke Vloot ons onder faveur van 't Bosch de passagie mocht willen beletten, of betwisten. Wy waren met de Vlood midden in de Rivier gesteeken, zulks dat zy aan wederzijde van ons konden zien: doch ontmoette geen Vyand. Op deze manier geraakten wy tot aan 't einde van het lange Rak, alzo geheeten om dat het een Vaart van meer als een uur vereischt. Hier vond ik eenige Christenen verzeld van weinige Indiaanen, afgevaardigd om my te gaan aflossen. 'k Wilde wel eens weten, waarom men niet een twintig a vijf-en-twintig van dat soort mee stuurde, om hier en daar omtrent het ontdekken van Vyanden dienst te konnen doen: want na veertien dagen tijdts zou men ieder ten hoogsten met een mes van twee stuivers hebben konnen betalen. Maar ieder zoekt om 't zeerst de gunst van de Heeren Patroonen, en, door weinige kosten in rekening te brengen, de zelve behouden. Terwijl wy hier ter plaatse een nieuwe Vloed afwachten, hadden d'anderen iets aan mijn Volk bekend te maken, 't geen ik niet mocht hooren. 'k Vatte hier eenig kwaad vermoeden uit op; en zijnde vervolgens van malkander gescheiden, riep ik den geen van mijne by-hebbende Christenen, daar ik 't meest op vertrouwde, en verzocht hem, dat hy my dit nieuws, 't mocht dan goed af kwaad wezen, wilde mede deelen. 't Bestond hier in, dat men my, zo haast als wy weder aan het Fort waren gekomen, op de zelve manier als den gedetineerden Commandant zou handelen. Ik was verheugd, dat ik wist, waar ik my na had te schikken: doch trachtende ook te weten, wie my deze part meende te speelen, vraagde ik den zelven mijnen vriend wijder, of hy my hier over ook eenige verlichting kon geven. Hy begon te grimlagchen, en zei, indien ik het kon raaden, dat hy my als dank de Man zou openbaren. d'Eerstemaal was raak: want ik wist ten naasten by, [99] wie mijne Vrienden of Vyanden waren. 't Was dan een zekere losbol, leggende op een plaats *Maikony* geheeten, aan wien ik veele Cargesoenen had gezonden, daar ik heel zelden Retouren af had gezien. Van alle deze gestuurde Goederen had ik een Rekening van hem, getekend met zijne eigene hand; waar over ik hem dikwijls had vermaand, dat hy zijn beleid in 't Vaderland niet en zou konnen verantwoorden, en dat ik, volgens mijne plicht, genoodzaakt was die in tijd en wijle te vertoonen. Ondertusschen gingen wy met de Vloed vast voort, en kwamen des avondts omtrent ten zeven uuren weder aan het Fort. Straks vervoegde ik my by den nieuwen Commandant, om hem wegens het voorgevallene, omtrent mijne Brandwacht te verstendigen: doch zijnde deze bezig met gastereeren, en al te druk in discours om op zulke vodderijen acht te geven, nam ik die gelegentheid waar; ging stilletjes na mijne Kamer; deed mijne Kist open; kreeg 'er de Boeken uit; en gaf de zelven over aan een vertrouwd Vriend, dien ik aan het venster hier op liet passen, om zo in de zijnen te sluiten. Dit geschiedde buiten iemandts weeten, behalven dat het gezien werd van een zekere Juffrouw, welke, niet van mijne Vyanden zijnde, aanstondst by my kwam, en my zei, dat zulks, indien het Volk het gewaar wierd, zeer kwalijk genomen zou worden. Ik voerde haar te gemoet, dat ik met het Volk niets te doen en had; sloot de Kist; en vervoegde my by het geselschap: na welkers scheiden het Opperhoofd, zijnde wy nu kwansuis in vrijheid, tegen my zei, dat ik doch niet in mijne Kist zou gaan, en dat hy my waarschouwde als een vriend. Ik vraagde hem de reden. Hy onschuldigde zich met te zeggen, dat hy 'er geen reden af wist; maar dat het Volk my in de Boeijen wilde zetten. Ik gaf hem het zelve antwoord, als ik aan de Juffrouw had gedaan: doch wetende ondertusschen wel, wat my te doen stond, ging ik aantsondts by den geen, die my dit gantsche spel brouwde, en vraagde hem, wat reden hy had om het Volk tegen my op te maken. Hy ontkende het stout en stijf, en swoer, dat hy 'er nooit de minste gedachte toe had gehad. 'k Zei, dat hy met my in de Kombuis zou gaan, en dat ik 'er hem met zijne eigene hand af zou overtuigen. Hier [100] toonde ik hem de Rekening, en smeet ze in 't vuur. Zie daar, voerde ik hem al lagchende te gemoet, den appel van tweedracht. Inderdaad, het was ze ook; en hier mee verdween de gantsche stormbuy.

XIX. HOOFDSTUK.

Aenkomst van twee Schepen. Staking van den gedetineerden Commandant, en aantelling van een nieuwen. Overkomst van een nieuwen Secretaris in de plaats van den Auteur. Vertrek van de zelven. Verschijning van een Vredevuur. Ontmoeting van drie Schepen. Komst van de Auteur voor Vlissingen, enz.

Terwijl de saaken in desen staat waren, kregen wy in de Maand January van den jaare 1674 tijding van het Fort wegens d'aankomst van twee Schepen: 't geen een ongemeen blijdschap veroorsaakten, betuygd door het lossen van drie kanon schooten. Straks de groote Boot na beneden gesonden, om de rechte sekerheid te hebben. Ondertusschen kwamen de gemelde Schepen vast opwaarts en lieten het Anker voor het Fort in de grond vallen: waar op den Commandant na Boord zijnde gesonden, om de Capiteynen te verwelkomen, vervoegde ik my eerst by den Vlagman, zijnde mijn eerste Opperhoofd; en vervolgens by den andere Bevelhebber, die weeleer zijn Stuurman en Lieutenant was geweest, en nu herwaarts gekomen om de plaats van Commandant voor den tijd van een jaar waarte nemen. Ik wierd aan beide de Schepen seer minnelijk ontfangen en met de Sloep van den Vlagman weder na land gevoerd; alwaar zich ook des anderendaags de twee Capiteynen lieten vinden: waar op de Heeren Raaden ontbooden zijnde, wierd in hare Vergadering goed gevonden, dat men den gedetineerden Commandant aantondts op vrye voeten sou stellen; vervolgens den nieuwen Commandant zijne Commis- [101] sie voorgelezen; en wyders de dag in vrolijkheid doorgebracht.

Met de gemelde twee Schepen was ook een nieuwe Secretaris overgekomen: want alzo mijn tijd verstreeken was, om dat ik geen genegentheid had om in die qualiteit langer aan *Rio de Berbice* te blijven, had ik al overlang verzocht, dat de Heeren Patroonen zich van een bekwaam Persoon, om in mijne plaats te succederen, geliefden te voorzien. Dezen begon ik aanstondts t'onderrechten wegens 't geen in de bediening van zijn Ampt hadde waar te nemen; doch zonder dat ik hem echter tot noch toe zich met eenige zaken liet bemoejen: behoudende de bestiering tot aan mijn ververtrek aan my.

Ondertusschen begon zich, na omtrent drie a vier weeken tijdts, de Capitein, die de Vlag had gevoerd, hebbende zijn Schip in de Rivier laten schoon maken, en eenige Suiker en Verw ingenomen, om geballast in Zee te gaan, (want hy was te kaap uitgerust, met zes-en-twintig stukken Geschut en honderd vier-en-twintig Man) tot zijn vertrek te bereiden; weshalven een Vergadering aangesteld zijnde, wierd (niet tegenstaande dat d'order van de Heeren Patroonen medegebracht, dat de gedetineerde Commandant als Capitein met het tweede Schip na 't Vaderland zou vertrekken) goed gevonden, day hy als Passagier met dit zou overgaan, en zijn verblijf in de Hut hebben; mitsgaders dat de Lieutenant het tweede Schip, waar op men my mijne plaats had verordend, in qualiteit van Capitein zou voeren. Dit aldus geschikt zijnde, staken zy zeven a acht dagen daar na in Zee, om op de kust van de *Barbados* te gaan kruissen.

Midlerwijl wierden wij ook bereidselen tot het vertrek van ons Schip gemaakt; en in het laatst van de Maand February de Koopmanschappen, of Cargesoenen, in handen van den nieuwen Secretaris overgeleverd hebbende, besteede ik den noch overigen tijd tot mijn vermaak, en met de Heeren Planters te gaan bezoeken, van de welken ik begiftig wierd met Honders, Endvogels, Kalkoenen, Ec. tot mijne provisie op de Reis. Den 15^den^ Maart vertrok [102] het Schip na den mond van de Rivier, doch ik, alzo ik noch eenige byzondere zaaken te verrichten had, niet eer als den 18^den^ wanneer ik, verzeld door het Opperhoofd, en de Heeren *Beekman* en *Heyn*, mijne voornaamste Vrienden, met een Kanoo aan Boord wierd gebracht. Den 22sten Maart, 's morgens met het aanbreeken van den dag, liepen wy in Zee; zijnde het Schip genaamd *d'Eendracht*, en de Capitein *Adriaen de Vyver*: en zijnde op zes a acht vademen waters gekomen, wierd het Anker in de grond gesmeeten. Hier kwam de groote Bark, of Boot, by ons aan Boord leggen, leverd ons het overige van de lading, mitsgaders noch eenige provisie voor de Reis. Thans wierd de laatste maaltijd gedaan, en het afscheid gedronken; waar na van wederzijde drie schooten zijnde gelost, van ons de laatsten, om de Vrienden te bedanken, wierd het Anker gelicht, en onder zeil gesteeken; en waren wy met den avond al buiten 't gezicht van 't land. Wij hadden doorgaans goed weêr, maar in de wind, en nu en dan voor een uur of twee vermengd met *Travanden*. 't Zijn schielijke sterke winden, die de Schepen slingeren, als of ze uit malkander gescheurd zullen worden; doch gemeenlijk niet zeer lang duuren. Maar op de hoogte van het Eiland *Barmudas* wierden wy beloopen door een sware storm, die zich van des middags ten twaalf tot des nachts omtrent ten elf uuren met een afgrijselijk geweld deed gevoelen. 'k Had geduurende dien meesten tijd, alzo men op het Schip noch gaan noch staan kon, in de Kooy gelegen; doch wierd 'er des avondts omtrent acht a negen uuren door den Capitein uitgehaald, die my zei, dat'er iets te zien was, 't geen dikwils van lieden, die twintig jaaren ter Zee gevaaren hebben, nooit gezien is. 't Was een Licht, gelijk een kaars, vertoonde zich op de top der Vleugel van de groote Mast, by de Hollanders een *Vredevuur* geheeten, en van d'oude Zee-luiden gehouden voor een teken dat de storm op zijn hoogst is. Inder-daad, de wind verminderde hand over hand; en des anderendaag morgens was het weêr gansch en al bedaard: hoewel de Zee echter noch geweldig ontsteld was, en met hooge golven voort rolde. Aldus zeilden wy negen weeken en twee [103] dagen, zonder dat wy Land of Schepen hadden gezien; en mocht ik toen met *Ovidius* wel gezegt hebben:

Quocunque aspicio, nihil est nisi pontus & æther.

Maar op den gemelden tweeden dag, in den achtermiddag wierd een Zeil gezien ; waar op wy aanstondts cours stelden. Een half uur daar na ontdekten wy 'er noch twee by dit eerste: weshalven wy alles klaar maakten om te staan. Wy hadden acht-en-twintig Stukken op, en vier-en-tachtig Eeters, daar onder twee Wijven; doch waren veertien voet diep gelaaden: 't geen ons niet weinig hinderlijk zou zijn geweest, indien 't 'er op aan had gekomen. 's Avonts ten negen uuren kwamen wy malkander onder 't bereik van 't Kanon. Wy toonden de Prinse-Vlag; de drie anderen 't Bourgondische Kruis, of de Spaansche Vlag. Hier op wierden de zeilen op de wind gebragt, en de Schippers van de Spaansche Schepen aan ons boord gesonden, om hunne Passen te toonen. Zy kwamen van *Bilboa*, en gingen na *Groenland*. Doch onze Capitein, hier meer noch niet vernoegd, liet de Schepen vistiteren, of 'er ook onvrije goederen in waren: maar men vond 'er niet anders als gereedschap tot de Walvischvangst. Dezen maakten ons bekend, dat wy vrede met Engeland hadden, gelijk ook dat wy 's morgens in 't gezicht van *Fero* zouden wezen. In-derdaad, wy bevonden ons, na dat wy des nachts van malkander waren gescheiden, 's anderendaags, zijnde Saturdag, in 't gezicht van de Eiland; en Zondags lagen wy 'er dicht onder met weinig wind: weshalven wy ons van deze gelegentheid bedienen, om ons Schip te krengen en schoon te maken, op dat het te beter mocht zeilen. Dien zelven avond gingen wy weder voort; en 's morgens, met het aanbreeken van den dag, zeilden wy door verscheidene Visschers, daar wy de versche zoode van Kabeljaauw af kreegen: waar tegen wy hen weder met enige klenigheden begiftigde. Dingsdags daar aan volgende kreegen wy een Franschen kaper boven wind in 't gezicht. Wy zetten 't na hem toe: doch hy terstond alle zeilen by; en smeet alles, wat boven was, overboord. [104] Ondertussen konden wy met laveren niet genoeg winnen, alzo hy te hoog, en onze laading te swaar was; waarom wy het dan, na hem een uur of anderhalf gejaagt te hebben, over staag smeeten, en onze cours vervolgden. Twee of drie dagen daar na kwam ons een Vinvisch op zy, daar wy heel vermaakelijk den tijd mee sleeten. Eindelijk, na noch eenige dagen zeilens en laverens, bevonden wy ons omtrent *Texel,* alwaar wy order hadden om in te loopen: maar dewijl er vier Oorlog Schepen bezig waren met uit te komen, laveerden wy na het Eiland *Schouwe.* Hier lieten wy ons Anker vallen, om bekwaam tij af te wachten. 's Anderendaags morgens maakten wy weder zeil, en kwamen omtrent den middag voor Vlissingen, alwaar wy het voor de laatstemaal in de grond smeeten; hebbende aldus elf weeken min twee dagen met de Reis bezig geweest.

EINDE.

[105]

AMERICAANSCHE
VOYAGIEN,
TWEEDE DEEL:
Behelzende een
REIS na SURINAME,
Gelegen in het Noorder Deel van het
Landschap
G U I A N A.

[106] blanco

[107]

REIS na SURINAME

I. HOOFDSTUK.

Begeerte van den Auteur om nochmaels na vreemde Gewesten te gaan. Krijgt daar door een zeker voorval gelegentheid toe. Word voor Opzichter van een Plantazie in Suriname aangenomen. Steekt in Zee. Komst in de Rivier Suriname, enz.

De lust om weder na vreemde Gewesten te gaan, was niet tegenstaande d'ongemakken die men aldaar dikwijls te lijden heeft, zodanig niet uitgedoofd, of ik had zich wel weer een gelegentheid willen zien opdoen om een nieuwe Tocht t'ondernemen. Ondertusschen wil ik evenwel wel bekennen, dat *Rio de Berbice* de plaats niet en was, daar mijne genegentheid zich heen strekte. d'Eenzaamheid was 'er te groot; en zijnde al mijn leven een liefhebber van Geselschappen en Menschen geweest, had ik 'er in mijne voorgaande Reis onbezield dingen genoeg gezien om 'er geen tweede Tocht te willen waagen, hoewel 'er my meer als eenmaal gelegentheid toe te vooren kwam: Want ik had de Heeren Patroonen zo kwalijk niet gediend, of hun huis stond ten allen tijden voor my open. Midlerwijl, gelijk men meesten tijd niet en kan 't geen men wil, en dat men niet altijd machtig is zijne eigene driften op te volgen, was ik zo lang in deze verwachting, dat ik de hoop verlooren begon te geven, en mijne dingen te schikken om met ernst een andere manier van leven by der hand te gaan vatten; wanneer zich heel onverwacht een gelegentheit opdeed om mijne lust te voldoen. Zekeren Heer, die een schoone Plantazie in *Suriname* had, viel, benevens eenigen zijner Bloedverwanten, een erffenis van een vry tamelijk belang te beurt, welke, indien hy [108] zich recht wilde zien geschieden, hem noodzaakte persoonlijk in *Zeeland* over te komen. Hy ondernam de reis; maar naauwlijks had hy voeten te land gezet, of hy verstond, dat de baatzucht zo zeer in de weer was geweest, dat het scheiden en deelen zo heel gemakkelijk niet zou vallen. In der daad, gelijk ieder even zeer hardebolde, of immers dat 'er ongemakkelijke Menschen onder waren, wierd het werk wel haast in proces gesmeeten: de toevlucht van onrechtvaardige lieden, die zich door dit middel meerder toeleggen, als hen van rechtswege toekomt. De winter, alreedts op handen toen de gemelden

Heer overkwam, verliep zonder dat men noch veel gevoorderd was; weshalven niet weetende wanneer men hier een eind af te gemoet mocht zien, en de Plantazie in *Suriname* niet konnende blijven zonder iemand die 'er het opzicht op had, begon hy na een bekwaam Persoon te vernemen: en hebbende zich ten dien einde gericht aan de Heeren Patroonen, wierd ik hem voorgedraagen, en des anderendaags morgens ontboden om dien avond met malkander over de zaak te spreeken. De conditien waren zo redelijk, dat men my na weinige woorden met het Opzichterschap van de Plantazie geluk wenschte: En alzo 'er ter zelve tijd een Schip, de *Juff. Sophia* geheeten, voerende ettelijke Bassen, in lading lag, 't geen voor eenige Particulieren derwaarts stond te gaan, kreeg ik order om my op mijn gemak klaar te maken. Het Contract luidde van vier jaren; 't geen my een mooye tijd dunkende te weezen, maakte ik zo veele bereidselen, als of ik mijn leven in deze Colonie geeyndigt zou hebben. Inmiddels geraakte het Schip vollaaden; en de Reeders eenmaal of twee met malkander aan boord vrolijk geweest zijnde, kreeg de Schipper, *Cornelis Blom* genaamd, order om met den eersten goeden wind in Zee te steeken. Dit geschiedde op den 17 April van den jare 1680. 't Weêr was gewenscht; de wind gunstig; 't Geselschap goed (want daar waren, benevens my, noch drie Passagiers t' scheep, braave lieden, die in *Suriname* gehuisvest waren) kort om, indien de gestadige beweeging der golven ons niet had doen gedenken, dat wy ons op de Velden van *Neptunus* bevonden, wy zouden onse Reis als een stille [109] verhuizing van het eene gewest na het ander hebben konnen aenmerken. Aldus raakten wy op de hoogte van de *Canarische Eilanden*, daar wy binnen korte dagen de *Passaad* aantreften, gelukkig dat wy ze wat hoog namen: Want naderhand vervielen wy by mistig weêr etttelijke mijlen, daar wy groote moeite mee gehad zouden hebben om ze weder te boven te komen. Eindelijk, na dat wy negen a tien weken op Zee waren geweest, zonder eenige gedenkwaardige ontmoeting gehad te hebben, wierpen wy op den 23 Juny het anker in den mond van de Rivier *Suriname*.

II. HOOFDSTUK.

Gelegenheid van de Rivier Suriname. Visschen in de zelve. Wonderlijke eigenschap van de Visch Torpedo. Menigte van Watervallen, enz.

De Rivier is gelegen op ses, of vijf en een halve Graad, Noorder breedte van de Linie. In het inkomen is zy beset met Zandbanken, doch echter met hoog water drei vademen diep, en ten tijde van Springvloeden noch dieper. Haare wydte is in den mond van omtrent een myl, welke zy doorgaans behoud tot aan de plaats daar ze zich in twee bochtige Armen verdeelt; waar af d'eene, die zich na 't Oosten strekt, de *Combuine*; en d'andere, schietende na 't Westen, *Suriname* geheten word. De Armen, waar langs zich een menigte van Plantazien heen strekt, en van welker eene men by goed weer over de *Savaanen*, of Weylanden, in een halven dag by d'andere kan komen, zyn ieder omtrent een halve myl breed, en zo diep, dat ze wel dertig myl opwaarts van de grootste Schepen bevaren konnen worden; wyders aan wederzyde met Bosschagien bezet. Ongevaar twee myl van den mond der Rivier, vlak tegen de Rivier *Suriname* aan, heeft men een Fort, van Steen opgehaald,

Parimari- [110] *bo* geheten, benevens een Dorp van vijftig a sestig Huisen; en wat hooger op, aan een spruit van de selve Rivier, een sterk Huis, geduurende het Gouvernement des Heeren van *Sommelsdijk* opgeworpen. Noch hooger opwaarts, aan de selve Rivier, legt de *Zandpunt* een Dorp van Christenen, bestaande uit 25 a 30 Huisen en een Kerk. Boven dit Dorp ziet men een oord, het *Joodenquartier* geheeten, ter oorsaak dat 'er veele Jooden woonen. Hier zyn de beste Plantazien van de gantsche Colonie. 't Was eertydts d'uiterste woonplaats : Maar de Zuster des Heeren van *Sommelsdijk* in den jaare 1684 overgekomen zynde, hebben de met haar overgekomene *Labadisten* noch hooger een Plantazie aangelegt, voerende den naam van hunne Secte. Op de samenvloeying van de twee Armen, of Rivieren, de *Combuine* en *Suriname*, legt het *Krabbebosch*, zynde verdronken land, 't welk geen Fort kan lyden: andersins souden 'er beide de Rivieren door verdedigd konnen worden. Maar op die van de *Combuine* en de *Cottica*, een Arm van den zelven monder der geheele Rivier, ziet men een Fort van een taamelijke sterkte. Langs desen Arm zyn ook veele Plantazien aangelegt, doch wel ter verte van 15 a 16 mylen; mitsgaders ook verscheidene langs een sekere kreek, *Piereka* geheeten, loopende uit de *Cottica* in de *Combuine*. Noch zyn 'er meerder Kreeken, daar ook Plantazien langs heen leggen, te lang om hier altemaal op te halen, en die men den Leser ook niet verstaanlijk genoeg voor oogen kan stellen.

Ziet daar de gelegentheid van de Rivier, die wyders seer vischrijk is, zynde wel voorsien met een ontallijke menigte van groote Visschen, ende oock van anderen die wel niet eetbaer, maar echter raar en siens waardig zyn, als onder anderen de *Swaart-Visch*, die soo genoemt wort van een been dat uit zyne snuyt wast, en een swaart gelijkct, ofte eerder een zaage, waar van ick gesien hebbe die wel een elle langh geweest zyn. Noch is 'er een andere aert van Visschen, Manaty genoemt, die langs de Rivier haer selven voedt met struycken of bladeren van dien: sy wort van harre jongen gesogen als een Koey, ende smaekt meer naar Vleesch als [111] naar Visch. De derde aart van Visschen sal ik hier slechts noemen; want het is sulk een vreemden slagh, dat het wel de pijne waart soude zyn in 't bysonder beschreven te worden. De naem daar van is *Torpedo*, ofte in 't Engelsch Num-eel, dat is te seggen, een beroerende Aal ofte Paling, dewelcke levendig zynde, en eenig ander Schepsel aanrakende, ofte daar van aangeraackt wordende, geeft aan alle leden van de selve een sulcke doofheit en beroerte, dat sy voor een tijdt lang t'eenemaal ongevoeligh ende niet te gebruycken zyn: ende het is gelooflijck, dat verscheydene luyden verdroncken zyn, die het ongeluk gehadt hebben van in 't swemmen over de Rivier door een van dese Visschen geraekt te worden. Sy doen desgelijcks, wanneer sy maar aangetast worden met het eynde van een lange stock, of wanneer een Man de hant slaet aan een ander die soo beroert is. Hier van hebben wy d'ervarenheit gehadt, wanneer soodanig een Visch gevangen en op 't lant geworpen zynde, een Hond die daar aan snuffeld, en hem in den mond nam, schielijk ter aarde viel. Den Heer van desen Hond, dit siende, ging daar na toe, en docht hem dar van af te trecken; maar hy wierd aanstonts beroert aan alle zyne leden, sonder dat hy zyn selven eenigsins bewegen konde. Een ander man, die by hem stont, en hem van daar trecken wilde, raackt 'er also wel aan vast: en dat duyrde soo lang, tot dat desen Aal het ontsnapte: ende doen quamen sy allegaar weder tot zich selven, en konden zich roeren en beweegen als te voren.

De Plantazien leggen wel dartig mijlen opwaarts langs de Rivier; en het schijnt, dat de Colonie hare grensen niet verder en sal uytstrecken, wegens verscheydene Cataracten ofte Watervallen aan weder zyden van de selve: waar door het water van den kanten der Steenrotzen nederstortende, de passage op de rivier, de beste wegh zynde om alle behoeften naar boven te brengen, t'eenemaal onbruyckelijck gemaakt wort. Want als 'er maar een enckele Water-val ware, soo soude met der tijdt raat daar tegens gevonden worden maar nu zyn 'er elcke vijf of ses mijlen eenige, en dat soo verre opwaarts als het lant eenigsins [112] bekent is. Het gebeurde eens, dat men ontrent dese Watervallen jacht maakte op eenige Indiaanen, die van boven gekomen waren, en een Engelsche Vrouw vermoort hadden, plonderende het huys daar sy in was. Hier toe hadden sich eenige Mannen gereet gemaakt, die van alles wel voorsien waren: ende naar dat zy hunne Vaartuigen over landt opgehaalt hadden, om seven of acht van dese Water vallen voor by te komen, moesten sy ten laatsten wederom keeren, sonder yetwes uyt gerecht te hebben, door dien sy geen Indiaan ter werelt te sien kregen. Wanneer nu sommige onder haar in het wederom komen zich verstonden door dese Water vallen met hunne Vaartuigen neder te sacken, wierden eenige van haar al vallende in stucken verbryselt: ende de overigen quamen naauwlijks met het leeven daar van. Sodanige Water vallen zyn meest in alle Rivieren op dese kust, ende beletten dat men dit rijcke landt niet ter deeg ontdecken kan.

III. HOOFDSTUK.

Van het klimaat of de getemperdheid des Landts, mitsgaders eenige bysonderheden welke daar betrekking toe hebben.

Van November tot in Julius is het hier maar matigh heet, ter oorsaacke van de wolcken die daar over het hooft hangen, en van de overvloedige regen die als dan valt en d'aarde ververscht, zo oock van wegen de geduyrige Noord Oosten wint, die de lucht niet weynig verkoelt. d'Ander vijf maanden, wanneer 'er geen regen en valt, en men de soete schaduwe van de wolcken koomt te missen, soo is't 'er al vry heet; en dat komt niet alleen van de reflectie ofte wederstuytinge der stralen van de Son op een meest sandig aartrijk, maar ook van de Son zelve, die als dan zo naby is: ja de hitte soude qualijck te verdragen zyn, ten ware sy door de voortsz[egde] Koelte eenigsins gematigt [113] wierde. Nademael dit Lant zoo na by de Linie is, zoo zijn dag en nacht al meest even gelijk, ofte verschillen niet boven een uyr; want de Son gaat noyt vroeger ofte later op, ofte onder, als een half uyr voor, ofte een half uyre na zessen. De onveranderlijke warmte maakt, dat dit Land veel vermaekelijker is voor oude als voor jonge luyden. Want het schijnt, of het Lant haer toelacht, en hare jaren vernieuwt: want die te vooren lam, mat, en swak waren, worden hier weder jeugdig, en vol van leven. De Jonge luyden daar ten tegen verliesen hier veel van hare krachten, ende komen eerder te vervallen als in de Noordsche Landen, hoewel *Suriname* anders gezont genoeg is voor wel getemperde gezonde lichamen.

De ziektens, die hier meest ommegaan, zijn koude en heete Koortzen, de *Jawes*, en het Water, 't welk men daer de *Land-siekte* noemt. Het Volck was in den eersten geweldig daer mede gequelt; maer ik gelove, dat het meer toequam by de slechte huyzinge en d'ellendige kost, als by d'ongetemperheyt van het Lant. De *Jawes* is bykans een en de zelfde ziekte met de Spaansche Pokken; ende men krijgt se maar al te licht door ommegang met de Indiaansche Vrouwen, die 'er van natuyre mede besmet schijnen te weezen: gelijck ook deze ziekte, die ons eerst door de Spanjaarden toegebracht is, tegenwoordig in geen deel van Europa voor vreemd gehouden wort. Sy komt ook voort uyt eenig Seer, daer niet wel na gesien wort; want het Lant is die dingen van natuyre zodanig tegen, dat het ze doet veranderen in deze droevige en bykans ongeneeselijcke ziekte. Het Water, ofte de Lantziekte, is, na mijn oordeel onder het Volk gekomen van d'ongezonde en slappe kost, waer mede zich d'arme Dienstboden hebben moeten behelpen, door gebrek van goede Heeren en Meesters in dat rouwe Landt; want ik hebbe daer op gelet, dat qualijk iemandt anders deze ziekte onderhevig is geweest, als dit slag van menschen. Want d'ongezonde kost maekt niet als zwaer bloet en bedwelmde geesten, waer door de luyden geen lust tot haar zelven hebbende, maer zich versloffende, hebben ze eyndelijk niet sterkte genoeg om de quade humeuren en vochtigheden uyt te drijven, die zulke [114] melancholijcke menschen hoe langer hoe meer broeden; ende over zulks moeten zy al meest sterven en vergaan, by aldien 'er niet in 't begin van de ziekte op gelet wort.

Het Land naast den mond van de Rivier is laag, Bosachtig, en vol van *Swampen*, of verdronkene plaatsen. Dartig mijlen hooger op is het hoog en Bergachtig, hebbende tusschen beiden groote en wijde Velden of Pleinen, die hier en dar met kleine Bosjes zoodanig bezet zijn, dat het lijkt, of het Eylandekens waren in een groene Zee. Het is een uytmuntend playzier, te zien de wonderbare en vermaekelijke werken van de Natuyre aen de kleyne Beesjes, die met kluchtige postuyren van den eenen tak op den andren springen op deze altijt groenende Boomen, aan de welken men ook noch ziet een geduyrig wassen en vallen van de Bladeren. Want zoo haast en valt 'er geen af, ofte daer komt een ander in de plaatze. Ondertusschen worden de Bomen nooit ontbloot van haer Somerlivrey. Aan zommigen zal men altijdt Bloessem vinden, en met eenen Vruchten, waer van eenige noch heel onrijp, en de rest d'eene rijper zijn als d'andere. Geen van s'menschen zinnen heeft 'er meer vermaek in deze Bosschen als de reuk; want de Bomen aldaer verspreyden haren kruydigen reuk een groot stuk wegs rontom in de lucht; zulks dat de Zeezieke luyden geweldig daer door verguikt worden.

Het is ook een wonder om sien, wat menigte van alderhande Gewormte dit heete en vochtige Lant voorteelt. Ik hebbe gezien een witte plekke, die in den eersten niet grooter was als een speldenhooft, en die op een nieuwen zachten uyt was van een wortel van een grooten Boom binnen den tijt van twee of drie dagen groeyde tot een aert van een Somer-vogel, oft Pepel, met schoone zwarte ende zaffraancoleur gesprickelde vleugels. Ik heb 'er anderen gevonden, die noch niet volwassen waren, maer zoo vast aen de schorze van den Boom kleefden, als of zy daer aan gegroeit waren. Daar is noch een ander slag, genaemt de *Cemelvliege*, van wegen haren langen hals; welke ik niet weet hoe zy geteelt wort: maer wanneer zy een tijt lang geleeft heeft, soo valt zy op de aerde, schiet een wortel, ende wort verandert [115] in een Plante. Buiten twijfel zal dit eenigen ongeloofelijk schijnen: maar ik kan verzekeren, dat het alzo waar is als de menigvuldige verandering der Zywurmen.

IV. HOOFDSTUK.

Van het Voedsel.

Dit bestaat in *James*, *Plantons*, en *Cassader*, in plaats van Broot. Het eerste is een Wortel, die een tros draagt gelijk Hop. Zy wort rijp binnen den tijt van acht maanden: ende wanneer ze gekookt ofte geroost wort, is ze droog en kruymachtig. Wat de smaak belant, daar valt niet veel af te zeggen: want ik heb 'er nooit veel smaak in konnnen vinden. *Planton* is de vrucht van een Boom, die wel een jaar van doen heeft eer zy volwassen is. Zy gelijkt wel na de bast ofte schale van een Boon, maer is grooter. Daer hangen veertig ofte vyftig aan een bos: maar de Boom en draagt 'er niet meer van als een. Men plukt ze af eer zy heel rijp worden, ende kookt of roost ze. Naer mijn gevoelen is deze zoort van Brood niet beter als de voorgaende. De laatste, namelijk *Cassader*, welke eygentlijk Broot genoemt kan worden, is van gelijken een Wortel zoo dik als een mans been; maer van verscheyde gedaante. Daer spruyt een Boom uyt, van de hoogte van acht voeten. De Wortel wort getrokken wanneer de Boom een jaer out is, en wort herplant met de stokken van den Boom, die men in de aarde legt. De Wortel, uytgetrokken, wort geschrapt, ende het zap daar uytgeperst, het welk een quaat venijn is. Daer na wort zy gedroogt, en gestooten, en van het meel op heete steenen ronde koeken gebakken, die een halven duym dik zijn. Het is aengenaem wanneer het nieuw bakken is; maar wanneer het een dag oudt is, zoo is 'er weynig smaeks in. Van deze *Cassader* maeken de Indiaanen verscheyde soorten van sterken Drank, waar van een seker slag, *Perrinoe* genoemt, in der daat goet is; gelijkende [116] niet qualijk na onze sterkste Maartsche Bieren, die een jaar oud zijn. Wy hebben in het Hooftstuk, 't geen wegens de Dranken van *Rio de Berbice* handelt, gezegt hoe deze Drank gemaakt word, en zullen het derhalven hier niet herhalen.

Vleesch en Visch moet haer geduyrig toegebracht worden uyt *Nieuw Engelant*, *Virginia*, ende andere plaatsen; hoewel de Bosschen en Rivieren genoegzaam van alles voorzien zijn: maar de gestadige regen ende Watervloeden beletten dat de Visch niet in zulk een menigte gevangen kan worden, als men ze wel zoude van doen hebben; hoewel 'er nochtans by dag zo veel te krijgen is, dat niemant, die een weynig moeite daer om doen wil, reden heeft om over gebrek te klagen. De Visschen zijn 'er heel goed van smaak: maar een, die wat lekker is, zal wel haast proeven, hoe veel beter het Vleesch in onze *Nederlanden* is, als hier ter plaatse: want de zelve soorten van Beesten, die aldaer gequeekt worden, hebben in deze heete Landen Vleesch dat heel slap is, ende geen smaak heeft, uytgezondert de Verkens, die hier veel vetter en beter van smaek zijn, als in 't Vaderland.

In een zekeren tijdt van 't Jaer worden 'er ook *Tortoises*, ofte Schild-padden, op de Zee-kust gevangen, niet van die waer van de schilden zoo kostelijk en dier zijn; maer egter wel 2 a 300 pont wegen. De Wijfkens houdt men voor best; en die hebben in 't gemeyn wel een kinneken met eyeren in haren buyk, waer van elk zoo groot is als een hennen ey, maar qualijk zoo goet. Deze eyeren leggen zy, uyt het water kruypende, in het zant, alwaer zy ze met het selve bedekken, ende laten ze zoo uytbroeyen door de hitte van de Son. Het gezouten Vleesch van de Schildtpadden kan by groot gebrek wel gegeten worden; want honger, segt men, maekt rauewe boonen zoet: maer versch zijnde, wort het van sommige zeer geprezen als een treffelijke kost; daar ik nochtans voor mijn part niet veel sin in hebbe: want hoewel de smaak zo heel onaengenaem niet en is, zo bezwaerde het my doch altijt de maeg, die anders nieuwers na de swackste is. Het en kan ook niet anders als een grof en slijmachtig voetzel geven, om dat het zoo lichtelijk verrot, ende dat het datelijk begint te stinken, wanneer men het [117] slegts twee uyren, naar dat het geslagen is, ongesouten leggin laat. Schapen kan men hier gants niet queeken, want het schijnt dat dese Beesten beter groeyen in een kout en droog, als in een heet en vochtig Lant. Ossen en Koeyen komen 'er wel voort, by namen aen de Zeekant: maar daer zijn 'er voor als noch niet soo veel, dat de Vleeschhouwers daar veel zouden te doen hebben: daar en tegen zou 'er een oneyndig getal van Verckens zijn, indien de Vledermuysen, die haer de Tepels afbyten, het niet beletteden.

V. HOOFDSTUK.

Van de Vogelen, en Dieren.

Ik geloove, dat 'er geen schoonder noch beter Vogels in de wereld gevonden worden, als in dit Gewest. Alleenlijk word 'er de Nachtegael met zijn lieflijk Keeltjen gewist; want het schijne, dat dit Landt al te rouwende wild is voor zulk een soeten gast. De Vogels, die hier zijn, maeken geen ander accoord ofte t'zamenstemmige, als waar door men verschrickt zoude konnen worden want d'eene huilt, d'anderre schreeuwt, de derde steent ende schreyt: maer allegaer maeken zy met malkander een geluyt, of het een muzijk uyt de Helle ware. Dan wat haer aen de zoetigheyt van de stemme gebreekt, waer van men niet vet en word, dat word met andere dingen herset, die goede en treffelijk zijn voor 's menschen leven vermaak: want d'Enden, Teelingen, Pijl staerten, Pinviers, of wilde Duyven, Sneppen, Faizanen, Pardrijzen, enz. veel grooter ende wel zo goet zijnde als eenige in 't Vaderland, zijn hier in meenigte op alle plaatzen. De Papegayen zijn 'er gemeener als de Krayen in Nederland. En aen de Zee-kust is een zeekere Vogel wiens naam ik niet onthouden hebbe, die zoo groot is, dat, wanneer eenigen daar van by malkander, ende wat verre van ons zijn, men zoude denken, dat 'er een Compagnie Soldaten op het sant quam aantreden; want haer veders van Scharlakenverwe, die door geen kunst [118] kan nagebootst worden, geven zodanigen glants van haar, dat zy al meest de oogen van de genen verblinden die haar aanzien. Noch is 'er een andere aert van Vogelen, die deze in schoonheyt te boven gaat, hoewel zy geweldig van d'andere in groote verschilt zijnde, niet grooter als een wilde Bye of Hommel. Deze zich in de

Bosschen hier en daar ommedraiende, vertoont zulk een menigte van de schoonste levenste couleuren, dat het onmogelijk is te beschrijven. Men noemt ze *Honig-Vogels*, om dat zy haer voetsel meest van de blommen haelen. Daer en boven is 'er een zeker slag van zwarte Vogels: die hangen hare nesten op het uyterste eynde van de takken der Boomen, uyt vreese vande diefsche Apen, welke de zelven anders vernielen souden. Ik zoude hier ietwes bygevoegt hebben van de *Fleder-muysen*; maar dewijl men als noch daar over twist, of het een Vogel ofte een Beest is, zo zal ik de beschrijvingen vandien uytstellen tot dat ik kome aan de schadelijke Dieren, denkende dat het beter te pas zal komen aldaar daar van handelen. Ondertusschen is *Suriname* soo wel met alderhande slag van Vledermuysen voorsien, dat, indien het tot lof van dit Land strekte, men zoude konnen seggen, dat de sterren aan den Hemel eerder te tellen waren, als de verscheydene zoorten van dit gedrochte. Doch ik zal het geduld van den Lezer niet langer misbruiken, maar hem daar mede geven een korte beschrijvinge van de voornaamste Dieren die my in de gedachten komen. Daer zijn den *Herten, Hasen, Konynen, Armadillas, Verkens, Buffels, Mierenbeeren, Tygers, &c.* Op de Boomen onthouden zich de *Meerkatten, Quottoes, Aapen, Marmezetts, Cuscharees, Luyarts,* en veel andere, waer van ik de namen vergeten hebbe. De Herten zijn al meest als d'onzen in 't Vaderland. De Hasen gelijken meer een Speen-Verken, als een ander Dier dat ik gezien hebbe. Sy zijn bruyn en zacht van hair, met wit gespickelt, grooter als de Vaderlandsche Hazen, met de welke zy geen gelijkenisse hebben als alleenlijk wegens de mont. Het is een uitmuntende goede kost, ende veel beter als een eenig viervoetig Dier 't geen in de Nederlanden by ons bekend is. De *Konynen* sijn rood van hair, niet van zo goede smaak, [119] ook kleynder als de Hasen, welken zy anderszins in gedaante gelijk zijn. De *Armadillaas* zijn van tweederhande zoorten, d'eenen groot d'anderen wat kleynder. Van de grooten heb ik 'er gezien, die tachtig pond woegen. Zy hebben korte beenen, en drie klaauwen aan hare voeten; een hoofd gelijk de Varkens, gene tanden, en een kleine mond. Zy zijn met schelpen over als beschermd, behalven het hooft en de buyk, daar geen spies of lancie doorsteken kan, ten ware dat juist tusschen de voegen van de schelpen haer quame te raken. Zy booren haar selven met de snuit en met de pooten in de aerd; ende het zoude een heel goede kost zijn, wanneer zy niet een strengen reuk van muscus hadden. De *Verkens* zijn van driederhande aert, waar af d'eene gelijk een Otter meest in 't water leeft. Deze worden zeer geprezen: maar ik en hebbe nooit het geluk gehad van haar te sien. De twee andere zoorten worden genaamt *Pakkyra*, en *Pinko*. De eerste heeft den navel op de rugge, is graauw van couleur, en maar tamelijke goede kost. De *Pinko* is niet zo groot als onze Verkens, maar wel immers zo goet. De Buffel wort gezegt zoo groot te zijn, als een onzer Runderen van twee jaren, en alzoo goede kost. Met meerder omstandigheden kan ik dit zoort van Beesten niet beschrijven, want zy zyn my noit te voor gekomen, zoo lang als ik daer geleeft hebbe; en ik hebbe ook verstaan, dat zy heel zelden zoo verre naar beneden komen als daar ik woonde.

De *Mierenbeer* is van de groote van een gemeyn Verken, donker graauw van verwe, hebbende een langen ruygen staert gelijk een Vos of Eekhoorn, waer mede hy het heele lijf bedekt voor den regen. Hy heeft een kleyn hooft; maar zijn snuit is wel een voet lang van d'oogen aen te reekenen; wijders geene tanden: zijne tong is lang en smal, en hy kan ze uytsteeken, wel ter lengte van een voet. Hy steekt ze in de nesten vande Mieren, die noodzakelijk daar op kleven moeten, en slingert ze alzoo in de krop ofte maeg, hebbende geen ander voetzel als deze Beesjes. Het is een sterk Dier, voornamentlijk in de voorste deelen van 't lighaam. Hy heeft scherpen klaauwen, de breedte van anderhalf duim lang, waar mede hy eenen gevaarlijk quetzen kan: [120] maar het beste is, dat hy langzaam gaat, zoo dat men hem lichtelijk kan ontgaan. Sijn vleesch is niet van het beste ofte zoetste; maar wanneer men grooten honger heeft, zo moet het al door de keel.

De *Tygers* zijn van dreiderley slag; de eene swart, de andere gespickelt, de derde roodt. De eerste zoort wort gehouden voor de wreedste, maar zelden gezien op plaatzen die bewoont worden. De gespickelde, geloof ik, dat misnoemt zijn; want het zijn eer Luipaarts als Tijgers, ende doen aan de luyden de meeste schade met haer Vee en Gevogelte, als Hoenderen, Ganzen, en diergelijke te vernielen. Sy zijn zo stark, dat 'er een zal springen over een tuin van vyf of zes voeten hoogte met een Verken in de mondt. Onder anderen kwam 'er een in de bevolkte plaatzen, die doodde een Rund van twee jaren, en sleepte hem verder als een quartier uire gaens in het Bosch. Sy zullen nochtans niemand by dag aanvallen, ten ware zy heel hongerig, ofte verwont waren; en ik hebbe nooit van meer als twee ofte drie Menschen gehoort die zy zouden verscheurt hebben, t' zedert dat deze Colonie opgeregt is. Een van die was een Huysman, een vlugge gast, die altijt gewenscht hadde dat hy eens een Tijger vinden mogte, ende hadde dikwijls daar over geklaagt, dat hy in alle sijne jachten nooit het geluk hadde gehad van een dezer Beesten aan te treffen. Een laatsten gebeurde het op een nacht, wanneer hy in zijn hamak lag met opene deuren, dat 'er een Tijger komt, vat hem aan, en draagt hem twee uiren gaens in het Bosch. Hy riep te vergeefs om hulp, hoewel een Engelsche Vrouw ter naaster deure in een gesloten huis hem hoorde, en zich verstoute met een musquet uit het venster te schieten. Maar die met deze Dieren te doen gehadt hebben, weeten dat een Tijger zijn roof niet zal laten op een klein geruchte. 's Anderendaags vond men den Man, wiens hooft en schouderen afgegeten waren. Daar wort opgelet, dat 'er niet meer zoo veel Tijgers zijn in die Gewesten, als te vooren, ten deele om dat zy zich verder van daan in de Bosschen begeven hebben, ten deele dat 'er veele van sijn gevangen geworden by de Wey-luiden. Eenen *Jan Millar*, dien men [121] my verhaalde een zeer stoutmoedig Man geweest te zijn, heeft 'er altoos niet minder als 12 of 14 met het roer ofte lancie gevelt, zijnde miraculeuzelijk van eenigen ontkomen met het leven, ende van anderen heel swaerlijk gequetst geworden. Daar zijn niet zoo veel roode Tijgers, als andere; ende deze zijn ook niet zoo wreed als de voorverhaalde.

In de Bosschen word een meenigte van *Land-Schildpadden* gevonden, maar die op de drie vierendeel na zoo groot niet zijn als aan de Zeekant. Hare schilden zijn zoo hart en stark, dat 'er een geladen karre mag over gaan, zonder haar te breken ofte te kreuken; ende daar mede beschermen zy haar zelven, zijnde anderzints weerloos voor alle hare vyanden, behalven zijnde anderzints weerloos voor alle hare vyanden, behalven voor de Menschen, en voor de Tijgers. De Menschen begaan haar een huysbraak met een Bijl; en de Tijgers keeren haar om, en verslinden het vleesch. Sy eten al wat haar voor komt; en d'Inwoonders zijn gewent een getal van haar op te sluyten in een kot, en zich daar van te bedienen, wanneer het te pas komt; wordende het daar voor gehouden, dat het geen van de quaatste kost in de Gewesten is.

Daar en boven zijn 'er *Porcupines*, die al meest met de Egels over een komen; maar zy zijn wat grooter, en over al gewapent met witte en swarte prickels, als de schachten van pennen, twee handen breet, lang en scharp als naalden, welken de Natuyr haar geleert heeft van alle kanten uit te schieten met een wonderbare gaauwheid, tegens de genen die haar zouden willen aentasten.

De *Aapen* en *Meerkatten* zijn zo wel bekent in 't Vaderland, en over al, dat men niet en hoeft haer in 't bysonder te beschrijven: dan een ding hebben de Meerkatten in dese Gewesten, waar in ik geloove dat zy van alle andere verscheyden worden, ende 't welk ik niet en kan voorby gaan om alhier gewag daar van te maken: Te weten, dat zy op een zeker uyre, zoo wel by dag als by nacht, sulk een ijsselijk geschreeuw voor hare holle keelen maken, dat den geen, die het niet gewent en is te hooren, niet lichtelijk iets vreemders en schrickelijkers kan voorkomen; wordende dit geschreeuw gehoort over twee mijlen weegs van die plaetze alwaar haar deze beesten onthouden. [122]

De *Marmazet* is een kleynaardig Diertjen, van een geele en groene couleur, veel kleynder als een Aep; en nochtans commandeert en beheerscht het alle dese Coorden-danssers, op haar enigszints rijdende, en met haar springende van den eenen boom op den anderen, haar daar en boven de spooren gevende, met haar in d'ooren te byten, niet konnende by haer of geschakelt ofte uyt de sadel geset worden.

De *Quotto* is swart in eenigerhande manieren, wat grooter als een Aep, heeft een langen steert, waar mede hy zich van den eenen tak van een Boom op den anderen swingt. Zy hebben een root bakkes, het hayr over het voorhooft hangende, siende uyt als een oud besjen. Haar geschreeuw is schitterend en geweldig luyde.

De *Cuscary* is swart, kleynder als een Marmazet, ende alomme geschapen als een Leeuw.

Den *Luyart* is een schepsel, zoo genaamt van wege zijn domme en slordige natuyr. Hy is wat grooter als een Meerkat, en heeft een vel van alderhande coleuren; wijders zoo luy, dat geen slag noch stoot hem zal doen rasser gaan als hy gewent is: ende men kan denken, dat hy geen van de voortvarendsten zijn moet, dewijle het een dag-reysens voor hem is op een Boom te klimmen, waar van hy heel selden nederdaalt, voor dat 'er niet meer op en is, daar hy sijn voetsel zoude van hebben konnen; want dan komt hy met een groote gravitey en deftigheyt weder naar beneden, ende gaat zo weder op een anderen, alwaar hy den legen tijdt (waar van al evenwel niet veel overschiet, wanneer men de gene dien hy tot eeten en slapen besteet rekenen wil) toebrengt met een deuntjen te fluyten, welk gefluyt echter niet zeer aangenaam voor het gehoor is.

Men heeft 'er noch meer andere soorten van Vogelen en Gedierte, die my niet altemaal te binnen schieten. Ook ben ik verzekerd, al verbleef de naarstigste Opmerker zeven jaaren lang in die Gewesten, dat hy altijd noch het een of ander Schepsel zou vinden, 't geen hy van te vooren niet gezien had, en zijne opmerking echter wel waardig ware. [123]

VI. HOOFDSTUK.

Van de Vruchten.

De Vruchten van 't Land zijn *Oranje-appelen, Limoenen, Limes, Pomcitrons, Water- en Muscadel-Meloenen*, mitsgaders sommige *Druyven*; alle de welke daar niet van natuyre, maar van buyten gebracht ende geteelt zijnde, nochtans zo goet zijn, ende zo wel dragen en voortkomen, als op eenige andere plaatzen. De Inlandsche vruchten zijn deze: *Plantons* ofte *Potatoes, Bonanoes, Semerrimars, Guavers, Pines*, ende overvloet van wilt goet, dat verplant zijnde mochte misschien niet zoo zeer te verachten zijn, als het tegenwoordig is. Van de Plantons hebb' ik alrede ietwes verhaalt. *Bonanoes* zijn bykants de zelve, ofte daar is altoos weynig onder scheyt onder dese twee als alleenlijk dat deze laatste wel zoo goet, ofte beter zijn als d'eerste, hoewel ik in geen van beyden sonderlingen smaak vinde. De *Semerrimars* wassen op een redelijken langen Boom: zy lijken wel Persiken, zyn van buyten wolachtig, konnen niet gegeten worden voor dat zy aangesteken, en gerot zijn, en dan hebben zy den smaak van Marmalade ofte Queen. De *Guaver* is omtrent zoo groot als een Mispel, geel, en vol saatjes. 't Is inderdaed een van de lekkerste vruchten die gevonden konnen worden; en wanneer ze rijp is, smaekt ze gelijk Aelbessen. Zy wast in *Savannas* of weyen.

De *Pine* of *Ananas* is wel de Prince van alle vruchten. Zy is zeer groot, zijnde in 't ronde wel acht duymen dik, ende heeft de lengte van een voet. Van buyten is zy groen en gespickelt, van binnen geel, sappig, vol van holligheden gelijk een Honigraet. Boven op den top heeft zy een fraay kroontje van bladeren, als of daar mede te kenne gegeven wierde de voortocht die zy voor andere vruchten heeft: ende zy heeft-ze met recht; want zy is verre de beste van de genen [124] die ik oyt gezien ofte gesmaakt hebbe. Zy wast op een kleyn bosjen ontrent vier voeten hoog. Den steel daar van komt uyt de wortel, gelijk die van de Artischokke. Het kroontjen afgesneden, en in d'aarde geplant zijnde, draagt binnen de tijd van tien maanden een nieuwe vrucht.

VII. HOOFDSTUK.

Van de Waaren en Koopmanschappen van dit Landt.

De Waaren van dit landt, waar mede men Koopmanschappen drijft, zijn, *Suycker, Speckle-wood* ofte gespickelt Hout, *Cattoenen, Tabak*, verscheyde *Gummen*, en *hout om te verwen.*

Suyker word 'er een aanzienelijke quantiteit gemaakt, en wordt door den bank tien par Cento beter gehouden als die van de Barbados.

Spekkle-wood is 'er ook overvloedig genoeg, en in *Engelant* eertijts verkocht geworden in gelijken prijs met de Zuyker; maar naar dat 'er een sulke menichte van overgebrocht is, is het vry wat afgeslagen.

De *Cattoenen* komen hier niet zoo wel voort als in de *Barbados* en ander Eylanden, mogelijk dewijle hier al te veel regen valt, ende dat zy al te verre van de Zee leggen, van waar een sout-achtigen dauw opstijgt, die de Rupsen en andere schadelijke gewormte van de Boomen verdrijft.

Tabak groeit 'er heel wel, doch is echter zo goed niet als die uit *Virginia* komt. En ik geloof, dat 'er voor als noch niet meer geplant word, als de Colonie voor zich zelve van daen heeft: want al de werelt, Mans, Vrouwen, Kinderen zijn daar liefhebbers van een pijpjen.

Met *Indigo* heeft men 't niet zonderling besocht.

Rum is een gedestilleerde vocht uyt het sap van Suykerriet, in 't gemeyn noch eens zoo sterk als Brandewijn, waarom het in Nieuw-Engelant *Kil-Divel,* ofte Duyvelsdoot genoemt word; ende wort aldaar verkocht een kanne van twee stoopen tegens 12 pont Suyker. [125]

Molasses wort van Suyker gemaakt, ende is het geene dat 'er van afdruypt wanneer de Suyker in potten gegoten is.

De mest bekende *Gummen* by onse Drogisten zijn *Montagne* en *Gummi Semnia.* Zy zijn beyde gaar wel te krijgen; ende daar zijn 'er buyten twijffel noch andere die beter zijn, en die metter tijdt door d'ervarentheid voor den dag gebracht sullen worden.

Cassia Fistula is 'er ook in overvloed, ende daar en boven een aart van *Balsem* die van een boom afdruypt. Geen van allen word 'er beter gehouden voor de versche wonden, als even dese.

Daer en is ook geen gebrek van alderhande slag van hout om te verwen; waar mede een tamelijke Koophandel gedreven zou konnen worden.

VIII. HOOFDSTUK.

Van de Bevolckinge.

Het getal der Huysgezinnen placht zich over eenigen tijd naauwlijks tot vier a vijf honderd uit te strekken: doch tegenwoordig worden 'er veel meer geteld, en onder de zelven wel drie honderd Plantazien, die geen klein profijt brengen aan hare Meesters, aangemerkt de eerijke renten die van een slecht capitaal binnen weinig jaren konnen getrocken worden, wanneer het werck maar voorzichtig beleit wort, ende die buiten ongeval veel hooger komen zullen als die van een grooter Bevolckinge, ende van een Lant daar meer moeite gedaan wort.

Den tijt om hout te kappen is tusschen April en Augustus: ten eynde van dien laat men 't leggen op de gront om droog te worden, tot in de maant van September, ende dan wort het aangesteken, ende d'assche verstrekt voor Mist. *Indiaansche Koorn* en *Zuyker-riet* worden geplant in de leegten; *Yamas* en ander voetsel op hooger-lant. Het *Koorn* groeyt [126] op een steel gelijk riet, in 't gemeyn zes ofte zeven voeten hoog: het draagt slechts twee Ayren op ieder steel, maar het graen is zoo groot als een erwte, en wort rijp in vier maanden. Men heeft er twee oogsten in een Jaar; ende het Koorn geeft ten minsten vyf hondert voor een. Het Suyckerriet is bequaam om gebroken of gesneden te worden, wanneer het ene Jaar out, en ontrent ses voeten hoog, en zo dik is als een mans arm ontrent de hant: het heeft een top als een vlagge, die afgesneden ofte gebroken, en geperst wort in een Molen. Het sap wort gekookt in kopere ketels tot een behoorlijke dikte, en daar na gegoten in houte bakken, die boven breed en vierkantig zijn, maar allensjens na beneden smaller worden tot op de grootte van een stuyver, aan de bodem, alwaar een gat is dat zoo lang toegestopt blijft met een klein houtjen, tot dat de Suyker kout en stijf is geworden: dan trekt men het houtjen uit, en laet de Siroop van de Suyker door het gat afsakken, die, wanneer hy ene tijt lang zo gehavent is, wort eindelijk uyt de bakken in Oxhoofden geslagen, en zo afgescheept word.

IX. HOOFDSTUK.

Van de Negros en de Slaven.

Desen worden daar meest gebracht uyt Guinea in Africa, en verkocht als Honden; gelijk zy dan ook niet meer geacht worden in haar werk, waar mede zy de heele week besig zijn, en daar zy toe gehouden worden met de grootste strafheit van de werelt, scherpelijk getuchtigd wordende over de minste fauten die zy begaan: en dat duurt tot Saturdags achter-middags, wanneer haer vergunt wordt haar eygen Tuinen en Plantingen waar te nemen; want zy en hebben anders niet waar van zy zouden leven konnen, behalven dat haar Meesters haar eens ofte tweemaal 's Jaars met wat stinkende soute Visch begunstigen, [127] ofte haar wat gebraats geven van een Koey of Paart die van haar selvne zijn komen te sterven. Haar huysvesting is een harde plank, en haar deeken haar eigen zwarte vel.

Door deze groote elende worden ze altemet bewogen, uit ene mismoedigheit, vertwijfelde dingen aan te gaan, om haar selven vry te maken; en wanneer zy vreezen gevat te mogen worden, verdoen zy haar zelven; ofte indien zy met hoop van vergiffenisse weder gebrocht worden tot hare Meesters, ende aldaar tot schrik en exempel gestraft worden, zullen zy hare stantvastigheid, ofte veel meer hare hartnekkigheid tonen, met de grootste tormenten, dier haar konnen aangedaan worden kloekmoedig uit te staan. Het is mengelmoes van alderhande Natien, die altijt in twist en strijt met malkanderen leven, ende daarom kan 'er geen conspiratie ofte t'samensweeringe onder haar gemaakt worden, of zy wort dadelijk ontdekt door de genen die om dies wille niet genegen zijn tot de verraderye, om dat eenige van hare vyanden deel daar in hebben; hoewel zy meest allegaar verraders en bloetdorstig van natuyr zijn, ende geen Religie altoos en hebben, niet tegenstaande verscheyden onder haar Gedoopt zijn. Maar veele zijn er die het oude gevoelen hebben van *Phytagoras*, nopende de verhuysinge van de ziele van 't eene lichaam in het ander, en dat zy, wanneer zy komen te sterven, herboren zullen worden, ende wederkeerende in haar Vaderlant, zo voorts in de werelt leven sullen in een gestadige veranderinge. Desе inbeeldinge doet haar dikwijls suchten en wenschen om hare doot, dewijle zy geen hoop en hebben van hare bedroefde slavernije andersints verlost te worden.

X. HOOFDSTUK.

Van vergiftige en schadelijke Beesten, en Wormen.

Het is geloofelijk dat de vruchtbare hitte van 't Lant, ende het kleyne getal van d'Inwoonders d'oorzaak zijn van het gekriel van zoo menigerley Wormen en [128] schadelijke Beesten, waar mede de Menschen aldaar gequelt en dikwijls in gevaar geset worden. Onder de geenen, die meest bekent zijn, worden deze naarvolgende gerekent: *Slangen, Crocodillen, Scorpioenen, Vledermuysen, Mieren, Muskytoes, Kreuten en Kickvorschen.*

Aangaande de Slangen, is het seker, dat 'er zijn dood geslagen geworden, die dertig voet lang waren, en dik naer proportie van de lengte. Het beste is, dat 'er geen zo groot gevaar is by deze vervaerlijke Beesten; want zy en zijn gants niet venijnig, ende ook, wanneer zy geen honger hebben, geensins bitsch. Het zijn eygentlijk Water-slangen, hoewel zy ook altemet op 't Lant kome weyden. Wat zy tot haar voetsel betrappen, geschiet met een gaauwigheid, niet met rasch loopen ofte wentelen: want ik hebbe nooit gehoort, dat iemant zo zot zoude geweest zijn als zich te laten beschadigen door een ongeval, dat men zo licht ontgaan kan als dat van deze Slangen. Maar daar is een ander slag dat kleinder, ende in groote meenigte is, daar men wel voor toezien mag; want daar zijn 'er onder die zoo venijnig zijn, dat haar niet te boven en gaat: gelijk wy daar van twee ofte drie reysen droevige ervarentheid gehad hebben, dat niet alleen de Menschen, die van haer zijn beschadigt geweest, korten tijdt daar aan gestorven zijn; maar dat het vleesch van de beenen, der geenen, die zy hebben gebeten gehadt, afgevallen is met stukken, binnen 24 uiren. Daar zijn 'er, die heel schoon van gesprikkelde levende verwe zijn; maar ondere deze schoone couleuren legt het doodelijkste vergif. Andere zijn 'er die zijn knoopigh en hebben hoorens aan haren steert, en slagtanden aan 't gehemelte van de bek, die twee duymen breet en lang sijn.

Daar zijn ook *Crocodillen*, maar niet zeer groot, noch in geen groote meenigte. Ik en behoeve ze niet te beschryven, want haar opgevulde vellen worden bykans in alle Apoteekers winckels ende elders gevonden.

De *Scorpioenen* zijn swart, ende gelijken wel een Kreeft. Zy schuylt meest in droog hout en Koorn. Haar prickel is de steert; ende wien zy daar mede steecken, die zal eenige uuren lang de grootste pijn van de wereld hebben; maar het [129] en raakt het leven niet. Het gemeyn genees-middel word genomen van het schepsel self: want men verbrijselt het selve, ende legt het op de wonde.

De *Vledermuizen* sijn schadelijke creaturen voor menschen en beesten; want zy trekken haar beyde gaar het bloet af, en dat zo behendig, dat men 't niet en voelt voor dat het te laat is. Het wordt geseyt, dat verscheyde luyden zijn genootzaakt geweest hare wooningen te verlaten, om het weynige bloet te behouden dat zy haar over gelaten hadden. Zy gelijken in de vlucht zoo groot te zijn als Duiven; ende, gelijk ik alreede verhaalt hebbe, zoo zijn zy d'eenige oorsaken waarom de Verkens niet in meerder getal in dat Landt konnen aangequeekt worden.

De *Mieren* zijn wel kleine schepselen, maar echter zo ontallijk, ende zo schadelijk, dat *Suriname* bykans van geen ding meer ongemaks heeft als van deze beesjes. De zandige gronden zijn boven anderen vol daar van: en de arme Luyden, die zulk landt is ten deel gevallen, ende die geen hulp van Dienstboden gehadt hebben om haar uyt te roeien, zijn gedwongen geworden haar landt te verlaten, ende beter plaatsen te zoeken.

De *Muskyta* is een soorte van Muggen, daar men 'snachts geen rust van hebben kan, zoo wort men van haar gebeten; ende daar loopen dadelijk groote puysten van op aan het vleesch. Met dit gewormte word men meest gequelt in de lage Landen en aan de Zeekant, waar de Zee over het Land op en afloopt; zoo dat de Visschers, om 's nachts te konnen slapen, het heele lijf moeten bedekken met slijk, behalven d'oogen ende den mondt.

Kreuten ende *Kik-vorssen*, het verschriksel van 't Vrouwen-volk, zijn hier, gelijk in Egipten, op alle plaatsen, zo wel in de huisen als in het veldt; ende zy maken 's avonts, naar dat 'er een regen-vlagen gevallen is, zulk een hel geluit, dat men zijn zelven qualijk hooren kan; ende zommige hebben zulk een vervaarlijken toon, dat men hen nieuwers mede vergelijken kan als met het steenen ofte gekerm van een mensch die op 't sterven leyt.

Dit is nu het alderquaadste, dat van *Suriname* kan ge- [130] segt worden: want het Landt is anders zodanigh van God gesegent, ende heeft zoo veel deugden, dat dese ongemakken niet daar by halen konnen. Daar sijn ook vooreenige van deselve uitgevonden volkomenen ende onfeylbare remedien ende hulp-middelen; ende tot de rest zal ook metter tijt raet wezen.

XI. HOOFDSTUK.

Omstandige verhandeling van alle de voornaamste byzonderlieden, welke tot de Huishouding, Levensmanier, enz. der Indiaanen behooren.

Men zegt, dat bloohartige menschen in 't gemeyn verraders zijn. Daar zijn verscheyde Natien, die met het Volk van deze Colonie verkeerren, ende Koopmanschap drijven; maar d'eigene Inwoonderen van 't landt zijn *Charibes*, ofte *Canibalen*, die ook wel de meeste in 't getal zijn van de genen die deze Landen bewoonen; ende die hebben haar selven verspreyt meest in alle Eylanden daar omtrent, ende op het vaste land langs de Riviere van d'*Amazones* aan, tot aan die van *Oronoque*. Sy gaan heel ende al naakt, behalven dat zy, eerbaarheidshalven, een lap dragen; maar de Vrouwen die een ofte twee kinderen gehadt hebben, werpense weg. Haar vel is van Orangiegeele verwe, haar hair zwart en zonder krullen. Het zoude een gelukkig Volk zijn, ten aanzien van de dingen van deze wereld, dat zy haar eigen geluk kenden; want de Natuur heeft haar zodanig met alle noodige dingen verzien, dat zy weinig moeite behoeven om haar zelven die te nut te maken. Het Vrouw-volk is in 't gemein geil; en daar zynder onder die zoo schoon zijn van gestalte, lijf ende leden, dat, wanneer de beste ende verstadingste Beeldthouwers haar sagen, zy niet met al daar op te zeggen zouden hebben. Haar beschaamtheid, in zonderheid die van Maagden, voor vreemden, geeft tot alle andere hare volmaaktheden, die zoo

[131] naakt ten toon gestelt worden, zulk een aantrekkende gratie ende aangenaamheid, dat de genen, die met haar omgaan, geen minder als Josephs Kuisheid van doen hebben, om tot geen verboden lust verwekt te worden. Sy zijn tot hier en toe zoo onnozel geweest, dat ze neffens alle andere vriendelijkheid, waar mede zy het Man-volk aanlokken, het zoetste ende puurste vermaak van kussen niet geleert en hebben; maar dewijle zy nu zoo veel niet d'Europers omme-gaan, ende van natuure geestig ende leerzaam zijn, zo is 't gelooflijk dat zy 't mettertijd wel leeren sullen. Sy hebben tweederhande huizen. Het eene voor de nacht, ende dit sijn kotten die met het dak bykants aan de grond leggen; ende het ander om 's daags daar in te zijn. Deze zijn wat hooger en wijder, om haar selven te beschermen, voor de heete stralen van de Son; ende zy zijn open aan alle kanten, ten einde de koele wind daar door zoude konnen gaan. Haar huisraat bestaat in fraey geschilderde aarde Potten en Schotels; ende haar Tafel-linden zijn bladeren van Boomen. Hare bedden of hamakken zijn gemaakt van Katoen, vierkantige gelijk een spreide van een bedde met boorden aan elk einde, waar door de hamak in 't vierkant stijf uitgespannen word. Haar Brood en Drank komt uyt hare Cassavetuinen; de Bosschen ende Rivieren verzien haar geduurig met vleesch ende Visch. Om haar zelven op te pronken, schilderen zy haar netjes met een roode couleur *Anotta* genoemt, dat op kleine Boompjes in schalen groeit, ende met het zap van verscheide Boomen. Sy booren haar zelven gaten door de neus, lippen ende ooren, ende hanger er glaze pendanten, stukken van kooper, ende andere beuzelingen in die zy van de Hollanders, met haren arbeid, verdienen. Den hals, d'armen, ende beenen beladen zy met Corrallen, schulpen van visschen, ofte met eenige koddige dingen die zy krijgen konnen. Sy en hebben geen andere Regeeringe ofte Wetten als die van de huis houding; ende over sulks leven heele Geslachten by malkanderen gelijk ten tijden van de oude Patriarchen; ende d'oudste van de Soonen treedt altijt in zijns Vaders plaats. Nochtans hebben zy onder haar eenige uitmuntende Mannen, welke [132] haar Capiteinen ofte Hooftluiden zijn, die haar in den Oorlogh voeren; ende dezer kloekmoedigheid wordt daar mede beproeft, dat men haar lustig met roeden geesselt; wanneer zy dat uitstaan konnen, zonder schreeuwen, ofte eenige andere merkelijke beweginge te maken, zoo worden zy voor brave luiden gehouden, ende van d'andere geeert die minder moed daar toe hebben. De Hoofden van de Geslachten hebben ordinaris drie of vier Wijven, daar d'anderen maar eene hebben; ende men mag ze allegaar met reden eer Dienaressen als Huisvrouwen noemen: want zy moeten al zonder zodanig zijn tot hare Mans, als de minste meid onder ons is tot haren Meester ofte Vrouw. De Man zal heel zelden zijne schouderen met eenige last ofte dracht beswaren, maar hy legt ze allegaar op die van de Vrouwen; ende die dragen zulk een eerbiedigheid tot hare Mans, dat zy haar altijd aan de Tafel opwachten, ende niet eerder en eeten, als wanneer de Mans gedaan hebben. De Vrouw in de Kraam gekomen zijnde, gaat zy dadelijk haar werk doen gelijk daar te vooren. Hare Taal luit niet vreemd, maar men kan ze qualijk leeren, omdat er veel woorden in zijn die verscheide dingen beduiden, ende die men niet anders onderscheiden kan, als by de verscheide uitspraak. Wanneer 'er een Veldtocht besloten is, zoo zend den Generaal ofte opperste Capitein op alle Dorpen, ende tot alle Huisgezinnen die vergadert zullen worden, eenen stok, daar

zo veel kerven in zijn, als hy haar dagen stelt om op de vergader-plaats by een te komen: van deze kerven snijden zy alle dagen een uit, tot zoo lang dat den tijd omme is, ende daar by konnen zy alleen weten, dat den tijd verstreken is; want haar getal ofte cyferen verstrekt zich ook niet boven de twintig, om dat zy tot de rest geen namen hebben, ende beduiden ook maar deze twintig met hare vingeren ende toonen, het zelve getal evenwel altemet verdubbelende ofte drievuldigende. Wat hooger gaat, daar is haar cijfer-kunst op een einde; ende dan bersten zy uit met haar *Ounsa awara*, dat is te zeggen, zoo veel als hair op ons hooft. Sij gaan in Zee met geschilderde *Canoas* ofte Boots, die van een stuk gemaakt zijn, uit een [133] Boom die uitgeholt is als een trog, ende die zoo groot is dat er altemet twee ofte drie last goedt kan in gevoert worden. Hare Wapens zijn Boogen met vergiftige pijlen, ende korte stokken van gespikkeld houdt. Sommige dragen tot haar beschermige Rondassen ofte Schilden, die fraai gemaakt en met figuren gesneden zijn. Sy en houden geen ordre in 't vechten, ende gaan ook op geen aanslag, 't en ware dat zy een merkelijk voordeel zagen, als by nacht. De Mans, die zy gevangen krijgen, brengen zy om 't leven, met de meeste wreedheid die bloode menschen bedenken konnen tegens hare vyanden die zy in haar gewelt hebben. De Kinderen ende Vrouwen maken zy tot slaven, ende verkoopen ze voor beuzelingen. Sy overvielen eens de Franschen in *Suriname*, end bezochten het ook met d'Engelschen, wanneer zy eerst daar quamen; maar zy wierden van deze laatsten zodaning bejegent, dat zy alsnoch berouw hebben van hare dwaasheid. Tegenwoordig, nu de Colonie machtig is geworden, durven zy niet wederkomen, maar dragen haar althans beleefdelijk. Sy zijn heel wraekgierig onder haar zelven, ende sullen het leet, dat haar gedaan wordt, wreeken den eenen tijd ofte den anderen; maar altijt verraderlijk, ende niet durvende haren Man onder d'oogen zien. Ik hebbe nooit konnen bemerken, dat zy eenige Religie ofte Gods-dienstigheid souden hebben, hoewel zy altemet praten van een Capitein van de wolken; maar zy en dienen nochte hem nochte eenig ander. Van den Duivel hebben zy eenige kennisse, ende noemen hem *Yarakin*; ende de Bedriegers van 't Volk, die zy *Peies* noemen, ende haar in plaats van Priesters ofte Papen verstrekken, maken haar wijs, dat zy groote gemeinschap met hem hebben. Of het inderdaad zoo is, often niet, en zoude ik niet konnen zeggen: het dient haar altijt daar toe, dat zy haar selven een aanzien maken by de rest, die haar laten voorstaan dat doodt, ziekte, ende alderhande ongelukken, onmiddelbaar van den Duivel vandaan komen. Sy hebben ook een klein vonkjen van kennisse van een ander leven, alwaar vergeldinge en straffe zijn zal van goet ende van quaat in dit leven bedreven; maar zy zijn wel wijser, als [134] dat zy begeeren zouden te weten wat voor vergeldinge en straffe het zijn zal, ende op wat plaatze dezelve geschieden zal. d'Inbeeldinge die zy hebben van der *Peies* gemeenzaamheid met den Duivel, ende van de kennisse die zy mogten hebben verkregen van Kruiden ende Medicijnen, maakt dat zy dezelve gebruiken als Doctoren. Maar zy en hoeven zich niet te verheffen op hare professie ofte kunst: want wanneer een van haar gehaalt wort by een ziek mensch, ende dat hy aldaar met sijne besweeringen ende tooverijen niet en kan uitrechten, en dat den Patiënt komt te sterven, zo krijgt de Doctoor van de overgeblevene vrienden den doodt tot loon voor zijne moeite, by aldien hy hem niet haast van daar maakt. Zy verbranden het doode lichaam, ende neffens het selve al het gene waar van d'overleden meester was in zijn leven; ende wat zy niet verbranden konnen, als ijserwerk ende diergelijken, dat zullen zy op eenigerhande manier vernielen, op dat den doode doch immers geen gebrek moge hebben van eenige dingen in 't ander leven. Indien hy ook eenige slaven ofte slavinnen gehadt heeft, die dooden ze mede, op dat zy haren Meester opwachten mogen. De Begraafnisse wordt gehouden met een Feest, met drinken, klinken, ende een kluchtig onordentlijk danssen, het welk onder haar zeer gebruikelijk is; terwijl de wyven, die den overleden naast bestaan, daar neffens zitten, ende maken een ijzelijke gehuil over het verlies van hare vrienden maegschap.

Ziet daar het aanmerkelijkste noopende de zeden en gewoonten der inboorlinge: laat ons nu tot andere dingen overtreden. [135]

XII. HOOFDSTUK.

Dood des Heeren van Sommelsdijk, Gouverneur van Suriname. Vruchtelooze aanslag der Franschen op deze Colonie. Ongeluk, den Heer van Châtillon by die gelegentheid overgekomen. Vertrek des Auteurs van Suriname, en wederkomst te Middelburg.

Na den Leezer aldus een beschrijving gegeven te hebben van al het voornaamste, 't geen in de Colonie van *Suriname* aan te merken is, zal ik overtreeden tot andere zaken, welke by mijnen tijd aldaar zijn voorgevallen: want het Contract, 't geen ik met mijnen Patroon gemaakt had, ten einde geloopen, en vervolgens vernieuwt zijnde, kan ik met een genoegsame zekerheid spreeken wegens de dood des Heeren van *Sommelsdijk*, Gouverneur der Colonie, als hebbende die met eygene oogen aangezien, mitsgaders wegens een aanslag der Franschen op *Suriname*, onder het Gouvernement van de Heer *Scherphuizen*; waar mede ik deze mijne Voyagien zal sluiten.

't Was al over lang dat de Soldaten van de bezetting, welken inderdaad een al te harden en slaafachtigen arbeid wierd opgelegt, geklaagd hadden over het slecht rantsoen; welke klachten eindelijk tot zo verre uitborsten, dat ze gezamenerhand, opgemaakt door eenige Belhamels; riepen, dat ze geen hand meer aan 't werk zouden slaan, indien ze niet beter van leeftocht voorzien wierden. Den Adjudant, die hen commandeerde, ziende dat het ernst was, beloofde na den Gouverneur te gaan, en voor hen te spreeken; gelijk hy ook inderdaad deed: maar deze, in plaats van hem zacht bescheid te geven, taste na een rotting, en dreef hem met veel kwade woorden ter kamer uit. Hy keerde dan weder na het Volk, en vertelde zijn wedervaaren; waar aan geen geloof wordende geslagen, stooven ze gelijk [136] kerhand na het Huis van de Gouverneur. Midlerwijl ontmoet hen de Commandeur *Verboom*, een Man, zo zeer by al de Wereld bemint, als der Heer van *Sommelsdijk* wegens zijnde onvriendelijkheid en hardheid gehaat was. Deze vraagt terstont met minnelijke woorden na de reden van hun misnoegen en hebbende die verstaan, belooft hy hen, dat hy rijkelijker rantsoen voor hen te weeg zal brengen; met verzoek, dat zy zich voor als toen ieder na zijn huis zouden vervoegen. De Krijgsknechten gehoorzamden; doch zijnde 'sanderendaags op de plaats van den arbeid gekomen, en vernemende geen bescheid, namen ze het besluit van zelven zich recht te doen, en met geweld te haalen 't geen ze met ootmoedig verzoek niet konden verkrijgen. Straks elk na zijn geweer en onder een afgrijselijk gevloek gezamenerhand na het Huis van den Gouverneur, die door den Commandeur *Verboom* op dit gezicht, en de schrikkeijke dreigementen der Soldaten welke na geen redenen meer wilden luisteren, nu meer als ooit aangemaand wierd om het verzoek van de Militie in te willingen: doch in plaats van voor den storm te wijken, vliegt de Gouverneur met de sabel in de vuist ter deur uit, en op de Muitelingen aan, waar van hy 'er een den kop meende te klooven. Deze, ziende dat het op hem gemunt was, lost zijn geweer, en jaagt den Gouverneur een kogel in de dy, welke hem aanstondts ter aarde deed storten; daar hy wijders in een oogenblik met zeven-en-veertig wonden, zonder een eenig woord te spreeken, afgemaakts wierd. In deze verwoedheid kreeg ook de Commandeur *Verboom*, hoewel hem de Soldaten toeriepen dat hy zich aan kant zou maken, een kogel in den buik; waar af hy negen dagen daar na kwam te sterven. Dit geschiedden den 19 July van het Jaare 1688 dag die by veelen noch wel in geheugenis is: want de Muitelingen hier mede niet vernoegd, rukten voort; bemachtigden het Fort; verstrekten zich tot 140 a 150 man; wierpen Keuroverstens in plaats der Officiers van het Fort, op; overweldigden twee Schepen op de Rivier; voorzagen ze met behoeften uit het Magazijn; persten den Burgers, na hen ontwapend te hebben, 3500 guldens af; en vervaar- [137] digden alles tot hun vertrek, de politijke Raaden van het Land, trachtende met zachtheid de zaak weder te recht te brengen, lieten hen weten, dat de geenen, die blijven wilden, kwijt gescholden zouden worden. Veertig a vyftig lieten zich gezeggen. d'Overigen geraakent' Scheep; maar gaven zich, op het samenrotten van de gantsche Colonie, en beloften dat alleen de schuldigen gestraft zouden worden, over. Inderdaad, acht van de Belhamels wierden opgehangen, die drie gerabraakt, en de rest ontslagen.

Negen a tien Maanden daar na, wanneer wy nu weder in openbaaren Oorlog met de Koning van Vrankrijk waren geraakt, bemachtigden eenige Fransche Oorlogschepen in *West-Indien* het Eiland *St. Christoffel*, den Engelschen toebehoorende, en meenden met *Suriname*, kort na d'aankomst des Heeren van *Scherphuizen*, nieuwen Gouverneur, even eens te handelen; waar mede het zich aldus toedroeg. Den 6 May van den Jaare 1689 wierd het Guarnisoen door den Schildwacht van *Motte-Crek*, twee mijlen benedenwaarts, gewaarschuwd, dat 'er een Fransche Konings Vloot van tien Zeilen na de Rivier wende. De Gouverneur beval derhalven aan alle de Capiteinen zich met hunne Compagnie omtrent het Fort te vervoegen. De Vyanden dreeven ondertusschen de Rivier op; lieten een Bombardeerschip, een van de tien, op het Fort schieten; en vermeesterden 's Landts Barck, *'t Wapen van Amsterdam*, op de Brandwacht gelegt. Den 7 haalden de bezettelingen hunne Schepen, zes nevens twee Branders sterk, aan de wal; en verdeelden zich, 78 Man onder de Capitein *Swart*, 84 Jooden onder Capitein *Samuel Nassi*, en 69 Soldaaten onder Capitein *Lucas Codri*, op de noodige Posten, alle wel gewapend en wel gemoed, te meer dewijl de Sterktens door de goede zorg der Heeren van *Vredenburg*, Commandeur van de Colonie, byna in gewenschten Staat waren. Den 8 speelde het Fransche Bombardeerschip des nachts hevig, doch des daags slapper, op het Fort en de zes Schepen: maar de Vyandelijke Vloot bleeft buiten bereik van het Hollandsch Geschut. 's Nachts daar aan zonder de Franschen Ver- [138] spieders uit; welke, ontdekt zijnde, wel haast weeken, en wegens de duisternis niet vervolgd konden worden. Den 9 vervaardigden zich de Vyanden tot het bestormen van het Fort, en wierpen, tot belemmering der Hollanders die uittoogen om hen t'ontfangen, eenige Bomben doch zonder vrucht. 's Avondts naderde het Bombardeerschip tot dicht aan 't Fort, gevolgd door d'andere Schepen. De Schildwacht gaf bericht, dat zy zich in een Halvemaan een Pistoolschoot van het Fort bevonden. 't Weer was donker. Twee van hen losten eerst; maar wierden, niet tegenstaande hun gestadig vruchteloos Bombarderen en Granaaten werpen, in twee uuren met over de drie duizent Kanonschooten zodanig begroet, dat ze hunne Ankers kapten, en met de eb afzakten. De bezettelingen kreegen vier a zes gekwetsten, doch van weinig belang, en des anderendaags twee van de vyf Vyandelijke Ankers, die zy zagen drijven, benevens eenige Mannen zonder hoofd, beenen, en handen, en meer andere tekenen der Frandsche schade. Den 10 keerde het Bombardeerschip, 't geen in alles 140 a 150 Bomben, meestendeel van omtrent honderd pond, na, doch niet een in, het Fort en de Schepen geworpen had, weder onder 't Fort; maar wierd door het hevig Kanonneeren wel haast te rug gedreeven. De Vyandlijke Schepen deinsden ook. Den 12 sworven de Franschen noch in 't gezicht van 't Fort; dreeven 's nachts na beneden; en staken des anderendaags, ziende dat 'er niets te verrichten viel, weder in Zee.

Beklaagelijk was het ongeluk, 't geen den Heer van *Châtillon*, Zoon des Heerre van *Sommelsdijk*, by deze gelegentheid overkwam. Hy had het gebied over een Batterij, die gestadig op de Franschen speelde; en willende voor de tweede-maal zelve een stuk Kanon afsteeken, vloog het voor den tijd in brand, nam hem twee vingers van de rechter en drie van de slinker hand weg, verschroeide zijn aangezicht, en kwetste hem deerlijk.

Drie a vier weeken na dit voorval nam mijn verblijf in *Suriname* een einde; want hebbende mijn Patroon ongevaar een Maand te vooren zelve zich weder daar vervoegd, [139] ik order om my tot mijne wedertocht na het Vaderland gereed te maaken: in welke Reis gelijk my niet aanmerkelijks wedervoer, zal ik alleenlijk zegen, dat ik, na tusschen de zes en zeven weeken onder weeg te zijn geweest, den 6 Augusti van den Jaare 1689 te *Middelburg* in *Zeeland* aan Land stapte.

EINDE.

[140]

REGISTER DER HOOFDSTUKKEN Deses Boeks.

I. HOOFDSTUCK

Register van de Hoofdstukken naar Suriname

I. HOOFDSTUK.

EYNDE.

Dutch Glossary

Van Berkel	[Page]	English
Abary	25	Abary village, also Abary River
Adriaen de Vyver	102	Captain of the *Eendracht*
Ael	15	ale, English beer
Aernocque, (Rio) Aarnocque	44, 86	Orinoco River
Allengskens	91	gradually
Anotta	131	annatto (*Bixa orellana*)
Appiteyt	28	appetite; from *appetit* (Fr.)
Aquewyen	19	Akawaios, Akawaio, Acawaio Indians dwelling in the interior of modern Guyana; their language is attributed to the Carib family
Armadillas	118	armadillo; from *armadillo* (Sp.)
Atestatien	58	attestation, proof; from *attestation* (Fr.)
Atty	9	Spanish garbled term for long peppers; from the Arawakkan *hatti* or *haçi*, de Goeje, p. 266
Ayren	126	cob of maize
Baalien	56	to bail water
Bagazie	25	baggage; from *bagage* (Fr.)
Bakeren	68	swaddling
Bakkers	80	monkeys that play with their hands, so-called 'bakers'
Bakoves	73	bacove, fig bananas
Balsam	125	balsamum
Balsamum Copeira	44	copal tree (*Copaifera* sp.)
Bandeliers	20	shoulder-belts to carry cartridges; from *bandelier* (Fr.)
Banketje	81	banquet; from *banquet* (Fr.)
Barbados	101	Barbados
Bark	61	barque; from *barque* (Fr.)
Barmudas	102	Bermudas
Bassen	108	small mounted cannon on a ship

Bassia	25, 74	beverage made of cassava, Hartsinck 1770, p. 25
Batterij	138	battery (of cannons)
Beekman	102	Samuel Beekman, the future commander of Essequibo (1690-1707) and a friend of Van Berkel
Begiftig wierd	101	to be presented with
Bekwaamelijk	67	rather well
Beltiery, Beltiry	22, 74	beverage made of cassava, Hartsinck 1770, p. 24; de Goeje 2009, p. 253
Benanes	73	bananas
Bennetje	30	small basket
Berbekot	21	barbecue
Bergen	94	during the *Third Anglo-Dutch War* (1672-1674) Dutch ships sailed to Bergen in Norway to join a convoy to reach the Netherlands safely
Berkemeyer	62	type of drinking glass
Beuzelingen	131	knick knacks
Bevesier	3	Beachy Head, or Bevesier (Fr.) in East Sussex
Bezemstuiver	20	penny with seven arrows symbolising the Dutch provinces
Bilboa	103	Bilbao (northern Spain)
Bley, Bleytje	31, 87	fish with many bones, bream (*Blicca bjoerkna*)
Bloohertig	97	cowardice; faint-hearted
Bockja watilly	25	'I am a man' in Arawakkan, see De Goeje 2009, p. 90
Boekmakers	vi	book writers
Bokjes	9	pejorative term (lit. small bucks) with which Europeans referred to Indians
Bonitos	2	bonitos; as mackerel and tuna of the *Scombridae* family
Boschagie	30	grove; from *bossage* (Fr.)
Bottelier	38	steward responsible for the victuals on a ship
Bourgondisch Kruis	103	Burgondy Cross, Spanish flag
Bourum	12	meal or soup

Bouteljes sek	15, 36	bottles of dry wine; from *bouteille* (Fr.) and *vinho secco* (P.)
Brandwacht	94	night watch or (temporary) front post on a river which warned the colony by firing cannons or lighting a fire
Broodtuin	22	'bread garden', slash-and-burn field
Busselen	92	bushels
Cajouw-appelen	72	cashew apples (*Anacardium* sp.)
Canarische eilanden	109	the Canaries; islands located off north-western Africa
Canje	17	Canje River
Capitein Lucas Codri	137	Captain Lucas Coudri (or Caudri); Commander of Berbice (1678) and Surinam (1689)
Capitein Samuel Nassi	137	Captain Samuel Nassi (or Nassy), son of David Cohen Nassi
Capitein Swart	137	Captain Swart
Cargesoen	17	load of merchandise or cargo; from *cargaison* (Fr.)
Caribischen	97	Carib Indians
Carsaay, Carsavy	70, 82	manioc tuber (*Manihot esculenta*)
Carsavybrood	74	cassava cakes
Cassader	115	cassava; see also *Carsaay*
Cassia fistula	125	*Cassia* sp.
Cassyry	75	beverage made of cassava cakes; *casiri* in Carib, see de Goeje 2009, p. 253; Hartsinck 1770, p. 25
Cataracten	111	waterfalls
Cemelvliege	114	camel fly (*Raphidiidae*)
Christenen	15	Christians
Combuine	109	Commewijne River
Commandant	31	Commander, head of the colony/post
Commandeur Verboom	136	Laurens Verboom (1654-1688) from Zierikzee, Zealand
Commany	74	cassava drink 'popular at the Essequibo River'
Commodyen	31	large ceramic pot, commodyen
Coppename	8	Coppename River
Coriaar	32	corial, canoe

Cornelis Blom	108	Master of *Madame Sophia*
Cornelis Marinus	2	Cornelis Marinusz or Marinussen; Master of the fregat *Nassau*
Corrallen	131	(glass) beads
Correntijn, Corentijn	8, 50	Corantyne River
Cottica	110	Cottica River
cs	36	*cum suis*; together with the crew members
Cuscary	122	*kussi* or *sapajou* (*Sanguinus midas*) ; see also *Bakkers*
Cuscharees	118	presumably the plural of *sapajou* or *kussi*
Dackje wathia	25	'I am also a man' in Arawakkan, de Goeje 2009, p. 90
Den Berg	24	plantation Den Berg
Depesches	17	quick message; from *dépêche* (Fr.)
Doodtshoofdjes	80	deadhead monkeys (*Saimiri sciureus*)
Dortsche mom	43	German 'Mum beer' brewed in Dordrecht, Holland
Dreef	13	drive
Droesem	92	dregs
Droogscheerders	76	wool carders
Duivels-eilanden	8	Devil Islands; now named Îles du Salut and situated off the Kourou River (French Guiana)
Duizendbeenen boomen	39	"Thousand-leg trees", red mangroves (*Rizophora mangle*)
Dwarlwind	7	whirl wind
Een roer op lossen	84	to aim at it with a gun
Een wyda dikke Payewats	29	presumably a printing error; it concerns the drink *payewar* which is carried in a calabash (*iwida*), de Goeje 2009, p. 264
Egipten	129	Egypt
Elbe	94	river on which the most important German port of Hamburg is situated
Endvogel	84	domesticated ducks
Equipagie	2	to equip or fit out a ship
Expresse	31	express letter
Farnerary	34	Demerara River
Fero	103	island of Pico de Ferro (the Açores)
Fort Nassau	13	*Fort Nassau* at the Berbice River

Gaauw	35	clever, handy
Geaffronteerd	18	insulted
Gebied	138	command
Gedood	59	to annul
Geproviandeerd	44	provisioned
Gijk	55	(main) beam
Ginnegabben	61	to sneer
Gitte-gamba	76	translated 'rubber' by Roth 1948, p. 79
Goejavis	72	guava (*Myrtaceae* sp.); see also *Guavers*
Gom of Gonje	3	the Goodwin Sands located off Foreland (Kent)
Gommen	76	gums
Graaf	23	'warrap' (G.), fermented syrup; see also Graap
Graafsche Wijn	75	red wine from the Graves region near Bordeaux (France)
Graap	88	syrup drink also known as 'warrap' (G.), see Hartsinck 1770, p. 24
Graveel	44	'gravel' formed in the urinary system; from *gravier* (Fr.)
Grimlagchen	98	to smirk
Groenland	103	Greenland
Grolders	80	howler monkeys (*Alouatta seniculus*)
Grollen	27	normally 'grollen' means pleasantries; here the calls produced by howler monkeys are referred to
Guavers	123	guava (*Psidium guajava*)
Guilen	48	blockheads
Gummi semnia	125	type of gum
Hair	23	hair
Hardebolde	108	stubbornness
Harig	37	'hairy' or full of small bones
Hasen	118	hares, labba (G.) (*Dasyprocta*)
Heer de Graaf	43	Master de Graaf; private plantation owner in Essequibo
Heer Scherpenhuizen	135	Johan van Scharpenhuizen [aka Van Scherpenhuizen] (?-1699), governor of Surinam (1689-1696)

Heer van Châtillon	135	François van Aerssen, Lord of Châtillon and Bernières (1669-1740); second son of Cornelis van Aerssen van Sommelsdijck
Heeren Planters	15	Lords Planters
Heeren Raaden	34	Lords Councillors
Heet zijn	6	to express disproportionate prediliction; to greatly desire something
Hegt	64	hilt
Hendrik Rol	42	commander of the Essequibo Colony
Heyn	102	friend of Van Berkel
Holle baar	56	pipeline, 'hollow wave'
Honing-vogel	118	hummingbird
Honslaarsdijk	85	the palace Honslaarsdijk was constructed between 1621 and 1647 by stadholder Frederik Hendrik and demolished in 1819
Hoofdplantazie	90	most important plantation
Hovaardig	20	proud
Hucken	46	to squat
In de asch brouwen	34	to make a mess of things
Indiaasche koorn	125	'Indian corn', maize; see also *Milie*
Indigo	124	indigo (*Indigofera* sp.)
Jammes, James	115	yams, tubers
Jan Hagel	2	a term perhaps here referring to common sailors
Jan Millar	120	John Millar, an English hunter
Jarouw	67	name of a fish, probably 'cascudo' (G.)
Jawes	113	yaws; chronic tropical disease which Van Berkel refers to as Spanish Pocks but also as French-Pox. See G. Warren, *An Impartial Description*, p. 4
Joeling	23	party; merrymaking
Joodenquartier	110	Jewish quarter on the Suriname River named 'Torarica' in Warren's *An Impartial Description* 1667
Josephs Kuisheid	131	Joseph's Chastity
Juff[rouw] Sophia	108	name of a ship
Kaarden	76	wool carding
Kaboutermannetjes	80	hobgoblin monkeys

Kakkebarretje	26	Shit Hat: an insulting nickname for an Indian Captain
Kalebas	11	calabash and a general term for all sorts of vegetables such as pumpkins
Kandeel	56	negus
Kano	14	canoe, small boat with a peddle; see *Coriaar*
Karsy	21	cassava; see *Carsaay*
Kartabak	87	Arawakkan name for 'characins' (*Characidae*); fish often found in waterfalls and also known as 'paku', see Schomburgk 1841, p. 241
Karvaane	36	caravan
Kattetijgers	80	(cat) tigers (*Leopardus* sp.)
Kerven	36	baskets
Ketelwacht	3	Night watch; see *Brandwacht*
Keuroverstens	136	officers chosen by soldiers
Kift	96	envy
Kilduivel	60	Kill devil, rum
Kinneken	116	Dutch measure linked to a small barrel; from *quintal* (Sp.)
Klappen	86	to talk
Klipsteenen	42	craggy rocks
Knoopigh	128	bony, 'knotty', see Warren, 1667, p. 21
Kondschap	10, 51	tidings, news
Konstapel	6	constable, gunman
Konynen	118	hares or *labba* (G.) (*Dasyprocta*)
Koopmanschappen	iii	merchandise
Kooy	30	cabin, bunk
Korael	19	(glass) bead
Korlen	5	grains
Koxswil	52	to be eaten; for the pot
Kraamvrouw	56	woman in childbed
Krabbebosch	110	Crabbush is an important strategic point located between the Commewijne and Suriname Rivers; in 1734 constructing the fort Nieuw Amsterdam began
Krap-boom	76	crab tree (*Carapa guianensis*), see also Hartsinck 1770, p. 76

Kreb	33	stable
Krengen	103	to careen
Kreuten	128	toads
Krevelkruid	71	itching weed
Krijgshuis	38	strong- or warriors house
Kwansuis, Kwansijs	vi, 27	negligence
Kweek	11	basket containing a certain quantity of vegetables
Labadisten	110	Labadists
Labber koeltje	2	light breeze
Landziekte	13	land disease or dropsy; original meaning: being tired of the sea (often concerning unexperienced sailors) but later interpreted as general laziness
Letterhout	75	snakewood (*Brosimum guianense*) often used in furniture making
Liguaanen	82	iguanas
Limes	123	lemon
Linie	109	line of the Equator
Loog	92	ley
Lootsmannen	80	pilot monkeys with 'long beards'
Losbol	99	carouser
Loulouw	40	'a fish that looks like a cod': Piratinga (G.) according to Roth 1948, p. 42; it may also refer to the *Siluridae* or *lau-lau*, see Schomburgk 1841, p. 193, or the catfish (*Pimelodidae* sp.) or Piraiba (P.)
Louwkiddy	37	common catfish (*Pimelodidae*), 'bagri' (G.); also known as *laukidi* in Arawakkan, Schomburgk 1841, p. 177
Lust mee boeten	51	to gratify their lusts
Luyart	122	either the two-fingered (*Megalonychidae*) or the three-fingered sloth (*Bradypodidae*)
M. de Feer	24	Matthijs de Feer; supervisor of plantation Den Berg
Maartsche bieren	116	March beer; in order to have sufficient stock, extra strong beer was brewed in Germany and England during the month of March
Maikony	99	Mahaikony River

Malen	85	to paint
Manaty	110	sea cow (*Trichechidae*); from *manatee* (Sp.)
Mangel	43	lack, want
Mannekole	31	manicole palm tree (G.) (*Euterpe oleracea)*
Manslag	68	manslaughter
Maquary	46	torch but presumably a whip, see Roth 1924, pp. 845-848; de Goeje 2009, p. 161
Maraan, marepaan	44, 96	old Dutch name for *Copaifera officinalis*
Markaay	19	now named Markaay Mountains (see map Rapkin 1851); a trading post situated up the Berbice River also known as the 'Accawaai Poort'
Marmezerts, Marmazet	118, 122	squirrel monkeys
Mars	9	top stays
Meby	93	Vine rope or *mibi* in Arawakkan, see de Goeje 2009, p. 198; often used to reinforce sugar barrels
Mebyky	38	Arawakkan name for chigoe fleas or jiggers (Eng.), de Goeje 2009, p. 263
Meerkatten	118	a general name presumably referring to the water opossom (*Chironectes minimus*) and to other animals considered similar e.g., coati (*Nasua nasua*), ayra (*Eira barbara*) or 'wood dogs' (*Procyon cancrivorus*, *Speothos venaticus*)
Midlerwijl	11	meanwhile
Mierenbeer	118, 119	ant bear or *tamandua* (*Myrmecophaga tridactyla*)
Mierenberg	49	Plantation *Mierenberg* or Plantation 'Anthill'
Mijlen	51	Dutch mile measuring 5.5 km
Milie	84	maize (*Zea mays*); from *milli* (Sp.)
Miskettery	48	firing of muskets
Mist	125	fertilizer (animal dung)
Mitsgaders	iii	together
Montagne	125	type of 'mountain' gum
Motte-crek	137	Mud Creek
Musketten	42	muskets; from *mousquet* (Fr.)
Musschieten, Muskytoes	14, 128	mosquitos
Naby	38	name of an Indian village

Natgieriger	15	more given to wine
Nooddruft	30, 32, 90	necessary victuals
Noodwendigheden	50	necessities, all matters required
Num-eel	111	numb eel; see also *Torpedo*
Ommegang	113	sexual intercourse
Onder schoot krijgen	77	to get within (gun) shot
Onpasselijk	21	indisposed
Ontsteken	14	broached
Opperhoofd	12	Commander of the colony or outpost
Oranje-appelen	123	oranges
Orewebbe	20	native term for shell bead ornaments also known as *quiripia* (Gassón 2000); compare to the Arawakkan *th-üyédi*, de Goeje 2009, p. 293
Oriane	18	annatto (*Bixa orellana*)
Ouden Amen	28	village of Ouden Amen; perhaps derived from Dutch 'aam', hence the referrence to the 'Old Barrel'
Ounsa awara	132	'very much' in Cariban
Oxhoofden	126	oxhead barrel
Paap	133	(Catholic) priest
Pagaaien	41	to row
Pagale, Pagaal	19, 29	*pagara*, square basket, see Davy 2007, p. 158
Pakkyra	119	*pakira* (Sr.) (*Tayassu tayacu*)
Palmyt, Palmijt-boomen	9, 72	*palmito* (G.), palm tree with edible heart
Pan	97	rifle pan for gun powder
Parimaribo	109	Paramaribo, capital of the Surinam colony
Passaad	109	trade winds
Patronen	1	Patrons or Directors of the colony
Pauyssen	84	*powissi, hocco* (G.) (*Crax elector*)
Payewa, Payewar	22, 38, 74	beverage made of cassava, Hartsinck 1770, p. 24; de Goeje 2009, p. 253
Peies	133	shaman, *piai* in Cariban; in Arawakkan *cemici*, de Goeje 2009, p. 39
Pepel	114	butterfly; from *papilio* (Lat.)
Peperpot	22	Pepperpot: traditional fare consisting of peppers and boiled manioc juice known as *kasiripo* in Cariban

Pernou	25, 31, 74	beverage made of cassava, Hartsinck 1770, p. 25
Perrinoe	115	manioc drink; see *Pernou*
Persing	88	disease with bad stool
Petaddes	71	(sweet) potatoes
Piereka	110	Perica River
Pines	123	pineapples
Pinko	119	*pingo* (Sr.), peccari (*Tayassu pecari*)
Plantazien	10	plantations, estates
Plantons	115	plantains; from *platanos* (Sp.)
Pleisterhuisje	16	shelter, *banab,* see Roth 1948, p. 17
Pomcitrons	123	pomcitrons: apples grafted onto lemon trees
Porcupines	121	porpucines (*Coendou prehensilis*)
Pottazie	10	meal, soup; from *potage* (Fr.)
Prinse vlag	103	Prince flag (Orange-White-Blue)
Puitaal	37	eelpout (*Zoarces viviparus*)
Quereman	41	mullet species according to Roth 1948, p. 43; see also Biet 1664, p. 422: *coñeréman* or *kwériman* in de Goeje 2009, p. 300
Quottoes	118	spider monkey (*Atelus paniscus*)
Rad	82	rapid, agile
Ravens	86	parrots, macaws; from *ravens* (Sr.) or *Ara* sp.
Resolveerden	45	to decide
Restantie	38	remnants
Rijksdaalder	20	thaler
Rio de Berbice	iii	Berbice River
Roede	72	Roe, a Dutch (Rijnlandse) roe measures *c.* 3,75 m
Roodsaaye kleed	68	dress consisting of a specific red dyed tissue
Roomsche-boonen	74	broad beans
Ruigte	71	vegetation; hairiness of the body
Savaanen	90	savannahs
Scheeps-biskuit	70	biscuits
Scheppers	36	oarsmen
Schielijke	102	unexpected, sudden
Schildtwacht	97	sentinel

Schouwe	104	island of Schouwen (Zeeland)
Seeswijnen	4	sea hogs, porpoises (*Phocoena phocoena*)
Segrein	5	shagreen; granular-like skin of rays or sharks; from *chagrin* (Fr.)
Semerrimars	123	unknown fruit; perhaps 'sapodilla'
Slofheid	vi	feigning
Snaphanen	96	flintlocks
Snoeijen	88	eating candy
Snorken	27	boasting, swagger
Somerlivrey	114	summer livery
Somer-vogel	114	summer bird, butterfly
Sommelsdijk	110	Cornelis van Aerssen van Sommelsdijck, governor of Suriname (1683-1688)
Spaanse pokken	88	Spanish pocks, syphillus
Speckle-wood	124	speckle-wood; see also *Letterhout*
Spinnekoppen	83	spiders
St. Christoffel	137	Saint Kitts
Steen	44	(kidney) stone; see *Graveel*
Stoop	60	old Dutch measure of c. 2.4 liter
Stout en stijf ontkennen	99	to ignore something at all costs
Stropvogels	85	birds caught with a noose (often parrots)
Stukken van achten	3	Spanish pieces of eight; from *ocho de reales* (Sp.)
Suramkeka	8	Saramacca River
Suriname	8	Suriname River
Swaart-visch	110	swordfish
Swampen	114	Swamps, 'zwampen' (Sr.)
Tafel-linden	131	table linen
Tannerary	30	Demerara River
Ter deeg	112	certainly, extensively
Texel	104	island of Texel, Holland
Tijding	96	tidings, news
Tijgers	80	tigers; generic term for all felines in the Guianas
Tomenaq	30	name of Indian Captain
Toonen	86	toes
Tormenten	54	to torment, torture
Torn	27	fury, wrath

Torpedo	111	torpedo, ray; from *topedo* (Fr.) (*Torpedinidae*)
Tortoises	116	land turtles
Travanden	102	fast winds; from *travado* (P.)
Trinidad	86	the island of Trinidad
Troup	79	troupe, herd of animals
Turf trappen	23	to prepare peat
Vaek	13	sleepy
Van Peere	1	Van Pere family; Zealander merchant family of which Abraham van Pere was the first Patron of Berbice in 1627
Van Ree	1	Van Ree family; name of an important Zealander merchant family
Velden of pleinen	114	plains, fields
Verguikt	114	to refresh
Verpozing	54	pause, break
Verstendigen	99	to inform
Verwittigen	67	to inform
Vierende den toom	95	to lead (bridle)
Vinvisch	104	whale (*Baleanopteridae*)
Virginia	72	Virginia, the English colony in North America
Voddery	38	bunch
Voor af schikken	28	to send ahead
Voorland	3	Foreland, Point of Dungeness, England
Voorttelling	86	to raise livestock
Voyagien	iii	voyages; from *voyage* (Fr.)
Vredevuur	102	Saint Elmo's fire
Vroedwijf	55	midwife
Wammen	7	guts
Warouen	66	Warau Indians
Water- en muscadel	123	water and muscade melons
Wederbaaringen	57	revelry
West-Indien	137	West Indies
Wijders	90	further(more)
Windbuil	17	braggart
Woeronje	49	Wironi: name of an Indian village, see also Hartsinck 1770, p. 281

Wynbraauwen	21	eyebrows
Yamas	125	yams, tubers
Yarakin	133	*yolokan* in Cariban; the spirit of the hurricane or 'huracan'
Yet-appelen	73	fruits of ité palm (*Mauritia flexuosa*)
Yetwes	112	somewhat
Ysekepe	24	Essequibo River; also the common name of the Dutch colony located on this river and in particular of fort Kyckoveral
Ytoeriës	22	howler monkeys, baboons, see Patte 2011, p. 95 (*Alouatta seniculus*)
Ytoerybalijs	80	probably spider monkeys with 'an old and hairless face'
Zandpunt	110	Sandy Point (toponym) situated in the vicinity of plantation La Simplicité and Torarica
Zeilree	16	ready to depart
Zied	92	'zieden': to cook
Zieken	38	chigoes (*Tungiasis* sp.); from *chique* (Fr.), also see jigger (Eng.) or *sika* (Sr.)
Zinkhout	75	sink-wood, very hard wood
Zoo, Zoode	37, 103	bunch
Zywurmen	115	silkworms

Eng. = English
Fr. = French
G. = Guyanese
P. = Portugese
Sp. = Spanish
Sr. = Surinamese
Lat. = Latin

Sources and bibliography

Archival Sources

Nationaal Archief

(Oude) West Indische Compagnie: NL-HaNA_1.05.01.01 Resoluties Kamer van Zeeland, pp. 28-32, 41

West Indische Compagnie: NL-HaNA_1.05.01.02_1025

Archief Rademacher: NL-HaNA_1.10.69_614_ Berbice

Regionaal Archief Leiden

NL-LdnRAL_501A

NL-LdnRAL_1004

Zeeuws Archief

NL-MdgZA 2035.1

NL-MdgZA_MS_182. Stapels, G., van, Jornael van onse viiasij begonnen in den iarre 1629 den 24 iannevaries met het schiep den iager en iacht denortsterre nar de amsones en andre kūsten godt verlen ons behoūden rese, 35 folios, Zeeuws Archief, Middelburg, c. 1630

NL-MdgZA_ 995 DTB Scherpenisse

Gids 102, Staten van Zeeland en Suriname, nr. 314, Johannes Heinsius to the commander of Essequibo, letter dated 31 December 1678.

Stadsarchief Amsterdam

NL-AsdSAA_231_294G; 231_2

Gemeente Archief Vlissingen

NL-VsGA_357_531

NL-VsGA_387_5673

Universiteit van Amsterdam

Special Collections, *Hollandse Mercurius*, Tome 39 (1688), Haarlem 1689

Special Collections, *Hollandse Mercurius*, Tome 40 (1689), Haarlem 1690

British Library

Williams Byam Journal of Guiana, Mss No. 3662, ff. 27-37

Maps

Map of British Guiana with engravings by J. Rapkin, London: J. & F. Tallis, 1851

Bibliography

Koninklijke Bibliotheek

Handelingen der Staten-Generaal, Bijlagen 1922-1923, No. 5, Koloniaal Verslag II, Suriname

Handelingen der Staten-Generaal, Bijlagen 1923-1924, No. 5, Koloniaal Verslag II, Suriname

Sumatra Post

La Gazette d'Amsterdam

Oprechte Haerlemsche Courant

Amsterdamsche Courant

Books

Anonymous

1667 *Waerachtich Verhael van de heerlijke overwinning van Pirmeriba* [...], 's Gravenhage: Johannes Rammazeyn

Anonymous

1676 *Een vertoogh van de considerable colonie, by de Staten van Hollandt uitgeset op de vaste kust van America* [...], Den Haag: Jacobus Scheltus

Balée, W.

1989 The Culture of Amazonian Forests, *Advances in Economic Botany* 7:1-21

Beeckman, I.

1989 *Journal tenu par Isaac Beeckman de 1604 à 1634, publication avec une introduction et des notes par C. de Waard,* IVième Supplément, La Haye: Martinus Nijhoff [1953]

Bel, M.M. van den, L.A.H.C. Hulsman

2013 Une colonie néerlandaise sur l'Approuague au début de la deuxième moitié du XVIIe siècle, *Bulletin de la société d'histoire de la Guadeloupe* 164:5-15

Benjamin, A.

1998 Fort Nassau and the Van Wallenburg Thesis: A Re-evaluation of the Evidence, *Archaeology and Anthropology* 12:8-21

Benjamins, H.D., J.F. Snelleman (eds)

1914-7 *Encyclopaedie van Nederlandsch West-Indië*, Den Haag/Leiden: Martinus Nijhoff/E.J. Brill

Berkel, A. van

1695 *Amerikaansche Voyagien, Behelzende een Reis na Rio de Berbice, Gelegen op het vaste Land van Guiana, Aan de Wilde-Kust van America, Mitsgaders een andere na de Colonie van Suriname, Gelegen in het Noorder Deel van het gemelde Landschap Guiana* [...], Amsterdam: Johan ten Hoorn

1948 *Adriaan van Berkel's Travels in South America between the Berbice and Essequibo Rivers and in Surinam 1670-1689*, Translated and Edited by Walter Edmund Roth (1925), The Guiana Edition 2 (3rd Impression) of reprints and original works dealing with all phases of life in British Guiana, Edited by Vincent Roth, Georgetown: The Daily Chronicle

Biet, A.

1664 *Voyage de la France Equinoxiale en l'Isle de Cayenne, entrepis par les françois en l'année MDCLII*, Paris: François Clouzier

Bolingbroke, H.

1807 *A Voyage to the Demerary, containing a statistical account of the Settlements there, and of those of the Essequibo, the Berbice, and other contiguous Rivers of Guyana*, Norwich: Richard Philips

Boomert, A.

1984 The Arawak Indians of Trinidad and Coastal Guiana, ca. 1500-1650, *Journal of Caribbean History* 19:123-188

2002 Amerindian-European Encounters on and around Tobago (1498-ca.1810), *Antropológica* 97-8:71-207

Bos, G.

1998 *Some recoveries in Guiana Indian ethnohistory*, PhD Dissertation Free University of Amsterdam, Amsterdam: VU University Press

Bosman, L.

1994 *Nieuw Amsterdam in Berbice (Guyana): de planning en bouw van een koloniale stad, 1764-1800*, Hilversum: Verloren

Boyer, P. Sieur du Petit-Puy

1654 *Véritable relation de tout ce qui s'est passé au voyage que monsieur de Bretigny fit à l'Amérique occidentale* [...]. Paris: Chez Pierre Rocolet

Brett, W.H.

1851 *Indian Missions in Guiana*, London: George Bell

Brinton, D.G.

1871 *The Arawack Language of Guiana in its Linguistic and Ethnological Relations*, Philadelphia: McCalla & Stavely Printers

Butt-Colson, A.J.

2009 *Land. Its occupation, management, use and conceptualization: the case of the Akawaio and Arekuna of the Upper Mazaruni District, Guyana.* Panborough: Last Refuge

Buve, R.

1962 *De positie van de indianen in de Surinaamse plantagekolonie gedurende de 17ᵉ en de 18ᵉ eeuw*, typoscript

1966 Gouverneur Johannes Heinsius. De rol van Van Aerssen's voorganger in de Surinaamse Indianenoorlog, 1678-1680. *Nieuwe West-Indische Gids* 45 (1966)

Cameron, A.J. McR

2007 *The Berbice Uprising 1763*, Georgetown: Caribbean Press

Carrico, C.

2011 Akawaio-European relations during the Dutch colonial Era in Guyana, *From Historical paths to the cultural processes between Brazil and Guyana*, Reginaldo Gomes & Ifill Melissa (Orgs.), Boa Vista: EdUFRR

Cats, J.

1828 *Dichterlijke Werken*, 2 Vols., Amsterdam: Gebroeders Diederichs

Colenbrander, H.T.

1911 *Korte Historiael ende Journaels Aenteykeninge van verscheyden Voyagiens in de Vier Deelen des Werelds-ronde, als Europa, Africa, Asia, ende Amerika gedaen door David Pietersz. De Vries.* In: Werken van de Linschoten Vereniging 3, Den Haag: Martinus Nijhoff

Condamine, C.M. de la

1778 *Relation abrégée d'un voyage fait dans l'intérieur de l'Amérique méridionale, depuis la Côte de la Mer du Sud, jusqu'aux Côtes du Brésil & de la Guyane, en descendant la Rivière des Amazones* [...], Maestricht: Jean-Edme Dufour & Philippe Roux

Dalton, H.G.

1855 *The History of British Guiana comprising a General Description of the Colony*, 2 Vols., London: Longman, Brown, Green & Longmans

Davy, D.

2007 *Vannerie et vanniers. Approche ethnologique d'une activité artisanale en Guyane française*, PhD Dissertation University of Orléans, ms

Donselaar, J. van

1993 De boeken van Warren (1667, 1669), Van Berkel (1695) en Herlein (1718) en hun onderlinge betrekkingen, *OSO Tijdschrift voor Surinamistiek en het Caraïbisch gebied* 12(1):87-94

2013 Woordenboek van het Nederlands in Suriname van 1667 tot 1876, Amsterdam: Meertens Instituut

Duyse, F. van

1903 *Het oud Nederlandsche lied*, Den Haag: Martinus Nijhoff

Edmundson, G.

1901 The Dutch in Western Guiana, *The English Historical Review* 16(64):640-675

Engelbrecht, E.A.

1973 *De vroedschap van Rotterdam 1572-1795*, Rotterdam: Gemeentelijke Archiefdienst

Farabee, W.C.

1918 *The Central Arawaks*. In: University Museum, Anthropological Publications 9, Philadelphia: University of Pennsylvania

Fermin, P.

1769 *Description générale, historique géographique et physique de la colonie de Surinam*, 2 Vols., Amsterdam: E. van Harrevelt

1770 *Nieuwe algemeene beschryving van de colonie van Suriname. Behelzende al het merkwaardige van dezelve, met betrekkinge tot de historie, aardryks- en natuurkunde*, Harlingen: V. van der Plaats jr

Ferreira, B.R. Miranda

2011 *Gente de Geurra: Origem, cotidiano e resistência dos soldados do exército da Companhia das Indias Ocidentais no Brasil (1630-1654)*, PhD Dissertation University Leiden, ms

Forest, R. de

1914 *A Walloon Family in America. Lockwood de Forest and his Forbears 1500-1848. Together with A Voyage to Guiana being the Journal of Jesse de Forest And his Colonists 1623-1625*, 2 Vols., Boston/New York: Houghton Mifflin Company

Fritz, S.

1922 *Journal of the Travels and Labours of Father Samuel Fritz in the River of the Amazons between 1686 and 1723*, Translated from the Evora Ms and edited by the Rev. Dr. George Edmundson. In: Works issued by The Hakluyt Society, Second Series 51, London

Gassón, R.A.

2000 Quirípia and Mostacillas: The Evolution of Shell Beads as a Medium of Exchange in Northern South America, *Ethnohistory* 47(3-4):581-609

Goeje, C. de

2009 *The Arawak Language*, Cambridge: Cambridge University Press [1928]

Goslinga, C.

1971 *The Dutch in the Caribbean and on the Wild-Coast (1580-1680),* Groningen: Van Gorcum

1985 *The Dutch in the Caribbean and in the Guianas 1680-1791*, Assen: Van Gorcum

Grenand, P.

2006 Que sont devenus les Amérindiens de l'Approuague? Réflexions autour d'une histoire peu documentée, *L'histoire de la Guyane, depuis les civilisations amérindiennes*, Serge Mam Lam Fouck & Jacqueline Zonzon (eds), pp. 105-126, Matoury: Editions Ibis Rouge

Grol, G.J.

1934-42 *De grondpolitiek in het West-Indische domein der Generaliteit*, 's-Gravenhage: Algemene Landsdrukkerij

Harlow, V.

1925 *Colonising expeditions to the West-Indies and Guiana, 1623-1667*. In: Works of The Hakluyt Society, Second Series 56, London

Harris, C.A., J.A.J. de Villiers

1911 *Storm van 's Gravesande, The Rise of British Guiana*, Vol. 1. In: Works issued by The Hakluyt Society, Second Series 26, London

Hartsinck, J.J.

1770 *Beschrijving van Guiana, of de Wilde Kust, in Zuid-America* [...], Amsterdam: Gerrit Tieleburg

Herlein, J.D.

1718 *Beschryvinge van de Volk-Plantinge Zuriname* [...], Leeuwarden: Meindert Injema

Heijer, H. den

1994 *De geschiedenis van de WIC*, Zutphen: Walburg Pers

Hilty, S.L.

2003 *Birds of Venezuela* (2nd Edition), New Jersey: Princeton University Press

Hoff, B.J.

1995 Language contact, war, and Amerindian historical tradition: The special case of the Island Carib, *Wolves from the Sea: Readings in the Anthropology of the Native Caribbean*, Neil L. Whitehead (ed.), pp. 37-59. In: Caribbean Series 14, Leiden: KITLV Press

Hulsman, L.A.H.C.

2009 *Nederlands Amazonia. Handel met indianen tussen 1580 en 1680*, PhD Dissertation University of Amsterdam, ms.

2011 Routes of the Guianas: a voyage from Suriname to the Rio Branco in 1718, *Dos Caminhos históricos aos processos culturais entre Brasil e Guyana*, Reginaldo Gomes de Oliveira & Melissa Ifill (eds), pp. 45-66, Boa Vista: EDUFFR

Husson, A.M.

1978 *The Mammals of Suriname*. Leiden: E.J. Brill

Im Thurn, E.F.

1883 *Among the Indians of Guiana, Being sketches chiefly anthropologic from the interior of British Guiana*, London: Kegan Paul, Trench & Co

Jameson, F.

1907 *Voyages of Samuel de Champlain 1604-1618*. In: Original Narratives of Early American History 4, New York: Charles Scribner's Sons

Kappler, A.

1854 *Zes Jaren in Suriname. Schetsen en tafereelen uit het maatschappelijke en militaire leven in deze kolonie*, 2 Vols., Utrecht: W. F. Dannenfelser

Kars, M.

2009 Policing and Transgressing Borders: Soldiers, Slave Rebels, and the Early Modern Atlantic, *New West Indian Guide* 83:191-217

2013 'Wij beleven hier droevige tyden': Europeanen, indianen en Afrikanen in de Berbice slavenopstand, 1763-1764, *Geweld in de West: een militaire geschiedenis van de Nederlandse Atlantische wereld, 1600-1800*, Victor Enthoven, Henk den Heijer, Han Jordaan (eds), pp. 183-216. In: Caribbean Series 33, Leiden: E.J. Brill

Knappert, L.

1926 De Labadisten in Suriname, *West Indische Gids* 8:193-218

Knuttel, J.A.N.

1913 Adriaan van Berkel, Amerikaanse Voyagien behelzende een reis na Rio de Berbice [...], *Proza uit de 17e eeuw*, Verzameld en toegelicht door J. Knuttel, Redacteur van het 'Woordenboek der Nederlandse taal', met reproducties van Titelbladen en Titelprenten, Amsterdam: S. L. van Looy

Korten, H.

2011 '*Boeckeniers zijn gaeuw in het schieten': Jan ten Hoorns uitgave 'Americaensche zee-roovers'*, Master Thesis University of Amsterdam, ms (http://dare.uva.nl/document/221204)

Kouwenberg, S.

2009 The invisible hand in Creole Genesis. Reanalysis in the formation of Berbice Dutch, *Complex processes in New Languages*, Enoch O. Aboh & Norvan Smith (eds), pp. 115-158. In: Creole Language Library 35, Amsterdam: John Benjamins Publishing Company

Langen. J.C. van

2004 *De Britse overname van de Nederlandse koloniën Demerary, Essequebo en Berbice (Guyana); van economische overvleugeling naar politieke overheersing (1740-1814),* Master Thesis University of Amsterdam, ms.

Leigh, C.

1906 Capitaine Charles Leigh his voyage to Guiana and plantation there. In: *Hakluytus Posthumus or Purchas His Pilgrimes. Contayning a History of the World in Sea Voyages and Lande Travells by Englishmen and others*, Samuel Purchas (ed.), Vol. 16, pp. 309-323, Glasgow: James MacLehose & Sons

Léry, J. de

1578 *Histoire d'un voyage faict en la terre du Brésil, autrement dit Amérique* [...], La Rochelle: Antoine Chuppin

2008 *Histoire d'un voyage faict en la terre du Brésil, autrement dit Amérique* [...], Frank Lestringant (ed.), Paris: Librairie Générale Française [1992]

Meiden, P. van der

2008 *Betwist bestuur. Een eeuw strijd om de macht in Suriname 1651-1753*, Amsterdam: De Bataafsche Leeuw [1987]

Moreau, J-P.

1992 *Les Petits-Antilles de Christophe Colomb à Richelieu (1493-1635),* Paris: Editions Karthala

Moretti, C., P. Grenand

1982 Les nivrés ou plantes ichtyotoxiques de la Guyane française, *Journal of Ethnopharmacology* 6:139-160

Nardeux, A.

2001 L'expédition aventureuse en Guyane de trois gentilhommes normands et de leurs vingt-six compagnons (1626-1630), *Les Normands et l'outre-mer, Annales de Normandie*, Jean Paul Hervieux, Gilles Désiré dit Gosset & Eric Barré (eds), pp. 299-304, Caen

Nassy, D.

1788 *Geschiedenis der Kolonie van Suriname*, (facsimile edition by S. Emmering, Amsterdam 1974)

Nederlands gedenkboek

1751 *Nederlandsch gedenkboek of Europische Mercurius, Vol. LXII, eerste deel van 't jaar 1751*, 's-Gravenhage: Frederic Hendric Scheurleer

Netscher, P.M.

1888 *Geschiedenis van de Koloniën Essequebo, Demerary en Berbice, van de vestiging tot op onze tijd*, Den Haag: Martinus Nijhoff

1929 *History of the Colonies Essequibo, Demerary and Berbice form the Dutch Establishment to the present day*, Translated by W. E. Roth, Georgetown: The Daily Chronicle

Nieuhof, J.J.

1682 *Gedenkweerdige Brasiliaense Zee- en Lantreize, behelzende al het geen op dezelve is voorgevallen, beneffens een bondige beschrijving van gantsch Neerlants Brasil* [...], Amsterdam: Voor de Weduwe van Jacob van Meurs

Oest, E.W. van der

2003 The Forgotten Colonies of Essequibo and Demerara, 1700-1814, *Riches from Atlantic Commerce: Dutch Transatlantic Trade and Shipping, 1585-1817*, Johannes Postma & Victor Enthoven (eds), pp. 343-346, Leiden: E.J. Brill

Oostindie, G.J.

2012 'British Capital, Industry and Perseverance' versus Dutch 'Old School'? The Dutch Atlantic and the Takeover of Berbice, Demerara and Essequibo, 1750-1815, *Low Countries Historical Review* 127(4):28-55

Oppenheim, S.

1907 *An Early Jewish Colony in Western Guiana, 1665-1666, and its relation to the Jews in Surinam, Cayenne, and Tobago*, Publications of the American Jewish Historical Society XVI:95-186

Oudeschans Dentz, F.

1918 Suriname vóór de verovering door Abraham Crijnssen, *Bijdragen en Mededelingen van het Historisch Genootschap* 39:173-213

1938 *Cornelis van Aerssen van Sommelsdijck*, Amsterdam: van Kampen

Paesie, R.

2010 De "Societeyt ter Navigatie op Essequebo en annexe Rivieren". Op- en ondergang van een Zeeuwse rederij, *Alle streken van het kompas* [...], Maurits Ebben, Henk den Heijer & Joost Schokkenbroek (eds), pp. 295-318, Zutphen: Walburg Pers

Patte, M.-F.

2011 *La langue arawak de Guyane. Présentation historique et dictionnaires arawak-français et français-arawak*. In: Collection Didactiques, Paris: IRD Editions

Penard, F.P., A.P. Penard

1907-8 *De menschetende Aanbidders der Zonneslang*, 2 Vols., Paramaribo: H. B. Heyde & J.H. Reisig

1793 *De Suikerraffinadeur, of volledige beschrijving van het suiker, deszelfs aankweking, bereiding en verzending...* , Dordrecht: A. Blussé en zoon

Pistorius, T.

1763 *Korte en zakelijke beschrijvinge van de Colonie van Zuriname*, Amsterdam: Theodorus Crajenschot

Reisig, J.H.

1793 *De Suikerraffinadeur, of volledige beschrijving van het suiker, deszelfs aankweking, bereiding en verzending* [...]. Dordrecht: A. Blussé en zoon

Renselaar, H. C. van

1966 Oude Kaarten van Suriname, *West Indische Gids* 45(1):2-13

Rochefort, C. de

1658 *Histoire naturelle et morale des îles Antilles de l'Amérique* [...], Rotterdam: Arnould Leers

Rodway, J., T. Watt

1888 *Chronological History of the Discovery and Settlement of Guiana, 1493-1668*, Georgetown: Royal Gazette Office

Roos, D.

1992 *Zeeuwen en de Westindische Compagnie (1621-1674)*, Hulst: van Geyt Productions

1996 *Nederlandse forten in Guyana*, Vlissingen: Stichting Menno van Coehoorn

Roth, W.E.

1915 *An Inquiry into the Animism and Folk-lore of the Guiana Indians*, Extract from the Thirtieth Annual Report of the Bureau of American Ethnology, Washington DC: Government Printing Office

1924 *An introductory study of the Arts, Crafts, and Customs of the Guiana Indians.* In: Thirty-Eighth Annual Report of the Bureau of American Ethnology to the Secretary of the Smithsonian Institution 1916-1917, Washington DC: United States Government Printing Office

Santos-Granero, F.

2009 *Vital Enemies: Slavery, Predation, and the American Political Economy of Life*, Austin: University of Texas Press

Schneider, M., J. Hemels

1979 *De Nederlandse Krant 1618-1978. Van 'nieuwstydinghe' tot dagblad.* Baarn: Het Wereldvenster

Schomburgk, R.H.

1841 *The Fish of Guiana, Part I.* In: Ichtyology, Vol. III, The Naturalist's Library 32, edited by Sir William Jardine, Edinburgh: W.H. Lizars

1922 *Richard Schomburgk's Travels in British Guiana, 1840-1844*, translated and edited, with Geographical and General Indices, and Route Maps by Walter E. Roth, Daily Chronicle, Georgetown.

Schuyl, F.

1727 *A Catalogue of all the cheifest* [sic] *rarities in the publick anatomie-hall of the University of Leyden*, Leiden: Diewertje vander Boxe

Sijpesteijn, C.A., van

1854 *Beschrijving van Suriname, Historisch-, Geographisch- en Statistisch Overzigt, uit officiele bronnen bijeengebragt*, Den Haag: De Gebroeders van Cleef

Sluiter, E.

1948 Dutch-Spanish Rivalry in the Caribbean Area, 1594-1609, *The Hispanic American Historical Review* 28(2):165-196

Staden, H.

1557 *Warhaftige Historia und beschreibung eyner Landtschafft der Wilden Nacketen, Grimmigen Menschfresser-Leuthen in der Newenwelt America gelegen*, Marburg: Kolb

Staehelin, F.

1918 *Die Mission der Brüdergemeine in Suriname und Berbice im achtzehnten Jahrhundert: eine Missionsgeschichte hauptsächlich in Auszügen aus Briefen und Originalberichten*, Teil II, Herrnhut

Steward, J.

1948 *Culture Areas of the Tropical Forests*, Handbook of South-American Indians, Julian Steward (ed.), Vol. 3, pp. 883-899. In: Bulletin Bureau of American Ethnology 143, Smithsonian Institution, Washington DC: United States Government Printing Office

Stoett, F.A.

1923-4 *Nederlandsche spreekwoorden, spreekwijzen, uitdrukkingen en gezegden*, Zutphen: W. J. Thieme & Cie

Thompson, A.O.

2002 *Unprofitable servants. Crown Slaves in Berbice, Guyana, 1803-1831*, Barbados: University of the West Indies Press

Verhoeven, G., S. van der Veen

2011 *De Hollandse Mercurius. Een Haarlems jaarboek uit de zeventiende eeuw.* Haarlem: Bubb Kuyper Veilingen

Vries, D. Pietersz de

1655 *Korte Historiael ende Journaels Aenteykeninge van verscheyden Voyagiens in de Vier Deelen des Werelds-ronde, als Europa, Africa, Asia, ende Amerika gedaen door David Pietersz de Vries.* Alkmaar: Symon Cornelisx Brekegeest

1853 *Voyages from Holland to America, A.D. 1633 1644*. Translated from the Dutch by Henry C. Murphy, New York: Billin & Brothers

1911 *Korte Historiael ende Journaels Aenteykeninge van verscheyden Voyagiens in de Vier Deelen des Werelds-ronde, als Europa, Africa, Asia, ende Amerika gedaen door David Pietersz de Vries*, H.J. Colenbrander (ed.). In: Werken van de Linschoten Vereniging 3, Den Haag: Martinus Nijhoff

Wallenburg, M., van

1995a Sites of Fortifications and Administrative Headquarters of Early Dutch Colonists on the Berbice River, *Archaeology and Anthropology* 10:1-18

1995b Het reisverhaal van Gelein van Stapels, *Zeeuws Tijdschrift* 1995(1)

Warren, G.

1667 *An Impartial Description of Surinam upon The Continent of Guiana in America. With a History of several strange Beasts, Birds, Fishes, Serpents, Insects, and Customs of that Colony, &c. Worthy of Perusal of all, from the Experience of George Warren Gent.*, London: Printed by William Godbid for Nathaniel Brooke at the Angel in Gresham-Colledge, in the second yard from Bishopsgate-street

1669 *Een onpartydige beschrijvinge van Surinam, gelegen op het vaste landt van Guiana in Africa: mitsgaders een verhael van alle vreemde beesten, vogels, visschen, slangen ende wormen* [...], Amsterdam: Pieter Arentsz

Weiland, P.

1828 Beknopt Nederduitsch Taalkundig Woordenboek, E-K, Dordrecht: Blussé & van Braam

Whitehead, N.L.

1988 *Lords of the Tiger Spirit: A History of the Caribs in Colonial Venezuela and Guyana 1498-1820*, PhD Dissertation University of Oxford (1984). In: KITLV Caribbean Series 1, Dordrecht: Foris Publishers.

1995 Ethnic plurality and cultural continuity in the native Caribbean: Remarks and uncertainties as to data and theory, *Wolves from the Sea: Readings in the Anthropology of the Native Caribbean*, Neil. L. Whitehead (ed.), pp. 91-111. In: Caribbean Series 14, Leiden: KITLV Press

Whitehead, N.L., M. Harbsmeier (eds)

2008 *Hans Staden's True History: An Account of Cannibal Captivity in Brazil*, Durham: Duke University Press

Whitehead, N.L., M.J. Heckenberger, G. Simon

2010 Materializing the Past among the Lokono (Arawak) of the Berbice River, Guyana, *Antropológica* 114:87-127

Williamson, J.A.

1923 *English colonies in Guiana and on the Amazon, 1604-1668,* Oxford: Clarendon Press

Wilson, J. of Wansteed

1625 *The Relation of Master John of Wansteed in Essex, one of the last ten that returned into England from Wiapoco in Guiana 1606*, Purchas His Pilgrimes: In Five Bookes: The First, Contayning the Voyages ... Made by Ancient Kings, ..., Others, to and thorow the Remoter Parts of the Knowne World, etc., Part 4, Chapter 14, pp. 1260-1265, London: W. Stansby for H. Fetherstone

Wolbers, J.

1861 *Geschiedenis van Suriname,* Amsterdam: De Hoogh (facsimile edition by S. Emmering, Amsterdam 1970)

Yzerman, J.W.

1911 Twee reizen van Paramaribo, een naar de Parima in 1718 en een naar de Boven-Corantijn in 1720, *Tijdschrift Koninklijk Nederlands Aardrijkskundig Genootschap* 28:648-661

Maps and illustrations